J. Ranade Workstation Series

To order or receive additional information on these or any other McGraw-Hill titles, in the United States please call 1-800-822-8158. In other countries, contact your local McGraw-Hill representative.

BC14BCZ

PowerPC

Concepts, Architecture, and Design

Dipto Chakravarty

Casey Cannon

McGraw-Hill, Inc.

New York   San Francisco   Washington, D.C.   Auckland   Bogotá
Caracas   Lisbon   London   Madrid   Mexico City   Milan
Montreal   New Delhi   San Juan   Singapore
Sydney   Tokyo   Toronto

To Bapi
—D.C.
To my family for their enthusiasm
and to Don Meyer for his encouragement
—C.C.

Library of Congress Cataloging-in-Publication Data

Chakravarty, Dipto.
    PowerPC : concepts, architecture, and design / Dipto Chakravarty, Casey Cannon.
      p.   cm. — (J. Ranade workstation series)
    Includes bibliographical references.
    ISBN 0-07-011192-8
    1. PowerPC (Microprocessor) I. Title. II. Series.
QA76.8.P67C48 1994
004.165—dc20   94-19135
                                                CIP

1 2 3 4 5 6 7 8 9 0   DOH/DOH   9 0 9 8 7 6 5 4

ISBN 0-07-011192-8

The sponsoring editor for this book was Jerry Papke and the production supervisor was Pamela A. Pelton. This book was set in Century Schoolbook by North Market Street Graphics.

Printed and bound by R. R. Donnelley & Sons Company.

Trademarks

Alpha and VAX are trademarks of Digital Equipment Corporation.

AFS and Transarc are trademarks of Transarc Corporation.

AIXwindows and AIXwindows Interface Composer/6000 are trademarks of International Business Machines Corporation.

AIX 3278/79 Emulation/6000 is a trademark of International Business Machines Corporation.

Apple, Appletalk, and Finder are trademarks of Apple Computer Corp.

C Set ++ is a trademark of International Business Machines Corporation.

CICS is a trademark of International Business Machines Corporation

Ethernet is a trademark of Xerox Corporation.

GL and Graphics Library are trademarks of Silicon Graphics, Inc.

HP is a registered trademark of Hewlett-Packard.

HP Precision Architecture and Laserjet are trademarks of Hewlett-Packard.

InfoExplorer is a trademark of International Business Machines Corporation.

Macintosh is a trademark of Apple Computer Corp.

Microsoft is a trademark of Microsoft Corporation.

Motorola and Motorola 88110 are trademarks of Motorola, Inc.

Micro Channel is a registered trademark of International Business Machines Corporation.

MIPS is a registered trademark of MIPS Computer Systems, Inc.

MS-DOS is a trademark of Microsoft Corporation.

NETBIOS is a trademark of International Business Machines Corporation.

NFS and SunOS are trademarks of Sun Microsystems, Inc.

OPEN LOOK is a trademark of AT&T.

Open Software Foundation, OSF, OSF/Motif and Motif are trademarks of Open Software Foundation, Inc.

Pentium is a trademark of Intel Corporation.

POSIX is a trademark of the Institute of Electrical and Electronic Engineers (IEEE).

POWER Architecture is a trademark of International Business Machines Corporation.

PowerOpen is a trademark of International Business Machines Corporation.

PowerPC, PowerPC Architecture, POWERserver, POWERstation are trademarks of International Business Machines Corporation.

PowerPC 601, PowerPC 603, PowerPC 604, and PowerPC 620 are trademarks of International Business Machines Corporation.

RISC System/6000 is a trademark of International Business Machines Corporation.

RT and RT PC are trademarks of International Business Machines Corporation.

SPARC is a registered trademark of SPARC International, Inc.

Taligent is a registered trademark of Taligent, Inc.

UNIX is licensed by and is a registered trademark of UNIX System Laboratories, Inc.

Wabi is a trademark of Sun Microsystems, Inc.

X Window System is a trademark of Massachusetts Institute of Technology

X11 is a trademark of Massachusetts Institute of Technology.

XPG3 is a trademark of X/OPEN Company Limited.

Contents

Part 2   Software

Preface

This book is a general-purpose reference for the computer professionals who wish to understand the PowerPC technology, which has evolved as a result of the IBM-Motorola-Apple alliance. The text is designed to serve as a single source of reference about the PowerPC hardware and its operating environments. A layer-by-layer introduction of the hardware, middleware, and software options unveils the diverse capabilities and features of this revolutionary technology. The subtitle, *Concepts, Architecture, and Design,* is quite appropriate, as the book contains a comprehensive overview of the hardware and the software *concepts* from both user as well as system perspectives. The text introduces the hierarchical *architecture* of the PowerPC microprocessor and explains the *design* rationales for the facilities and features that enable Power-PC to achieve the paramount level of performance.

Architecture and implementation of a computer are two distinct entities. Perhaps the most popular distinction between the terms was made in a *Communications of the ACM* journal.*

Computer architecture

... is defined as the attributes and behavior of a computer as seen by a machine language programmer. This definition includes the instruction set, instruction formats, operations codes, addressing modes, and all register and memory locations that may be directly manipulated by a machine language programmer.

Implementation

... is defined as the actual hardware structure, logic design, and data path organization of a particular embodiment of the architecture.

Thus, architecture is a definition that describes the behavior of all possible implementations, as compared to implementation that typically references a single microprocessor. The discussions of PowerPC architecture and its implementations have been kept separate for maximum benefit to the reader. A survey of operating systems and user interfaces has been provided to present to the reader with a system-level picture of the PowerPC-based computer systems.

---

* *Communications of the ACM,* vol. 36, no. 2, p. 33, February 1993.

WHY THIS BOOK

The publicity generated concerning the PowerPC microprocessor has resulted in the dissemination of a wide variety of information among vendors and developers in the computer industry. What has not been disseminated is a reference that ties all the aspects of this nascent technology together in a comprehensive source of reference. *Hence, this book.*

OBJECTIVES OF THIS BOOK

The first objective of this book is to describe the principles of the PowerPC architecture (and its implementations), which evolved out of the POWER architecture. Introduced in 1990, the POWER technology used in the RISC System/6000 product line acquired a quick reputation for itself in the marketplace by virtue of its advanced RISC-based design and achievable level of performance. PowerPC is a flexible derivative of the POWER architecture and shares a wide spectrum of traits with its parent architecture.

The second objective of this book is to depict a system-level picture of computers based on the PowerPC processor with emphasis on the operating systems, software development tools, standards, and user interfaces. An array of technologies is available today, in terms of hardware as well as software, that can be optimized by using PowerPC as its core. With a proliferation of PowerPC-based computer systems in the marketplace, end users will be faced with a choice of whether to opt for a computer that is PowerPC reference platform compliant or a computer that uses the PowerPC as its core. Both types of systems offer the power of the PowerPC microprocessor, the difference being in the varying degrees of compatibility that exist among the applications.

USES OF THIS BOOK

The intended use of this book is threefold:

- It can be used by the computer professionals working on or transitioning to the PowerPC-based development environment.
- It can be read by the general audience of the computer community wishing to get acquainted with PowerPC technology. The material delves into adequate depth to serve a novice as well as a knowledgeable user.
- It can be used as supplemental reading material in a computer system architecture course.

ORGANIZATION OF THIS BOOK

The first part of the book introduces the PowerPC in light of RISC technology. The second part explains the PowerPC architecture and discusses its available and planned implementations, including a comparative study with the POWER offerings to explain how POWER developed into the PowerPC. The third part of the book covers the user interfaces, standards, and tools. It also discusses the several operating systems that can/will run on the PowerPC. The final chapter wraps up the concepts by giving a tutorial on how to go about building one's own PowerPC platform. The contents of each of the parts are stand-alone and can be studied individually.

The book is organized into 12 chapters:

1. Presenting the PowerPC

2. RISC Technology

3. Architectural Definition

4. Processor Implementations

5. User Interfaces

6. Choice of Operating Systems

7. Development Tools

8. Supported Standards

9. Design of AIX: A PowerOpen Implementation

10. AIX Process Subsystem Internals

11. AIX File, Memory, and I/O Subsystem Internals

12. What You Need to Build a PowerPC

Chapter 1 introduces the PowerPC, discusses its evolution through the formation of the IBM-Motorola-Apple alliance, compares its standing with the Pentium, and addresses some of the important highlights such as the PowerOpen Environment, the application binary interface (ABI), and the application programming interface (API) definitions. Chapter 2 discusses the RISC technology in light of its unique traits, performance tradeoffs with CISC, pipelined implementation of the execution units, and the significance of reduced instruction set cycles. Chapter 3 explains how the layered architecture defines the varying degree of compatibility from an instruction set level, to the virtual environment level, all the way up to the operating environment level. Chapter 4 describes the implementations of the PowerPC architecture, such as the 601, 603, 604, and the 620, while contrasting them with some of the POWER implementations, the RS 1, RS .9, and RSC. Chapter 5 discusses the functionality and illustrates the leading industry standards of user interfaces including the Common Desktop Environment, Wabi, X Windows, and Macintosh Application Services.

Chapter 6 reviews the PowerOpen Application Binary Interface and then highlights five of the 32-bit operating systems that the PowerPC platform is intended to support, including Taligent, Windows NT, Solaris, AIX, and Workplace OS. Chapter 7 provides a broad overview of the most widely used development tools for UNIX operating systems, including discussions of (among others) the XL C optimizing compiler, assembler, and debuggers. Chapter 8 discusses the compatibility, portability, and interoperability standards for the PowerPC, followed by an overview of the interconnectivity functionalities of the PowerPC. Chapters 9, 10, and 11 cover in detail the PowerOpen-compliant AIX operating system, which is based on the COSE (Common Open Software Environment) version of UNIX. Chapter 9 presents the design of AIX, with in-depth discussions on components of the kernel, structural layout and characteristic features of the kernel, internal representation of files, related kernel tables, interprocess communication mechanisms, and allied data structures. Chapter 10 explains AIX process management principles, with emphasis on process structure, process state, context switching, scheduling principles, affiliated kernel structures and their positioning in the kernel address space, the art of monitoring processes by traversing through the *kmem* (running kernel's memory), and handling of threads. Chapter 11 discusses the file, memory, I/O, and device subsystems of the AIX kernel. It begins with a detailed discussion on the AIX file system in light of its memory mapped files, journaled file system, and the logical volume manager. The memory architecture topics include the addressability of the segmented memory, followed by the virtual memory management, page replacement, and memory load control schemes. The I/O subsystem topics include asynchronous I/O and I/O pacing, followed by the device subsystem, which discusses device drivers and the object data manager. In conclusion, Chapter 12 wraps up the concepts, architecture, and design of the PowerPC by providing a description of the devices and interfaces that are recommended for designing and building a PowerPC based computer system.

The content of Chapter 1 serves as an introduction to PowerPC for everyone. The material in Chapters 2, 3, and 4 will be of maximum benefit to hardware engineers who need to know about the registers and the architectural traits of the PowerPC microprocessor. The information in Chapters 5, 6, 7, and 8 are meant for end users and system integrators/designers. Chapters 9, 10, and 11 are geared for UNIX gurus who wish to understand how the internals of the PowerOpen compliant AIX operating system works. The content of Chapter 12 provides an account of the aspects to be considered when building one's own PowerPC-based computer system.

In conclusion, this book can be thought of as a single source of information about all technical aspects of the PowerPC. Professionals requiring an immersion training in PowerPC, as well as those keen on gaining an insight into the internals of this complex system, will benefit from this book.

A few caveats need to be mentioned. No attempts have been made to cover details of implementation-specific hardware components or release-specific software components. Such attributes are likely to change over a period of time. For an implementation-specific dependency of a microprocessor, or a release-specific dependency of an operating system or software component, one is encouraged to refer to the corresponding product reference manuals. Although we have avoided predicting the future development of the hardware and software, trends in many of the characteristics are obvious. In that case, this book will serve as the baseline technical reference for future products based on the PowerPC architecture.

The IBM-Motorola-Apple alliance has resulted in the birth of the PowerPC, and, consequently, has brought the RISC technology to the desktop computing world. By blending together the cost-performance and scalable aspects of the architecture, along with the interoperable software base, the PowerPC has made the biggest impact in the personal computer industry since the original Intel-based personal computer itself.

Acknowledgments

The genesis of PowerPC has generated an enthusiastic community worldwide. The technology, which evolved as a result of the IBM-Motorola-Apple alliance, is rapidly penetrating the computer industry's relentless pursuit for cost-performance computing.

The inspiration and support for writing this book came from our colleagues and friends too numerous to mention. Of the many individuals who helped us author this book, we would like to express our gratitude to our colleagues at IBM, Motorola, and Apple who willingly answered questions about this emerging subject.

We express our sincere thanks and gratitude to each of the following people whose timely help enabled us to march to an ambitious production schedule.

Gary Leikam provided timely guidance and review of the standards encompassing the PowerPC technology.

Art Adkins provided ongoing advice and help whenever we needed. He also reviewed the information pertaining to PowerPC reference platform specification and operating systems.

Morris Grove reviewed the material on architectural definition of the PowerPC and provided useful suggestions regarding the format of the material.

John McKeeman reviewed the material on PowerPC-based embedded controllers.

Paul Lugo, Dave Thompson, and Mark Wieland reviewed the material on Wabi, Macintosh Application Services, and Common Desktop Environment.

Richard Swann helped us with the material on Windows NT.

Mark Hevesh and Sanjoy Chatterji perused the material on PowerOpen Association and PowerOpen Environment.

Jim Shaffer reviewed the material on AIX process subsystem internals and helped fine-tune the topics on processes and threads.

Our warmest thanks to the team at North Market Street Graphics, especially Virginia Carroll, Anne Friedman, Christine Furry, and Nathanael Waite,

xx   **Acknowledgments**

who adhered to a tight schedule to get this book out on time. A special mention should be made of editors Gerald Papke, Jay Ranade, and Rachel Hirshfield at McGraw-Hill.

A recognition or an acknowledgment will not be enough, but it will have to do for my wife, Aloka Chakravarty, without whose support this book would not have happened.

—D.C.

Special thanks to my management team—Pat Birdsall, Mark Akers, and Tom Cross—for their support.

—C.C.

Introduction

PowerPC is the result of the 1993 Apple, IBM, and Motorola alliance that has paved a path for a high-performance, low-cost RISC-based chip to penetrate the desktop market in high volume across a wide variety of operating environments. The revolutionary PowerPC technology was launched to offer users and vendors access to binary compatible platforms in the marketplace—a phenomenon in the UNIX arena.

The Apple-Motorola-IBM alliance is centered at the Somerset Design Center in Austin, Texas (Somerset being the county in England where King Arthur's Knights of the Round Table gathered to strategize). Motorola's manufacturing expertise, Apple's software support, and IBM's processor architecture make the alliance a formidable challenger in the microprocessor market.

This chapter discusses the PowerOpen Environment, the PowerOpen Association which promotes the environment, the evolution of POWER to PowerPC, and the comparison of PowerPC 601 (which is the first member of the family) with the Pentium processor.

1.1 OVERVIEW OF THE PowerPC

PowerPC technology is based on a RISC (Reduced Instruction Set Computer) architecture which is derived from IBM's POWER (Performance Optimized With Enhanced RISC) architecture. Note that performance was and still is the core driving force behind RISC-based systems. With a superior cost-performance balance, RISC processors have proven to be a peerless choice for systems ranging from entry-level personal computers to high-end servers, and embedded control applications.

Since the advent of the 8080 microchip, compatibility with existing architectures has been a major issue in microprocessor design. While Intel maintained an upward compatibility within generations of its own product line of 8086, 80286, 80386, 80486, and Pentium, Intel made the architecture more complex than it would have been otherwise. This is the reason that Motorola's 68000, upon its introduction into the marketplace, featured a much cleaner and simpler design than the 8086, and not surprisingly had an easier time maintaining compatibility in its 68020, 68030, and 68040 chips. History repeats itself, as this decade of computing offers us a new beginning with RISC processors.

Much of RISC's success is tied in with UNIX. Since much of UNIX (over 90 percent) and most UNIX software is written in C, a new microprocessor architecture poses less of a problem than would have been the case for MS-DOS and Macintosh worlds where the system software is in assembly language. The other significant advantage that RISC processors like the PowerPC offer is the ease of emulating existing instruction sets. Since RISC processors have outdistanced CISC processors in terms of performance, a comparable-speed emulation of CISC instruction sets becomes plausible, which is a monumental advantage for compatibility in the marketplace. AIX (Advanced Interactive Executive), IBM's version of UNIX, has been chosen to become the underpinning of the PowerOpen Environment.

1.2   PowerOpen ENVIRONMENT

The PowerOpen Environment is an application platform specification enabling binary-compatible applications to run on multiple vendor PowerPC-based systems. The PowerOpen Environment consists of the combination of any binary-compatible PowerOpen multiuser, multitasking UNIX operating system running on a PowerPC-based platform.

The PowerOpen Environment offers an optional extension, Macintosh Application Services, which allows users to run Macintosh applications within the PowerOpen Environment. At the same time, users can run OSF/Motif-based applications, and character-based applications. No matter what the user interface, each application rides on the PowerOpen Environment. The PowerOpen Environment specification includes an application binary interface, an application programming interface (which includes XPG4, XTI, and XNFS), and the PowerPC RISC microprocessor. See Fig. 1.1 for a conceptual layout of the PowerOpen Environment.

The PowerOpen Environment is designed to enable software vendors to produce shrink-wrapped software and powerful server systems to give users access to UNIX and Macintosh software. To promote the concept of shrink-wrapped applications in the high-powered workstation market, the PowerOpen Association is focusing on the concept of application binary compatibility—a concept taken for granted in the PC world, but elusive in the UNIX environment.

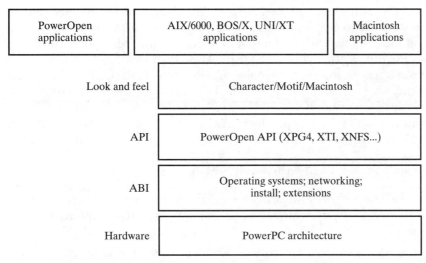

Figure 1.1 PowerOpen Environment. *(Copied with permission from IBM.)*

Using the PowerPC technology and PowerOpen system standards (derived from AIX), the PowerOpen Association has goals for a large application base supported and endorsed by major suppliers. The bottom-line question the PowerOpen Association wants to deliver on is: "What is needed for shrink-wrapped applications?" The group is modeling their efforts after the PC world model—to jump start acceptance of the PowerPC in the market, resulting in a larger base of shrink-wrapped applications (see Fig. 1.2).

1.3 PowerOpen ASSOCIATION

The PowerOpen Association is a not-for-profit association resulting from the 1991 PowerPC technology alliance of Apple, IBM, and Motorola. The Power-Open Association promotes the growth of the PowerPC marketplace, and develops and supports the PowerOpen specification. Launched in March 1993, the PowerOpen Association also performs compliance certification or branding (platform certification based on OSF's Test Environment Toolkit).

The PowerOpen Association is primarily concerned with making the PowerOpen Environment the most pervasive RISC-based open systems envi-

Figure 1.2 Jump starting the volume cycle.

ronment in the industry. The PowerOpen Association is not in business to create standards or to compete with standards groups; rather, the PowerOpen Association harmonizes with and defers to official standards groups including X/Open's XPG, ISO 9945-1 (POSIX), OSF's AES/OS, and Motif X-Windows.

The PowerOpen Association includes Apple, Bull, Harris, IBM, Motorola, Tadpole, and Thomson/CSF. Apple, Bull, IBM, Motorola, and Thomson/CSF function as sponsor companies, and Harris and Tadpole as principal members. The association functions independently in order to cooperate in establishing the PowerOpen Environment Standard while simultaneously competing in the marketplace.

PowerOpen's goals for software developers include:

- An independent corporation providing high-value services (porting assistance; ABI compatibility verification tools; branding program; environment promotion)
- Application development investment leverage (multiple platforms with a single port)

PowerOpen goals for end users include:

- Broad selection of applications (Macintosh desktop applications; UNIX-based workstation/server class applications)
- Vendor independence (multiple vendor platforms with binary compatibility)
- Scalable binary-compatible architecture (laptop to high-end multiprocessing)

Technical deliverables of the PowerOpen Association include the PowerOpen Environment Specifications, the PowerPC System Information Library, the PowerOpen 890 System Verification Test Suite (platform certification), the PowerOpen Application Verification Test Suite (application certification), and PowerOpen Cross Platform Technical Support (including fee-based technical support and porting assistance).

1.4 POWER TO PowerPC ARCHITECTURE

The first seeds for RISC were sown during the development of a telephone switching network in the midseventies. The progress made on the design of a prototype machine was taken up as a research project at the T. J. Watson Institute. The low cost-performance ratio of this prototype processor was exceedingly encouraging and, as a result, a system called the IBM 801 emerged. Although the 801 design could handle one instruction per cycle for specialized code, the rate fell short when used with general purpose code. In the continuing effort to smooth out the delays caused by storage access and conditional branching with additional pipelines, a new design was formulated. Referred to as the AMERICA architecture, this new design made use of three semi-autonomous processors. The design of AMERICA later evolved into RIOS, which came to be known as the POWER RISC System/6000 in the commercial world. The success of the POWER architecture led researchers and designers to develop a more flexible and cost-effective derivation of it. The result was the PowerPC.

The primary enhancement of the PowerPC architecture is the extension to 64 bits. All processors run 32-bit applications as a minimum; the 64-bit implementations have a 32/64-bit mode switch selectable from supervisor code. 32-bit applications can run on a 64-bit kernel. The extension simply increases the size of the registers to 64 bits and adds a few new instructions for 64-bit operations. In addition, PowerPC specifically extends the POWER architecture to directly support multiprocessing.

1.5   POWER-PowerPC DELTAS

The conventional traits of POWER architecture adhered to the fundamental RISC characteristics, and featured fixed-length instructions, a load-store architecture, and a generous number of general purpose registers.* It was also organized around the idea of superscalar instruction dispatch, pipelined implementation of instruction processing, and the presence of multiple independent execution units to increase the throughput for instruction processing. Finally, the architecture featured a set of unique facilities for handling branches via condition registers and leading to the concept of zero-cycle branches, and availability of a set of unique compound instructions that can be executed atomically.

The PowerPC uses the POWER architecture as its baseline and sculptures it to address the evolving needs of the computer industry. The IBM-designed POWER architectural definition was the logical starting point, as it already offered much of what the multicorporate alliance of Motorola, Apple, and IBM had in their vision for the next generation of desktop computing. New features, such as support for 64-bit computing, a more flexible microprocessor design for the Open Systems marketplace, and enhanced portability for running multiple operating systems, have been made available to the PowerPC architectural definition.

From a standpoint of comparative computer architecture, the POWER architecture featured a performance-crafted design, whereas the PowerPC architecture emphasizes a more cost-effective and flexible approach. To achieve this, some of the complex logic was removed and some new features were introduced.

The process of slimming the POWER architecture to formulate the PowerPC derivative consisted of the following highlights:

■ Elimination of "load-string and compare-byte" instruction which was the most complex instruction in the POWER architecture

---

* Refer to Chap. 2 for a detailed discussion on the RISC characteristics.

- Elimination of multiply-quotient (MQ) register and all extended precision shifts and integer multiply-and-divide instructions which use it
- Elimination of instructions whose operation was dependent on source operand value (to reduce cycle time)
- Elimination of several bit-field instructions that had three source operands

Add-ons to the PowerPC architecture beyond the POWER predecessor consisted of the following features:

- Extension of the architecture to a true 64-bit model
- Addition of single-precision floating-point instructions (POWER only supports double-precision, which precludes implementations with fast single- and slower double-precision)
- Addition of unsigned integer multiply and divide
- Provision for a fast-trap-and-emulate mechanism for implementing complex operations such as string operations (for low-cost implementations)
- Addition of an improved set of instructions for explicitly scheduling data into and out of the cache under user control
- Definition of a weak storage memory model (to simplify dynamic reordering of memory operations in hardware) with user storage locking and synchronization (for multiprocessors)
- Addition of a little-endian addressing mode switch

The charter of the PowerPC architecture group was to come up with a more cost-effective derivative of the POWER architecture. Therefore, the features of POWER architecture that were too restrictive and not as cost-effective, have

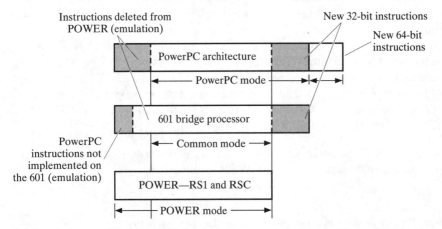

Figure 1.3 PowerPC and POWER architecture relationship. *(Copied with permission from IBM.)*

been eliminated in the PowerPC. Refer to Fig. 1.3 for a conceptual illustration of the POWER to PowerPC relationship.

The PowerPC initial focus is on the high-volume, single-chip implementations characteristic of the PC and low-end workstation markets building on the RSC. The benefits inherent in RISC architectures make the 601 microprocessor much easier to design and to fabricate at a given clock rate than Pentium, an implementation of the Intel CISC x86 architecture.

The PowerPC programming model and instruction op-code assignments remain fully POWER-compatible, enabling PowerPC users to access approximately 4000 AIX applications. However, there are some incompatibilities between PowerPC and POWER such as:

- Different alignment requirements
- Different interrupt mechanism
- Different I/O structure
- Different page table and cache model
- 32-bit and 64-bit implementations
- Support for single-precision floating point
- Instruction set differences

A complete set of POWER and PowerPC instructions is provided in App. C for reference.

1.6   PowerPC PERFORMANCE

The PowerPC architecture has been designed to support computers ranging from pen-based systems to desktop PCs to multiprocessing servers to multiprocess supercomputers, including real-time systems and server systems. The 601 and 604 microprocessors give desktop designers a chip for office computing and have extensive support for multiprocessing. The 603 microprocessor is targeted towards low-end desktop computers and laptops. The 620 microprocessor is targeted to the high-end workstations, server, and multiprocessor systems market.

The PowerPC microprocessor architecture goals include:

- Simplify architecture (smaller chips, faster cycle times, and more aggressive superscalar implementations)
- Improve architecture (for example, 32-bit single-precision floating-point, bi-endian addressing, low-power modes)
- Maintain compatibility of ABI with POWER (trap and emulate removed instruction)
- Incorporate multiprocessor support (strong multiprocessor comparabilities for scalability)
- Add 64-bit extensions (compete with competitive 64-bit architectures including MIPS R4000 and DEC Alpha while maintaining 32-bit compatibility)

1.6.1 Why the RISC-based PowerPC is faster

PowerPC CPUs achieve their performance by processing instructions faster than CISC CPUs. The chips adhere to RISC-specific design principles, whose goal is to complete one instruction every CPU clock cycle. To complete one instruction every CPU clock cycle, RISC chips employ uniform instruction size, which expedites the fetching of instructions. RISC processors do not have to pause and retrieve additional words to complete a pending instruction, as CISC processors sometimes do.

The reduced complexity of instructions simplifies instruction processing. RISC chips have little if any of the microcode instructions. Simple memory-addressing methods allow quicker access to main memory on the system board. RISC methods do not include complex calculations and multiple memory references, as the most sophisticated CISC methods do. Limited memory-access instructions reduce instruction size and simplify instruction processing. RISC instructions that manipulate data never get or put data in memory, but many CISC instructions combine those functions. An abundance of registers lessens memory access. Compared with CISC programs, RISC programs keep more interim results on the chip in registers and fewer off the chip in main memory.

To gain further understanding of these characteristic traits, refer to Chap. 2.

1.6.2 601 microprocessor

The 601-based machines target Intel's market—601s are for use in desktop computers, portable systems, and low-end multiprocessor systems. The PowerPC 601-based machines are not the first RISC systems to specifically target Intel's desktop hold, but they are the most formidable challengers. Designing competitive systems is not the problem; the problem is winning market share from the firmly entrenched Intel and getting independent software vendors to port their applications to PowerPCs.

However, the benefits inherent in RISC architectures make the superscalar 601 the microprocessor of choice. The 601 microprocessor (see Fig. 1.4 for an illustration) includes the following highlights:

- Capable of running at 50 to 80 MHz
- Bridge support for POWER applications
- Multiprocessing enablement
- Concurrent fixed-point, floating-point, and branch instruction execution capability
- 32-KB unified eight-way associative cache

1.6.3 603 microprocessor

The 603 microprocessor offers higher performance at low power level. The 7.4-by 11.5-mm chip features on-chip 8-KB instruction and data caches coupled to a high-performance 32/64-bit system bus. Peak instruction rates of three

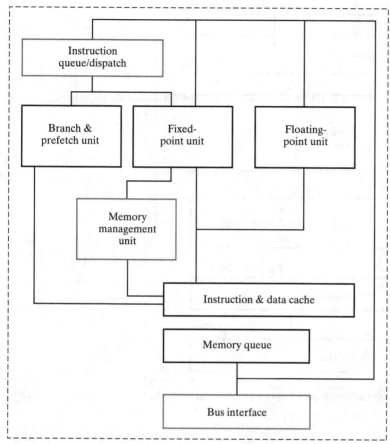

Figure 1.4 601 microprocessor architecture. *(Copied with permission from IBM.)*

instructions per cycle, with power levels below 3 W at 3.3 V, offer unparalleled notebook and portable computer performance at the current time.

The 603 microprocessor, a low-cost, low-power processor primarily for laptops and low-end desktop systems, includes the following highlights (see Fig. 1.5 for an illustration):

- Capable of running at 75 MHz
- Low-cost uniprocessor
- Nap and Doze mode for power saving
- 8-KB I-cache and 8-KB D-cache

1.6.4 604 microprocessor

The 604 microprocessor architecture uses superscalar design techniques to achieve high performance. It is a medium-sized, relatively high-performance

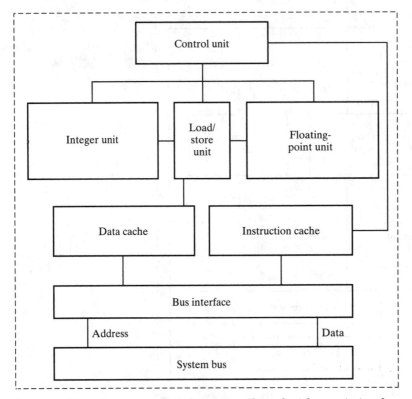

Figure 1.5 603 microprocessor architecture. *(Copied with permission from IBM.)*

part for mainstream personal computers, midrange workstations, and multiprocessor systems, including the following highlights (see Fig. 1.6 for an illustration):

- Capable of running at 100 MHz
- Multiprocessing support
- Fast L2 secondary cache
- 16-KB I-cache and 16-KB D-cache

1.6.5   620 microprocessor

The 620 microprocessor includes .5-μm CMOS process technology and an embedded secondary cache controller. The 620 microprocessor implements full 64-bit high performance for high-end workstations, servers, and multiprocessor systems including the following highlights (see Fig. 1.7 for an illustration):

- Capable of running at 150 MHz
- Single-chip modular 64-bit implementation

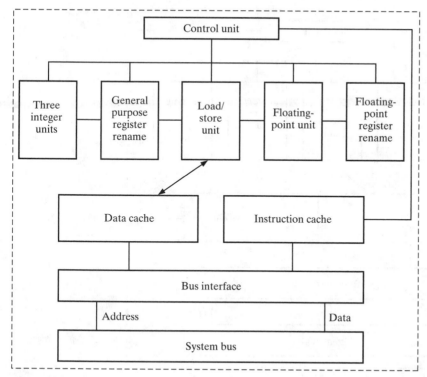

Figure 1.6 604 microprocessor architecture. *(Copied with permission from IBM.)*

- Dual fixed-point and floating-point execution units
- Multiprocessing support
- On-chip support for secondary cache
- Eight-way associative cache
- 32-KB I-cache and 32-KB D-cache

1.6.6   601 versus the Pentium

1.6.6.1   Market comparison

Intel's Pentium is primarily for use in servers and high-end microcomputers. Most of the first Pentium models are on existing systems with Pentiums added via daughter- or processor cards. Pentium is fully compatible with the existing suite of x86 software.

An advantage of Intel's Pentium is user acceptance—users have consistently been moving from 8080 to i286, i286 to i386, and then i386 to i486. A second primary advantage is the enormous x86 user base—Intel's x86 is the premier processor architecture in the mainstream computing market, with over 50,000

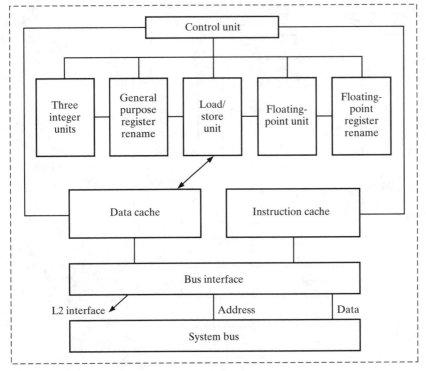

Figure 1.7 620 microprocessor architecture. *(Copied with permission from IBM.)*

supported DOS and Windows software products, and an installed base of over one hundred million PCs. PowerPC is a brand new technology. It is difficult to convince users to risk their heavy investments in software for moves to emerging platforms.

1.6.6.2 Architecture comparison

Both the PowerPC and Pentium are based on superscalar architectures. The PowerPC 601 has three pipelined execution units capable of issuing and retiring three 32-bit instructions per clock cycle. These instructions include one integer, one floating-point, and a branch processing unit which can be either integer or floating-point. Each of Pentium's two instruction pipelines includes an arithmetic logic unit, address-generation circuitry, and data cache interface. The Pentium's dual pipelines can only process two integer or one floating-point instruction per clock cycle. This two-to-three difference in instructions per clock cycle represents a definite performance advantage for the PowerPC 601.

Although both the PowerPC and Pentium include an on-chip cache, the Pentium's 8-KB data and 8-KB instruction cache is only half of that offered by the PowerPC 601's 32-KB, 8-way, set-associative, physically addressed unified cache. The on-chip cache memory acts as a buffer for instructions and data that can be accessed at high speeds to avoid loading another segment from the slower main memory. A larger cache translates into a smaller wait state, which improves overall processor performance.

The Pentium's floating-point processor, a redesigned version of that found in the i486, is still much slower than the PowerPC 601's. Its eight-stage pipeline can execute only one floating-point operation per clock cycle. Not surprisingly, the Pentium's 56.9 SPECfp92 is almost 40 percent slower than the 81 SPEC-int92 found on the PowerPC 601.

The PowerPC is based on a .65-μm complementary metal oxide semiconductor (CMOS) technology, while Intel's Pentium uses .8-μm BiCMOS (a combination of bipolar logic and CMOS) technology. The PowerPC 601 has four levels of metal wiring compared with three on the Pentium. See Fig. 1.8 for an overview of the 601 versus Pentium architecture.

The PowerOpen alliance is counting on most microcomputer buyers finding that Intel's i486 processor family can still meet their price and performance requirements and that the PowerPC support of multiple operating systems and applications running on high-performance hardware is worth the investment.

1.7   SYSTEM ENVIRONMENT OVERVIEW

While PowerPC and PowerOpen directly impact the workstation market, software running via emulation or natively on the PowerPC promises to break the x86 software applications barrier. Among the most important developments, SunSoft's Windows translator, Wabi, opens the Windows x86 application library to UNIX or any other software or hardware environment. Users can choose to work in either an OSF/Motif user environment, a Macintosh user environment, or a combination of both. Once in the Macintosh window, users interact with the Macintosh look and feel. Using the multifinder, users can cut and paste between the Macintosh window environment and virtually any other

Features	PowerPC 601	Pentium
Millions of transistors	2.8	3.1
Size of die	11 × 11 mm	16.6 × 17.6 mm
Power consumption	9W at 66MHz; 3.6-V	16W at 66MHz; 5-V
Cache size	32-K combined cache	8-K Instr; 8-K Data
Maximum instr/cycle	3	2
User registers	32 GPRs; 32 FPRs	8 GPRs; FP Stack
Architecture	RISC	CISC/RISC
Technology	CMOS	Bi-CMOS
Instruction format	Fixed length	Variable length
Data bus; Address bus	64 bits; 32 bits	64 bits; 32 bits

Figure 1.8   601 versus Pentium. *(Copied with permission from IBM.)*

X-client application on the PowerOpen system. Refer to Chap. 5 for details concerning the PowerPC end-user environment and to Chap. 6 to learn more about the PowerPC operating environments.

The PowerOpen Association's promise of promoting application availability is primarily achievable by the wide range of operating systems that are PowerPC functional. The PowerPC platform supports numerous 32-bit operating systems (which must be based on the PowerOpen base operating system ABI specification), including AIX, Solaris, Windows NT, Workplace OS, and Taligent. All the operating systems can run DOS and Windows under emulation, giving users an unending range of applications to choose from.

1.7.1   PowerOpen ABI and API

The application binary interface (ABI) defines the structure of the application as it was in the PowerOpen Environment. This includes such key definitions as loading and linking, conventions, object formats, the execution environment, networking infrastructure, and installation and packaging information. The PowerOpen ABI technical support is provided by a PowerOpen Cross Platform Support Center which answers questions or concerns about general ABI compliance issues and provides a specific company contact for platform-unique support.

The application programming interface (API) defines the set of system calls, library function, header files, commands, and utilities that an application developer is allowed to use to develop a compliant application. The PowerOpen API supports the following industry standards: XPG4, XNFS, XTI, and X11R5. The networking API provides the commands and parameter-passing definitions for intersystem operations. Both stream and sockets are used for networking in the PowerOpen Environment. TCPI/IP (discussed in Chap. 10) is one of the underlying protocols used for networking. See Fig. 1.9 for an illustration of how the ABI and API are aligned.

1.7.2   International language support

The PowerOpen Environment includes international language support. Character representation is handled by both UNIX's standard 7-bit ASCII, and also

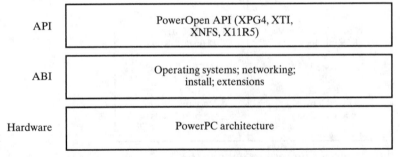

Figure 1.9 API and ABI alignment. *(Copied with permission from IBM.)*

by the ISO 8859 family of 8-bit extended ASCII code sets, as well as the de facto standard PC code set (IBM-850). For Asian languages, character encodings are supported by the Extended UNIX Code set, including support for Chinese, Japanese, and Korean characters.

Language customs and conventions support is provided for Chinese, English, French, German, Japanese, and Spanish. The same tools that are used to develop the language support are provided as a part of the environment, allowing further customization of customs and conventions. Software developers may also choose to develop additional language support.

1.8   SUMMARY

The PowerOpen alliance has promised to deliver support for binary applications running across PowerOpen compliant systems from multiple vendors. In an unprecedented effort in the UNIX environment, the evolution of the PowerOpen effort has geared up to encompass the hardware, system, software, and applications interfaces required to run both UNIX and Macintosh applications supporting any look and feel a user wants.

The delivery of the 601 and 603, with the 604 and 620 follow-ons, launches the PowerOpen alliance directly into the PC desktop mass market with an eye on the low-end laptop and high-end multiprocessing markets as well. IBM's formation of the PowerPersonal Systems Division to exclusively sell PowerPC-based systems competes directly with the marketing of IBM's own Intel-based systems highlighting IBM's commitment to the PowerPC products.

PowerPC compatible technology includes Apple's System 7, IBM's OS/2, DOS via emulation, AIX with the Macintosh GUI, Solaris, NetWare, Taligent, and Wabi, to name a few. The PowerOpen Environment allows users to work simultaneously with graphical applications based on a Macintosh- or OSF/Motif-based interface. Supported by the seven suppliers and backed by the POWER architecture, users have access to a large base of applications running on proven hardware—users have a standards-driven, open environment today.

Hardware

RISC Technology

The PowerPC features a RISC-based design. This chapter introduces some of the key concepts behind RISC architecture. The traditional notion of RISC was to create a machine with a very fast clock cycle that can process instructions at the rate of one per cycle. To achieve this, the idea of *pipelining* became a default trait of this type of architecture, since it is a natural technique to achieve the goal of executing one instruction per machine cycle. Understanding the underlying philosophy of RISC-based designs of microprocessors makes the study of PowerPC concepts, facilities, and design more useful and interesting.

2.1 EVOLUTION OF RISC

The first seeds for RISC were sown as a result of the development of a telephone switching network in the midseventies. Maybe nobody remembers the telephone switching network anymore, but the progress made on the design of a prototype machine at that time was taken up as a research project at the T. J. Watson Institute. The low cost-performance ratio of this prototype processor was exceedingly encouraging and, as a result, a system called the IBM 801 emerged. The term "RISC" was coined shortly thereafter by a University of California research group that was working on a similar project; their system was called the RISC I. So, when the IBM 801 was further refined and released commercially as the IBM RT, it was appropriately called a RISC-based system. Although the 801 design could handle one instruction per cycle for specialized code, the rate fell short when used with general purpose code. In the continuing effort to smooth out the delays caused by storage access and conditional branching with additional pipelines, a new design was formulated. Referred to as the AMERICA architecture, this new design made use of three semi-autonomous processors. The design of AMERICA later evolved into RIOS, which came to be known as the POWER RISC System/6000 in the commercial world. Very shortly after its introduction into the market, the success of the POWER architecture led researchers and designers to develop a more flexible and cost-effective derivative of it. The result was the PowerPC.

The architectural heritage of the PowerPC-based systems allows all the existing software applications for POWER architecture to work this new system, while taking additional advantage of PowerPC's new features.

2.2   RISC CHARACTERISTICS

What makes a machine a RISC machine is a set of its characteristic traits. They all have fixed-size instructions. For performance reasons, instructions are typically implemented in the hardware instead of being microcoded. A desired side effect of doing this is that it frees up a lot of the chip area, which would have been used to store the microcode. Also, a generous supply of general purpose registers was inherent to the design of RISC machines, since their architectural design called for instructions to be brought in to registers before being able to process them. These traits are further elaborated in the ensuing sections.

Most of the commercially available RISC processors, such as the HP Precision Architecture, Sun SPARC, DEC Alpha, and IBM POWER, incorporate a few hybrid features from non-RISC types of architectures, marrying the best of available technologies into one microprocessor to deliver optimal cost-performance ratio. An example of this is the implementation of the integer division logic in the POWER architecture in microcode instead of in the hardware. Note that there is nothing wrong with doing this, but the term *RISC* is thereby weakened from a purist's perspective on RISC architecture.

2.2.1   Load-store architecture

Load-store computer architecture is also referred to as a register-register architecture or RR architecture. In this class of machines, operands and results are retrieved indirectly from the main memory through the use of a large number of scalar or vector registers. In contrast to an RR architecture, there is a class of architectures called the storage-storage architecture in which source operands' intermediate and final results are retrieved directly from the main memory. The shorter notation for this class of machines is SS architecture. RISC machines are of the RR type of architecture.

2.2.2   Fixed-length instructions

Fixed-length instructions make it easier for the machine to decode them. By having simple instructions, it may take more instructions to do the same piece of work, but exploiting the fast, less-expensive memory devices makes it possible to execute a larger piece of code (a larger number of instructions) faster. This is consistent with the age-old principle: KISS (keep it simple, stupid!).

2.2.3 Hardwired control

RISC machines feature hardwired controlled instructions, as opposed to microcoded instructions. Contrary to the idea of using more complex (and often variable-length) instruction sets to maximize the semantic efficiency of the processor, simple instructions are found to be easier for the machine to interpret. Also, the work done in executing fewer instructions is not necessarily less, as there is microcode interpretation time involved; therefore, implementing instructions in hardware—although more expensive—offer a better performance equation in terms of execution time. Adding to this is the free-up of the microstore area on the chip and elimination of the time needed to interpret the microcode.

2.2.4 Fused instructions

Hardwired control also results in a higher degree of accuracy. This facilitated the implementation of *fused* or *compound instructions* in the design of the POWER and PowerPC architectures. By making certain frequently occurring instructions execute atomically as fused instructions, the gain on clock cycle savings is doubled.

Consider a basic floating-point multiply and floating-point add operation on a classical machine (Fig. 2.1). Now consider how a greater accuracy could be achieved. If the two steps of the classical multiplier and adder can be combined into a fused implementation of a multiply-add logic, an accuracy gain is achieved by reducing six connections to four connections in the instruction logic. Figure 2.2 explains this notion by showing how the fused multiply-add logic is actually implemented. In terms of accuracy, the reduction from six connections to four in the fused multiply-add instruction logic of the floating-point unit of the PowerPC is consistent with the RISC philosophy of producing heavily optimized units to tackle the most frequently required functions.

Classical FP multiply	Classical FP add
1. Add exponents.	1. Subtract exponents.
2. Multiply significands.	2. Shift significand with smaller exponent to right by the difference of exponents.
3. Normalize	3. Add significands. Larger exponent is the exponent of the result.
4. Round.	4. Normalize.
	5. Round.

Figure 2.1 Comparison of steps involved in a classical floating-point multiplication and a floating-point addition.

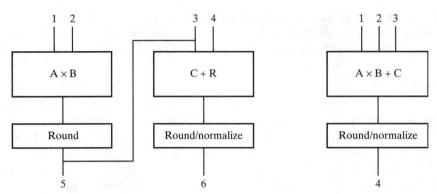

Figure 2.2 Implementation of classical multiplier and adder versus fused multiply-add implementation.

2.2.5   Pipelined implementation

Instruction execution in the PowerPC takes place in a way that is quite different from the classical machines that executed one instruction at a time with a *program counter* pointing to the instruction currently being executed. A pipelined architecture of the three execution units of PowerPC adds a new set of complexities to its instruction execution mechanism while yielding a high degree of performance. In order to best explain the functions, features, and benefits of pipelining, we first explain its basic design philosophy, followed by the implementation.

The basic principle of pipelining is quite natural; it is not specific to computer technology. The notion of a pipeline can be conceptualized using quite a few real-world examples. The first analogy can be made with petroleum pipelines where a sequence of hydrocarbons is pumped through a pipeline of treatment phases. The last product may be entering the pipeline before the first product has been removed from the terminus. Our second analogy is made with an assembly line in an industrial plant. Consider automobile manufacturing plants that build cars using an assembly line consisting of phases. The initial phase could be molding of the chassis itself, with the final phase being assembly of the engine. The last automobile may very well enter the pipeline before the first vehicle has been removed from the terminus. In both analogies, notice the fact that the net yield will be directly proportional to the number of phases of the pipeline or the assembly line.

The most significant contribution of pipelining is that it provides a way to start a new task before an existing one has been completed. Hence, the completion rate (or throughput) is not dependent on the total processing time, but rather on how soon a new process can be introduced in the pipeline.

To further illustrate this concept, consider the aspects of a general purpose processing operation. Figure 2.3 depicts a (simplified) sequential process done step-by-step over a period of time. Assume that three distinct stages in the automobile assembly are molding of the chassis, painting of the frame, and

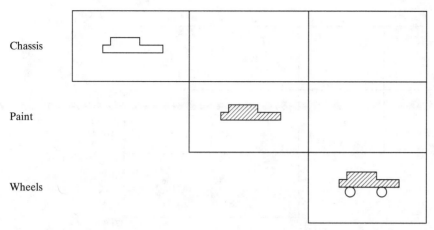

Chassis

Paint

Wheels

Figure 2.3 Pipelined execution for a three-stage automobile assembly line.

installation of the engine. If each stage takes one time unit, then the total time for the processing will be three units. So, to build three automobiles it will take nine time units.

To perform the same process using pipelining technique, imagine a continuous stream of the jobs going through the three stages. In this case, each horizontal row in Fig. 2.3 represents the time history for one job. Each vertical column represents the activity at a specific time. Note that up to three independent jobs may be active at any time in our example. Hence, to build three automobiles using this three-stage pipelining technique, it will definitely take less time than the nine time units that were required in the earlier case using sequential processing.

Relating the general ideas presented in Fig. 2.3 to computer design is quite straightforward. Formulate an analogy between executing a single computer instruction and the sequence of the automobile assembly line. Instruction processing is done in a number of pipeline stages. Each phase of computer instruction processing is conceptualized as a stage in the pipeline. Typically, an instruction is first fetched, then decoded, and subsequently executed. So, the three pipeline stages (1) *instruction fetch,* (2) *instruction decode,* and (3) *instruction execute,* can be correlated to the three stages in the assembly pipeline.

Figure 2.4 illustrates the analogy by substituting the names of the stages. In a specific sense, each of the three instruction-processing stages is significant. The instruction fetch stage consists of obtaining a copy of the instruction from memory when the program begins. The instruction decode stage comprises examining the instructions and initializing the control signals that are required to execute the instruction in the subsequent step. The instruction execution essentially executes the specific instruction in the processor. In this generic example, we assume that each of the stages takes one time unit to complete. This time unit is referred to as a *clock cycle* throughout the remaining discussion.

	1	2	3	4
Fetch	i_1	i_2	i_3	i_4
Decode		i_1	i_2	i_3
Execute			i_1	i_2

Figure 2.4 Pipelined execution of computer instructions.

In the normal mode of operation, the first stage of the pipeline will continuously fetch instructions, the second stage will decode instructions, and the third stage will continue to execute the decoded instructions. If you were to have a sequential stream of instructions, this pipelining scheme would be adequate to handle a program execution efficiently. But in the real world almost all programs have branches that lead to nonsequential execution of the code. When a conditional branch instruction is detected, its address cannot be determined until it is executed. If the branch falls through, the sequence of instructions will remain unaffected. However, if the branch is taken and it happens to be a forward branch, its address will remain unresolved. As a result, we will end up with a *hole* in the pipeline. The holes are also known as *bubbles*.

Figure 2.5 illustrates a simplified instruction stream that contains a forward branch instruction. Its pictorial representation is portrayed in Fig. 2.6, illustrating the temporal positioning of bubbles in a two-stage pipeline. If too many of these bubbles were to develop in the pipeline, the performance penalties (encountered by the idle clock cycles) will increase significantly. Although we can guarantee the proper execution of the instruction stream in the pipeline by interlocking the execution of the conditional branch fetched by the first stage such that no further fetches take place until the execution of the branch instruction in the next stage, we are penalized by acute performance costs. The method guarantees proper instruction execution, but it wastes too many clock cycles. So, one has to be able to deal with these bubbles in the pipeline in a reasonable way.

Dealing with bubbles in a pipeline requires an understanding of the fact that when a processing stage lies idle on a particular cycle due to the lack of available input rather than to a potential future collision, the idleness eventually propagates through the entire pipeline and deteriorates the overall pipeline efficiency. Some techniques exist to handle this problem.

A *delayed branching* technique that is suitable to sustain high performance is discussed first. It is based on the attempt to manipulate the sequence of

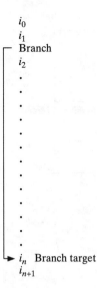

i_0
i_1
Branch
i_2
.
.
.
.
.
.
.
.
.
.
i_n Branch target
i_{n+1}

Figure 2.5 Simplified instruction stream containing a forward branch instruction.

instructions in the instruction stream at compilation time. An optimizing compiler is used to perform this feat. Figure 2.7 shows how a normal instruction stream is altered by realigning an independent instruction to execute immediately following the branch instruction fetch. The branch instruction is now followed by an independent instruction, i_2, so that the execution phase following the decode phase always remain full, as shown in Fig. 2.8. The machine attempts to execute one instruction per cycle, and the delay in the execution pipeline is two or more stages. This technique is well suited for early RISC processors. When the depth of the pipeline gets longer, it becomes exceedingly difficult to find independent instructions that can fill up all the bubbles. As a general rule of thumb, this technique becomes difficult to design for pipelines with a depth of three or greater.

Another way to sustain high performance is a *branch prediction* technique, in which the branch target is guessed in advance and the instructions in the pipeline are marked provisionally. After the outcome has been resolved, the

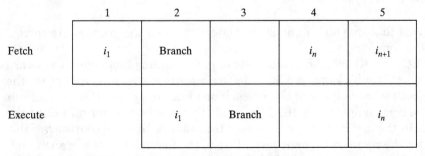

	1	2	3	4	5
Fetch	i_1	Branch		i_n	i_{n+1}
Execute		i_1	Branch		i_n

Figure 2.6 A two-stage pipeline showing bubbles generated by an instruction stream.

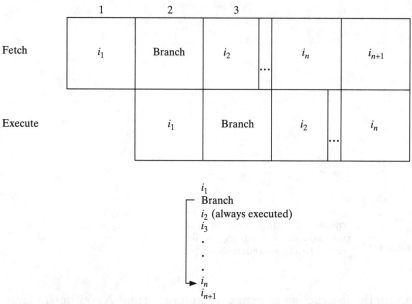

Figure 2.7 Delayed branching technique that allows a potential bubble to be replaced with an independent instruction that can be made to execute.

temporarily tagged results are made permanent if the guessed outcome was true; these tentative results are purged if the guessed outcome was false and the operations in progress are all canceled. The algorithm looks like this:

```
guess branch outcome
proceed on that path
.
.
.
if prediction correct
   < no bubble in the pipeline >
if prediction incorrect
   partially executed instruction cancelled
   < bubble left in the pipeline >
```

It is obvious that this technique is very effective when the guesses are correct most of the time.

In the FOR or DO/WHILE statements in programming languages, backward branches are usually loops. All loop-closing branches are taken except for the last one. So, for these types of branches, if one were to predict that the default case is the branch not taken, then the prediction will be true for all except the last case. In the last iteration of the loop, the value of the loop control variable will render the comparison logic false. Due to the availability of a branch-and-count instruction in some of the RISC machines' instruction sets, counting the number of loops becomes easy. The process becomes challenging when branch

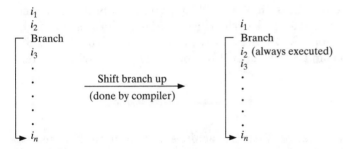

Figure 2.8 Outcome of realigned instruction processing (1) with and (2) without delayed branching technique.

instructions are used differently by different software, particularly when generated by different compilers. The IF/THEN statements that generate forward branches allow a guess to be correct only 50 percent of the time. Moreover, the branch address of a jump instruction might be the normal-case branch produced by one compiler and might be the exceptional-case branch in the code produced by another compiler. Which case should the hardware guess to be the normal case when deciding whether the branch is to be taken or not? With a random chance of guessing the outcome, there is the probability of being right half of the time.

Of the two methods of dealing with bubbles in the pipeline, the PowerPC makes use of the branch prediction method. For FOR and DO/WHILE loop constructs, it assumes that a branch is not taken. Due to the availability of its branch-and-count instruction, counting the number of loops is easy. So, for a loop of 100 iterations, all but the last iteration will succeed, thereby yielding a 99:1 success ratio. For IF/THEN constructs, the outcome has a 50:50 chance of succeeding. In real life, the instruction mix usually consists of three different types of branches: (1) unconditional, (2) loop-closing, and (3) forward branches. With all three branches occurring in equivalent proportions, it is imperative that the unconditional branches occur a third of the time, the loop-closing branches occur a third of the time, and the forward branches occur for the remaining third of the time. As the probability of the untaken forward branches is 0.5, the total likelihood that the branches will be predicted correctly is $\frac{1}{3} + \frac{1}{3} + (\frac{1}{2} * \frac{1}{3}) = \frac{5}{6}$. So, only $\frac{1}{6}$ of the branches (taken conditionals) may waste cycles and cause bubbles in the pipeline.

2.3 SUPERSCALAR IMPLEMENTATION

The availability of three independent execution units in the PowerPC that are capable of concurrent execution of instructions enables the processor to handle an instruction set so rich that it could execute multiple instructions in a single clock cycle. In addition to this parallelism, each of the individual execution units is pipelined, implying that they have the ability to process multiple instructions simultaneously. This implementation, i.e., the ability to process multiple instructions in a single clock cycle, is referred to as *superscalar* architecture. Available VLSI and CMOS technology is exploited to provide this feature—parallel execution of up to five operations per clock cycle—with the ideal instruction mix.

2.4   RISC/CISC TRADEOFFS

One of the typical characteristics of RISC machines is their simplified instruction set. This notion that a large set of simplified instructions can deliver a higher degree of throughput is best explained with the help of a practical everyday-life scenario. Consider an option to build a wall five feet high using either (1) a large number of small bricks or (2) fewer large concrete blocks. The amount of work done in each case is quite different. The larger blocks would be slower to carry (performance deterioration) but there would be fewer to fetch (performance amelioration). Likewise, the small bricks would be much faster to haul (performance amelioration), but there would be more to fetch (performance deterioration). Now if the rate at which the fetches are performed can be increased, then the latter method will end up being faster.

This is exactly how the performance metrics for RISC and CISC machines compare. The pros for CISC machines may be that there are fewer instructions to fetch and the size of the object code is smaller. But the cons are the time required to decode variable-length complex instructions and the slower rate of execution for its microcoded instructions. Table 2.1 describes some of the typical RISC and CISC characteristics.

2.5   EFFECT OF PIPELINING

A pipelined architecture for the three independent execution units of PowerPC has produced a significant yield from the instruction processing rate. In the earlier sections, the concept of a pipeline was explained in that a yield was shown to be directly proportional to the number of phases of the pipeline. If the pipeline can be kept full for any of the execution units, then every clock cycle will result in multiple instruction processing. The pipeline gains occur not only

TABLE 2.1   Typical RISC and CISC Characteristics

	RISC	CISC
Number of instructions	under 100	over 200
Number of address modes	1–2	5–20
Instruction formats	1–2	3+
Average cycles per instruction	near 1	3–10
Memory access	load/store only	most CPU ops
Registers	32+	2–16
Control unit	hardwired	microcoded
Instruction decode area	10%	over 50%

within an execution unit, but also result from the cumulative effect of multiple execution units processing as many instructions as their pipeline's depth will allow, per clock cycle.

2.6   REDUCED INSTRUCTION SET CYCLES

Most of the performance leverage resides in making optimal tradeoffs between instruction set functionality (the power of each instruction) and the clock cycles per instruction. Hence, the design of the PowerPC instruction set focuses on optimal functions per instruction. Minimizing the cycles per instruction (CPI) and reducing the path length as much as possible demonstrates how the net program execution time is affected.

The overall *program execution time* is really the number of instructions executed (*path length*), each using the given number of clock cycles that the architecture supports, while the *cycle time* is fixed for the given architecture. Thus, the performance metric can be expressed as

$$\text{program execution time} = \text{path length} \times \text{CPI} \times \text{cycle time}$$

All three variables contribute equally to the overall performance of the system. Note that the first two variables, the path length and cycles per instruction (CPI), can be controlled, while the third variable will remain constant for a given architecture. Minimizing the first two variables augments the overall performance. Having understood that this performance leverage results from making optimal tradeoffs between instruction set functionality and cycles per instruction, it is easier to appreciate how the PowerPC architecture is defined with as much function per instruction as possible. This reveals the parallelism that exists among the three independent execution units of this machine with the compilers, in order to harness the machine's ability to handle multiple operations per clock cycle.

2.7   SUMMARY

The advent of RISC architecture marks a new milestone in the field of hardware technology for computer systems. The architectural traits of a RISC design have their obvious benefits—so much so that RISC-based architecture has now reached the level of desktop machines from its original application in research and engineering environments. With the best cost-versus-performance ratio, RISC-based personal computers are on their way to becoming the de facto standard for the forthcoming decade.

The biggest advantage of RISC-based architecture is that we now have the speed-matching peripheral components to take advantage of the raw performance that the processor is capable of delivering. Because the RISC architecture of the PowerPC is scalable, it emerges as a possible leader, not only in the entry-level market, but also in the high-end computing arena. In the last few years it has been proven that megahertz is no longer the key criterion for speed, since a 20-MHz RISC-based processor (whether it is IBM's POWER or Hewlett Packard's HP-PA) is able to deliver a completely different level of performance than an Intel 80386 running at the same 20 MHz. The parallelism achieved through the presence of multiple independent execution units propels the effective performance of the machine above and beyond what was previously characterized as CPU throughput. In time, this parallelism will be expanded into massively parallel systems, which would then reach a new zenith of achievable performance.

Architectural Definition

This chapter focuses on the architectural definition of the PowerPC design and explains how the layered architecture defines varying degrees of compatibility, from an instruction set level, to a virtual environment level, all the way up to the operating environment level.

The domain of 32-bit and 64-bit architectural definition includes the instruction set, addressing modes, and all register and memory locations. The implementation, which is the actual hardware structure, logic design, and data path organization of a particular embodiment of the architecture, is discussed elsewhere in the book.

3.1 EVOLUTIONARY ROAD MAP OF PowerPC

When the POWER architecture was introduced in the form of the RISC System/6000 product line in 1990, its design philosophy, based on functionally partitioned execution units to separate the functions of program flow, remained unique and state of the art. It was unique because it attempted to minimize the overall throughput of a task instead of executing instructions at the fastest possible clock rate. It was state of the art because it delivered the best performance in the marketplace at that time. There were two implementations of the POWER architecture offered—namely, the RS 1.0 and the RS .9. The RS 1.0 implementation had a wider memory bus, a bigger data cache, and a dedicated instruction cache reload bus, while the RS .9 featured a memory bus half as wide, a half-size data cache, and a shared-instruction cache reload bus.

A year later, the subsequent generation of POWER processors offered a single-chip version of the silicon, in which the execution units were integrated on a single chip, along with the cache and memory management unit. This implementation was referred to as the POWER RSC (refer to Fig. 3.1).

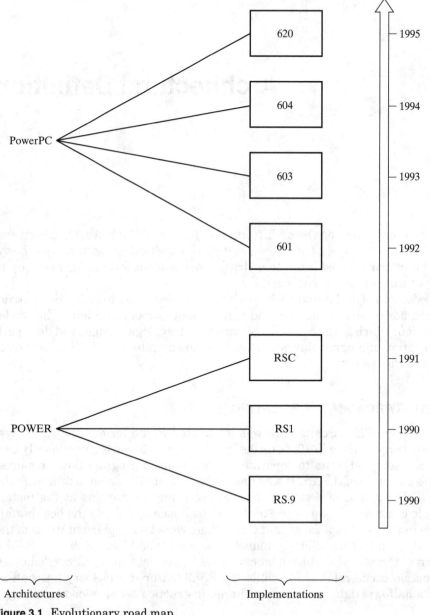

Figure 3.1 Evolutionary road map.

The third generation of POWER processors arrived with the advent of the PowerPC architecture. Although a slimmer and trimmer derivative of the POWER architecture, the PowerPC featured a more flexible design, while preserving full binary compatibility. The initial implementations consisted of four offerings, the 601, 603, 604, and 620.*

The common reference architecture that defines the design of PowerPC is specified at three different levels. From a bottom-up perspective, they are classified as follows:

- Instruction set architecture
- Virtual environment architecture
- Operating environment architecture

The lowest level, the *instruction set architecture,* refers to the programmer-visible instruction set. It defines the base user-level instruction set, user-level registers, data types, and addressing modes. Note that the components defined at this level form the fundamental elements of any software program, specifying what registers can be used and how address references can be made. As this is a baseline definition, it is legitimate for each implementation of the PowerPC architecture to add its own set of features. The next level, which is the *virtual environment architecture,* describes the semantics of the storage models that software programs have to adhere to. It defines some of the additional instructions, explains the timing facilities, and covers the memory and cache models as seen by the application programmer. The third level, the *operating environment architecture,* describes the structure of memory management, supervisory level registers, and the exception model. It goes into the details of privileged facilities not available to the application programmer, which include interrupt and exception handling mechanisms. Viewing this hierarchical definition, each higher level can be thought of as a superset of the previous level (Fig. 3.2). In the three following sections, the multilayer PowerPC architecture is unveiled layer by layer.

There are two computational modes supported by the PowerPC architecture: a 32-bit implementation and a 64-bit implementation. This scalable design provides a major benefit in terms of a structured road map for future enhancement with the same underlying architecture.

- 32-bit implementation
- 64-bit implementation

3.2   THE PowerPC INSTRUCTION SET

The complete instruction set is provided in Table 3.1.

---

* Their unique implementations are explained elsewhere in the book.

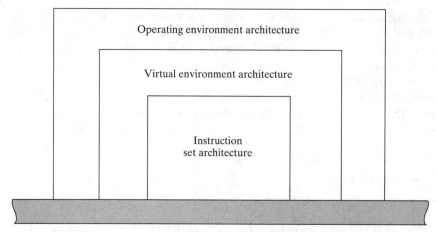

Figure 3.2 The common reference architecture of PowerPC illustrated as layered definitions to emphasize the varying degrees of compatibility from an application perspective.

3.3 THE 32-BIT PowerPC ARCHITECTURE

In this discussion of the 32-bit computational mode, all three layers have been described individually, providing a full view of the 32-bit architecture.

3.3.1 Instruction set architecture

All registers are 32 bits long, as they were in the original POWER architecture (the only exceptions are the floating-point registers, which are 64-bits for double-precision computations).

3.3.1.1 Processor implementation

The processor implementation consists of three independent execution units. The first is referred to as the *branch processing unit* because it processes the branch instructions. The second execution unit is called the *fixed-point unit* or the *instruction unit*. It executes fixed-point instructions and the load-and-store instructions. The third processor, the *floating-point unit,* is tasked with processing the floating-point instructions.

The data flow in the logical processing model (Fig. 3.3) for the PowerPC is essentially identical to that of the POWER architecture. Instructions are fetched from storage and fed into the branch processing unit, which in turn dispatches the nonbranch (fixed-point and floating-point instructions) to the fixed-point and floating-point units for subsequent processing. Together, the execution units orchestrate the code execution for the PowerPC processor.

A point to be noted here is that the PowerPC architecture does not include any specific I/O definitions.

The processor implements three classes of instructions: branch instructions, fixed-point instructions, and floating-point instructions. All instructions are

TABLE 3.1   PowerPC Instruction Set

Instruction	Mnemonic
Add	add[o][–]
Add carrying	addc[o][–]
Add extended	adde[o][–]
Add immediate	addi
Add immediate carrying	addic
Add immediate carrying and record	addic.
Add immediate shifted	addis
Add to minus one extended	addme[o][–]
Add to zero extended	addze[o][–]
AND	and[–]
AND with complement	andc[–]
AND immediate	andi.
AND immediate shifted	andis.
Branch	b[l][a]
Branch conditional	bc[l][a]
Branch conditional to count register	bcctr[l]
Branch conditional to link register	bclr[l]
Compare	cmp
Compare immediate	cmpi
Compare logical	cmpl
Compare logical immediate	cmpli
Count leading zeros doubleword	cntlzd[–]
Count leading zeros word	cntlzw[–]
Condition register AND	crand
Condition register AND with complement	crandc
Condition register equivalent	creqv
Condition register NAND	crnand
Condition register NOR	crnor
Condition register OR	cror
Condition register OR with complement	crorc
Condition register XOR	crxor
Data cache block flush	dcbf
Data cache block invalidate	dcbi
Data cache block store	dcbst
Data cache block touch	dcbt
Data cache block touch for store	dcbtst
Data cache block set to zero	dcbz
Divide doubleword	divd[o][–]
Divide doubleword unsigned	divdu[o][–]
Divide word	divw[o][–]
Divide word unsigned	divwu[o][–]
External control in word indexed	eciwx
External control out word indexed	ecowx
Enforce in-order execution of I/O	eieio
Equivalent	eqv[–]
Extend sign byte	extsb[–]
Extend sign halfword	extsh[–]
Extend sign word	extsw[–]
Floating absolute value	fabs[–]
Floating add	fadd[–]
Floating add single	fadds[–]
Floating convert from integer doubleword	fcfid[–]
Floating compare ordered	fcmpo
Floating compare unordered	fcmpu

TABLE 3.1   PowerPC Instruction Set (*Continued*)

Instruction	Mnemonic
Floating convert to integer doubleword	fctid[–]
Floating convert to integer doubleword with round toward Zero	fctidz[–]
Floating convert to integer word	fctiw[–]
Floating convert to integer word with round toward zero	fctiwz[–]
Floating divide	fdiv[–]
Floating divide single	fdivs[–]
Floating multiply-add	fmadd[–]
Floating multiply-add single	fmadds[–]
Floating move register	fmr[–]
Floating multiply-subtract	fmsub[–]
Floating multiply-subtract single	fmsubs[–]
Floating multiply	fmul[–]
Floating multiply single	fmuls[–]
Floating negative absolute value	fnabs[–]
Floating negate	fneg[–]
Floating negative multiply-add	fnmadd[–]
Floating negative multiply-add single	fnmadds[–]
Floating negative multiply-subtract	fnmsub[–]
Floating negative multiply-subtract single	fnmsubs[–]
Floating reciprocal estimate single	fres[–]
Floating round to single-precision	frsp[–]
Floating reciprocal square root estimate	frsqrte[–]
Floating select	fsel[–]
Floating square root	fsqrt[–]
Floating square root single	fsqrts[–]
Floating subtract	fsub[–]
Floating subtract single	fsubs[–]
Instruction cache block invalidate	icbi
Instruction synchronize	isync
Load byte and zero	lbz
Load byte and zero with update	lbzu
Load byte and zero with update indexed	lbzux
Load byte and zero indexed	lbzx
Load doubleword	ld
Load doubleword and reserve indexed	ldarx
Load doubleword with update	ldu
Load doubleword with update indexed	ldux
Load doubleword indexed	ldx
Load floating-point double	lfd
Load floating-point double with update	lfdu
Load floating-point double with update indexed	lfdux
Load floating-point double indexed	lfdx
Load floating-point single	lfs
Load floating-point single with update	lfsu
Load floating-point single with update indexed	lfsux
Load floating-point single indexed	lfsx
Load halfword algebraic	lha
Load halfword algebraic with update	lhau
Load halfword algebraic with update indexed	lhaux
Load halfword algebraic indexed	lhax
Load halfword byte-reverse indexed	lhbrx
Load halfword and zero	lhz

TABLE 3.1   PowerPC Instruction Set (*Continued*)

Instruction	Mnemonic
Load halfword and zero with update	lhzu
Load halfword and zero with update indexed	lhzux
Load halfword and zero indexed	lhzx
Load multiple word	lmw
Load string word immediate	lswi
Load string word indexed	lswx
Load word algebraic	lwa
Load word and reserve indexed	lwarx
Load word algebraic with update indexed	lwaux
Load word algebraic indexed	lwax
Load word byte-reverse indexed	lwbrx
Load word and zero	lwz
Load word and zero with update	lwzu
Load word and zero with update indexed	lwzux
Load word and zero indexed	lwzx
Move condition register field	mcrf
Move to condition register from FPSCR	mcrfs
Move to condition register from XER	mcrxr
Move from condition register	mfcr
Move from FPSCR	mffs[−]
Move from machine state register	mfmsr
Move from special purpose register	mfspr
Move from segment register	mfsr
Move from segment register indirect	mfsrin
Move from time base	mftb
Move to condition register fields	mtcrf
Move to FPSCR bit 0	mtfsb0[−]
Move to FPSCR bit 1	mtfsb1[−]
Move to FPSCR fields	mtfsf[−]
Move to FPSCR field immediate	mtfsfi[−]
Move to machine state register	mtmsr
Move to special purpose register	mtspr
Move to segment register	mtsr
Move to segment register indirect	mtsrin
Multiply high doubleword	mulhd[−]
Multiply high doubleword unsigned	mulhdu[−]
Multiply high word	mulhw[−]
Multiply high word unsigned	mulhwu[−]
Multiply low doubleword	mulld[o][−]
Multiply low immediate	mulli
Multiply low word	mullw[o][−]
NAND	nand[−]
Negate	neg[o][−]
NOR	nor[−]
OR	or[−]
OR with complement	orc[−]
OR immediate	ori
OR immediate shifted	oris
Return from interrupt	rfi
Rotate left doubleword then clear left	rldcl[−]
Rotate left doubleword then clear right	rldcr[−]
Rotate left doubleword immediate then clear	rldic[−]
Rotate left doubleword immediate then clear left	rldicl[−]
Rotate left doubleword immediate then clear right	rldicr[−]

TABLE 3.1   PowerPC Instruction Set (*Continued*)

Instruction	Mnemonic
Rotate left doubleword immediate then mask insert	rldimi[–]
Rotate left word immediate then mask insert	rlwimi[–]
Rotate left word immediate then AND with mask	rlwinm[–]
Rotate left word then AND with mask	rlwnm[–]
System call	sc
SLB invalidate all	slbia
SLB invalidate entry	slbie
Shift left doubleword	sld[–]
Shift left word	slw[–]
Shift right algebraic doubleword	srad[–]
Shift right algebraic doubleword immediate	sradi[–]
Shift right algebraic word	sraw[–]
Shift right algebraic word immediate	srawi[–]
Shift right doubleword	srd[–]
Shift right word	srw[–]
Store byte	stb
Store byte with update	stbu
Store byte with update indexed	stbux
Store byte indexed	stbx
Store doubleword	std
Store doubleword conditional indexed	stdcx.
Store doubleword with update	stdu
Store doubleword indexed with update	stdux
Store doubleword indexed	stdx
Store floating-point double	stfd
Store floating-point double with update	stfdu
Store floating-point double with update indexed	stfdux
Store floating-point double indexed	stfdx
Store floating-point as integer word indexed	stfiwx
Store floating-point single	stfs
Store floating-point single with update	stfsu
Store floating-point single with update indexed	stfsux
Store floating-point single indexed	stfsx
Store halfword	sth
Store halfword byte-reverse indexed	sthbrx
Store halfword with update	sthu
Store halfword with update indexed	sthux
Store halfword indexed	sthx
Store multiple word	stmw
Store string word immediate	stswi
Store string word indexed	stswx
Store word	stw
Store word byte-reverse indexed	stwbrx
Store word conditional indexed	stwcx.
Store word with update	stwu
Store word with update indexed	stwux
Store word indexed	stwx
Subtract from	subf[o][–]
Subtract from carrying	subfc[o][–]
Subtract from extended	subfe[o][–]
Subtract from immediate carrying	subfic
Subtract from minus one extended	subfme[o][–]
Subtract from zero extended	subfze[o][–]
Synchronize	sync

TABLE 3.1 **PowerPC Instruction Set (Continued)**

Instruction	Mnemonic
Trap doubleword	td
Trap doubleword immediate	tdi
TLB invalidate all	tlbia
TLB invalidate entry	tlbie
TLB synchronize	tlbsync
Trap word	tw
Trap word immediate	twi
XOR	xor[–]
XOR immediate	xori
XOR immediate shifted	xoris

four bytes long and word-aligned. As stated earlier in Chap. 2, the PowerPC architecture does not have any computational instructions that modify storage, since it follows a load/store architectural model. So, values must be loaded into registers before they can be manipulated. To facilitate this, a large number of user-level registers are available.

3.3.1.2 User-level registers

The branch processing unit contains several registers. The first one is called the *link register* (LR), and it contains the return address from subroutine calls. A set link bit in the branch instruction causes the next instruction address to be placed in the link register. The second register is called the *count register* (CTR), and it is used for counting loop iterations. It treats loop iterations as conditional branches, and causes all enumerated loops to be closed with a branch-and-count instruction, which, in turn, causes the CTR to decrement by one each time and branch on the resulting value. This naturally augments the performance level for code execution by a significant extent. The third register, the *condition register* (CR), enhances the traditional branch handling mechanism by providing register-level speed to resolve the results. It is worthwhile to mention here that the aforementioned set of registers in the branch processing unit form the baseline for the instruction-set-level architecture. As we build up the architectural definition layer by layer, the additional set of privileged registers that are not visible to the application programmers will be introduced. They are explained later in the definition of the operating environment architecture of PowerPC.

The fixed-point unit's main feature consists of the 32 general purpose registers (referred to hereafter as GPRs), which can be used by the application programmer. There is also an exception register (XER), which deals with the carry and overflow flags and contains byte count and comparison byte used by string instructions. As in the case of the branch processing unit, there are additional registers in the fixed-point unit that are outside the scope of the PowerPC's instruction set architecture.

The floating-point unit contains 32 floating point registers, which are referred to as the FPRs. These are used as source and destination operands

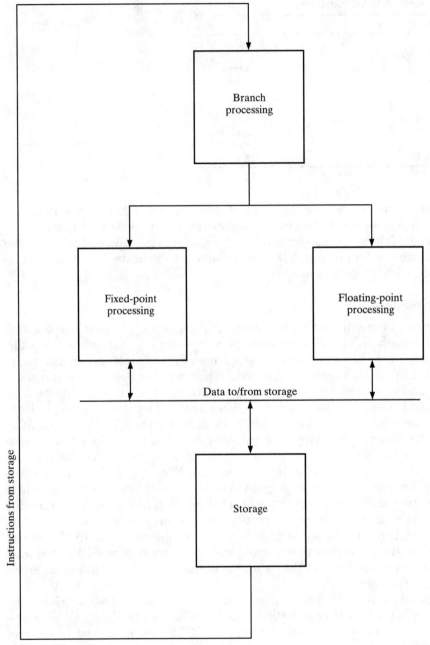

Figure 3.3 Common logical processing model for PowerPC and POWER architectures.

for all the arithmetic floating-point operations and their results. There is also a floating-point status and control register (FPSCR) which handles floating-point exceptions and records status resulting from the floating-point operations.

Figure 3.4 presents all the pertinent user-level registers in the three execution units of PowerPC's 32-bit implementation.

3.3.1.3   New instructions for 32-bit implementations only

It should be noted that most of the instructions are available in both the 32- and the 64-bit modes, although their implementation-specific formats differ. Those instructions that are provided only for 32-bit implementations are illegal in 64-bit implementations. Currently, there is only one instruction defined (see Table 3.2) that is exclusive to the 32-bit implementation.

3.3.2   Virtual environment architecture

The concept of storage was oversimplified in the earlier section (instruction set architecture), where it was expressed as an array of bytes ranging from 0 to $(2^{32} - 1)$ for its 32-bit implementation. In this section, the idea of storage (i.e., memory) is further expanded in light of how it is viewed by the virtual environment architecture.

The storage model encompasses cache(s), virtual storage, and shared storage multiprocessors.

3.3.2.1   Cache model

The typical implementation of a cache consists of a partitioned *set* of *lines,* where each set contains one or more lines. Lines (also referred to as *blocks*) are the basic unit of transfer between the cache itself and the main memory. The organization of the cache (refer to Fig. 3.5 for an example) is determined by three parameters: the number of sets in the cache *N,* the number of lines present in a set *K* (i.e., the associativity of the cache), and the size of each line *L.* The cache size is given by the formula

$$\text{cache size} = L \times K \times N$$

The PowerPC architecture does not specify any rigid cache organization in terms of its associativity and size. Although many flexible implementations are allowed, a programmer is expected to assume that there are separate instruction and data caches in the system. This type of model, which uses two separate memory spaces to allow simultaneous access of data and instructions,

TABLE 3.2   New Instructions for 32-Bit Implementations Only

mfsrin	Move from segment register indirect

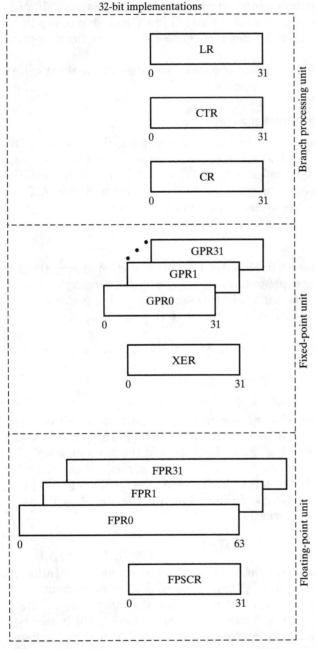

Figure 3.4 User-level registers in the three execution units in a 32-bit implementation: LR = link register; CTR = count register; CR = condition register; GPR0–31 = general purpose registers; XER = exception register; FPR0–31 = floating-point general purpose registers; FPSCR = floating-point status and control register.

is commonly referred to as the Harvard architectural model (refer to Fig. 3.6). Some PowerPC implementations, like the 601, use a unified instruction and data cache (also referred to as a Von Neumann machine model) to gain the flexibility of allowing data and instructions to take variable amounts of the same space at the cost of compromising half the bandwidth of the Harvard architecture. The cache management instructions still depend on the Harvard cache model.

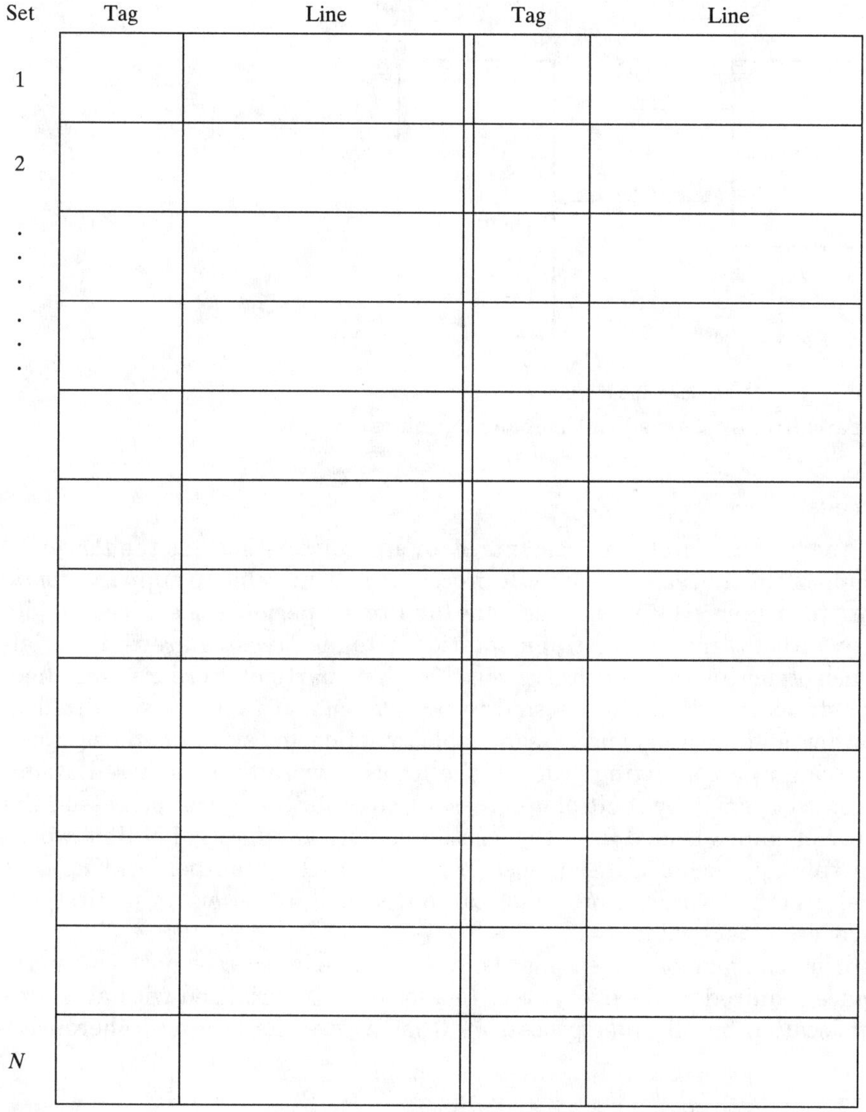

Set	Tag	Line	Tag	Line
1				
2				
.				
.				
N				

Figure 3.5 Organization of a two-way set-associative cache with N sets.

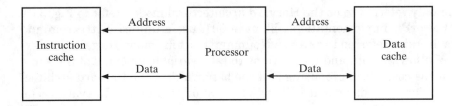

Harvard architecture

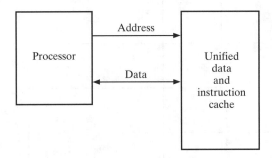

Von Neumann machines

Figure 3.6 Harvard architecture versus Von Neumann machines.

3.3.2.2 Memory model

One of the fundamental requirements of an architecture such as the PowerPC that supports a shared storage multiprocessor is being able to support *atomic updates* to memory locations—i.e., the ability to perform the access to its entirety without any visible fragmentation. Atomic accesses are thus serialized, each occurring to its entirety even though no particular order is specified. Atomic stores to a location are said to be *coherent** if they are serialized in some order, and no (other) processor is able to notice any subset of those stores as occurring in a conflicting order. If the location were to be accessed atomically and coherently by multiple processors, then for any given processor, the sequence of values loaded from the location during any interval of time would form a subsequence of the sequence of values the location held during that interval. In other words, a processor can never load a "newer" value first, followed by an "older" value.

There are two memory access modes. When a page is accessed in the memory-coherence-required mode, every store to a location is serialized with all stores to that location by all other processors (that access the location coherently).

---

* Memory coherence refers to the ability of all processors to "see" the latest update to a location in memory, regardless of caching.

This is implemented by an ownership protocol that ensures that, at most, one processor stores to that location at a time. On the other hand, when a page is accessed in the memory-coherence-not-required mode for software performance reasons, the processor does not impose any storage coherence. However, it is the software's responsibility to ensure that relevant cache management instructions have been executed to put the memory in a consistent state.

The PowerPC architecture specifies that the memory coherence is managed in terms of logical units called *coherence blocks,* whose size is implementation-dependent.

In terms of shared memory support, different instances of the same or separate program(s) running on one or more processors may share memory. The basic unit of memory sharing is blocks. Also, a location may be accessed using different effective addresses. This is a noteworthy trait, since by using this feature (called *address aliasing*), each application can be assigned separate access privileges to aliased pages.

A weakly consistent storage model specified in PowerPC offers an increased performance level by allowing the processor to run very fast for most storage accesses. However, the tradeoff is that the programs have to guarantee proper placement of the ordering or synchronization instructions. In this architecture, the actual order in which a storage access is issued, executed, and viewed could be completely different. This is a strategy for sharing resources (storage in this case) among multiple participants, and is referred to as *storage access ordering*.

3.3.3   Operating environment architecture

At this level of abstraction, the PowerPC architecture encompasses the supervisory level registers, explains the exception model, and details the structure of memory management.

3.3.3.1   Privileged registers

In PowerPC architecture, there are several privileged registers that are not visible to the application programmers. These registers control special attributes of the machine.

The branch processing unit features a register called the machine state register (MSR) that describes the state of the processor by describing system states like user/supervisory mode, interrupt enable/disable mode, and address relocate on/off status.

The next set of registers worth mentioning is the set of machine status save and restore registers (SRR). The SRR0 and SRR1 save the old value of MSR and the address of the interrupted instruction in the event of an interrupt. Upon returning from the interrupt, they restore the MSR value and resume execution from the interrupted instruction.

Finally, there is a processor version register (PVR), which identifies the version and revision model of the microprocessor. Unlike the rest of the privileged registers, the PVR is a read-only register and is always 32-bit (even in the 64-bit implementation, discussed later).

The fixed-point unit's list of privileged registers consists of a data address register (DAR), which specifies the address of storage access that caused a data storage or alignment interrupt.* Another privileged register, the data storage interrupt status register (DSISR) defines the actual cause of the data storage or alignment interrupt. Note that the DSISR is always 32-bit (even in the 64-bit implementation). In addition, there are four 32-bit special purpose registers (SPRG0 to SPRG3) provided for the operating system's use.

The floating-point unit contains a special register called the floating-point status and control register (FPSCR). It enables/disables floating-point exceptions and records status resulting from the floating-point operations, which is required by the IEEE 754 standard.

Figure 3.7 shows the pertinent privileged registers within the three execution units of PowerPC's 32-bit implementation.

3.3.3.2 Interrupt handling strategies

A standard interrupt processing and exception handling model is provided by the PowerPC architecture to allow change of state under unusual conditions.

There are several types of interrupts supported by the PowerPC architecture. Some of the interrupts are caused by the system (system-caused interrupts), while the others may be caused by instructions (instruction-caused interrupts).

Upon the generation of an interrupt, control is transferred to a set of privileged routines called *interrupt handlers*. The interrupt handler routine services the interrupt and, after completion, may transfer control back to the software to continue execution. In general, information (such as the instruction that should be executed after control is returned to the original program and the contents of the machine state register) is saved to the save/restore registers (SRR0 and SRR1), program control passes from user to supervisory level, and the software continues execution at an address predetermined from each interrupt.

Occurrence of instruction-caused interrupts in classical machines is not a new concept, since the program counter is able to maintain a pointer to the precise location of the instruction stream. But on the PowerPC, there is no program counter per se. With three separate independent execution units, processing a single instruction stream makes recovering from interrupts not a simple task. Recognize that since different instructions are executed by different (and independent) execution units, the instruction stream can be left fragmented. So, this fragmented state requires the architecture to provide a means for reconstructing the instruction stream around the point of the interrupt so that the postinterrupt processing code can recreate the sequential state. Due

---

* A *data storage interrupt* is a hardware interrupt that occurs because of a nontranslatable virtual address access, a storage protection violation, an access denial owing to data locking, or an I/O exception condition. An *alignment interrupt* is another type of hardware interrupt that occurs when the effective address generated by a load or a store violates a storage boundary.

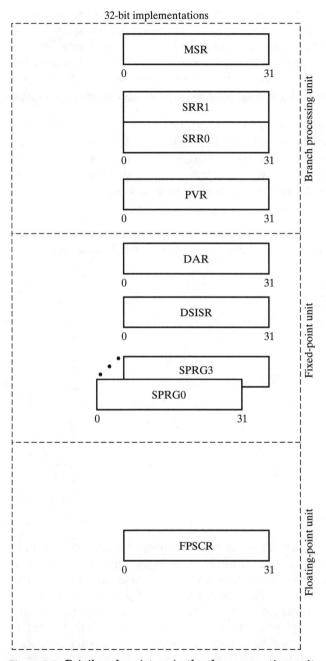

Figure 3.7 Privileged registers in the three execution units of the Power PC microprocessor: MSR = machine state register; SRR0 and SRR1 = save and restore registers; PVR = processor version register; DAR = data address register; DSISR = data storage interrupt status registers; SPRG0–3 = special purpose registers; FPSCR = floating-point status and control register.

to the pipeline complexity of the machine organization, architecting a method for handling interrupts in an imprecise manner gets costly and complex. Therefore, the architecture has to enforce generation of precise interrupts. Despite the fact that out-of-order instruction dispatches are supported by the architecture and interrupt conditions are recognized out of order, interrupts are handled in program order. Except for a catastrophic condition causing a system reset or machine check interrupt, only one exception is handled at a time. If, for example, a single instruction encounters multiple interrupt conditions, those conditions would be encountered sequentially. Following the processing of an interrupt, the instruction execution will continue until the occurrence of the next interrupt condition. In this way, recognizing and handling interrupt conditions sequentially guarantees that interrupts are recoverable.

3.3.3.3 Types of interrupts

The following types of interrupts are specified in the PowerPC architecture:

- System reset
- Machine check
- Data storage
- Instruction storage
- External
- Alignment
- Program
- Decrementer
- System call
- Trace
- Floating-point assist
- Floating-point unavailable

The *system reset interrupt* causes a system reset (causing the system to reboot), which can happen in the event of an unlikely catastrophic failure. Sometimes byzantine anomalies may cause the system to enter a checkstop state* by issuing what is called a *machine check interrupt*. A *data storage interrupt* is another type of hardware interrupt that occurs because of a nontranslatable virtual address access, a storage protection violation, an access denial owing to data locking, or an I/O exception condition. An *instruction storage interrupt* occurs because of a nontranslatable effective address, a storage protection violation by a fetch access, or fetch access owing to a direct-store segment. An

---

* This is a special state in which instruction processing is suspended till the processor has been reset. It freezes the contents of registers in order to aid in problem determination.

external interrupt is generated when there is no higher priority exception. An *alignment interrupt* occurs when the effective address generated by a load or a store, violates a storage boundary. There is a *program interrupt* that can occur when the system encounters an illegal instruction, a privileged instruction, or a trap instruction. A *decrementer interrupt* occurs when no higher priority interrupt exists and the decrementer register has completed decrementing. A *system call interrupt* is generated whenever there is a system call instruction encountered in the program. A *floating-point unavailable interrupt* takes place whenever a floating-point instruction is executed and the floating point unit is disabled. A *trace interrupt,* if implemented, is caused in the event of a branch-and-trap instruction or from single-stepping through instructions. A *floating-point assist interrupt,* if implemented, renders a degree of software assistance to implemented floating-point instructions that require assistance in order to complete operations such as those involving denormalized numbers, and unimplemented floating-point instructions that are not optional.

Note that, except for the system reset, machine check, external, and decrementer interrupts, all other types of interrupts are regarded as instruction-generated interrupts.

3.3.3.4   Structure of the memory management model

The memory model and its management policies form the infrastructure for any program's execution. Software programs would have to reference storage using an effective address that is computed by the processor. This effective address is translated to a real address, as per a set of address translation rules, and, consequently, accesses are made to location(s) in memory.

In order to best understand the memory management scheme, a set of parameters needs to be explained. Some of these parameters are consistent across the architecture, while some depend on the implementation (32-bit or 64-bit) of the architecture.

The design of the memory layout in PowerPC architecture uses a segmented scheme, with a set of special registers called the *segment registers* (SRs). There are 16 SRs that divide the total addressable memory into *segments,* each of which is 256 MB in size. Segments can be of two types: (1) Ordinary storage segment (or regular storage segment) and (2) Direct-store segment.

Direct-store segments are meant for access to an external address space like an I/O bus or device, while the ordinary storage segments refer to internal address space in memory.

The basic unit of addressing real memory is referred to as a *page frame* or simply a *page,* the size of which is 4 KB. Since the 256-MB segment is accessed in 4-KB chunks, it can be also be viewed as if there are 64,000 (2^{16}) pages that a single segment can access. The rest of the description for the memory model is implementation-specific, i.e., it varies with 32-bit versus 64-bit implementations, summarized in Fig. 3.8.

In this discussion of 32-bit implementations, the maximum real memory size is limited to 4 GB. Segments totalling 2^{24} can be accessed, with an effective address range of 2^{28} and virtual address range of 2^{52}.

	32-bit	64-bit
Maximum real memory size	4 GB	16 EB
Number of addressable segments	2^{24}	2^{52}
Effective address range	real 2^{32} relocate 2^{28}	2^{64}
Virtual address range	2^{52}	2^{80}

Figure 3.8 Comparison of memory model parameters that are implementation-specific.

3.3.3.5 Address translation concept

An address generated by the processor (which is referred to as an *effective address*) must undergo a translation step before being able to access an actual location. The address translation scheme in PowerPC comprises two available approaches that proceed in parallel (for performance reasons). The two simultaneously progressing translations are referred to as *segmented address translation* and *block address translation*. Typically, one of them ought to succeed, otherwise, a storage exception will be encountered. If both succeed, then the block address translation takes precedence.

- Segmented address translation
- Block address translation

When a segmented address translation occurs, it accesses either an ordinary storage segment or a direct-storage segment. Depending on which type of segment is accessed, this address is either converted into a real address through an intermediate step and then used to access storage, or it is converted directly into an I/O address and passed to the I/O subsystem for further action. When a block address translation occurs, the effective address is directly converted into a real address, and then used to access storage. Figure 3.9 further illustrates these various modes of storage access.

In both cases, a set of four privileged bits, called the *mode control bits,* are used to assign a context-specific meaning to the effective address (such as determining whether a coherence is required for the address).

3.3.3.6 Segmented address translation

The steps consist of starting with a 32-bit effective address and generating a 52-bit virtual address, to get access to a 32-bit real address. Refer to Fig. 3.10 for an overview of the address translation process, and to understand how the 32-bit segment registers play a strategic role in the translation.

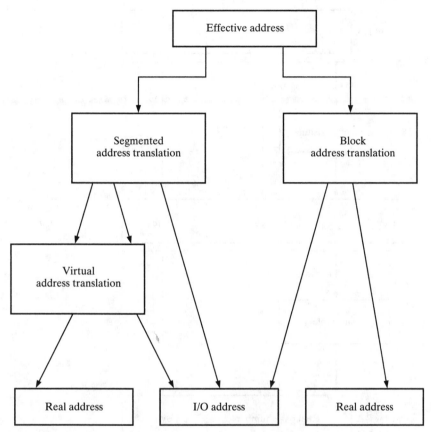

Figure 3.9 Types of address translations in PowerPC.

For segmented address translation, out of the 32 bits of the address, 4 bits (0–3) are used to index into one of the 16 segment registers to yield a virtual segment ID. A 24-bit segment ID, when concatenated with 16 additional bits (4–19) of the effective address, yields a 40-bit virtual page number within that segment. This in turn, is indexed into a structure called the *page table* to yield a 20-bit real page number. When the offset, i.e. the remaining 12 bits (20–31), from the effective address is concatenated to this real page number, the result is the corresponding real address that can access the storage. Figure 3.11 illustrates the steps involved in the process of translating the effective address into a virtual address.

This segmented address translation scheme is used for the 32-bit implementation only. For 64-bit architectures, the scheme is significantly different.

3.3.3.7 Block address translation

Typically, the smallest unit used to map ranges of virtual addresses into real memory is a page (where a page is 4 KB in size). The dynamics of program exe-

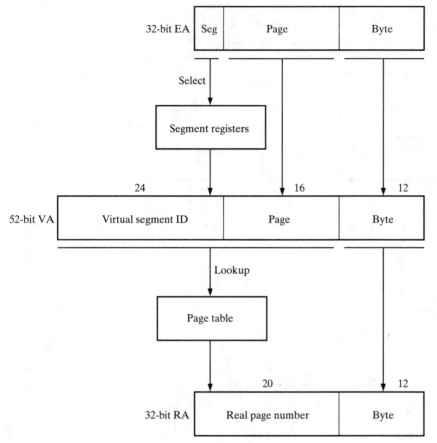

Figure 3.10 Address translation in 32-bit implementation.

cution typically references a selected set of pages periodically. The block address translation feature allows clusters of pages to be accommodated onto contiguous areas of real memory. In this way, it augments the performance of accesses to nonpageable areas of memory. In general, candidates for this type of access are memory mapped files or large arrays of numerical data.

The newly introduced *block address* paradigm imposes some specifications, the principal one being that the variable size of a block must be boundary-aligned, and consist of a minimum of 32 pages (128 KB) to a maximum of 65,536 pages (256 MB) with a finite set of allowable intermediate sizes. As is apparent by now, the block address translation areas are all in powers of 2.

The size of, as well as access to, a block address translation (BAT) area is controlled by a set of special purpose registers called the BAT registers. The mechanisms for interpreting the block length and address are essentially the same for the 32-bit and the 64-bit implementations; it is the number of bits in each field that is different. Figure 3.12 illustrates how a pair of BAT registers is used to interpret information in the 32-bit implementations.

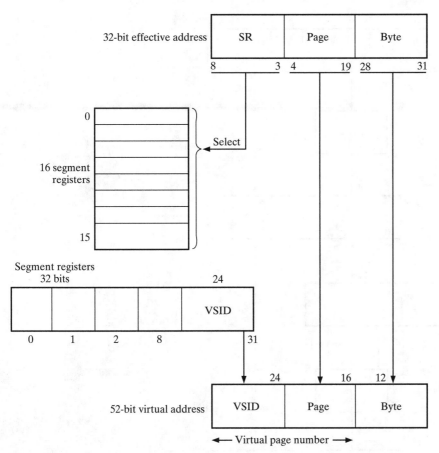

Figure 3.11 Translation of 32-bit effective address to virtual address.

3.4   THE 64-BIT PowerPC ARCHITECTURE

In this discussion for the 64-bit computational mode, all three layers are described individually, enabling an overall focus on the 64-bit architecture in its entirety, without having to cross-reference the 32-bit counterpart.

3.4.1   Instruction set architecture

The two computational modes (32-bit and 64-bit) supported by the PowerPC architecture provide not only a scalable design but also a structured road map for future enhancement using the same underlying architecture.

The 64-bit implementation features all 64-bit registers, with effective addresses of 64 bits long. The 64-bit implementations have two modes of operation:

- a 64-bit mode
- a 32-bit mode

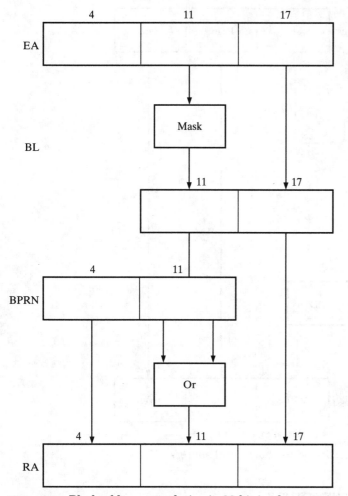

Figure 3.12 Block address translation in 32-bit implementation.

These modes control how the effective address is interpreted and how status bits are set.

The two computational modes view storage merely as an array of bytes, where each byte is identified by its index, called its *address*.

3.4.1.1 Processor implementation

The processor implementation consists of three independent execution units. The first of the three execution units is referred to as the *branch processing unit,* because it processes the branch instructions. The second execution unit is called the *fixed-point unit* or the *instruction unit,* and it executes fixed-point instructions and the load-and-store instructions. The third processor, which is the *floating-point unit,* processes the floating-point instructions.

The data flow in the logical processing model (Fig. 3.3) for the PowerPC is essentially identical to the POWER architecture. Instructions are fetched from storage and fed into the branch processing unit, which in turn dispatches the nonbranch (fixed-point and floating-point) instructions to the fixed-point and floating-point units for subsequent processing. Together, the execution units orchestrate the code execution for the PowerPC processor.

Note that the PowerPC architecture does not include any specific I/O definitions.

The processor implements three classes of instructions:

- branch instructions
- fixed-point instructions
- floating-point instructions

The PowerPC architecture does not have any computational instructions that modify storage, since it follows a load/store architectural model. So, values must be loaded into registers before they can be manipulated. To facilitate this, a large number of user-level registers are available.

3.4.1.2 User-level registers

The branch processing unit contains several registers. The first one is the link register (LR), which is a 64-bit register and contains the return address from subroutine calls. A set link bit in the branch instruction causes the next instruction address to be placed in the *link register*. The second register, called the *count register* (CTR), is used for counting loop iterations. It treats loop iterations as conditional branches, and causes all enumerated loops to be closed with a branch-and-count instruction. This causes the 64-bit count register to decrement by one each time and branch on the resulting value. This naturally augments the performance level for code execution to a significant extent. The third register, the *condition register* (CR), is a 32-bit register. It enhances the traditional branch handling mechanism by providing register-level speed to resolve the results. It is worth mentioning here that this set of registers in the branch processing unit forms the baseline for the instruction-set-level architecture. As the architectural definition is constructed layer by layer, the additional set of privileged registers that are not visible to the application programmers will be introduced. They are explained in the next architectural definition, the operating environment architecture of PowerPC.

The fixed point unit's main feature consists of the thirty-two 64-bit general purpose registers (GPRs), which can be used by the application programmer. There is also an exception register (XER), which deals with the carry and overflow flags, and contains byte count and comparison byte used by string instructions. Note that the exception register is 32-bit. As in the case of the branch processing unit, there are additional registers in the fixed-point unit that are outside the scope of the PowerPC's instruction set architecture, and are therefore discussed in later sections.

The floating-point unit contains thirty-two 64-bit floating point registers, which are referred to as FPRs. These are used as source and destination operands for all the arithmetic floating-point operations and their results. There is also a floating-point status and control register (FPSCR) which handles floating-point exceptions and records status resulting from the floating-point operations. Note that the floating-point status and control register is 32-bit.

Figure 3.13 shows all the pertinent user-level registers within the three execution units.

3.4.1.3   New instructions for 64-bit implementations only

It should be noted that most of the instructions are available in both the 64- and the 32-bit modes, although their implementation-specific formats differ. Those instructions that are provided only for 64-bit implementations are illegal in 32-bit implementations.

Refer to Table 3.3 for a list of instructions that are exclusive to the 64-bit implementation.

3.4.2   Virtual environment architecture

The concept of storage was oversimplified in the earlier section (instruction set architecture), where it was expressed as an array of bytes ranging from 0 to $(2^{64} - 1)$ for its 64-bit implementations. In this section, the idea of storage (memory) is further expanded with respect to the virtual environment architecture.

The storage model includes cache(s), virtual storage, and shared storage multiprocessors.

3.4.2.1   Cache model

The typical implementation of a cache consists of a partitioned *set* of *lines,* where each set contains one or more lines. Lines (*blocks*) are the basic unit of transfer between the cache itself and the main memory.

The PowerPC architecture does not specify any rigid cache organization in terms of its associativity and size. Although many flexible implementations are allowed, a programmer is expected to assume that there are separate instruction and data caches in the system. In fact, the cache management instructions depend on a Harvard cache model with separate caches for instruction and data.

3.4.2.2   Memory model

There are two memory access modes. When a page is accessed in the memory-coherence-required mode, every store to a location is serialized with all stores to that location by all other processors (that access the location coherently). This is implemented by an ownership protocol that ensures that, at most, one processor stores to that location at a time. On the other hand, when a page is

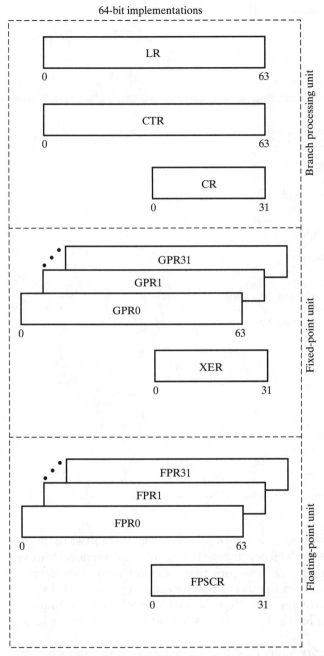

Figure 3.13 User-level registers in the three execution units in a 64-bit implementation: LR = link register; CTR = count register; CR = condition register; GPR0–31 = general purpose registers; XER = exception register; FPR0–31 = floating-point general purpose registers; FPSCR = floating-point status and control register.

TABLE 3.3   New Instructions for 64-Bit Implementations Only

cntlzd	Count leading zeros doubleword
divd	Divide doubleword
divdu	Divide doubleword unsigned
extsw	Extend sign word
fcfid	Floating convert from integer doubleword
fctid	Floating convert to integer doubleword
fctidz	Floating convert to integer doubleword with round toward zero
lwa	Load word algebraic
lwaux	Load word algebraic with update indexed
lwax	Load word algebraic indexed
ld	Load doubleword
ldarx	Load doubleword and reserve indexed
ldu	Load doubleword with update
ldux	Load doubleword with update indexed
ldx	Load doubleword indexed
mulhd	Multiply high doubleword
mulhdu	Multiply high doubleword unsigned
mulld	Multiply low doubleword
rldcl	Rotate left doubleword then clear left
rldcr	Rotate left doubleword then clear right
rldic	Rotate left doubleword immediate then clear
rldicl	Rotate left doubleword immediate then clear left
rldicr	Rotate left doubleword immediate then clear right
rldimi	Rotate left doubleword immediate then mask insert
slbia	SLB invalidate all
slbie	SLB invalidate entry
sld	Shift left doubleword
srad	Shift right algebraic doubleword
sradi	Shift right algebraic doubleword immediate
srd	Shift right doubleword
std	Store doubleword
stdcx	Store doubleword conditional indexed
stdu	Store doubleword with update
stdux	Store doubleword with update indexed
stdx	Store doubleword indexed
td	Trap doubleword
tdi	Trap doubleword immediate

accessed in the memory-coherence-not-required mode for software performance reasons, the processor does not impose any storage coherence. However, it is the software's responsibility to ensure that relevant cache management instructions have been executed to put the memory in a consistent state.

The PowerPC architecture specifies that the memory coherence is managed in terms of logical units called *coherence blocks,* whose size is implementation-dependent.

In terms of shared memory support, different instances of the same or separate program(s) running on one or more processors may share memory. The basic unit of memory sharing is blocks. Also, a location may be accessed using different effective addresses. This is a noteworthy trait, since by using this feature (called *address aliasing*), each application can be assigned separate access privileges to aliased pages.

A weakly consistent memory model specified in PowerPC offers an increased performance level by allowing the processor to run very fast for most memory accesses. However, the tradeoff is that the programs have to guarantee proper placement of the ordering or synchronization instructions. In this architecture, the actual order in which a memory access is issued, executed, and viewed could be totally different. This is a strategy for sharing resources (memory in this case) among multiple participants, and is referred to as *memory* or *storage access ordering*.

3.4.3 Operating environment architecture

At this level of abstraction, the PowerPC architecture encompasses the supervisory level registers, explains the exception model, and details the structure of memory management.

3.4.3.1 Privileged registers

In PowerPC architecture there are several privileged registers that are not visible to the application programmers. These registers control special attributes of the machine.

The branch processing unit features a register called the machine state register (MSR) that describes the state of the processor by describing system states like user/supervisory mode, interrupt enable/disable mode, and address relocate on/off status. The MSR is 64-bit. The next set of registers worth mentioning is the set of machine status save-and-restore registers (SRR). The SRR0 and SRR1 save the old value of MSR and the address of the interrupted instruction in the event of an interrupt. Upon returning from the interrupt, they restore the MSR value and resume execution from the interrupted instruction. Like the MSR, the SRR0 and SRR1 are 64-bit in case of 64-bit implementation of the architecture. Last, there is a processor version register (PVR), which identifies the version and revision model of the microprocessor. Unlike the rest of the privileged registers, the PVR is a 32-bit read-only register.

The fixed point unit's list of privileged registers consists of a data address register (DAR), which is 64-bit in size and specifies the address of storage access that caused a data storage or alignment interrupt.* Another privileged register, data storage interrupt status register (DSISR) defines the actual cause of the data storage or alignment interrupt. The DSISR is a 32-bit register. In addition, there are four 64-bit special purpose registers (SPRG0-3) provided for the operating system's use.

The floating point unit contains a special register called the floating-point status and control register (FPSCR). It enables/disables floating-point excep-

---

* A *data storage interrupt* is a hardware interrupt that occurs because of a nontranslatable virtual address access, a storage protection violation, an access denial owing to data locking, or an I/O exception condition. An *alignment interrupt* is another type of hardware interrupt that occurs when the effective address generated by a load or a store violates a storage boundary.

tions and records status resulting from the floating-point operations, which is required by the IEEE 754 standard.

Figure 3.14 presents a comprehensive view of all the pertinent privileged registers within the three execution units of PowerPC's 64-bit implementations.

3.4.3.2 Interrupt handling strategies

A standard interrupt processing and exception handling model is provided by the PowerPC architecture to allow change of state under unusual conditions. There are several types of interrupts supported by the PowerPC architecture. Some of the interrupts are caused by the system, while others may be caused by instructions.

Upon the generation of an interrupt, control is transferred to a set of privileged routines called *interrupt handlers*. The interrupt handler routine services the interrupt and, after completion, may transfer control back to the software to continue execution. In general, information (such as the instruction that should be executed after control is returned to the original program and the contents of the machine state register) is saved to the save/restore registers (SRR0 and SRR1), program control passes from user to supervisory level, and the software continues execution at an address predetermined from each interrupt.

Occurrence of instruction-caused interrupts in classical machines is not a new concept, since the program counter is able to maintain a pointer to the precise location of the instruction stream. But on the PowerPC, there is no program counter per se. With three separate independent execution units, processing a single instruction stream makes recovering from interrupts not a simple task. Recognize that since different instructions are executed by different (and independent) execution units, the instruction stream can be left fragmented. So, this fragmented state requires the architecture to provide a means for reconstructing the instruction stream around the point of the interrupt so that the postinterrupt processing code can recreate the sequential state. Due to the pipeline complexity of the machine organization, architecting a method for handling interrupts in an imprecise manner gets costly and complex. Therefore, the architecture has to enforce generation of precise interrupts. Despite the fact that out-of-order instruction dispatches are supported by the architecture and interrupt conditions are recognized out of order, interrupts are handled in program order. Except for a catastrophic condition causing a system reset or machine check interrupt, only one exception is handled at a time. If, for example, a single instruction encounters multiple interrupt conditions, those conditions would be encountered sequentially. Following the processing of an interrupt, the instruction execution will continue until the occurrence of the next interrupt condition. In this way, recognizing and handling interrupt conditions sequentially guarantees that interrupts are recoverable.

3.4.3.3 Types of interrupts

The following types of interrupts are specified in the PowerPC architecture.

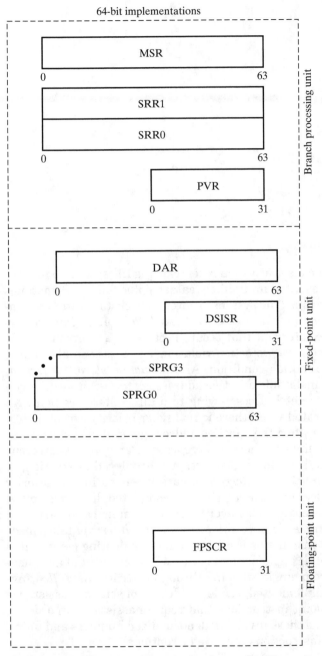

64-bit implementations

Figure 3.14 Privileged registers in the three execution units of the PowerPC microprocessor: MSR = machine state register; SRR0 and SRR1 = save and restore registers; PVR = processor version register; DAR = data address register; DSISR = data storage interrupt status register; SPRG0–3 = special purpose registers; FPSCR = floating-point status and control register.

- System reset
- Machine check
- Data storage
- Instruction storage
- External
- Alignment
- Program
- Decrementer
- System call
- Trace
- Floating-point assist
- Floating-point unavailable

The *system reset interrupt* causes a system reset (causing the system to reboot), which can happen in the event of an unlikely catastrophic failure. Sometimes byzantine anomalies may cause the system to enter a checkstop state* by issuing what is called a *machine check interrupt*. A *data storage interrupt* is another type of hardware interrupt that occurs because of a nontranslatable virtual address access, a storage protection violation, an access denial owing to data locking, or an I/O exception condition. An *Instruction storage interrupt* occurs because of a nontranslatable effective address, a storage protection violation by a fetch access, or fetch access owing to a direct-store segment. An *external interrupt* is generated when there is no higher priority exception. An *alignment interrupt* occurs when the effective address generated by a load or a store violates a storage boundary. There is a *program interrupt* that can occur when the system encounters an illegal instruction, a privileged instruction, or a trap instruction. A *decrementer interrupt* occurs when no higher priority interrupt exists and the decrementer register has completed decrementing. A *system call interrupt* is generated whenever there is a system call instruction encountered in the program. A *floating-point unavailable interrupt* takes place whenever a floating-point instruction is executed and the floating point unit is disabled. A *trace interrupt,* if implemented, is caused in the event of a branch-and-trap instruction or from single-stepping through instructions. A *floating-point assist interrupt,* if implemented, renders a degree of software assistance to implemented floating-point instructions that require assistance in order to complete operations such as those involving denormalized numbers and unimplemented floating-point instructions that are not optional.

---

* This is a special state in which instruction processing is suspended till the processor has been reset. It freezes the contents of registers in order to aid in problem determination.

Note that, except for the system reset, machine check, external and decrementer interrupts, all other types of interrupts are regarded as instruction-generated interrupts.

3.4.3.4 Structure of the memory management model

The memory model and its management policies form the infrastructure for any program's execution. Software programs would have to reference storage using an effective address that is computed by the processor. This effective address is translated to a real address, as per a set of address translation rules, and, consequently, accesses are made to location(s) in memory.

In order to best understand the memory management scheme, a set of parameters needs to be explained. Some of these parameters are consistent across the architecture, while some depend on the implementation (32-bit or 64-bit) of the architecture.

The design of the memory layout in PowerPC architecture uses a segmented scheme, with a set of special registers called the *segment registers* (SRs). There are 16 SRs that divide the total addressable memory into segments, each of which is 256 MB in size. Segments can be of two types: (1) ordinary storage segment (or regular storage segment) and (2) direct-store segment.

Direct-store segments are meant for access to an external address space like an I/O bus or device, while the ordinary storage segments refer to internal address space in memory.

The basic unit of addressing real memory is referred to as a *page frame* or simply a *page,* the size of which is 4 KB. Since the 256-MB segment is accessed in 4-KB chunks, it can be also be viewed as if there are 64,000 (2^{16}) pages that a single segment can access. The rest of the description for the memory model is implementation-specific, i.e., it varies with 32-bit versus 64-bit implementations, summarized previously in Fig. 3.8.

In 64-bit implementations, the real memory size is extended to 16 EB. There are 2^{52} segments that can be accessed, with an effective address range of 2^{64} and virtual address range of 2^{80}.

3.4.3.5 Address translation concept

An address generated by the processor (which is referred to as an *effective address*) requires a translation step before being able to access an actual location. The address translation scheme in PowerPC comprises two available approaches that proceed in parallel (for performance reasons). The two simultaneously progressing translations are referred to as *segmented address translation* and *block address translation.* Typically, one of them ought to succeed, otherwise a storage exception will be encountered. If both succeed, then the block address translation takes precedence.

- Segmented address translation
- Block address translation

When a segmented address translation occurs, it accesses either an ordinary storage segment or a direct-storage segment. Depending on which type of segment is accessed, this address is either converted into a real address through an intermediate step and then used to access storage, or it is converted directly into an I/O address and passed to the I/O subsystem for further action. When a block address translation occurs, the effective address is directly converted into a real address and then used to access storage. Refer back to Fig. 3.10 to see how these various modes of storage access operate.

In both cases, a set of four privileged bits, called the *mode control bits,* are used to assign a context-specific meaning to the effective address (such as determining whether a coherence is required for the address).

3.4.3.6   Segmented address translation

The basic steps involve using a 64-bit effective address to generate an 80-bit virtual address, to get access to a 64-bit real address. Refer to Fig. 3.15 for an overview of the process.

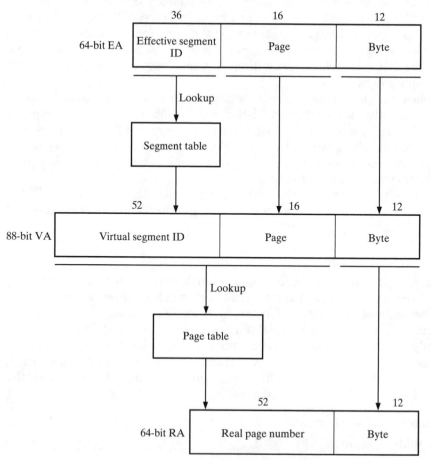

Figure 3.15 Address translation in 64-bit implementation.

For segmented address translation, out of the 64 bits of the address, 36 bits (0–35) are used to index into a data structure called the *segment table* (instead of segment registers, as in the case of the 32-bit implementation), which yields a 52-bit virtual segment ID. This virtual segment ID, when concatenated with 16 additional bits (36–51) of the effective address that are the page number within the segment, forms the virtual page number. This virtual page number, in turn, is indexed to the *page table* to yield a real page number. When the byte offset—i.e., the remaining 12 bits (52–63)—from the effective address is concatenated to this real page number, the corresponding real address to access the storage is generated. Figure 3.16 illustrates the steps involved in the process of translating the effective address into a virtual address.

3.4.3.7 Comparative anatomy of page table and segment table

As stated in earlier, the scheme for segmented address translation in the case of 64-bit implementation of PowerPC varies quite a lot from that of the 32-bit

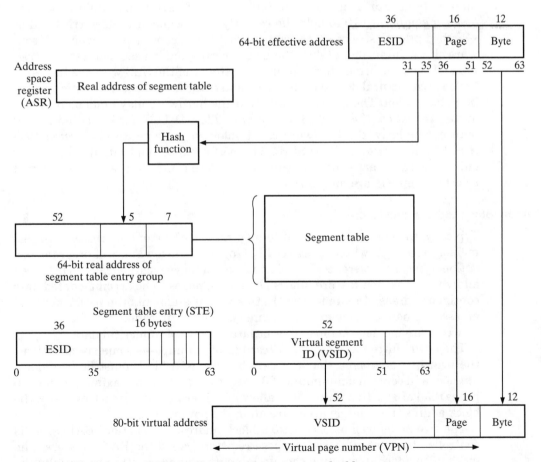

Figure 3.16 Translation of 64-bit effective address to virtual address.

implementation. These two structures, the page table and the segment table involved in the 32-bit and 64-bit address translation schemes of the PowerPC processor, have similar as well as dissimilar traits.

A *page table* is a variable-sized data structure that defines the mapping between virtual page numbers and real page numbers. The hashed page table consists of a number of page table entry groups, each of which contains eight page table entries. Conceptually, the page table is searched by the page relocation hardware to translate every reference. So from a performance standpoint, it makes sense for the hardware to maintain a *translation lookaside buffer* (TLB) that holds the recently used page table entries and is searched prior to scanning the page table.

A segment table is a one-page (each page is 4 KB in size) data structure that defines the mapping between effective segment IDs and virtual segment IDs. The table consists of 32 segment table entry groups, which in turn contain eight 16-byte segment table entries, each of which maps one effective segment ID to a virtual segment ID. Essentially, the segment table is searched by the address relocation hardware to translate every reference. So from a performance standpoint, it is useful to have the hardware to maintain a *segment lookaside buffer* (SLB) to hold the recently used segment table entries and be searched prior to scanning the segment table. As a consequence, when the software alters the segment table, changes to corresponding segment table entries must also be performed to maintain consistency of the SLB with the tables.

The architectural design of the TLBs and SLBs imposes no restriction on the implementation. Thus, it is possible that the hardware may implement a separate *instruction TLB* (I-TLB) and a *data TLB* (D-TLB) for increased performance. Similarly, the hardware can implement a separate *instruction SLB* (I-SLB) and a *data SLB* (D-SLB). The performance implication—separating out the caching area for dedicated instructions and data accesses—is that selection conflicts are minimized.

3.4.3.8   Block address translation

Typically, the smallest unit used to map ranges of virtual addresses into real memory is a page (where a page is 4 KB in size). The dynamics of program execution typically references a selected set of pages periodically. The block address translation feature allows clusters of pages to be accommodated onto contiguous areas of real memory. In this way, it augments the performance of accesses to nonpageable areas of memory. In general, candidates for this type of access are memory mapped files or large arrays of numerical data.

The newly introduced *block address* paradigm imposes some specifications, the principal one being that the variable size of a block must be boundary-aligned, and contain a minimum of 32 pages (128 KB) to a maximum of 65,536 pages (256 MB) with a finite set of allowable intermediate sizes. Obviously, the block address translation areas are all in the powers of 2.

The size of, as well as access to, a block address translation (BAT) area, is controlled by a set of special purpose registers called the BAT registers. The mechanisms for interpreting the block length and address are essentially the same for the 32-bit and the 64-bit implementations; it is the number of bits in each field that is different. Figure 3.17 illustrates how a pair of BAT registers is used to interpret information in the 64-bit implementations.

3.5   TIMER FACILITIES

The timer facilities in PowerPC consist of a 64-bit register called a *time base* and a 32-bit register called the *decrementer* (shown in Fig. 3.18).

The time base and the decrementer are counters that are driven by an implementation-specific frequency. Updates occur periodically, during which the low-order bit is incremented in the time base. There is no specification stating any correlation between the frequency at which the time base ought to be

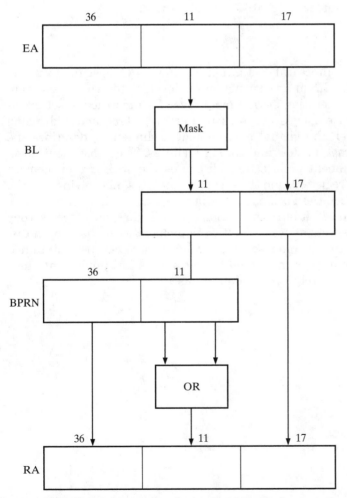

Figure 3.17 Block address translation in 64-bit implementation.

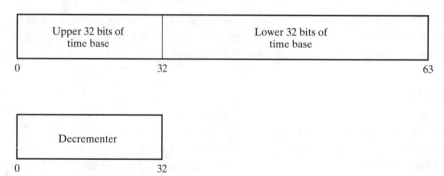

Figure 3.18 Timer facilities in PowerPC.

updated and other frequencies like the CPU clock. In fact, the update frequency of the timer is under the control of the hardware.

3.6 SUMMARY

The multilayered architectural definition of PowerPC specifies varying degrees of compatibility from an instruction set level, to the virtual environment level, up to the operating environment level. The instruction set architecture defines the base user-level instruction set, registers, and addressing modes. The next level, the virtual environment architecture, describes the semantics of the storage models and timing facilities. The subsequent level, the operating environment architecture, discusses the structure of memory management, special registers, and the exception model, while delving into the details of privileged facilities such as interrupt handling mechanisms.

While the 32-bit and 64-bit implementations are alike in some respects, they differ in numerous aspects as well. The two implementations have been discussed separately in this chapter so that a cohesiveness can be maintained with respect to the context of individual (32-bit and 64-bit) implementations and the semantics of the architectural definitions.

Processor Implementations

This chapter focuses on the implementations of the PowerPC architecture. It discusses the internal hardware structure, logic design, and data path organization of the 601, 603, 604, and 620 microprocessors. In order to contrast the implementations of PowerPC, a brief discussion on the implementations of POWER is also provided.* This is only appropriate because a PowerPC implementation resembles the POWER architecture in more respects than it differs from it. The POWER architecture features a performance-crafted design, whereas the PowerPC architecture emphasizes a more cost-effective and flexible approach. In the discussion that follows, each implementation is described individually, along with the supported design of cache layout and implementation-specific features that are not imposed by the PowerPC architectural definition.

The implementations of PowerPC are discussed in their order of evolution and appearance in the industry. This is done for the convenience of the reader, as the evolving description of functions and features makes it easier to follow and understand the trend.

4.1 UNDERSTANDING THE COMMON CPU MODEL

The PowerPC microprocessor achieves an exceedingly high level of performance in both commercial as well as scientific computing areas using a common CPU

---

* For a detailed description of the POWER architecture and implementation internals, refer to the text titled *POWER RISC System 6000 Concepts, Facilities, and Architecture* (ISBN 0-07-011047-6) from McGraw-Hill, Inc.

model. As stated earlier, in PowerPC and POWER architectures there is no single component that can be called the CPU per se, as the microprocessor harnesses its power from separate execution engines, each performing dedicated duties. From a neophyte's perspective, the basic CPU model features: (1) a branch processing unit which processes the branch instructions and dispatches instructions to the other execution units, (2) a fixed-point unit that executes integer instructions and performs the loads/stores, and (3) a floating-point unit that processes the floating-point instructions. Collectively, these three units are referred to as the *execution units*. They form the core of the central electronic complex. Refer to Fig. 4.1 for a conceptual view of how all the PowerPC and POWER chips operate.

4.2   THE POWER RS 1 MICROPROCESSOR

The RS 1 is a full-scale implementation of the POWER architecture. In additional to being the principal predecessor of the PowerPC design, it also serves as the core of the RISC System/6000 and POWERparallel systems.

4.2.1   Organization

The RS 1 implementation of the POWER processor features multiple execution units that include: (1) an instruction cache, (2) a branch processing unit, (3) a fixed-point unit, (4) a floating-point unit, (5) a data cache, (6) a memory management unit, (7) a sequencer unit, and (8) a COP (common on-chip processor) unit.*

- branch processing unit
- fixed-point unit
- floating-point unit
- instruction cache
- data cache
- memory management unit
- sequencer unit
- COP unit

The memory bus on this implementation is 128 bits wide and serves as the interface between the instruction cache and the main memory from which instructions are loaded via the instruction reload bus. A two-word-wide data path connects the branch processor with each of the floating-point and fixed-point execution units. A one-word data path connects the fixed-point unit with the data cache, while a two-word data path is present between the floating-point unit and data cache. Refer to Fig. 4.2 for a block diagram of the POWER

---

* The embedded COP is a processor-independent logic whose function is to control the built-in self-test, debug, and test features of the chip at boot time.

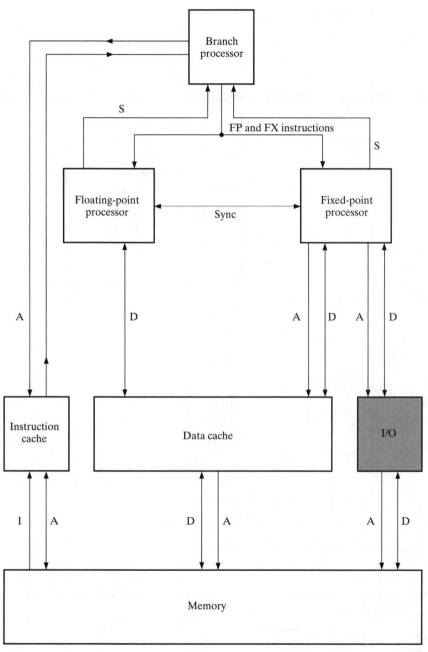

Figure 4.1 How all PowerPC and POWER processors operate. A = address; D = data; I = instruction; S = status. *Note:* The I/O unit (shaded) is outside the scope of the processor architecture.

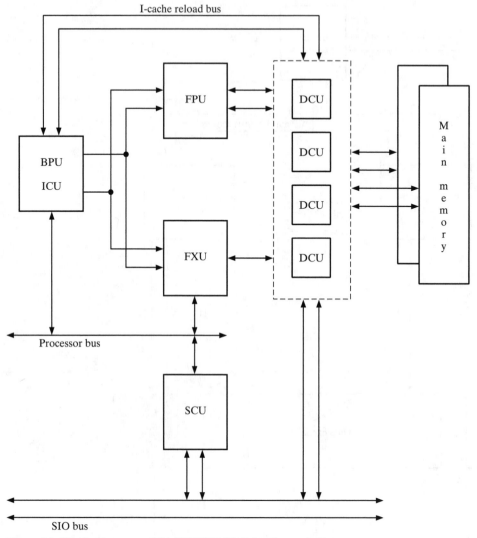

Figure 4.2 Block diagram of the POWER RS 1 implementation.

RS 1 chip set. Each line represents a one-word-wide path and the arrowhead indicates the direction of the instruction/data flow.

4.2.2 Instruction cache

The instruction cache is a 2-way set-associative cache. This layout gives the I-cache a total of 128 lines. As there are 64 bytes per line, the total cache size adds up to 8 KB. For machine models configured with a bigger I-cache, the number of sets is increased to 256 KB; that way, the total cache size is increased to 32 KB. Figure 4.3 explains the breakdown of set and line mapping.

Type 1 cache organization:

- 2-way
  } 128 lines
- 64 sets
  } 8 KB
- 64 bytes/line

Type 2 cache organization:

- 2-way
  } 512 lines
- 256 sets
  } 32 KB
- 64 bytes/line

Figure 4.3 Description of I-cache on RS 1 implementation in terms of its sets and lines.

4.2.3 Data cache

The data cache is a 4-way set-associative cache, consisting of 128 sets. This blueprint gives the D-cache a total of 512 lines. With 128 bytes per line, the total cache size adds up to 64 KB. Figure 4.4 explains the breakdown of set and line mapping in further detail.

4.2.4 Fixed-point unit

The fixed-point unit (FXU) consists of several registers and affiliated components. The first set of components includes 32 general purpose registers (GPRs) that can be used by general programs for assists. Second, there is a set of

Cache organization:

- 4-way
  } 512 lines
- 128 sets
  } 64 KB
- 128 bytes/line

Figure 4.4 Description of the D-cache on RS 1 implementation in terms of its sets and lines.

segment registers (SRs), which aid in address translation. Subsequently, there is a set of special purpose registers. A data address register (DAR) specifies the address of storage access that caused a data storage or alignment interrupt. The data storage interrupt status register (DSISR) defines the actual cause of the data storage or alignment interrupt. Also, there is an exception register (XER) which deals with the carry and overflow flags, and contains byte count and comparison bytes used by string instructions. In addition, there are two more registers present in the RS 1 implementation. The first one is called the transaction identifier register (TID) and it holds the transaction ID of the currently executing process in the system. The second one is a multiplier-quotient register (MQ), which is used by multiply, divide, and extended shift instructions, and also as a temporary storage by store string instructions.

Among the key components of the FXU is the arithmetic logic unit (ALU), which is used for arithmetic and logic operations. The next component is the fixed-point multiply/divide unit, and it is used in conjunction with the ALU. The ensuing component, which is the data translation lookaside buffer (D-TLB), works together with the segment registers (SRs) to aid in address translation, page protection, and data locking. Note here that the page table lookups for the D-TLB and the instruction translation lookaside buffer (I-TLB) reloads and page table updates are all performed by the FXU hardware. The FXU chip also contains the directory part of the D-cache. The address generation task and D-cache controls for both fixed- and floating-point load/store instructions as well as for cache operations are performed by the FXU. In addition, there is a store buffer in the FXU that is used to hold the data and address of a single fixed-point store instruction while waiting to write it into the D-cache. Consequently, the fixed- and floating-point loads can get ahead of the fixed-point stores, and the FXU and FPU can obtain the data they need sooner. But note that the instructions are not executed out of order; only the D-cache access is made out of order (to save cycles).

4.2.5 Floating-point unit

The floating-point unit (FPU) includes a set of registers and dedicated elements, each contributing to the overall performance-crafted design of the execution unit. The first group of components consists of a set of general purpose registers called the floating-point registers (FPRs). These are used as source and destination operands for all the arithmetic floating-point operations and their results. There are 32 FPRs available for the use of instructions. Each FPR is 64 bits in size and, thus, is able to deliver double-precision results, with the only exception being in the case of load-and-store operations, because they are handled by the fixed-point unit. The next key component of the FPU is a special register called the floating-point status and control register (FPSCR). It handles floating-point exceptions and records status resulting from the floating-point operations, which is required by the IEEE 754 standard. The FPSCR is 32 bits in size; its bits 0–19 are status bits and the remaining bits 20–31 are used as control bits.

Representation for a floating-point number consists of a signed exponent and a signed significand. The quantity expressed by this number is the product of the significand and the number $2^{exponent}$. Encodings are provided in the data format to represent finite numeric values, ±infinity, and values which are not a number.

4.2.6 Packaging

The hardware electronics and circuitry related to the central electronic complex are laid out on three different planars for this machine: (1) the CPU planar, (2) the I/O planar, and (3) the standard I/O planar. Direct benefits of this modular design are maintainability, serviceability, and scalability. The components of each of the three planars are described in Fig. 4.5.

The CPU planar houses the fixed-point unit and floating-point unit as individual chips, located adjacent to each other. The branch processing unit is integrated with the instruction cache unit and implemented as a single chip. The data cache unit is implemented as four separate chips on the planar. The data cache is 64 KB in size, while the instruction cache can be 8 or 32 KB, depending on the specific model. Last, the storage control unit, which serves as the central system controller to arbitrate the CPU-bound and I/O-bound communications, is located adjacent to the pair of data cache chips. Additional components worth mentioning on the CPU planar are the memory slots and a special diagnostic port called the ESP (engineering support processor) port.*

The I/O planar houses the Micro Channel slots which allow end users to configure and customize their systems appropriately. The I/O planar connects to the CPU planar via a 278-pin in-line connector. It also features a component called the on-card sequencer (OCS); essentially, it is a microcontroller whose primary task is to initialize the processor complex at boot time and carry out a self-test to verify proper operation of the modules located on the planar. There are three additional modules in the I/O planar. They are the nonvolatile RAM (referred to as NVRAM) for configuration, the operator panel interface for error display, and the real-time clock for time-of-day functions. The NVRAM stores vital system information which may be required for the system boot process (commonly referred to as initial program load or IPL). The 32-KB NVRAM unit normally derives its power from the system power supply. When the system is powered off, the NVRAM remains powered by a battery. The operator panel interface, which is another module on the I/O planar, displays error codes through the light-emitting diodes (LEDs). The next module, which is the clock, provides the time-of-day (TOD) functions. Like the NVRAM, this clock

---

* The ESP socket, though seldom used, plays a vital role when the processor needs to be debugged. It debugs the processor by loading test programs, single-stepping through the system's instruction stream, and monitoring the system interactively. The process is performed by connecting a separate stand-alone workstation via the ESP port.

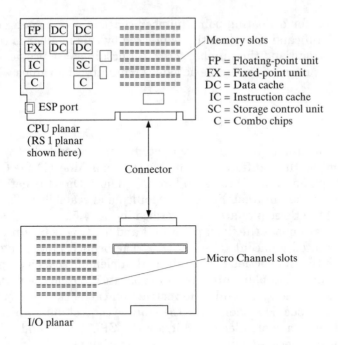

FP = Floating-point unit
FX = Fixed-point unit
DC = Data cache
IC = Instruction cache
SC = Storage control unit
C = Combo chips

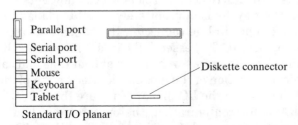

Figure 4.5 Packaging of POWER RS 1 and RS .9 implementations. Diagram shows the CPU planar, I/O planar,
and the standard I/O planar.

also remains powered by battery while the system is powered off. In fact, it is the
same battery unit that provides power to both the NVRAM and the TOD clock.

The standard I/O planar connects to the I/O planar through a common interface connector, which fits underneath the I/O planar and contains the interfaces and connectors to mouse, keyboard, tablet, diskette, parallel port, and
two serial ports.

4.3 THE POWER RS .9 MICROPROCESSOR

The RS .9 is a cost-reduced version of the original POWER architecture that
serves as the core for low-end RISC System/6000 computer systems.

4.3.1 Organization

This implementation is very similar to that of the RS 1; they share a lot of common features. It has multiple execution units on multiple chips assembled on a single planar. The components include the following:

- branch processing unit
- fixed-point unit
- floating-point unit
- instruction cache
- data cache
- memory management unit
- sequencer unit
- COP unit

The memory bus is 64 bits wide (as compared to 128 bits for the RS 1 implementation) and serves as the interface between the instruction cache and the main memory. The path leading from the branch processor to each of the floating-point and fixed-point execution units is two words wide. A two-word data path from the floating-point unit and a one-word data path from the fixed-point unit are dotted together, and in turn connect to the data cache. Refer to Fig. 4.6 for a block diagram of the POWER RS .9 chip sets. Each line in the diagram represents a one-word-wide path and the arrowhead indicates the direction of the instruction/data flow. The instruction cache is reloaded using the SIO (standard I/O) bus.

The RS .9 implementation is also referred to as a "cost-reduced" version of the POWER processor. Its memory interface is half as wide; therefore, some of the bit-scattering features which are applicable for the full-size CPU do not apply here. Also, note that the fixed-point and floating-point buses are dotted together, while interfacing with the data cache. Also, instructions are fetched into the instruction cache via a dedicated instruction-reload bus, whereas in the RS .9, the SIO bus is used as a shared resource to load instructions.

4.3.2 Instruction cache

The instruction cache is a 2-way set-associative cache. This layout gives the I-cache a total of 128 lines. As there are 64 bytes per line, the total cache size adds up to 8 KB. For models configured with a bigger I-cache, the number of sets is increased to 256 KB; that way, the total cache size is increased to 32 KB. Figure 4.3 explains the breakdown of set and line mapping in further detail.

4.3.3 Data cache

The data cache is a 4-way set-associative cache, consisting of 64 sets. With 128 bytes per line, the total cache size adds up to 32 KB. Figure 4.7 explains the breakdown of set and line mapping.

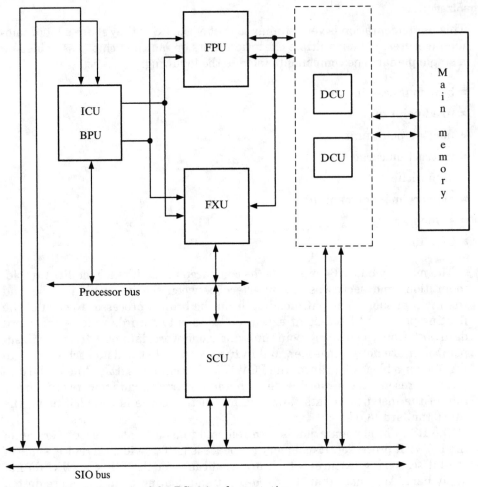

Figure 4.6 Block diagram of the RS .9 implementation.

Cache organization:

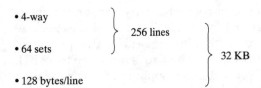

- 4-way
- 64 sets   256 lines
- 128 bytes/line   32 KB

Figure 4.7 Description of the D-cache on RS .9
implementation in terms of its sets and lines.

4.3.4 Fixed-point unit

This fixed-point unit consists of several registers and affiliated components. Its organization is identical to that of the RS 1 implementation. First, there are the 32 general purpose registers (GPRs). Then there is a set of segment registers (SRs) which aid in address translation. Next, there is a set of special purpose registers. A data address register (DAR) specifies the address of storage access that caused a data storage or alignment interrupt. The data storage interrupt status register (DSISR) defines the actual cause of the data storage or alignment interrupt. Also, there is an exception register (XER), a transaction identifier register (TID), and a multiplier-quotient register (MQ).

Additional components include the arithmetic logic unit (ALU) that is used for arithmetic and logic operations, the multiply/divide unit that is used in conjunction with the ALU, and the data translation lookaside buffer (D-TLB). Note that the fixed-point unit also contains the directory part of the D-cache. The address generation task and D-cache controls for both fixed- and floating-point load/store instructions, as well as for cache operations, are performed by the fixed-point unit. In addition, there is a store buffer that is used to hold the data and address of a single fixed-point store instruction while waiting to write it into the D-cache. Consequently, the fixed- and floating-point loads can get ahead of the fixed-point stores, and the FXU and FPU obtain the data they need sooner.

4.3.5 Floating-point unit

The floating-point unit for the RS .9 implementation is essentially the same as that of the RS 1. First, there are thirty-two 64-bit general purpose registers called the floating-point registers (FPRs). Each FPR is able to deliver double-precision results, with an exception in the case of load-and-store operations, because they are handled by the fixed-point unit. Also, there is a special register called the floating-point status and control register (FPSCR) that handles floating-point exceptions and records status resulting from the floating-point operations, which is required by the IEEE 754 standard.

4.3.6 Packaging

The mechanical packaging of the hardware is laid out on three different planars, as in the case of the RS 1 implementation. There are three planars: (1) the CPU planar, (2) the I/O planar, and (3) the standard I/O planar.

The CPU planar houses the execution units as individual chips, located adjacent to each other. The branch processing unit is integrated with the instruction cache unit and implemented as a single chip. The data cache unit is implemented as two separate chips on the planar. The data cache is 32 KB in size, while the instruction cache can be 8 or 32 KB, depending on the specific model. Finally, the storage control unit, which serves as the central system controller to arbitrate the CPU-bound and I/O-bound communications, is located adjacent to the pair of data cache chips. The additional components, like the memory slots and the ESP (engineering support processor) port, are the same as those described for the RS 1 implementation.

The I/O planar which houses the slots for add-on cards, the OCS for processor-complex initialization, the NVRAM for configuration, the operator panel interface for error display, and the real-time clock for time-of-day functions are also the same as those in the RS 1 implementation. Likewise, the standard I/O planar connecting to the I/O planar through a common interface connector is the same as the RS 1 implementation.

4.4 THE POWER RSC MICROPROCESSOR

The name "RSC" has been derived from *RISC single chip,* which appropriately describes the microprocessor. The design of RSC is particularly intended to address high computational requirements along with reduced system cost.

4.4.1 Organization

The implementation integrates the execution units (a fixed-point unit, a floating-point unit, and a branch unit), a cache, and a memory management unit on a single die. The memory bus on this implementation is 72 bits wide and connects directly to memory SIMMs. The I/O bus is 32 bits wide and connects to buffering and bus conversion chips.

The principal functional units in the RSC implementation are: (1) the cache, (2) the branch processing unit and instruction fetcher, (3) the instruction queue and dispatch logic, (4) the fixed-point unit, (5) the floating-point unit, (6) the memory management unit, (7) the memory interface unit, (8) the sequencer unit, and (9) the COP (common on-chip processor) unit. Their organization is depicted in Fig. 4.8.

- combined instruction and data cache
- branch processing and instruction fetch unit
- instruction queue and dispatch logic
- fixed-point unit
- floating-point unit
- memory management unit
- memory interface unit
- sequencer unit
- COP unit

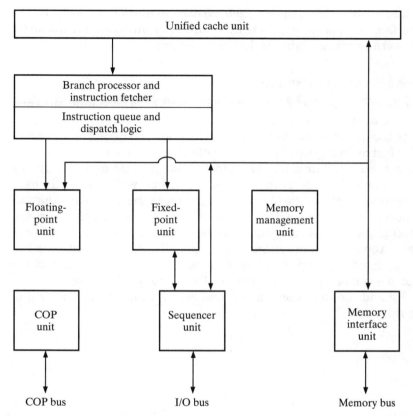

Figure 4.8 Block diagram of RSC implementation.

4.4.2 Cache

This implementation features a unified cache for instruction and data. The cache structure in RSC is a 2-way set-associative cache, consisting of 64 sets. This layout gives the I-cache a total of 128 lines. As there are 64 bytes per line, the total cache size adds up to 8 KB.

The cache is managed with no reload on a store miss, and an LRU (least recently used) replacement scheme. It is kept coherent with all I/O traffic. Up to four words can be read from the cache and up to two double words can be written to it, per cycle. The cache features two different interfaces: one is a path with the instruction fetcher, and the other is a multiplexed path with the fixed-point unit and the memory interface unit. Cache access policy for loads is delicately balanced among its potential requestors, which can be any one of the functional units (listed in the previous section). As far as the cache access policy for stores is concerned, a lazy-write approach is implemented in which the instruction is processed by the fixed-point unit and the information is stored away in a store queue, which, in turn, gets written to memory or cache by the memory interface, as appropriate. Note that coherency with the store queue for subsequent operations is maintained in the hardware.

4.4.3   Branch processing and instruction fetch unit

Commonly referred to as the branch processing unit or branch unit, the component consists of two separate logics. It performs two principal functions: (1) coordinate the execution of the branch instructions and (2) get new instructions into the instruction queue by what is called a *prefetch step*.

The branch processing unit has two pipeline stages and executes all the branch instructions. In-page branches, i.e., branches within a 4-KB page boundary, are completely handled by the branch processing unit, while the out-of-page branches are resolved with the help of the fixed-point unit. A *branch prediction* technique is when the branch target is guessed in advance and the instructions in the pipeline are marked provisionally. After the outcome has been resolved, the temporarily tagged results are made permanent if the guessed outcome is true; these tentative results are purged if the guessed outcome was false and the operations in progress are all canceled. The algorithm looks as follows:

```
guess branch outcome
proceed on that path
 .

 .

 .
if prediction correct
    < no bubbles in the pipeline >
if prediction incorrect
    partially executed instruction cancelled
    < bubble left in the pipeline >
```

To facilitate the productivity of this branch prediction scheme, a static prediction algorithm (prediction taken if displacement is negative) is implemented that can be reversed by setting a bit in the instruction.

The instruction fetch unit generates the next sequential address in the event that no branch or interrupt has occurred. In the event of a branch, the address is provided by the branch processing unit or the fixed-point unit. Once an address has been selected, it is forwarded to the cache arbitration logic for possible access. If a cache hit results from it, the instructions are brought in for consequent processing by the instruction queue and dispatch logic. If a cache miss were to happen, the item gets fetched after an address translation step, via the fixed-point unit and the memory management unit. Note that once an address translation has happened, all subsequent references to that page require minimal access time because of the presence of a translation shadow buffer.

4.4.4   Instruction queue and dispatch logic

This component forms the second half of the branch processing unit. The instruction queue has two functional components: a primary queue and an instruction queue. The former is used to dispatch instructions, while the latter is used for providing buffering in the event of higher-priority operations.

The dispatch logic forwards instructions into the three execution units. Note that some floating-point and branch instructions may fold directly out of the instruction queue and without entering the pipeline.

4.4.5   Fixed-point unit

The instructions received through the dispatch logic enter the fixed-point unit's pipeline. They pass through a three-stage pipeline, which features a decode, an execute, and a writeback stage. An optional *cache access* stage that is contingent upon the data item being found in the cache can occur. If data is found, the cache is accessed and the data is returned to the fixed-point unit or floating-point unit, as the case may be.

4.4.6   Floating-point unit

The instructions pass through a four-stage pipeline that features a decode, a multiply, an add, and a writeback stage. The decode stage contains the instruction decode logic; the multiply stage houses the alignment shifter logic; the add accepts the sum and carry values to produce an intermediate result; and the writeback stage performs the rounding, normalization, and register update.

The floating-point unit complies with the IEEE floating-point standards. Unlike most floating-point coprocessor chips, this floating-point processor is tightly coupled with the fixed-point unit. It is able to achieve a dramatic degree of concurrency by being able to handle two separate task-pairs simultaneously. Its design enables it to exploit (1) floating-point load operations in parallel with floating-point arithmetic operations, and (2) floating-point multiply operations pipelined with floating-point add operations. The other distinctive feature about it is its ability to deliver a higher degree of accuracy beyond the capabilities of other currently available IEEE-compatible double-precision floating-point units. Although the floating-point unit operates independently of the fixed-point unit and can concurrently execute instructions, a synchronization scheme allows for the progressive execution of the two units, and can still achieve the effect of precise interrupts.

4.4.7   Memory management unit

The function of the memory management unit is to translate the virtual addresses into real addresses. It remains tightly coupled with the fixed-point unit, so that the address translation can happen in parallel with the cache access. The address translation process begins with accessing one of the segment registers to form the 52-bit virtual address. This address is then hashed and indexed into a page frame table to yield a 32-bit real address. A TLB (translation lookaside buffer) structure is maintained here to accelerate the address translation process.

4.4.8   Memory interface unit

The function of this component is to handle operations that require access to or from memory. It pipelines memory requests in an effort to overlap the address bus and data bus. Data is requested from memory in quadword blocks into a four-word reload buffer. When the reload buffer gets full, the memory interface unit arbitrates for access to the cache to write the data into it. Since a store-through cache is implemented in RSC, all store operations update the cache and get reflected back in main memory.

4.4.9   Sequencer unit

This component is essentially an embedded support processor that assists the core CPU in handling many of the algorithmic and area-intensive functions of the chip.

The sequencer unit on the 601 chip features a 3-KB RAM, a 3-KB ROM (containing microcode), 16 general purpose registers, and the control logic to execute its instruction set.

The sequencer unit's multifarious functions include: (1) sequencing of operations between the memory bus and the I/O bus, (2) performing the required tablewalks for I/O address translation, (3) providing the system interrupt controller function, (4) sequencing the power-on reset during the built-in self-test (BIST) phase, (5) maintaining the real-time clock, (6) handling the sequencing of interrupts and errors, and (7) assisting the fixed-point unit in executing selected (i.e., less frequently used) instructions.

4.4.10   Packaging

The RSC implementation is based on 0.8-μm CMOS technology with three levels of metal wiring. The chip uses about 1 million transistors and is implemented on a 14.9- by 15.2-mm die. Its typical power consumption is around 4 W at 33 MHz.

4.5   THE PowerPC 601 MICROPROCESSOR

The 601 microprocessor is the entry-level member of the PowerPC family and is positioned to be a bridge platform between the original POWER and the trimmed-down PowerPC architecture. It harnesses its CPU subcomplex power from the existing POWER RSC technology and its I/O subcomplex attributes from the 88110 microprocessor bus interface. Its highlights include a 32-bit cache interface to the fixed-point unit, a 64-bit interface to the floating-point unit, and a 256-bit interface to both the instruction queue and the memory queue. In terms of I/O interface, a 32-bit address data bus and a 64-bit data bus are provided. Figure 4.9 illustrates the organizational layout of the processor complex.

4.5.1 Pipelines

There are three separate pipelines in the processor complex, which together provide a degree of instruction-level parallelism in the execution of programs. The pipelines are two, three, and four stages deep. Figure 4.10 gives the pipeline structure of the 601 microprocessor.

- Branch processing unit—two-stage pipeline
- Fixed-point unit—three-stage pipeline
- Floating-point unit—four-stage pipeline

The two-stage branch instruction pipeline can dispatch, decode, execute, and, if necessary, predict the direction of a branch instruction in the first of the two cycles. In the subsequent cycle, new instructions can be accessed from the cache. This allows the processor to handle branches in a more efficient manner and reduce latency of subsequent instructions.

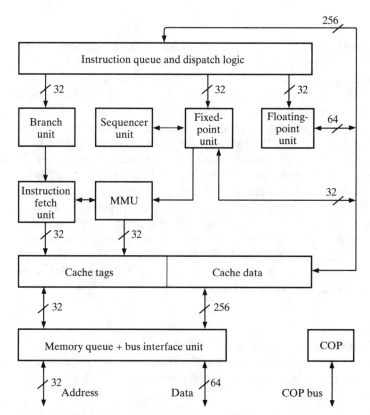

Figure 4.9 Block diagram of the PowerPC 601 microprocessor.

Branch instructions

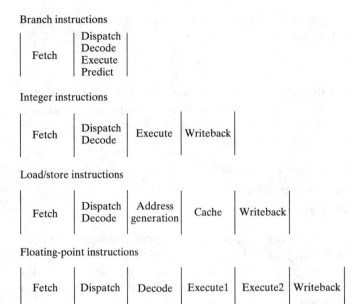

Integer instructions

Load/store instructions

Floating-point instructions

Figure 4.10 601 pipeline structure.

The three-stage fixed-point pipeline has several functions to perform in its dispatch, execute, and writeback stages. In addition to handling all the ALU (arithmetic logic unit) operations, it performs all the load-and-store instructions for the 601.* Note that this pipeline can optionally be a four-stage pipeline, when it must handle load instructions that need a cache access to occur following the address generation phase. The pipeline also manages the synchronization control that allows the processor to achieve precise interrupts.

The four-stage floating-point pipeline is the deepest of all the pipelines. It handles the floating-point instructions. The first stage of the pipeline (*decode*) consists of the instruction decode logic and the main pipeline control for the floating-point unit. The second stage (*execute1*) is the multiply stage and contains the carry-save adder tree, an alignment shifter, and the booth encoder. The third stage (*execute2*) is the add stage, which produces a single result from the sum and the carry values of the previous stage. Finally, the fourth stage (*writeback*) finishes up the operation by rounding the result obtained from the previous stage, normalizing it, and updating the registers.

4.5.2 Organization

The implementation integrates the three execution units along with a cache and a memory management unit on a single die. The 601's organizational highlights include a 32-bit cache interface to the fixed-point unit, a 64-bit interface

---

* This includes all the floating-point loads and stores as well.

to the floating-point unit, and a 256-bit interface to both the instruction queue and the memory queue. The I/O interface is similar to the RSC implementation, providing a 32-bit address data bus and a 64-bit data bus. Figure 4.9 gives a block diagram of the processor complex. The principal functional units consist of: (1) the instruction queue and dispatch unit, (2) the instruction fetch unit, (3) the branch processing unit, (4) the fixed-point unit, (5) the floating-point unit, (6) the memory management unit, (7) the cache, (8) the memory queue, (9) the bus interface unit, (10) the sequencer unit, and (11) the COP (common on-chip processor) unit. Each is described individually.

- instruction queue and dispatch unit
- instruction fetch unit
- branch processing unit
- fixed-point unit
- floating-point unit
- memory management unit
- combined instruction and data cache
- memory queue
- bus interface unit
- sequencer unit
- COP unit

4.5.3 Instruction queue and dispatch unit

The cache feeds into the instruction queue structure. The structure, which is in the form of a queue, can hold up to eight prefetched instructions. At every cycle, the dispatch logic considers the bottom four entries for dispatch. As out-of-order dispatches supported by this microprocessor, branches can be predicted ahead of time to reduce the delay due to dispatches.

4.5.4 Instruction fetch unit

The function of this component is to coordinate instruction fetching from the cache and to aid in address translation of instruction fetch addresses. It features a structure called the *translation shadow array* (TSA) that tracks the recently used instruction address translations and renders support to the page- and block-oriented address translations.

4.5.5 Branch processing unit

The function of the branch processing unit is to execute all the branch instructions. Branch instructions can be conditional or unconditional in their nature. Unconditional branches are no problem. But a conditional branch may depend on the condition register, the count register, or both. Since this branch processing unit executes independently of the fixed-point unit, it is necessary to be able to guarantee correct program operation when a preceding fixed-point instruction depends on the outcome of a count and/or condition register. This is achieved using a *register renaming* scheme, in which architected values of these registers are synchronized with the fixed-point unit, and the values are restored in the event of an exception.

As far as performance goes, the unconditional branches can be executed in a single cycle, and, as a result, give the effect of *zero-cycle branches* on the system. For the conditional branches, if they can be resolved at the time of dispatch, their performance is equivalent to that of the unconditional branches; otherwise, they are assumed to be "not taken" if the displacement of the branched address is positive, and "taken" if it is negative. This static branch prediction algorithm is supplemented by the presence of additional performance enhancement features, such as fast alternate address restore mechanisms, to facilitate the overall performance on the 601.

4.5.6   Fixed-point unit

The fixed-point unit is responsible for executing all fixed-point instructions in the system and for generating addresses for all the load-and-store instructions. Note that while most of the instructions are able to execute in a fully pipelined manner, some instructions (like multiply, divide, and multiple-word storage) may have to spend several cycles in the execute stage of the pipeline.

4.5.7   Floating-point unit

The floating-point unit processes all the floating-point operations. It receives instructions from the instruction dispatch unit. The floating-point unit is able to pipeline most single-precision operations with the exception of the divide operation. For double-precision operations, it can pipeline all except the multiply and divide operations.

Note that the register renaming scheme (present in the POWER architecture) is absent in the floating-point unit of the 601.

Although the floating-point unit operates independently of the fixed-point unit and can concurrently execute instructions, a synchronization scheme allows for the progressive execution of the two units, and can still achieve the effect of precise interrupts. The two units are able to cooperate in the execution of floating-point load/store instructions and process their respective portions of the operations independently.

4.5.8   Memory management unit

The role of the memory management unit is to translate virtual addresses to real addresses for load-and-store instructions. It remains tightly coupled with the fixed-point unit. If an address translation has to occur in the execute phase of the fixed-point unit pipeline, the cache access takes place in the subsequent

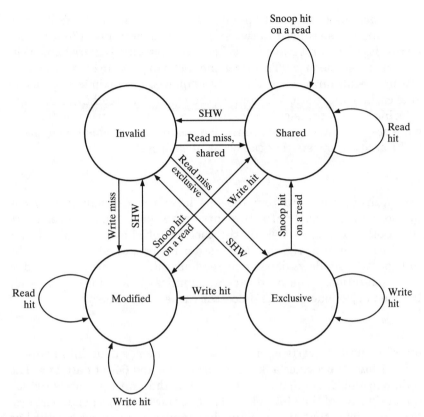

SHW = Snoop hit on a write, or read-with-intent-to-modify

Figure 4.11 Four-state MESI protocol.

cycle (thereby stretching the fixed-point pipeline to a four-stage pipeline for that access).

4.5.9 Cache

The unified cache is implemented as an 8-way set-associative structure. The line size is 64 bytes and each line is split into two 32-byte sectors. The cache is indexed with a real address and the tags are associated with the real address as well. One of the distinctive features is that a four-state MESI* (modified, exclusive, shared, invalid) cache coherency protocol is used to maintain coherency on a sector basis. The state diagram of the four-state MESI protocol is given in Fig. 4.11.

---

* It is a four-state status of cache sectors in a cache. The acronym MESI stands for modified/exclusive/shared/invalid. The four states indicate the state of the cache block as follows: *modified*—the cache block is modified with respect to system memory; *exclusive*—this cache block holds valid data that is identical to the data at this address in system memory, and no other cache has this data; *shared*—this cache block holds valid data that is identical to this address in system memory and at least one other caching device; *invalid*—this cache block does not hold valid data. This MESI protocol guarantees coherency in multiprocessor implementations.

This cache is nonblocking. Burst operations to the cache are buffered such that the cache update is reduced to two single-cycle operations of four words. That is, the results of the first two and the last two bursts are buffered and written to the cache in a single piece. This frees the cache to perform other functions in the meantime. Multifarious functions are employed to maximize the use of the available cache bandwidth. When all of the eight-word read interfaces are not in use during certain transient cycles, they are used for instruction fetching and snoop pushes. Also, a balanced arbitration scheme is implemented to prioritize the cache access requests that can occur in each cycle.

4.5.10 Memory queue

Operations requiring access to/from the bus interface are managed by the memory queue, which consists of a two-entry read queue and a three-entry write queue. Both queues, as well as the cache itself, have to arbitrate for access to the bus. Note that rigid program order is not a consideration in the arbitration logic, which allows dependent read operations to proceed ahead of pending write operations. The hardware automatically maintains coherency between the memory queue and the processor cache and memory.

4.5.11 Bus interface

The bus interface unit converts operation in the memory queue into transactions on the 601 bus. It provides a 32-bit address bus and 64-bit data bus. The buses remain decoupled from one another so that the unit's protocols (which are mostly a derivative of the Motorola 88110 microprocessor) can support system bus organizations that use pipelined, nonpipelined, or even split-bus transactions. Usually, the bus is operated at integer multiples of the processor cycle, so that it may allow use of simple bus structures using minimal external control logic.

4.5.12 Sequencer unit

The significance of the sequencer unit is greatly reduced from that in the RSC microprocessor. But its presence allows the 601 chip to minimize redesign efforts by making use of its existing functions, such as (1) the power-on reset during the built-in self-test (BIST) at the time of initialization; (2) maintaining the real-time clock; (3) handling the sequence of interrupts, context synchronizing events, and errors; and (4) assisting the fixed-point unit in executing selected instructions.

The sequencer unit on the 601 chip features a 1-KB ROM (containing microcode), a 1-KB RAM, eight general purpose registers, and the control logic to execute its instruction set.

4.5.13 Multiprocessor capabilities

The 601 microprocessor is equipped with the capabilities to facilitate symmetric multiprocessor systems. Typically, all multiprocessors have to be able to maintain *memory coherency,* i.e., the ability to perform atomic memory operations and the ability to control the order in which the storage operations are presented onto the interface.

Memory coherency is maintained in several ways. The processor performs bus snooping and adheres to a four-state MESI cache coherency protocol. Also, the processor provides support for a full range of cache control operations (including a broadcast on a shared address bus to all coherency participants). Furthermore, there is provision for allowing page- or block-level control of cacheability and coherency. In terms of storage access, the 601 follows a weakly ordered storage model that allows a more effective utilization of available bus bandwidth.

The 601's multiprocessing features provide enough flexibility to address a broad spectrum of multiprocessor-based system organizations. Asymmetric rather than symmetric multiprocessor systems are also feasible. The 601's multiprocessing solution focuses on providing a tightly coupled shared memory system organization. A typical PowerPC multiprocessor system (601-based) is shown in Fig. 4.12. The highlights of such a system are shared memory for uniform address space; shared bus to facilitate hardware-enforced coherency between a number of tightly coupled processors, each with their own local cache; cache control operations defined on the bus to allow other processors or external hardware to control the local cache state; and a low latency path to the shared memory.

4.5.14 Packaging

The 601 implementation uses a 0.6-μm CMOS technology with four levels of metal wiring. The 601 package is a 304-pin ceramic quad flat pack. The chip uses 2.8 million transistors and is implemented on a 10.95- by 10.95-mm die. Its typical power consumption is about 6.5 W at 50 MHz.

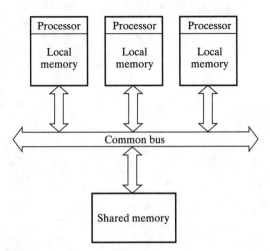

Figure 4.12 601-based multiprocessor system.

As with any microprocessor, various clock speeds of the 601 are available. Although the currently offered speeds are 50, 60, 66, and 80 MHz (see Fig. 4.13), this list is likely to grow over a period of time.

4.6   THE PowerPC 603 MICROPROCESSOR

The 603 microprocessor is the second member of the PowerPC family and has been designed with the intent of being used in portable computers, notebook PCs, and mobile systems. The implementation represents a new microarchitecture organization of the PowerPC architecture family. It offers high performance at a low power level; even with peak instruction rates of three instructions per cycle, its power consumption remains well below any other comparable processors in the industry at the current time.

The 603 chip retains the basic three execution units, but adds two dedicated components. A *load/store unit* is employed to handle the data movement between the data cache and the general purpose registers. A *system unit* is incorporated to handle all system register operations. In terms of cache, a dedicated instruction and data cache is implemented. The processor features a generalized dispatch/rename scheme which utilizes simple rename buses and autonomous functional units. Perhaps the most distinguished feature in the 603 is the use of a dynamic power management system to control the processor clocks so that functional unit clocks need run only when specific instructions are dispatched to the corresponding unit.

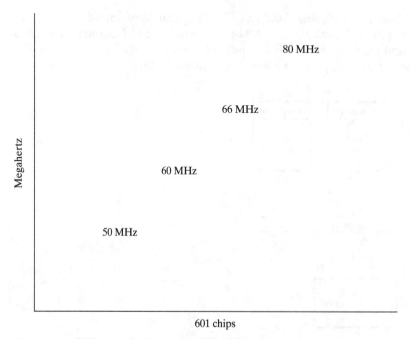

Figure 4.13 Different clock speeds of the 601 microprocessor.

4.6.1 Pipelines

There are four different pipelines in the processor complex:

- branch processing unit—two-stage pipeline
- fixed-point unit—three-stage pipeline
- floating-point unit—six-stage pipeline
- load/store unit—five-stage pipeline

The first stage of all the pipelines is the same and involves fetching the instruction(s). The branch instruction pipeline, which is a two-stage pipeline, can decode, execute, or, if necessary, predict the direction of an unresolved branch. This allows operation beyond a conditional branch without a delay.

The fixed-point instructions flow through a four-stage pipeline. The first two stages of the pipeline handle the fetching and decoding/dispatching. The third stage handles the execution of the fixed-point operation that can include arithmetic, logical, compare, shift, or rotate instructions. The fourth stage writes back the result to the registers.

The single-precision and double-precision floating-point operations are processed by a six-stage pipeline (it is the deepest of all the pipelines in the processor). Like the fixed-point pipeline, the first two stages of the floating-point pipeline handle the fetching and decoding/dispatching tasks. The execution phase consists of three stages, as shown in Fig. 4.14. The *execute1* stage involves the multiply. (Note: It is double-pumped for double-precision operations.) The *execute2* stage involves the carry-propagate-add. The *execute3* stage performs the rounding and normalization functions. In the subsequent stage (*writeback*), the results are written back to the registers.

Branch instructions

Fetch	Decode Execute Predict

Fixed-point instructions

Fetch	Decode Dispatch	Execute	Writeback

Load/store instructions

Fetch	Decode Dispatch	Address generation	Cache	Writeback

Floating-point instructions

Fetch	Decode Dispatch	Execute1	Execute2	Execute3	Writeback

Figure 4.14 603 pipeline structure.

To process the load/store instructions, the first two stages of the pipeline handle the fetching and decoding/dispatching. The third stage calculates the address for the element to be accessed. The fourth stage involves accessing the cache, followed by the stage that writes back values to the registers.

4.6.2 Organization

603's organizational highlights include a 64-bit interface from the instruction cache to the instruction fetch and branch unit, which, in turn, feeds into to the dispatcher. The dispatcher's interface to the fixed-point unit, load/store unit, floating-point unit, and the system unit is also 64 bits wide. Figure 4.15 gives a block diagram of the processor complex. The principal functional units consist of (1) the instruction cache, (2) the data cache, (3) the instruction fetch and branch unit, (4) the dispatcher unit, (5) the completion/exception unit, (6) the fixed-point unit, (7) the floating-point unit, (8) the load/store unit, (9) the system unit, (10) the bus interface unit, (11) the external bus, and (12) the COP unit. Each is described individually.

- instruction and data caches
- instruction fetch and branch unit

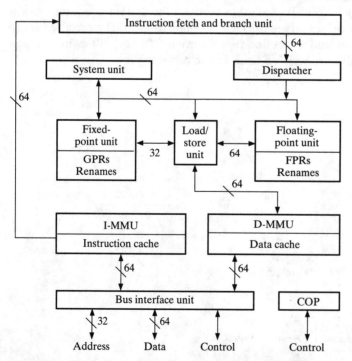

Figure 4.15 Block diagram of the PowerPC 603 microprocessor.

- dispatcher unit
- completion/exception unit
- fixed-point unit
- floating-point unit
- load/store unit
- system unit
- bus interface unit
- external bus
- COP unit

4.6.3 Instruction and data caches

The instruction and data caches are both 2-way set-associative caches with 32-byte cache lines. Because there are 32 bytes per line, the total cache size adds up to 8 KB. Figure 4.16 explains the breakdown of set and line mapping in further detail.

The coherency protocol used to update the contents of the cache is a compatible subset of the MESI (modified, exclusive, shared, invalid) four-state protocol. This means that this protocol can operate coherently in systems using the MESI protocol. Since the 603 does not have to broadcast cache operation instructions to support symmetric multiprocessing in the hardware, a three-state coherency protocol is implemented. A state diagram of the three-state MESI protocol is provided in Fig. 4.17.

4.6.4 Instruction fetch and branch unit

The function of the instruction fetcher is to manage the instruction prefetching from the instruction cache. The function of the branch unit is to execute the branch instructions.

Instructions are fetched into a prefetch buffer from the instruction cache (or main memory on a cache miss). Then these instructions are acted upon. The branch instructions are processed by the branch unit, and, consequently, the instructions are forwarded to the dispatcher.

Cache organization of 603 microprocessor:

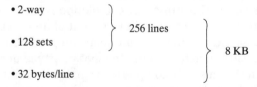

- 2-way
- 128 sets
- 32 bytes/line

256 lines

8 KB

Figure 4.16 Description of the I-cache and D-cache of the 603 in terms of its sets and lines.

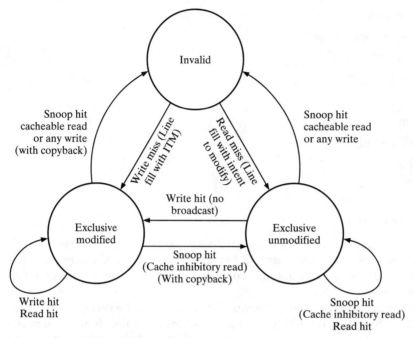

Figure 4.17 Cache coherency state diagram.

4.6.5   Dispatcher unit

The functions of the dispatcher are to decode instructions, decide whether they can be dispatched to an available execution unit, and manage the register renaming task. Note that the concept of register renaming is necessitated to keep the pipeline full and devoid of any stalling owing to the unavailability of load instructions. This technique of architected registers (used in instructions) getting mapped to physical registers is achieved by having a pool of free physical registers available beyond the proclaimed number of 32 floating-point registers.

4.6.6   Completion/Exception unit

The role of this component is to render a mechanism to track instructions from dispatch through execution, then retire them in program order. Recognize that completing an instruction implies updating appropriate architectural registers with the results of that instruction. An in-order completion scheme is used to ensure that the correct state can be preserved in the event of an exception or a mispredicted branch. Also, adequate information about an instruction has to be maintained in the completion registers owing to a possibility of out-of-order execution. This is the reason that a single completion register is maintained for every dispatched instruction. As far as exceptions and interrupts are concerned, they are monitored separately by the exception logic. The exception unit's interrupt mechanism allows the processor to change state as a result of external errors or any byzantine conditions.

4.6.7   Fixed-point unit

The fixed-point unit is responsible for executing all fixed-point instructions in the system. It is capable of processing all arithmetic, logical, compare, shift, and rotate instructions in a single cycle, and multiply instructions in two to five cycles. The execution unit interface consists of accepting instruction(s) from the dispatch unit, performing the specified operation on the operands, placing the result onto the specific rename bus, and notifying the completion unit and the dispatch unit, respectively, of the completion status of the current operation.

4.6.8   Floating-point unit

The floating-point unit processes all the single-precision and double-precision floating-point operations. Hardware support is provided for divide, float-to-fixed conversion, denormalization, and exceptions. Additionally, the PowerPC architecture enhancement for graphics is supported with three new floating-point instructions. Although the floating-point unit operates independently of the fixed-point unit and can concurrently execute instructions, a synchronization scheme via the load/store unit allows for the progressive execution of the two units, and still achieves the effect of precise interrupts.

The floating-point unit interface accepts instruction(s) from the dispatch unit, performs the specified operation on the operands, places the result onto the specific rename bus, and subsequently notifies the completion unit and the dispatch unit, respectively, of the completion status of the current operation.

4.6.9   Load/store unit

The load/store unit is responsible for data transfer between the data cache and internal (fixed-point and floating-point) registers, processing of external access instructions for graphics applications, as well as handling of the cache and memory management unit control instructions. The load/store unit calculates the effective addresses and handles the data alignment to and from the cache. It also contains the logic to perform normalization and denormalization of floating-point store data.

4.6.10   System unit

The function of the system unit is to execute a set of miscellaneous instructions (for example, move to/from special purpose registers instructions). Since these instructions are relatively infrequently encountered, renaming logic is not provided here.

4.6.11 Bus interface unit

The bus interface unit is responsible for accepting bus requests from the instruction and data caches, placing the requests on the external bus, and handling the addresses for snooping in the cache.

4.6.12 Packaging and power management

Two levels of power management are implemented in the 603 chip: (1) a dynamic power management logic, which uses power thriftily everywhere possible during normal operation, and (2) software selectable static power management modes that can be incorporated for periods of processor inactivity. Using the dynamic power management logic, execution units like the floating-point unit clock logic can be turned off when there are no destined instructions for that unit. By making use of the static power management logic and its three varying power modes (doze, nap, and sleep), processor state information can be maintained during the power-down modes. This power management capability makes the 603 chip an ideal choice for portable PCs and mobile systems.

The 603 implementation uses a 0.5-μm CMOS technology with four levels of metal wiring. The package is a 240-pin ceramic pack. The chip uses 1.6 million transistors and is implemented on a 7.4- by 11.5-mm die. Its typical power consumption is about 3 W at 80 MHz. The various available speeds of the 603 microprocessor are 50 and 80 MHz.

4.7 THE PowerPC 604 MICROPROCESSOR

The 604 microprocessor is a 32-bit implementation specifically designed for mainstream computing environments, including midrange workstations and multiprocessor systems. It features multiple integer units to harness optimal performance. It also contains a 16-KB data cache and 16-KB instruction cache. Refer to Fig. 4.18 for its block diagram.

4.7.1 Pipelines

There are six different pipelines in the processor complex; much of it is the same as that of the 603, except for the number of integer (i.e., fixed-point) pipelines:

- Branch processing unit—two-stage pipeline
- Integer unit—three separate three-stage pipelines
- Load/store unit—five-stage pipeline
- Floating-point unit—six-stage pipeline

4.7.2 Organization

The 604 features six execution units, the two new ones being the inclusion of a second and a third integer unit for superior fixed-point performance. Avail-

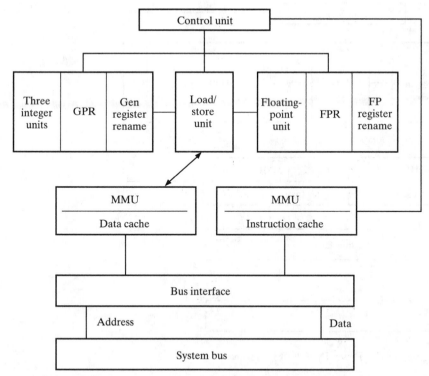

Figure 4.18 Block diagram of the PowerPC 604 microprocessor.

ability of three separate integer units in the processor augments the extent of instruction-level parallelism that modern applications and compilers exploit.

In the 604, both instruction and data caches contain 16 KB organized as 4-way set-associative, 32 bytes per line.

4.7.3 Packaging

The 604 implementation uses a 0.5-μm CMOS technology with four metal layers. The package is a 304-pin ceramic quad flat pack. The chip uses 3.6 million transistors and is implemented on a 12.4- by 15.8-mm die. Its power consumption is around 10 W at 100 MHz.

4.8 THE PowerPC 620 MICROPROCESSOR

The 620 microprocessor is a 64-bit implementation designed for high-end machines and multiprocessor systems. In addition to the standard cache, it includes an embedded secondary cache controller that interfaces to standard SRAM chips. Multiple integer units are utilized to harness optimal performance. Figure 4.19 gives a block diagram of the processor.

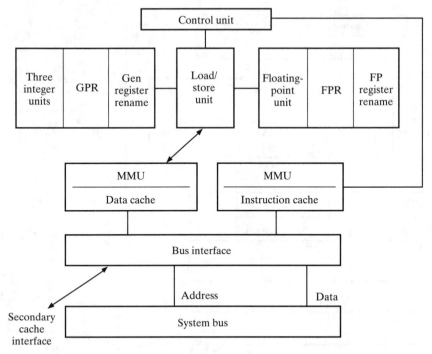

Figure 4.19 Block diagram of the PowerPC 620 microprocessor.

4.9 PowerPC EMBEDDED PROCESSORS

A suite of embedded controllers has been developed based on the PowerPC architecture. They are collectively referred to as the 4xx family of PowerPC processors.

Using the PowerPC as the core yields a flexible RISC-embedded controller that can be used in application-specific processors and ASIC cores. Since the nucleus of the embedded controller is based on the PowerPC technology, it harnesses all the power consumption advantages of the PowerPC microprocessor at a lower price than the competition. Not surprisingly, the 4xx family of embedded processors has become a favorite choice for cost-sensitive applications like printers, copiers, facsimiles (faxes), personal communicators, personal digital assistants (PDAs), video games, camcorders, video cassette recorders (VCRs), networking systems, and much more. (See Fig. 4.20.)

It is the scalable nature of the PowerPC architecture that makes it a realistic choice not just for the personal computer industry, but also for the consumer electronics and embedded controller market. The 4xx family of PowerPC embedded controllers integrates caches and system-level logic to simplify the system design, lessens the total number of components, and reduces the overall system power consumption. A business benefit of this is that, beginning with a family of general purpose embedded controllers, custom systems based on it can preserve the coherence of application development efforts.

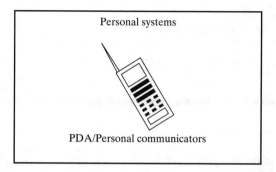

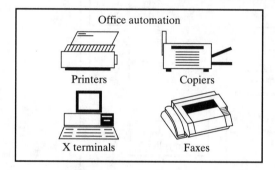

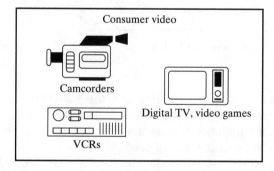

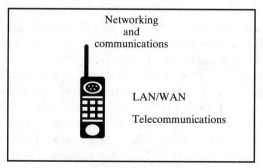

Figure 4.20 PowerPC embedded controller target markets.

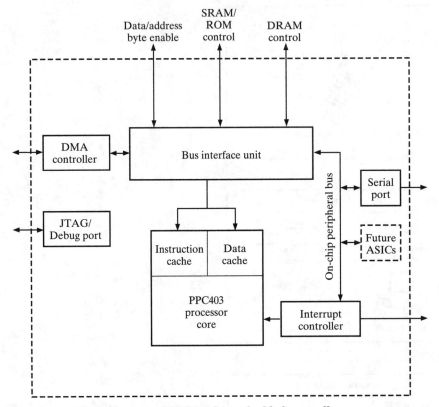

Figure 4.21 Block diagram of PPC403GA embedded controller.

4.9.1 The embedded controller 403

Based on the PowerPC instruction set architecture, the EC403 processor family offers a low-range series and a midend series. Each series can have more than one member in it. Each member acts as the core and may include system peripherals and application-specific logic as needed.

Consider the midrange embedded controller family, the EC403M, which features individual members like the EC403MA and the EC403MB. Each member retains the basic instruction set architecture, but is tailored to application-specific logic by featuring varying cache sizes, system peripherals, and registers. A description of the EC401MA is provided here, in terms of its core and peripherals. Figure 4.21 provides a block diagram of it.

The core consists of techniques such as instruction pipelining, branch prediction, and branch folding to achieve a sustained performance approaching one clock cycle per instruction (CPI) for most applications. Low latency interrupt performance is achieved by providing hardware assist for context switches and by terminating multicycle instructions which are executing when an interrupt is received. In terms of on-chip caches, a separate 2-KB instruction cache (2-way set-associative) and a 1-KB data cache (2-way set-associative and writeback) are employed to reduce bus contention and maximize system performance. In terms of operations, the integer, logical, shift, and rotate/mask are implemented as single-cycle operations. As far as the interrupt structure goes, it is optimized for embedded applications with a worst-case interrupt latency less than 1.2 μs at 25 MHz.

The system peripherals consist of a direct memory access (DMA) controller, JTAG interface, bus interface unit, serial port, and an interrupt controller. The DMA controller contains four independent DMA channels, which operate in buffered, fly-by, and memory-to-memory nodes, and have programmable priority levels for bus access. One DMA channel also supports DMA chaining. The JTAG interface is a debug interface to the processor core and allows user access to the 403 system. The bus interface unit controls the external bus interface, and the internal on-chip peripheral bus (OPB) that attaches to application-specific ICs (ASICs). The bus interface unit contains logic which allows SRAM, ROM, DRAM, and system peripherals to be directly attached to the 403. The serial port is a memory mapped I/O device attached to the on-chip peripheral bus and can operate at data rates up to 1/32 of the processor clock. Note that this serial port is the first of the multifarious ASICs that can attach to the on-chip peripheral bus. Future members of the 4xx family may contain customer-designed ASICs that interface directly with the on-chip peripheral bus.

4.10 SUMMARY

This chapter discussed the individual implementations of the PowerPC architecture. It explained the internal hardware structure, logic design, and data path organization of the available PowerPC implementations (601, 603, 604, 620, and 403), along with a comparative anatomy of the POWER implementations (RS 1, RS .9, and RSC), from which the PowerPC evolved.

Every implementation of the PowerPC architecture should be viewed as an enhancement to the original POWER architecture, optimized for single-chip implementations and extended to 64 bits. Instructions that restrict superscalar implementations have been eradicated. Furthermore, instructions that were deemed as "rarely used" have been removed or altered to improve performance. System flexibility has been increased dramatically by maintaining data storage consistency in hardware and implementing primitives to enable atomic storage access. Also, most implementations of the PowerPC have been equipped to support multiprocessing. These attributes together constitute an efficient and scalable processor, regardless of whether it is a 603, a 620, or any other implementation of PowerPC. As each implementation of PowerPC is a little different and unique, the implementation-specific description of each one has been discussed separately.

It is only the beginning of the era for PowerPC-based processors, and diverse implementations will evolve in the future. When they do, each will feature unique enhancements while preserving the core baseline technology.

Software

User Interfaces

The PowerPC end user environment enables users to run many of their favorite applications, to use simple drag-and-drop and double-click, to recognize a consistent industrywide look and feel, and to exchange data across these applications on one computer on one screen. The PowerPC user can run Windows, DOS, and AIX applications through the use of emulators, translators, binary-to-binary converters, and source code port and adaptation.

User interfaces compatible with the PowerPC operating environment include:

- Common Open Software Environment's Common Desktop Environment
- Wabi
- X Windows
- Macintosh Application Services

These user interfaces provide powerful features while enhancing ease-of-use for PowerPC users. The ability to pick and choose from the array of application environments available and the ability to cut and paste between applications gives PowerPC users endless advantages over systems running only DOS, Windows, UNIX, or Macintosh operating systems and, by default, applications compatible with those single operating systems.

The Common Desktop Environment provides an industrywide consistent look and feel by supporting AIX, DOS, Macintosh, and Windows applications. The Common Desktop Environment provides smooth application integration, interoperability, and data exchange. The Common Desktop Environment's seamless environment supports "shrink-wrapped" end user applications including AIX applications, MS Windows 3.1 applications, x86 DOS applications, 680x0, and PowerPC Macintosh applications.

The operating system is crucial to effective computer usage—operating systems enable multiple applications to run simultaneously, determine how CPU time is distributed, store files, and enable users to access information. The operating systems compatible with the PowerPC enable any Common Desktop Environment, Windows, MS-DOS, X, or Macintosh users to format, access, retrieve, and archive information without relearning a new environment.

5.1   COMMON DESKTOP ENVIRONMENT

5.1.1   Overview

Developed as a Common Open Software Environment (COSE) technology, the Common Desktop Environment is a response to industry and user demands for a powerful, industry-standard desktop environment for UNIX. Based on X Window System 11.5 and OSF/Motif 1.2, Common Desktop Environment incorporates technology from IBM, HP, SunSoft, and Novell, Inc.

The UNIX community got its first taste of the Common Desktop Environment by attending a public developer's conference that included education, documentation, and a CD containing a common-source Common Desktop Environment Snapshot (portable across multiple platforms and the technology openly licensable to the industry). Together, leading desktop architects portrayed the Common Desktop Environment desktop as an environment and user interface providing significant benefits to end users, system administrators, and application programmers.

With the Common Desktop Environment, end users can access networked devices and tools without having to be aware of their location. Users can exchange data across applications by simply dragging and dropping objects. With the right software support, users can even run DOS, Windows, Macintosh, and other environments within the Common Desktop Environment.

System administrators will find that many tasks that previously required complex command line syntax can now be done more easily and similarly from platform to platform. They can also leverage their investment in existing hardware and software by configuring centrally and distributing applications to users. They can centrally manage the security, availability, and interoperability of applications for the users they support.

Application developers will find that they can migrate exiting applications easily—opting to simply port their applications onto the desktop or take advantage of full desktop services through program design.

5.1.2   Getting started with Common Desktop Environment

The standardized Common Desktop Environment desktop components provide a single API for developers and support an installed base of applications. The Common Desktop Environment user interface is based on the OSF/Motif style of user interface, with pervasive use of the drag-and-drop paradigm. The desktop starts up in a default configuration, which is adapted to the screen size of the particular display in use, but which is fully configurable by the user. An integral part of the desktop is the hypertext-based help system which may be invoked from the front panel at any time.

The *front panel* (see Fig. 5.1) contains a collection of frequently used controls and services. By default, the front panel appears at the bottom of the screen and contains a useful set of services. The contents and layout of the front panel are fully configurable. The front panel makes it easy to start applications, use desktop features such as workspaces and the screen lock, and log out of your session.

The front panel exists in all workspaces. (Workspaces are logical screens in which you can place groups of windows.) Many of the controls in the front panel are push buttons for starting applications. Some are drop zones—you can drag a file from file manager or application manager to the control. Others, such as the clock, date, and busy light, are indicators.

The front panel includes the following controls and indicators. (Note that the Common Desktop Environment can be configured for single- or double-click, with the default being single-click.)

The *clock* displays the current time (Fig. 5.2).

The *date* displays the current date (Fig. 5.3).

Clicking on the *file manager* opens an iconic version of your home directory (Fig. 5.4). You can specify another directory once the home directory displays. Most of the desktop basic operations are performed by accessing or invoking files represented in an open directory.

The *personal application* subpanel functions as a control for the personal application of your choice (Fig. 5.5). You can add to or customize the default list of executable programs listed in this subpanel by simply dragging the executable icon and dropping it on the *install icon* area. You can select any of the installed application's toggle buttons to cause that application to be the default application to be invoked from the front panel.

Figure 5.1 Common Desktop Environment front panel.

Figure 5.2 Clock.

Figure 5.3 Date.

Figure 5.4 File manager icon.

Figure 5.5 Personal application subpanel.

Figure 5.6 Mailer.

Clicking on the mail icon starts the *mailer* (Fig. 5.6). This icon can also be used as a drop zone and will accept a file icon to mail.

Clicking on the *lock* (Fig. 5.7) freezes your workstation, preventing unauthorized input. Access your workstation by issuing a password.

The *busy light* (Fig. 5.8) blinks to indicate an activity in progress. If you are trying to open a very large directory, for instance, you will notice that progress is occurring because the green light is blinking.

Clicking on the *exit* button (Fig. 5.9) begins the logout process.

Dropping a file on the *printer control* (Fig. 5.10) prints it on the default system printer. Click on the control to display the printer job status on the default printer.

Clicking on the *style manager icon* (Fig. 5.11) starts the style manager, which can be used to customize the appearance and behavior of desktop sessions. The style manager lets you tailor fonts, background, colors, mouse speed, click volume, screen saver parameters, and other general desktop environment characteristics.

Clicking on the *application manager icon* (Fig. 5.12) opens a directory of easy-to-use tools supporting end user and system administration tasks.

Clicking on the *on-line help icon* (Fig. 5.13) displays the *help manager*—a hypertext-linked list of all of the help volumes that support the desktop. Clicking on the pointer above the icon displays the top level of the hierarchy of help information.

Clicking on the *trash can icon* (Fig. 5.14) opens the trash can window. You can drop an object on the control to put the object in the trash can. You can use the trash can window to restore or permanently delete objects that

Figure 5.7 Lock.

Figure 5.8 Busy light.

Figure 5.9 Exit session button.

Figure 5.10 Printer control.

Figure 5.11 Style manager icon.

Figure 5.12 Application manager icon.

Figure 5.13 On-line help icon.

Figure 5.14 Trash can icon.

you've moved to the trash can. The trash can collects the files and directories that you delete. They are not actually removed from the file system until the trash is "emptied." If you change your mind and want to restore a file you've put in the trash, you can restore it if the trash hasn't been emptied.

5.1.3 Common Desktop Environment services

Common Desktop Environment desktop and application services include session management, window management, data interchange, network services, customization, on-line help, printing, and application integration. Integrated Common Desktop Environment services enable end users to run existing application binaries—applications look and feel the same on Common Desktop Environment as they did on previous platforms. Users can:

- Locate and launch applications quickly and intuitively—click on file manager, click on the application icon, and begin work.

- Focus on manipulation of data and objects, not on execution and command line arguments—users manipulate a file from an icon, not from a path.

- Exchange data across applications using direct manipulation—users can drag-and-drop much more quickly than memorizing command parameters and performing keystrokes.

In essence, interaction of Common Desktop Environment services maximizes end user productivity. End users can now get transparent access to network services and devices on their desktops (such as printers and shared application folders) and can run stand-alone and networked applications without having to be aware of the difference. The Common Desktop Environment enables end users to run X, Motif, OPENLOOK, and character-based applications—and with additional software support, DOS, Windows, Macintosh, and other application environments.

5.1.3.1 Session manager and workspace manager

Session manager (Fig. 5.15) preserves the state of the application at logout (end of session). When the user logs back in, session manager restores the application's state automatically. For an application to be saved and restored by session manager, the application must participate in a simple Inter-Client Communication Conventions Manual (ICCCM) session management protocol.

Session manager supports the notion of a current session and a home session. The current session enables the user to log in to the same session that was running when the user last logged out. The home session enables the user to log in to the same session every time. The user may choose whether the current or the home session is started at login by customizing the *startup* dialog in style manager.

A Common Desktop Environment desktop session starts when the user logs in. The Common Desktop Environment desktop session manager takes over after login manager recognizes the login and password. Session manager provides the ability to manage sessions—to remember the state of the most recent session and return the user there the next time he or she logs in.

Session manager saves and restores:

- The appearance and behavior settings—for example, fonts, colors, and mouse settings

- The window applications that were running—for example, file manager and text editor windows.

Figure 5.15 Session manager.

Certain types of applications can't be saved and restored by session manager. For example, if the vi editor is started from a command line in a terminal emulator, session manager cannot restore the editing session.

A *workspace* is the screen area where you bring the applications needed for your work, arrange them to suit your preferences, and put them away when you're done. Common Desktop Environment initially comes with four workspaces as illustrated in Fig. 5.15 (session manager).

You can organize application windows by choosing which applications belong in each workspace. For example, a workspace could contain applications used for correspondence, such as a mailer and text editor. Or, you could choose to set up your workspaces according to projects, such as budget presentations, marketing demonstrations, and specific in-house project work.

The workspace menu contains commands that help manage the workspace. (Access the workspace menu by holding down the right mouse button while positioning the cursor in the workspace area.) These commands include:

Shuffle up	Puts the bottom window (in a stack of overlapping windows) on the top of the stack
Shuffle down	Puts the top window (in a stack of overlapping windows) on the bottom of the stack
Refresh	Repaints the screen should the display become unreadable
Minimize/restore front panel	Turns the front panel into an icon; when selected a second time, restores the front panel
Restart workspace manager	Stops, then restarts, workspace manager after configuration files have been customized
Log out	Begins the logout process, the same as pressing the exit button in the front panel

5.1.3.2   File manager

File manager (Fig. 5.16) is a desktop application that lets you create, locate, organize, and work with desktop objects such as files and directories. The file manager main window is a view of a directory on your system. The directory you are currently viewing is called the current working directory. To remove a file from file manager and place it on the desktop, do the following:

1. Point to the object's icon.

2. Press and hold the right mouse button, known as the *drag* button. (On a two-button mouse, press both buttons simultaneously.)

3. Drag the icon to the location where you want to drop it, then release the mouse button.

The motion for dropping an object is press..drag..release. To cancel a drag in progress, press the Esc key before releasing the mouse button.

To move a file to a certain directory in file manager, drop a file into an open file manager window or into a directory icon. If you drop an object onto the

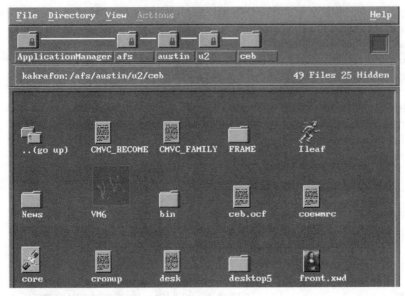

Figure 5.16 File manager.

workspace backdrop, you are placing a reference to it on the desktop in the current workspace.

5.1.3.3 Style manager

Style manager (Fig. 5.17) makes it easy to customize the visual elements and system behavior of the desktop. You can choose from lists of color palettes, change your mouse's double-click speed, or perform other tasks to customize the desktop according to your preferences. Options that can be customized include:

- Workspace (screen) colors
- Application font sizes
- Workspace backdrops
- Mouse button click settings, double-click speed, pointer acceleration, or pointer movement threshold
- Beeper volume, tone, or duration

Figure 5.17 Style manager.

- How a window acquires focus, if the window raises when it receives focus, or where window icons are placed
- Number of minutes before your screen times out or whether or not your screen is covered and locked at time out
- How your session begins and ends

5.1.3.4   On-line help

You can use desktop on-line help topics in a variety of ways including:

- Press F1, also known as the *help* key. The quickest and easiest way to get help is to press F1. When you press F1, the application you are using responds by displaying the help topic most closely related to your current activity. Some computers have a dedicated help button on the keyboard which may take the place of the F1 key.
- Choose a command from application help menus. Most applications have a help menu that contains additional commands for requesting specific kinds of help, such as *Introduction, Tasks,* and *Reference.* To learn more about using help windows, choose *Using Help* from the help menu in any Common Desktop Environment application. Or, press F1 while using a help window.
- Double-click on the help manager icon to browse all the available help. The help manager is a special help window that lists all of the on-line help that has been installed on the system. To browse the Common Desktop Environment help volumes:
  1. Choose the help control in the front panel.
  2. Choose Common Desktop Environment to display the list of help volumes for the desktop.
  3. Browse the list of titles. To open a volume, choose its title.
- Select the arrow above the help manager icon.

See Fig. 5.18 to view the help subpanel options available when you select the arrow above the help manager icon.

The help subpanel provides the following:

Install icon	Drop an object on the control to install it into the subpanel. You can install icons representing applications (actions), files, and directories.
Top level	Choose the control to open the top-level help window, which is a browser window that lets you access any Common Desktop Environment compliant help registered on your system.
Desktop introduction	Displays the help volume entitled "Introducing the Common Desktop Environment Desktop," which contains topics covering basic desktop concepts and skills.
Front panel help	Displays the help volume for the front panel, which contains topics covering how to use and customize the front panel.

Figure 5.18 On-line help pop-up.

5.1.3.5 Application manager

Application manager (Fig. 5.19) contains all the applications registered on your system. The top level of application manager contains a set of *application groups,* which is a special directory containing the application and, optionally, other useful files such as sample data files, templates, and readme files.

The application groups in your application manager are either built in or have been placed there by your system administrator. When an application group is in your application manager, it is said to be *registered* on your system.

Figure 5.19 Application manager.

The actual applications and other files may be located on your own system or can be elsewhere in the network. The registration of application groups into your application manager occurs each time you log in.

The various types of tools that are distributed by default with Common Desktop Environment support a broad range of tasks routinely performed by users and system administrators. There is a UNIX tools directory that contains a variety of icon and action associations that enable users to easily capture and display screens, tar files, uncompress files, and search on strings. The desktop also provides a graphical means to create icons, associate the icon with a desired command string, and refresh the user's environment with the new action definitions.

5.1.3.6 Messaging with ToolTalk

ToolTalk is designed to make it easy for applications on one or more hosts to easily exchange information or control each other by supporting multicast and point-to-point communication. Through the use of messages and patterns, requests and notices, handlers and observers, and scope of delivery, ToolTalk:

- Integrates global workspaces
- Is completely transparent to end users
- Supports procedural and object-oriented messaging
- Provides high performance and throughput
- Guarantees message delivery

The ToolTalk service enables independent applications to communicate with each other without having direct knowledge of each other. Applications create and send ToolTalk messages to communicate with each other. The ToolTalk service receives these messages, determines the recipients, and then delivers the messages to the appropriate applications.

ToolTalk messages are simple structures that contain fields for address, subject, and delivery information. To send a ToolTalk message, an application obtains an empty message, fills in the message attributes, and sends the message. Senders need to know little about the recipients because applications that want to receive messages explicitly state what message they want to receive. This information is registered with the ToolTalk service in the form of message patterns.

Applications can provide message patterns to the ToolTalk service at installation time and while the application is running. When the ToolTalk service determines that a message needs to be delivered to a specific process, it creates a copy of the message and notifies the process that a message is waiting. If a receiving application is not running, the ToolTalk service looks for instructions (provided by the application at installation time) on how to start the application.

Before your application can utilize the interoperability functionality provided by the ToolTalk service and the Common Desktop Environment Messaging Toolkit, it needs to know where the ToolTalk libraries and Common

Desktop Environment Toolkit reside. To use the ToolTalk service, an application calls ToolTalk functions from the ToolTalk API. The Common Desktop Environment messaging toolkit provides functions to register with the ToolTalk service, to create message patterns, to send messages, to receive messages, to examine message information, and so on.

5.2 WABI

5.2.1 Overview

Wabi allows users to run Microsoft Windows 3.1 software-based applications on the PowerPC operating system platform. An execution environment for Microsoft Windows 3.1 API compliant applications, Wabi includes a layer of code that maps the Microsoft Windows APIs onto X11. Wabi converts Windows programming calls to equivalent X Windows calls that are then executed in the host processor. Time spent in the operating system requesting services is remapped to native UNIX operating system calls. Wabi relies on native services, using the same instructions as the native instructions on top of the PowerPC.

Wabi's features include:

- Reimplementation of MS Windows dynamically linked libraries (dlls)
- Reimplementation of the following MS Windows executables: program manager, control panel, task manager, and write
- Support of cut, paste, and copy between MS Windows applications and AIX applications
- Support of DOS diskettes and CDROM for easy installation of MS Windows and 3.1 applications
- Full access to systems resources including PostScript printers
- Support of MS Windows enhanced (80386) mode applications
- Integration into the Common Desktop Environment

Wabi software resides between an application and the native operating system. There it redirects an application's requests for services and resources to the appropriate operating system location. As users work with applications, Wabi intercepts instructions and requests and translates them into a language understood by the native operating system. Wabi then directs these requests to the appropriate operating system location.

Wabi currently supports PostScript printers attached to the native operating system. Wabi takes the PostScript file created by an application and passes it on to the system's print queue, which, in turn, performs the normal printer control and management. The operating system carries out the print request, making available print resources in the form of a device or driver.

5.2.2 Wabi capabilities and functions

The Wabi program can run a variety of programs, including Windows 3.1 applications and additional dlls. As a result, the Wabi program can provide a variety of functions. However, the functions available during a Wabi session depend on the functions supported by the application you are running.

For example, if you are using an application that supports dynamic data exchange (DDE) and that includes DDE program libraries, the Wabi program will support DDE operations. The same is true for object-linking and embedding (OLE) operations. If your application supports OLE 1.0 operations, and includes OLE resources, the Wabi program uses the OLE dll supplied by the end user or the application.

In essence, the Wabi program supports two groups of functions: (1) *configuration functions* intrinsic to the Wabi program, and (2) *operational functions* supplied by applications. Configuration functions include the following:

- COM port settings
- Printer settings
- Drive connections
- Diskette connections
- Mouse settings
- Sound settings
- DOS emulator connection

Operational functions supplied by installed applications include:

- Many Windows 3.1 program manager functions
- Windows 3.1 accessory group programs
- Windows 3.1 main group programs
- Windows 3.1 games group programs
- Dynamic data exchange functions
- Object linking and embedding 1.0 functions

Access the configuration functions through the Wabi configuration manager. Each configuration function is represented by an icon appearing in configuration manager, and also by a menu item in the configuration manager options menu.

If you have a Microsoft Windows 3.1 license, you can access many Windows 3.1 applications and functions. These are available through Wabi's application manager, which replaces the need to use the MS Windows 3.1 program manager.

5.2.3 Getting started with Wabi

The Wabi program presents the familiar screens, dialog boxes, and menus of a graphical user interface (GUI). Make menu choices and icon selections by pointing and clicking with a mouse, or by using keyboard accelerator commands.

5.2.3.1 Configuration manager

Use the Wabi configuration manager to establish or change Wabi settings and connections. The Wabi configuration manager functions as the dashboard of the Wabi program, where most facets of program operation are controlled.

Some configuration manager settings require you to supply operating system device names. In most cases, the Wabi program identifies your operating system and supplies the appropriate default settings. Infrequently, you may need to enter a unique or unusual setting.

Because of the way your native operating system works, you must change certain system settings through your native desktop or from the native operating system command line. Examples of such system settings include the system date and time, desktop (non-Wabi) screen colors and fonts, and the exporting and mounting of remote filesystems. If a setting you want to change does not appear within configuration manager, refer to your operating system documentation for information about how to change the setting. The Wabi configuration manager is illustrated in Fig. 5.20.

5.2.3.2 Application manager

The Wabi program provides its own program environment called application manager. Use application manager to install and run applications. From application manager the Wabi configuration manager can be accessed.

You don't have to use application manager. You can run an application directly. You may find application manager useful, however, for organizing and managing your applications. Use application manager to manage applications by organizing them into groups. You can create application groups using the

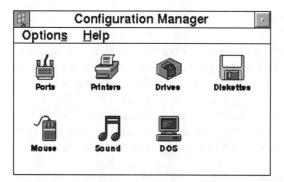

Figure 5.20 Wabi configuration manager.

new command from the *file* menu. Once you create a group, you can place an application item (program) or data file within the group. Application manager initially contains one group: the *tools group*. More groups appear in application manager as you install your Windows applications.

All application manager commands and functions are accessible through key combinations (called *keyboard accelerators*) as well as through the mouse pointer. Each menu title, menu choice, and dialog box function contains an underlined character. This character designates an accelerator key. By pressing the Alt key and the key represented by an underlined letter, you access the command or function.

Application manager provides several menus:

File
: Provides a way to create new application groups and items; open application groups; move, copy, and delete application items and groups; examine group and item parameters; run an application; and exit the Wabi program.

Options
: Allows you to automatically control the layout of icons within a group window, minimize an application on use, and save the window and icon layout on exiting the Wabi program.

Window
: Allows you to control the arrangement of windows and the layout of icons within a window.

Help
: If required program files are installed, help provides access to the Wabi on-line help system's table of contents, and allows you to search for a topic. Instructions about using the help system are also provided.

The Wabi application manager and menu bar is illustrated in Fig. 5.21.

5.2.3.3   Tools group

The tools group is contained within application manager. A tools group application item is a utility program that allows you to perform a specific Wabi task. An example of a task is installing the Windows 3.1 program. Application items within the tools group include:

Configuration manager
: A program through which you establish and change most Wabi program settings and connections. Use this program to set up a drive, assign a port, establish a default printer, and more.

Windows install
: A program used to install the Microsoft Windows 3.1 program. You must use this tool to install the Windows software.

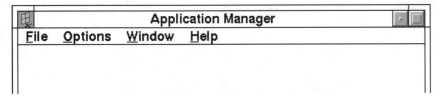

Figure 5.21   Wabi application manager.

DOS session
A program that starts a DOS session by starting the DOS emulator specified in the Wabi configuration manager.

File viewer
A program you can use to view and print text files having a .wri or a .txt file extension. Files with these extensions serve as *readme* files in many application programs. You can also use this program to view initialization (.ini) files.

The Wabi tools group is illustrated in Fig. 5.22.

When you install an application, it's informative to view the various readme files included with the application. These files contain information about the application, and usually some caveats about using the application. Use the *file viewer* to view and print an application's readme files. File viewer will selectively search for files with the following extensions:

.wri—Files in the Windows 3.1 write format.

.txt—Files in ASCII text format.

.—Files with any file extension. (This combination of wildcard characters represents all files, no matter what the file extension.)

To view a file, start file viewer by double-clicking the file viewer icon in the tools group. When the file viewer window opens, select *open* from the file menu.

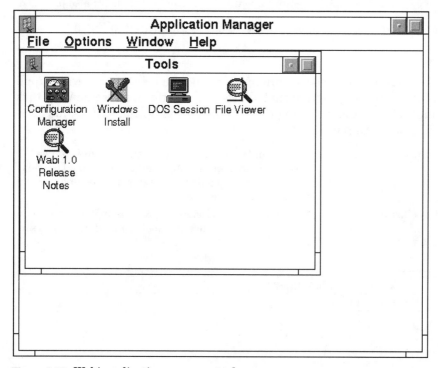

Figure 5.22 Wabi application manager tools group.

The Select File for Viewing dialog box opens. This dialog box is a file browser, which is used to locate the file you want to view or print. This Select File for Viewing dialog box has several panels:

Directory	Displays the directory path currently selected. You can enter a path in this panel or construct a path by browsing a file system.
File	Displays the name of the file selected for viewing in the search list.
Directory layout	A browser that displays the directories within the current directory available for browsing. Double-click [..] to move up one level in the directory hierarchy. Double-click a directory to select it.
Search list	Displays a list of files within the current directory that have the file extension specified in the *file types* panel.
Drives	Displays a list of Wabi drives and their assignments. Select a drive for browsing from this list.
File types	Displays a list of file extensions, from which you can select an extension. Selecting the wildcard item (*.*) returns for viewing a list of all files in the selected directory, regardless of extension.

You can print a readme file using the *export as* command located in the *file viewer* file menu. The *export as* command converts the file you are viewing to ASCII format and saves the file with a .txt file extension. Once the file is saved, you can print it using operating system tools such as vi or a text editor.

5.2.3.4 Wabi installed with Windows 3.1 program installed

If you are running Wabi with Microsoft Windows 3.1 installed, you can access many of the accessories and programs available in the Windows 3.1 program. For example, you can use Program Manager as your Wabi operating environment. In addition, you can use most accessory programs and games, including Paintbrush, Write, Notepad, Calculator, Solitaire, and Minesweeper.

You can also use the Windows *control panel color function* to change the color scheme of Wabi windows. This is the only control panel function you can use. Although additional functions (date/time, printers, international, etc.) appear in the control panel when Windows 3.1 software is installed under the Wabi program, these functions are managed by the Wabi program or by your operating system. Note that if you do not install Microsoft Windows 3.1 software, you will not have access to Microsoft Windows 3.1 accessories and programs.

You do not need to use the Wabi application manager or the Windows 3.1 program manager to run an application. By specifying the -s argument when starting the Wabi program, you can run an application directly. If you start the Wabi program in this way, the initial window that opens is the application window. You can use this technique to run a Windows application from your native desktop, or from any other UNIX program. Once you've established Wabi settings and connections, you may find running an application from your desktop to be a convenient way of using the Wabi program.

5.2.3.5 Wabi on-line help

The Wabi program provides comprehensive, context-sensitive on-line help. On-line help explains the tasks and procedures required to use Wabi functions. If you have installed Windows 3.1 software in conjunction with the Wabi program, you will be able to access Wabi on-line help and the help provided with your applications. Even if you can't access Wabi on-line help, you can view Wabi error messages and, when using configuration manager, *status panel help.*

A *manual (man) page* of information is available for the Wabi program. This man page describes command-line options, provides examples of various start-up modes, and describes the Wabi environment. To access the Wabi man page, add the Wabi man page directory to the `manpath` environment variable. This variable is located in either your `.login` file or your `.cshrc` file. Once you've modified this variable, you can view the Wabi man page.

A Wabi error message appears when you try to perform an "illegal" procedure or when Wabi software cannot complete a task. For example, you'll see an error message if you try to assign a Wabi drive to a file system that you do not have permission to access.

Status panel help is available within the Wabi configuration manager. Each configuration manager dialog box includes a help panel. This panel displays information about the dialog box item that is under the mouse pointer. As you move the pointer around a dialog box, the displayed help message changes.

5.3   X WINDOW SYSTEM

The X Window System (or X) is a hardware-independent, vendor-independent, and network-transparent operating environment developed at the Massachusetts Institute of Technology in 1984 as a cooperative effort funded by major computer manufacturers to build a network of graphical workstations. The enormous success of this program made the X Window System a UNIX-based windowing standard which is now available on virtually every workstation in the industry. Several versions of X have been developed, of which X Version 11 (X11) is the most recent. The X Consortium was formed in 1988 to foster development and support of the X Window System.

X offers many benefits to users. It solves the problem of having a common interface across a heterogeneous range of computers and operating systems. It provides a mechanism upon which one can build different user interface styles. It also addresses the issue of sharing resources among multiple programs—X allows multiple applications to run simultaneously and permits applications to be device-independent. X is operating-system-independent, encouraging the portability of its software to diverse platforms. Hence, X is one of the most popular and widely available user interface standards in the workstations arena.

X provides the ability to generate multifont text and graphics in monochrome or in color on a bitmap display. Graphics such as points, lines, arcs, and polygons can be generated in a hierarchy of windows. Each window can be considered a "virtual screen" and can, in turn, contain subwindows of an arbitrary depth. They may overlap each other and can be moved, resized, or restacked dynamically. Since windows are relatively inexpensive resources, applications utilizing several thousand subwindows are common and are often used to implement user interface components.

X, a network-oriented windowing system, consists of an X server, which manages a visual display, and client application programs. Client application programs can perform a variety of tasks, such as processing electronic mail, managing a database, or simply displaying the current time. Each application appears in its own window or in a family of associated windows. The server conveys user input information, such as a click of the mouse or keystroke, to the appropriate client application. Client applications communicate their needs for display actions to the server. The X server and client applications can reside on the same computer or on different computers connected by a network. An illustration of the X environment follows (see Fig. 5.23).

The interprocess communication used by the X server and client is defined by a network protocol. Programmers interface with this protocol using *Xlib,* the C language programming interface to X and higher-level "toolkits," such as Xt and OSF/Motif. Xlib functions as a procedural interface, hiding the details of the protocol-encoding and transport interactions, and automatically handling the buffering of requests for efficient transport to the server.

The X Window System architecture is based on a simple client-server relationship. The display server is the program that controls and draws the output to the display monitors, tracks client input, and updates the windows accordingly. Clients are application programs that perform specific tasks. Since X is, by design, a distributed environment, its clients and server do not necessarily have to run on the same machine.

The terminology in the world of X may be somewhat confusing to programmers from the traditional host or mainframe environment. The location of the *server* in the context of X is the reverse of servers in local area network environments. Consider a traditional database environment in which the server

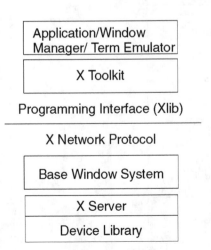

Figure 5.23 X environment.

lives on the remote host and the client application resides locally on the PCs that are attached to it. In X, the server lives on the local workstation, while the clients run on the remote host machines.

Although X is fundamentally defined by a network protocol, most application programmers think about it as a GUI. For ease of use, a higher-level layer is used to abstract the protocol layer and insulate it from programmers building X-based interfaces. This higher-level layer is referred to as the Xlib, or, more correctly, as the Xlib Interface Library (refer to Fig. 5.23). This library provides a familiar procedural interface that masks the detail of the protocol-encoding and transport interactions. It also automatically handles the buffering of requests for efficient transport to the server, much as the C language standard I/O library buffers output to minimize system calls. The library also provides an array of utility functions and primitive constructs that do not directly relate to the protocol but aid in building applications.

5.3.1 AIXwindows Environment

AIXwindows Environment provides a graphical interface to AIX for the Power-PC (see Fig. 5.24). Based on and compatible with the industry-standard X Window System and the OSF/Motif 1.2 GUI, AIXwindows can interact with other AIX and X-based equipment manufacturer systems implementing the X Window System and OSF/Motif interfaces. AIXwindows provides a graphical desktop that can be customized to integrate and launch applications. AIXwindows enables users to develop and execute X applications, OSF/Motif applications, or applications requiring Display PostScript support.

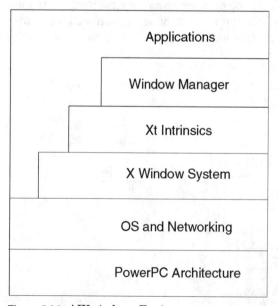

Figure 5.24 AIXwindows Environment.

The current AIXwindows environment (Version 1.2.5) provides support for X Windows Release 5 (X11R5) and is binary-compatible with X11R4. AIXwindows supports 2-D as well as 3-D applications.

AIXwindows is a set of guidelines and tools that specify how a user interface for graphics computers should look and feel. These specifications focus on the design of the objects that make up the user interface: the menus, buttons, dialog boxes, text entry, and display areas. AIXwindows implements a flexible software system layered on top of the X Window System to create individual visual components, such as *scroll bars* and *menus.*

In addition to providing users with the ability to run several applications simultaneously on the screen, the AIXwindows environment supports various services that can enhance applications including:

- *AIXwindows Style Guide.*   Provides a framework of behavior specifications to guide application, widget, user-interface system, and window-manager developers in the design and implementation of new products consistent with the operating system user interface. The *Style Guide* is based on the *OSF/Motif Style Guide.*

- *AIXwindows Customizing Tool.*   Helps to customize the look of an application. Provides a simple method for users to change attributes including colors and fonts.

- *AIXwindows National Language Support.*   Enables programmers to write internationalized applications that can port easily across systems, each of which supports a different native language. The environment clients are internationalized so they can run in the native environment of the user.

5.3.2 AIXwindows 3-D

The most apparent distinguishing characteristic of AIXwindows is its 3-D appearance. The AIXwindows 3-D feature provides facilities for the development and execution of 3-D applications using a variety of industry-standard APIs. This includes hardware support for PEXlib, graPHIGS, and GL as well as a pure software implementation of OpenGL, PEXlib, and graPHIGS referred to as Softgraphics. Softgraphics allows all 3-D functions to be performed by software, in which the graphics adapter is used simply as a frame buffer to display the image. This implementation makes it possible to run 3-D applications on any 2-D graphics adapter.

 Softgraphics provides a uniform development environment for 3-D applications on systems with entry-level graphics adapters. Programmers can develop advanced 3-D applications for industry APIs, which can then be moved to any 3-D graphics adapter with little or no change to the source code.

5.3.3 AIXwindows interface composer

The AIXwindows Interface Composer (AIC) is a software development application that enables application or systems programmers to readily create and generate graphical user interfaces and graft them onto existing programs, or create the interfaces in tandem with code generation. The AIC package provides a library of code modules (objects) that a programmer can use and reuse to build a graphical user interface. The AIC development package is itself graphically driven so that a programmer can build a graphics interface by selecting and working with menus, windows, buttons, and other types of graphic objects.

5.4 MACINTOSH APPLICATION SERVICES

5.4.1 Overview

The primary advantage of Macintosh Application Services is the availability of shrink-wrapped applications, as well as the new generation of PowerPC Macintosh applications. Another powerful feature brought to the PowerOpen system by Macintosh Application Services is the ability to cut and paste information from the Macintosh window environment to and from any other X client application. Both text and graphics can be copied from or pasted to the Macintosh clipboard, which then can be made available from within other X client applications on the system.

From a system perspective, Macintosh Application Services is a layered application execution environment that integrates Macintosh applications into the X Window System without requiring that the Macintosh environment be the dominant personality or desktop. The windowing extensions for the PowerOpen environment consist of a window manager, application commands and parameters, and the communication protocol. The PowerOpen windowing system is derived from the X Window System Release 11 Version 5 (X11R5), which provides a client/server-based graphical windowing system. There is a native mapping of Macintosh's Toolbox APIs onto X11. A 680x0 instruction set emulator is provided to support Macintosh applications.

5.4.2 Capabilities and functions

When using Macintosh Application Services, users see the familiar Macintosh graphical environment inside an X Window on the screen. Within this window, the user can run several Macintosh programs concurrently, and create new windows inside the Macintosh environments, just as with any other Macintosh computer. Macintosh Application Services uses System 7 software, making the look and feel of the PowerPC Macintosh environment identical to that of a Macintosh system.

Also available to users are the productivity features of the Macintosh interface, enabling users to manipulate files and move information throughout the PowerOpen environment. For example, users can move files on the system from one directory or folder to another, copy a file by clicking and dragging a file icon, cut and paste information between Macintosh and PowerOpen operating system documents, and use Macintosh commands to locate or manipulate information. Users can also launch both Macintosh or UNIX applications on the PowerPC by clicking on the appropriate document or application icon.

Apple Macintosh applications run through the Macintosh application services extension. Macintosh Finder, the Macintosh desktop creator and manager, runs within a single window. Both PowerPC and 680x0 Macintosh applications can be run simultaneously from the same system. The Macintosh Finder provides the familiar Macintosh Desktop Graphics User Interface within an X Window on the PowerOpen system. All files (including non-Macintosh documents and applications) appear as icons; users simply double-click on a Macintosh or UNIX icon to open a file or launch an application.

5.4.3 Getting started with Macintosh Application Services

The Macintosh Application Engine includes the toolbox, a 68040 emulator, and a multimode switcher that allows both 680x0 applications and PowerPC applications to run simultaneously. The Macintosh system software component maps the fundamental services such as memory management and I/O to files and devices to the underlying operating system. See Fig. 5.25 for an illustration of the Macintosh Application Services architecture.

There are three main components that make up the Macintosh Application Services software, including:

- Macintosh Desktop Services (the graphical interface through which users interact with the Macintosh environment)

- Macintosh Application Engine (functions as an intelligent switching device, ensuring that applications spend the maximum possible time carrying out functions in native PowerPC code)

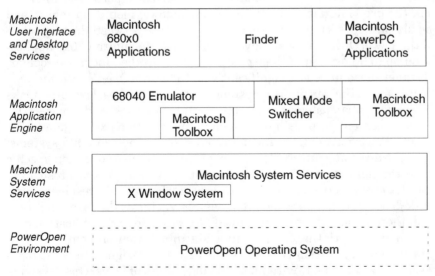

Figure 5.25 Macintosh application services architecture.

- Macintosh System Services (handles interaction with physical devices such as printers and disk drives, as well as memory management and file management)

The first layer, the Macintosh Desktop Services, enables users to manage both Macintosh and PowerOpen files and launch applications. The primary component of the Macintosh Desktop Services is the *finder,* based on Macintosh System 7 system software. The finder is the graphical interface (including the Macintosh desktop) through which users interact with both Macintosh and PowerPC applications. When the Macintosh Application Services application is launched, the desktop area created by the finder appears in the POEmac X window. All finder features are confined to this window, enabling the POEmac window to function as a self-contained Macintosh environment on the PowerOpen screen.

The second layer, the Macintosh Application Engine, consists of the Macintosh toolbox, the Macintosh 68040 emulator, and a multimode code switcher, which determines if the application instructions from the Macintosh Desktop Services layer are Macintosh 680x0 application code on PowerPC Macintosh code, and routes the code accordingly. The Macintosh Application Engine is the core of the Macintosh Application Services. It maximizes the speed of running Macintosh 680x0 applications on a PowerOpen system. All Macintosh 680x0 applications are supported by an emulator, which interprets the 680x0 code to instructions usable by the PowerOpen platform. The system is designed to minimize the time spent in the emulator, and to maximize the time spent executing application commands in native PowerOpen code, allowing increased application performance speed.

Included in the Macintosh Application Engine is the Macintosh toolbox (an interface written in native PowerOpen code) which enables applications to interact with the PowerOpen system layer. The toolbox supports user interface calls from the user interface layer to provide windows, menus, graphics, and fonts and also provides a native PowerPC code interface between the user interface and the PowerOpen hardware layer. Since most Macintosh 680x0 applications spend up to 90 percent of their processing time in the Macintosh toolbox, the application speed increases significantly on the PowerOpen platform.

The third layer, the Macintosh System Services, handles low-level tasks such as memory management and input/output to files and devices. Its resource management responsibilities include information exchange and file management to various devices including hard disks, network file systems, and printers. Native Macintosh files are displayed with an application-specific icon, while the nonnative files are shown with a standard Macintosh icon. Access to files remains transparent regardless of whether it is resident in the native disk drive or on network-mounted devices. As far as the print facility is concerned, there is no difference in printing from Macintosh Application Services as compared to printing from a native Macintosh environment.

The Macintosh Application Services GUI software, designed to work cohesively with the PowerOpen Environment, enables users of PowerOpen systems to take full advantage of the Macintosh environment while harnessing the power and speed of the PowerOpen Environment.

5.5 SUMMARY

The user interfaces compatible with the PowerPC provide powerful features while enhancing ease-of-use for users. The ability to pick and choose from the array of application environments available and the ability to cut and paste between applications gives PowerPC users endless advantages over systems running only DOS, Windows, UNIX, or Macintosh operating systems, and, by default, applications compatible with those single operating systems.

The Common Desktop Environment is a specification providing open systems users with an easy-to-use desktop computing environment that remains consistent across UNIX platforms and applications. The Common Desktop Environment will give developers the advantage of working with a single set of programming interfaces, allowing them to bring products to market faster and with lower support costs. The Common Desktop Environment was one of several specifications outlined in March 1993 when the Common Open Software Environment process was announced. The Common Open Software Environment was formed in order to expedite the adoption of standards and promote greater consistency and interoperability among UNIX system products.

The Common Desktop Environment incorporates major elements of Hewlett-Packard's Visual User Environment (VUE); IBM's Common User Access (CUA) model and Workplace Shell; SunSoft's DeskSet productivity tools and ToolTalk interapplication communication product; Open Software Foundation's Motif Toolkit and Window Manager; USL's UNIX SVR4.2 desktop manager components and scalable systems technologies; the X Window System V11; and Novell's client software for UNIX.

The COSE process was announced by the Hewlett-Packard Company, IBM, SunSoft, Inc., The Santa Cruz Operation, Univel, and Unix System Laboratories in March 1993 to expedite the adoption of standards and promote greater consistency and interoperability among UNIX system products in the industry.

Wabi allows users to run Microsoft Windows 3.1 software-based applications on the PowerPC operating system platform. An execution environment for Microsoft Windows 3.1 API compliant applications, Wabi includes a layer of code that maps the Microsoft Windows APIs onto X11. Wabi converts Windows programming calls to equivalent X Windows calls that are then executed in the host processor. Time spent in the operating system requesting services is remapped to native UNIX operating system calls. Wabi relies on native services, using the same instructions as the native instructions on top of the PowerPC.

Wabi's features include reimplementation of MS Windows' dynamically linked libraries (dlls); reimplementation of MS Windows executables such as program manager, control panel, task manager, and write; support of cut, paste, and copy between MS Windows applications and AIX applications; support of DOS diskettes and CDROM for easy installation of MS Windows and 3.1 applications; full access to AIX systems resources, including PostScript printers; support of MS Windows enhanced (80386) mode applications; and integration into the Common Desktop Environment.

Wabi software resides between an application and the native operating system, where it redirects an application's requests for services and resources to the appropriate operating system location. As users work with applications, Wabi intercepts instructions and requests and translates them into a language understood by the native operating system. Wabi then directs these requests to the appropriate operating system location.

X is a hardware-independent, vendor-independent, and network-transparent operating environment that solves the problem of having a common interface across a heterogeneous range of computers and operating systems by providing a mechanism on which one can build different user interface styles. It also addresses the issue of sharing resources among multiple programs by allowing multiple applications to run simultaneously and permitting applications to be device-independent. X is operating-system-independent, encouraging the portability of its software to diverse platforms, which makes it one of the most popular and widely available user interface standards in the workstations arena.

Macintosh Application Services is a graphical user interface that is compliant with the UNIX-based graphical interface, X Windows. It brings the functionality of the Macintosh environment to PowerOpen systems. With Macintosh Application Services, users of PowerOpen systems are able to take full advantage of the Macintosh environment—the graphical interface, the Macintosh System 7 system software and the wide range of software applications—and combine these advantages with the power and open system architecture of the PowerOpen Environment. Once Macintosh Application Services is installed, users will be able to run PowerPC Macintosh applications, as well as off-the-shelf Macintosh 680x0 applications, inside a window on the screen of a PowerOpen platform.

Operating Systems

The PowerOpen Association's promise of promoting application availability is primarily achievable through the wide range of operating systems that have been ported to the PowerPC. Based on the PowerOpen application binary interface (ABI), the operating systems will run DOS and Windows under emulation, giving users an expanded range of applications to choose from. See Sec. 6.1 for a discussion of the PowerOpen ABI.

The layered architectural definition and design of the PowerPC defines varying degrees of compatibility starting from the instruction set level, to the virtual environment level, up to the operating environment level. This layered approach to the processor's architectural framework makes it possible to run almost any application with minimal porting effort. (See Chap. 3 for more information concerning this new paradigm defined as *architectural abstraction.*)

The PowerPC platform is intended to support numerous 32-bit operating systems (based on the PowerOpen base operating system ABI specification). Candidate operating systems include:

- AIX
- Taligent
- Solaris
- Windows NT
- Workplace OS

The PowerPC support of 32-bit operating systems means that better memory management, preemptive multitasking, and multithreading/multiprocessing are now available to PC users. What do these terms mean to users? With a 32-bit *memory management* scheme, programmers are presented with a set of logical memory addresses that start at 0 and end at 4 GB. This is referred to as a *flat memory model.* The lack of segmentation in the memory model means that an application's code and data no longer need to be broken into 64-KB chunks.

Preemptive multitasking means that the PC's CPU is in total control of application execution. When the operating system is loaded, it establishes a special scheduling program that uses the memory-management hardware of the CPU to coordinate how applications operate. In a preemptively multitasking environment, each application is assigned its own region of system memory and the operating system scheduler allows the application to execute for a certain period of time before it interrupts the application and allows another task to execute. A *thread* is a single, sequential flow of control or task within a process. *Multithreading* is a paradigm given to self-contained tasks that can execute concurrently. *Symmetrical multiprocessing* complements multithreading by distributing threads across multiple processors.

6.1   PowerOpen APPLICATION BINARY INTERFACE

The PowerOpen environment (POE) provides a platform and I/O-independent application interface. The POE application binary interface (ABI) enables software developers to produce shrink-wrapped software without taking platform-specific functions and I/O bus dependencies into consideration. The ABI defines the structure of the application as it is in the POE, thereby defining a system interface for compiled application programs. This includes such key definitions as loading and linking, conventions, object formats, execution environment, networking infrastructure, and installation and packaging information.

The ABI consists of the PowerOpen application programming interface (API), which defines the set of system calls, library function, header files, commands, and utilities that an application developer is allowed to use to develop a compliant application. The POE API also contains the kernel programming interface which defines the kernel process environment. The PowerOpen API supports the following industry standards: XPG4, XNFS, XTI, and X11R5.

Through the use of the POE ABI execution environment, applications programs compiled and packaged for POE implementations support all of the PowerOpen execution environments, interfaces, and headers defined and listed within the ABI specification. Additionally, systems implementing the PowerOpen ABI may provide additional or enhanced interfaces, headers, and facilities.

Adherence to the PowerOpen ABI guarantees application portability to future versions of an ABI-conformant system and to future PowerPC architecture implementations. This portability is guaranteed at the following levels, depending on the application's origin, as follows:

- *ABI conforming system.*   A system that provides all the binary system interfaces for application programs described in the ABI specification and the PowerOpen API.

- *ABI conforming programs.*   A program written to include only the following system routines:

  Commands and other resources included in the ABI.

  Programs compiled into an executable file that has standardized object file formats and characteristics specified for such fields, as defined by the extended common object file format (XCOFF).

  Programs whose behavior complies with the rules given in the PowerOpen ABI specification. A program cannot have the routines defined in the shared libraries of the PowerOpen ABI statically bound into the program.

- *Binary compatibility.*   Application is a "load-and-go" application—only the physical availability of the application is needed. Applications adhering to this level of compatibility can be moved across compliant systems.

AIX, Taligent, Solaris, Windows NT, and Workplace OS operating systems have been ported to the PowerPC platform through modification of their ABIs to be POE ABI compliant. Recognize that complying with the PowerOpen ABI is necessary for an operating system to run on the PowerPC. A discussion introducing the features of AIX, Taligent, Solaris, Windows NT, and Workplace OS follows.

6.2 AIX

The AIX Personal Productivity Client (the version of AIX which will run on the PowerPC) is a fully PowerOpen-compliant operating system based on the Common Open Software Environment's (COSE) version of UNIX that includes COSE's Common Desktop Environment (discussed in Chap. 5). Based on System V Release 3 UNIX, the AIX customization facility is tied in with the X11R5 implementation. From the X Windows desktop, it is possible to customize features of X Windows applications through a graphical interface. AIX also includes the AIX system management tool (*smit*), which consists of a series of menus linked to an object database that builds UNIX commands in an interactive way. *smit* controls almost all system management functions and is also available in a character-based version. *smit* can be used as a diagnostic readout tool and configuration manager was well.

6.2.1 AIX personal productivity client configuration

The PowerPC implementation of the AIX personal productivity client comes in the following configurations:

1. *ASCII client workstation.*   This system consists of a one- to two-user system that operates as a stand-alone or client in a network. Software includes a base

run-time system, utilities, journaled file system, logical and physical volume manager, TCP/IP and NFS client support, system management (including support for remote boot/system management), and UNIX shell user interface.

2. *Graphical client workstation.*   This system consists of the ASCII client workstation functions plus 2D X Windows, Motif GUI, the Common Desktop Environment, Wabi, and a personal productivity user interface, including visual system management utilities. This configuration is referred to as Personal AIX.

3. *ASCII server.*   This system includes the ASCII client workstation functions plus TCP/IP and NFS server functions, multiuser support, and additional base system and system management utilities.

4. *Graphical server.*   This system includes the functionality of the ASCII server plus 2D X Windows, Motif GUI, Common Desktop Environment, and a personal productivity user interface, including visual system management utilities.

5. *Application development kit.*   The XL C compiler plus debuggers and software development utilities. These will run on any of the four base operating system packages.

The client workstation requires at least 16 MB of main memory; the developer workstation, 24 MB; and a LAN server, 32 MB. The main memory should start at address zero and should be continuously populated through the maximum amount in the configuration. A secondary cache (L2 cache) exterior to the processor is optional on a PowerPC configured system. However, to optimize performance for the developer workstation, include a 256-KB L2 cache, and to optimize performance for the LAN server, include a 512-KB L2 cache.

All configurations should have an alphanumeric input device. Note that if a LAN server does not function as a developer or client workstation, a simple console (for example, an ASCII terminal) may be used. A pointing device (typically a mouse) is required on the client and developer workstations.

The client workstation requires a graphics system capable of at least 800×600 pixels; a developer workstation, 1024×768 pixels; and a LAN server, only an ASCII character video system (unless it also functions as a client or developer workstation).

Only the developer workstation requires a serial port for the kernel debugger. However, all configurations require a parallel port and a minimum of one network interface.

The AIX personal productivity client supports a SCSI interface and some IDE disks. All configurations require one PCI bus; the ISA bus is optional for all configurations. However, the ISA bus decoder is required for native I/O support for such interfaces as parallel, serial, keyboard, and mouse.

6.2.2   Operating environment

The AIX software distribution is arranged in a hierarchical structure, resembling an inverted tree. Program modules are grouped in directories in this file tree. This logical organization of data and files allows control over the management of multiple directories and files at one time. The basic layout of vital programs has not changed from the standard UNIX file structure. However, a set of modifications has been made in terms of file organization to optimize storage, accommodate enhancements, and comply with standards.

6.2.2.1 Layout of files

The root directory in AIX is represented by a slash (/) symbol. All directories under this root directory are considered subdirectories and may contain files and/or directories in them. At the top of the AIX file system hierarchy is the system-defined root directory. This root directory contains a set of standard subdirectories. Described here are the names and functions of some of the main directories found under root:

bin	Contains binary programs that the users use as commands
dev	Holds special files for I/O devices
etc	Contains miscellaneous files for system initialization and system management (the name *etc* being derived from *etcetera*)
mnt	Provides a place to mount devices or external data from other machines
lib	Contains common libraries; later releases of AIX have linked /lib with /usr/lib
sbin	Holds system utilities and files needed to boot the machine
tmp	Contains temporary files that may get created by the users or the system itself; typically this directory is purged on a periodic basis
home	Contains login directories for the system users; for compatibility reasons, later releases of AIX have linked /u to /home
usr	Contains system programs and licensed program products that users would use
var	Serves as a mount point for directories and files which change size, such as things found in the /usr/spool directory of UNIX or older AIX systems.

An individual system may also have some additional directories occurring under root. However, the general convention for system maintenance is to keep the root directory as clean as possible. The standard layout of an AIX file tree, as it appears on the PowerPC, is shown in Figs. 6.1, 6.2, and 6.3.

6.2.2.2 Command language interpreters (shells)

In addition to providing a computer-human interface, a shell offers a variety of tools which may be used to automate repetitive user activities at the keyboard. The shell is a hard casing that provides a private workspace for the user. This private workspace is also referred to as the user's *environment*.

Shell commands can be thought of as filters. As Fig. 6.4 depicts, the commands have a single input, called *standard input* (abbreviated to *stdin*), that accepts characters one at a time. Each shell command also has two outputs including *standard output* (abbreviated to *stdout*) and *standard error* (abbreviated to *stderr*). The typical control flow in a shell command execution involves

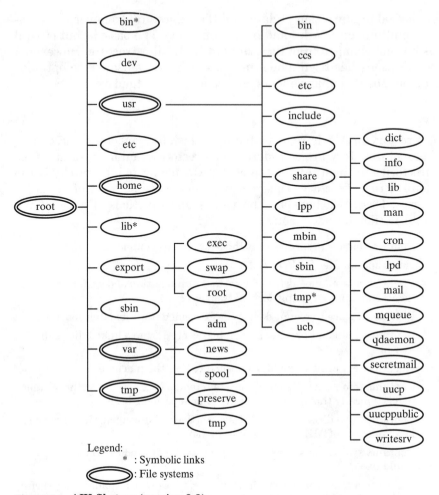

Figure 6.1 AIX file tree (version 3.2).

three discrete phases. The first stage is when data is input from stdin, the second is when the data is acted upon by the shell, and the final phase is passing data to stdout. In this way, each shell command acts upon the data that comes in from the stdin stream, and subsequently hands it off to the stdout stream.

The three primary shells provided by AIX for end users include the Bourne shell (sh), C shell (csh), and the Korn shell (ksh). While the basic functionality of each shell is similar, the actual look and feel of particular shells vary.

The Bourne shell, developed by S. R. Bourne of Bell Labs, is referred to as "sh." The Bourne shell is available on every AIX and UNIX system and is the industry-standard shell.

The C shell (called "csh") syntax is very much like the C language, since it was developed primarily for the use of C programmers at the University of California at Berkeley. The C shell provides some added functionalities to minimize repetitive typing of commands and to optimize job control. Although the

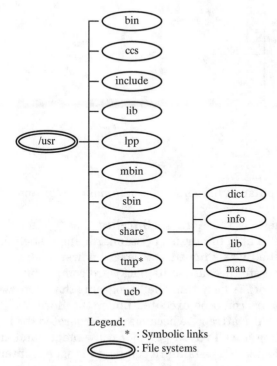

Legend:
   * : Symbolic links
   : File systems

Figure 6.2 *usr* file system.

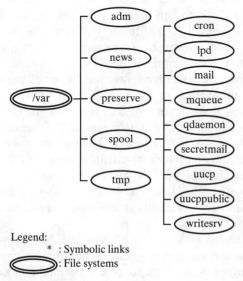

Legend:
   * : Symbolic links
   : File systems

Figure 6.3 *var* file system.

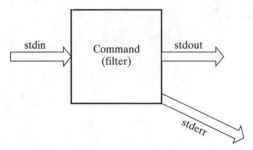

Figure 6.4 Shell filter.

C shell became quite popular in universities and among programmers, it has never been standardized in industry.

The newest of the shells is the Korn shell (called "ksh"), named after its developer S. Korn of Bell Labs. In pursuit of standardizing a shell for industrywide use, the Korn shell was shipped with every newer version of UNIX. The Korn shell was successful because of its backward compatibility with the Bourne shell (C shell is not). All existing shell programs that were written in Bourne shell over the years could be executed under the Korn shell without modification. The Korn is also attractive because it incorporated the best of the C shell features, providing a well-paved path for convergence and standardization of this shell as the industry-standard command language interpreter.

6.2.3 End-user environment

6.2.3.1 Positioning of programs and utilities

The PowerPC layout of programs and utilities resembles a doughnut as shown in Fig. 6.5. The hollow core represents the hardware. The outer layer represents the application programs, which can also be user commands. The inner layer depicts the system programs. The insulation between the two layers is provided by a command language interpreter (also referred to as a shell) that provides an interface between the user and the system.

For a more detailed view of AIX, consider a sectional view of the doughnut model and imagine it under magnification. At this level of detail, some additional components of the system software can be identified. In the sectional view (Fig. 6.6), the outermost layer of the figure consists of application programs and utilities that users use. When invoked, these perform a designated task. Flow of control passes from the user's application program down to the system programs through the shell layer. The vehicle used for this transfer of control is referred to as a system call. Use of system calls is the primary means of requesting information from the operating system and its resources. Details on system calls are covered in Chap. 9.

The third layer in the sectional view of the doughnut model serves as the manager who is responsible for supervising and scheduling requests from application programs. This layer is referred to as the kernel. The kernel services request and subsequently coordinate with the resources in the machine to schedule access to physical devices for information retrieval or storage.

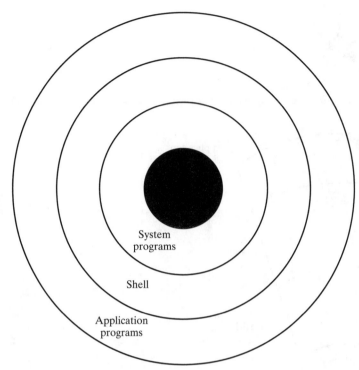

Figure 6.5 Doughnut model.

The fourth level in the sectional view consists of a set of low-level privileged system programs. Once a request has been scheduled by the kernel to access a device, these low-level routines take over the active control. These routines access the physical device (platters on a hard drive) upon request and send up the retrieved information via the same path it was sent down. These low-level routines are highly device-dependent and are collectively referred to as *device drivers.* For every device on the system, there are device drivers responsible for that physical device and for shielding applications from the hardware specifics of the machine.

To consider AIX from a user's point of view, consider a typical scenario: a document is created using a text editor. First, the editor program is invoked by the shell when its name is typed in at the user's command line prompt. New text is typed in and saved, and the editor program is terminated. This may seem like a trivial task to the user, but how do the layers of the doughnut model depict this scenario? Upon initiation of the editor (the application program) by the shell (the command language interpreter), a request to create a document is made to the operating system. Upon the granting of this request (from the operating system), new text is added into storage (a buffer in memory) set aside for this task. Each character typed at the terminal gets sent to some device driver (low-level routines) which is responsible for the terminal device I/O. In this way, a document is created.

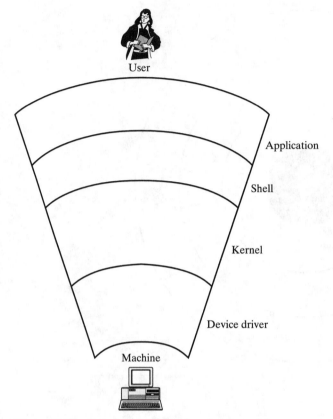

Figure 6.6 Sectional view of the doughnut model.

6.2.3.2 Moving files between DOS and AIX

Moving files between DOS and AIX is achieved using the suite of facilities that permit reading and writing of files in DOS format, that allow users access to DOS directories, and that give users the ability to format diskettes in DOS format. To use these utilities, some conflicting conventions between UNIX and DOS were resolved. As the backslash character (\) can have special meaning to the AIX operating system, the slash character (/) was used as the delimiter to specify subdirectory names in a DOS path name. For other functionality, DOS file-naming conventions were used consistently. AIX utilities used for moving files between DOS and AIX include:

dosread	Copies the contents of a DOS file to a specified AIX file
doswrite	Copies the contents of an AIX file to the specified DOS file
dosdir	Displays information about the specified DOS directory
dosformat	Formats a diskette with the DOS format
dosdel	Deletes DOS files

6.2.3.3 AIX file editors

Four editors are included with AIX: **ed, ex, vi,** and **sed.** In addition to these editors, a wide variety of other editors may be obtained from commercial or public domain sources. The **ed** editor is the original editor under UNIX that was developed at Bell Labs and was shipped with the very first distribution of UNIX. The **ed** editor is found on every UNIX and AIX system. As a line editor, **ed** is able to alter files without full-screen terminal support. The **ed** editor works on only one file at a time by copying it into a temporary edit buffer and making changes to that copy. It does not alter the file itself until you exit the editing session.

The **ex** editor was developed at the University of California at Berkeley. It was the first step toward full-screen editing. Shortly thereafter, the **vi** editor was developed (also at Berkeley). This **vi** editor was built on the primitives of **ed** and **ex.** It provides full-screen editing capabilities, multiple file editing, and many other features. If you're choosing an editor to start with, **vi** is a good choice.

The final AIX standard editor is **sed,** which is a noninteractive stream-oriented editor that is used more like a filter than like an actual text editor. The **sed** editor interprets a script that controls the actions performed. Use **sed** if you need to automate editing actions to be performed on one or more files or to write conversion programs that would be used like filters on input or output data streams.

In addition to the standard AIX text editors, one can acquire commercially available editors. One worth mentioning is **emacs.** The **emacs** editor can be obtained through the Free Software Foundation or from the public domain sites on the Internet.

6.2.3.4 Help access

Two kinds of help facilities will be discussed in this section: the standard facility available on all UNIX machines and InfoExplorer, the AIX-specific online library.

UNIX man pages. UNIX machines are usually shipped with a set of standard manuals for reference. However, these multivolume manuals are not always the most convenient option for end users. So, in addition to these manuals, an on-line help facility has also been provided on most UNIX systems. This on-line help facility is referred to as *man* pages—"man" being short for manual. man pages are a subset of the standard UNIX documentation and contain synopses of the commands and tools used by users and programmers.

To access the man pages on a specific command, you must type in the **man** command, followed by the name of the command on which help is being sought.

```
$ man who
```

A scrolling screen appears, displaying the text on the usage of the **who** command (**who** command shows the currently logged-on users on the system). At

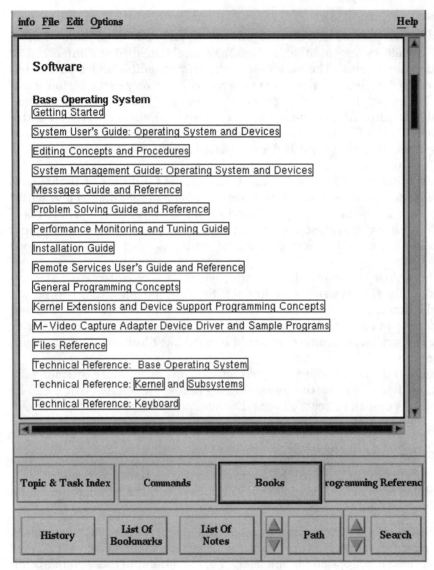

Figure 6.7 InfoExplorer books listing interface.

this time, one may continue to scroll through the documentation by pressing the spacebar or quit out of it at any time by hitting the "q" key.

InfoExplorer. AIX includes a Motif system navigator called InfoExplorer, which provides on-line hypertext documentation via point-and-click interface. The InfoExplorer text retrieval tool contains more than 35,000 pages of articles, tutorials, and technical references on machine- and software-specific topics. See Fig. 6.7.

The essential difference between InfoExplorer and standard UNIX man pages is that instead of being a mere subset of the AIX documentation, Info-Explorer contains the complete set of AIX and PowerPC documentation. This on-line access to the entire AIX and PowerPC library is made possible by the design and implementation of a text retrieval system based on hypertext. Hypertext technology provides a nonsequential method of organizing text in a manner that enables rapid retrieval and efficient storage. Users point and click on selected items such as topics, books, and commands, and the selected information is displayed in a browsable GUI.

To access the InfoExplorer facility, enter the **info** command:

```
$ info
```

To use InfoExplorer, simply follow the menu selections. Note that the screen drawing process that occurs is based on the type of terminal that you are using. In addition to supporting ASCII terminals, the InfoExplorer also provides an interface for X terminals. When using an ASCII terminal, a character-based user interface menu appears which may be operated using the hot keys that appear in inverse video. In an X environment, the InfoExplorer tool displays an X-based graphical user interface with icons that support the mouse and other standard X features (see Fig. 6.8).

In addition to being a completely menu-driven help facility, InfoExplorer also offers compound word(s) searches to locate key words across multiple documents, bookmarks to index selected pages, user notes to tag bookmarks with comments, on-line tutorials for beginners, and a built-in print facility for printing out selected documents.

InfoExplorer can be placed either on the hard drive or be made available on a removable medium like CD-ROM. The latter is generally preferred as it frees up a significant amount of valuable disk space.

6.2.4 Optimizing AIX

To fine-tune the AIX operating system, first identify the workloads on the system. Characterizing this workload is often the most time-consuming phase of performance tuning, as it involves queueing effects of network-mounted file systems and LAN traffic beyond the system's native I/O. Once the workload is defined, formulate a set of objectives to determine how the results are to be measured. The next step is to identify the "critical" resources that are limiting the system's performance with the help of one or more of the AIX performance monitoring, analysis, and tuning tools. Having identified the hot spots, the subsequent aim is to minimize the workload's critical resource requirements, while modifying the allocation of resources to reflect priorities. This allocation and reallocation of resources is termed *performance tuning*. The most commonly tuned critical resources are the disk drive subsystem, real memory, running processes, and communications I/O.

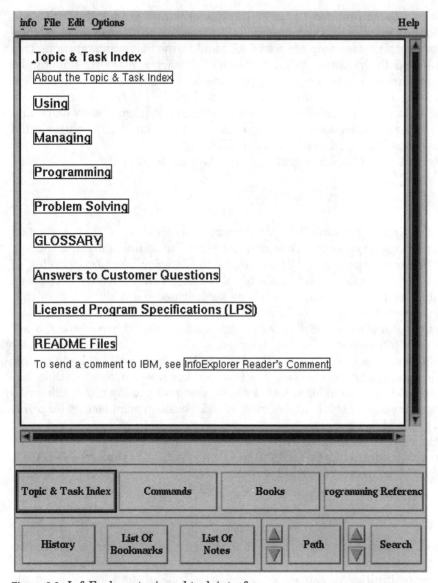

Figure 6.8 InfoExplorer topic and task interface.

Disk drives in traditional UNIX systems have always needed periodic atten-
tion. Since the logical organization of bytes in a file can be completely different
than the physical layout on the disk, data can get fragmented over a period of
time. When this occurs, file access results in longer seeks and, as a result, deteriorates I/O performance. The typical remedy for this is to recompact the disks
and, if needed, redistribute the frequently accessed components across multiple
disk drives. However, AIX is different because AIX implements what is known
as *memory mapped I/O* and *I/O pacing* paradigms. The memory mapped file

concept maps files directly in memory, thus bypassing traditional block I/O and kernel buffers. It alleviates the I/O penalties due to the effect of a file's placement and possible fragmented state on disk. All files are memory mapped by default. The second paradigm, I/O pacing, prevents I/O-intensive programs from building up long I/O queues. It ensures a fair share of I/O resources for both heavily demanding as well as less demanding programs. If a workload is performing poorly because it constitutes an uneven mix of acutely I/O-bound and lightly I/O-bound tasks, one should look into enabling the I/O pacing option in *smit* by experimenting with the high-water/low-water marks to suitable values (other than the default value of zero, which disables the feature).

Fine-tuning communications I/O is primarily a matter of configuration. Most network protocols use sockets to communicate across the network, which are made up of smaller memory buffers called *mbufs*. It is the availability of *mbuf* pools in the network subsystem that governs the performance of the communications I/O. Since the *mbufs* store traffic for inbound and outbound network traffic, having *mbuf* pools of the right size can have a very favorable effect on network performance. The key element to tuning *mbufs* is to know how and when to adjust them. Since *mbuf* pools consist of pinned pieces of virtual memory, they always remain in physical memory and are never paged out, reducing the real memory size. For ideal network performance, the minimum number of free buffers should be maintained in the pools, without degrading network performance. There are options (refer to the **no** command) to specify the minimum number of free buffers for the pool and to control the amount of memory that is to be allocated for *mbuf* management. When or if the number of buffers in the pool drops below the specified threshold level, the pools are expanded by the same amount.

6.3   TALIGENT

Formed by Apple Computer, Inc. and IBM in 1991, Taligent combines the leading-edge technology from both companies. The name Taligent comes from the combination of the two words "talent" and "intelligent." Taligent's object-oriented software environment is a result of a radical paradigm shift from structured procedural programming to object-oriented programming that inherently supports networked environments distributed across heterogeneous platforms.

Taligent provides a complete and integrated object-oriented environment. The operating system is built around the core elements of the object-oriented programming paradigm, and includes the following:

- Objects
- Classes
- Messages
- Inheritance
- Polymorphism

Objects provide an abstraction of state and behavior, in which a state is represented by an aggregated set of data elements and a behavior is depicted by functions—a set of rules that can alter the state. The object's methods provide the interface, and the programs that use this interface are referred to as its clients. The strength of the object paradigm is that new items can be added to the state without changing the interface.

Class is an abstraction of objects. Since reusing object definitions for every program can be tedious, a higher-level abstraction is made available, thereby allowing the class paradigm to be used as a template for the object. It is essential to note that a class is not an entity on its own; it exists only to make object definitions possible.

Communication between clients and objects takes place in the form of a series of *messages,* in which a message can be thought of as an instruction to the object to execute one of its methods.

Inheritance refers to the genealogical relationship that exists between newly created classes and old ones. It is an abstraction of the relationship between objects.

Polymorphism (the occurrence of different forms or stages) is a technique for allowing the specialized behavior of new classes to be used in existing procedures, even if they were written without knowledge of the new subclass. This attribute provides a framework for basic activities that can later be extended in ways not considered by the original designers.

Together, these five attributes reflect the architectural framework of Taligent. It does not use screen icons masquerading as objects, or monolithic procedural codes encapsulated with object code. Its entire infrastructure is object-based. From the bottom layer to the top layer, the design of Taligent emphasizes extendibility, portability, adaptability, and scalability as its key attributes.

Taligent's native implementation is based on the Mach kernel. The Mach kernel has been slimmed down and turned into a true microkernel implementation. It makes use of the standard protocols and supports OSF's DCE, Sun's RPC and NFS, AppleShare, Apple Events, and the Object Management Group's Common Object Request Broker Architecture mechanism for distributed computing.

6.3.1 Microkernel paradigm

The term *microkernel* implies a highly modular and extensible architecture as compared to the traditional operating system kernel. Extensibility allows many of the traditional kernel-based operating services to reside outside the kernel at the user process level. In traditional operating systems like AIX or UNIX, standard services—such as process management, virtual memory management, and file and device management—are all built into the kernel.

The microkernel operates on system resource objects, such as virtual memory space, files, and processors. User-level tasks access these objects by sending messages over communication channels, called *ports*. Even the device drivers are implemented at the user process level, thereby greatly increasing the ease of portability across heterogeneous hardware platforms.

6.3.2 Operating environment

As an object-oriented operating system, Taligent's microkernel architecture is portable and scalable. The Taligent kernel—as opposed to layered products—acts as the hardware-specific interface in place of current operating systems. Application interfaces such as the Apple Macintosh user interface and workplace shell are modules that run on top of these kernels. The kernel retains as little code as possible. The kernel code is used for execution management, memory management, and communication services with all other system services. They execute as threads, eliminating the distinction between user and system code.

The operating environment has two distinct layers designed to enhance the portability of application software and the operating environment itself. The software layer that directly supports the processor hardware on which the system runs is the kernel, called the *operating environment system* (OES). The systems programming interface (SPI) functions as the interface from the OES to the second layer of the operating environment, the *application environment system* (AES), which can run on multiple kernel layers. See Fig. 6.9 for an illustration of the Taligent OES.

The Taligent OES provides programmers with *object frameworks,* which are a set of classes that are designed to execute some particular activity. Programmers then provide objects to accomplish specific tasks not completely provided by the object frameworks. During program execution, object frameworks call the code necessary to complete a task. Rather than the code containing the entire programming function, programmers add code wherever it is needed to change or extend the framework's behavior to suit a particular program.

The Taligent run-time environment provides programming language support, including the object programming model of C++, storage allocation and memory management, a system of shared libraries, semaphores for synchronization of share memory, support for debuggers, and support for handling of software exceptions and hardware (processor) faults. The run-time environ-

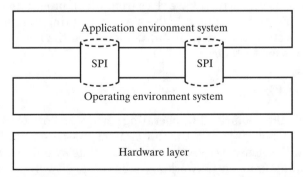

Figure 6.9 Positioning of the Taligent operating environment layers.

ment includes the standard C, C++, and SANE (Standard Apple Numerics Environment) function libraries.

6.3.3 End-user environment

Users organize their data in documents on the Taligent *workspace*. The workspace is defined by classes whose actions are determined by predefined protocols. The workspace provides services such as access to documentation, communication between documents, tool organization, and hardware configuration.

Taligent's workspace user interface is based on the concept of users (the primary user of the computer and other users with whom the primary user collaborates or who simply share the environment), places (desktop environments), and things (workspace tools, icons, applications). This environment enables a user to have a multiple-desktop environment with the workspace people, places, and things providing the ability to create, manage, and navigate among documents.

The *document* is the fundamental user-level program entity of the Taligent Operating Environment. Users see documents as data holders. A user wanting to deal with some data looks on the desktop to find the appropriate document. When the document is opened, the code and tools associated with the document start and are displayed to the user. The code and tools associated with the document have been integrated into the "document as object" framework which is organized into models, presentations, selections, and commands. Simply put, programmers encapsulate the information needed to manipulate data in a document object, giving documents a particular behavioral procedure.

Taligent's use of a document approach for the end-user environment deemphasizes the role of the application and reemphasizes the role of information. Users deal directly with information—the data in which they are interested—and the information is contained in documents. The executable routines that operate on the data reside in individual shared libraries. The system automatically starts and stops these programs to respond to user actions and other events.

Note that actual data exchange is accomplished using the class of *TModel* as the data type. (*TModel* is an abstract base class from which programmers derive their own classes.) This protocol supports the standard editing commands: **cut, copy, past, clear, push data,** and **pull data,** alleviating the need to reimplement these commands for each new data type.

6.4 SOLARIS

SunSoft introduced the Solaris 1.0 operating environment in 1991 and announced delivery of Solaris 2.3 in the fall of 1993. Based on SunOS 5.1, a derivative of System V Release 4 (SVR4), Solaris 2.3 offers symmetric multiprocessing, multithreading, built-in networking, a suite of software development tools, ToolTalk interapplication software, and LIVE! multimedia. Additional fea-

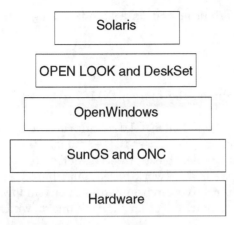

Figure 6.10 Solaris platform.

tures of Solaris 2.3 include Adobe Display PostScript, security, networking, system administration, and multimedia capabilities.

6.4.1 Operating environment

The SunSoft Solaris platform is a distributed computing environment featuring the SunOS; ONC (open network computing), a suite of networking products and services which includes NFS (network file system); the OpenWindows windowing environment; and the DeskSet desktop productivity applications. The SunOS adheres to the SVR4 standard, enabling the SunOS code to run on any platforms having the same CPU architecture. The Solaris platform is illustrated in Fig. 6.10.

The SunOS kernel handles system operation support including the file system, interprocess communications, devices, processes and protection, and memory management. The ONC networking services include NFS and remote execution service (REX). The ONC networking services provide access to distributed data and computer resources, as well as RPC (remote procedure call) technology.

RPC is a library of procedures from which one process (the caller process) can have another process (the server process) execute a procedure call, as if the caller process had executed the procedure call in its own address space. Two forms of RPC are available: secure RPC and transport-independent RPC. Secure RPC implements user ids and passwords in a distributed environment; transport-independent RPC provides a single programming interface to multiple network protocols with distributed applications, determining the appropriate network transport protocol at run-time using system software.

NFS is a network protocol that allows a user at one machine to work with files on other machines connected to the network. NFS's biggest asset is that it is independent of hardware, operating systems, and network architectures. This independence was achieved through the use of two lower-level protocols:

remote procedure call (RPC) protocol, and data standardizing external data representation (XDR) protocol.

6.4.2 End-user environment

OpenWindows Version 3.0 includes the merged X11/NeWS window system, which combines the X Window System Version 11 with the PostScript version of NeWS. It also includes the OPEN LOOK GUI, similar to the system application architecture (SAA) common user access (CUA) model. Based on OPEN LOOK, OpenWindows places a simple, object-oriented shell on top of a complex operating system. OpenWindows is a network-based, distributed window system providing a complete interactive environment—OpenWindows enables software applications to run on a machine other than the one on which the user interface is displayed.

Based on the client-server model, OpenWindows client applications communicate with the display server through a connection transporting X messages. Communications to the client applications are managed by two adjacent interpreters, which share a common underlying graphics library. The software application is stored centrally on a server with the user's individual desktop workstation functioning as the server's client.

OpenWindows includes an extensive set of desktop utilities, including a text editor and calendar program. The OpenWindows file manager resembles the Windows file manager; it allows users to navigate the UNIX file system graphically, supports drag-and-drop, and enables configuration of object properties using object menus.

The standard window manager provided for OpenWindows is the OPEN LOOK window manager (OLWM). The OPEN LOOK standard exists independently of any software with the OPEN LOOK GUI defining what the various controls and buttons of the user's interface should look like and how they should behave. Note that the OPEN LOOK GUI is not architecture-dependent or vendor-dependent. The *OpenWindows Developer's Guide* user interface design editor enables programmers to build and test interfaces using icons rather than writing code.

OpenWindows offers a single window server to create and manage windows: X11/NeWS. X11/NeWS provides both Xlib and PostScript graphics in a single window server by combining the X11 Window System with NeWS. The OpenWindows architecture includes the DeskSet environment, which enables developers to create applications, built on top of the user interface toolkits. Toolkits provided for building user interfaces include XView, the NeWS Toolkit (TNT), and the OPEN LOOK Intrinsics Toolkit (OLIT). OpenWindows offers two imaging models, Xlib and PostScript, that you can use to create graphic images and text. Scalable fonts can be rendered using the OpenFonts package. See Figure 6.11 for an illustration of the OpenWindows Architecture.

ToolTalk, the interapplication messaging service, is a key feature of OpenWindows. ToolTalk allows applications to exchange information and automatically update one another using procedural multicast or object-based messaging technology.

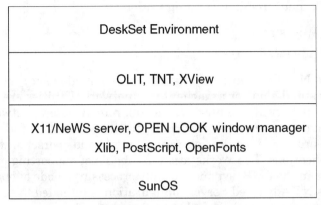

Figure 6.11 Solaris OpenWindows architecture.

Applications that use the ToolTalk service cooperate by sending and receiving messages; they do not share stored data. As long as message protocols are observed, cooperating applications can be modified without affecting one another. Applications can use ToolTalk directly, calling functions from the ToolTalk API library to create, send, and receive messages. Applications can also use a service built on top of the ToolTalk service. These application services use the ToolTalk service as a communication backbone and object manager. These types of services can provide linking, drag, and drop.

The ToolTalk service is built on top of SunSoft's ONC remote procedure call product. While both provide communication capabilities, the ToolTalk service has a higher-level interface for application developers. ToolTalk allows application developers multicast messaging for developers of procedure-based, self-contained applications and object-oriented messaging for developers of applications based on a distributed object paradigm.

6.5   WINDOWS NT

Microsoft Windows NT is a 32-bit, preemptive, multitasking operating system with an architecture based on modular design principles. It is extensible and provides compatibility with several other operating systems, file systems, and networks. Windows NT also includes security and networking, peer-to-peer services as fundamental components of the base operating system.

Additionally, Windows NT is portable across heterogeneous processor architectures and runs on both CISC and RISC computers. Windows NT also supports high-performance computing by providing kernel support for computers that have symmetric multiprocessor configurations.

Although the Windows NT user interface is similar to the standard Windows user interface and can support 16-bit DOS and Windows applications, Windows NT does not require DOS or any other operating system or network software in order to interface on a LAN. In addition, Windows NT is capable of supporting OS/2 and POSIX applications.

Windows NT is delivered in two configurations:

- Windows NT Workstation
- Windows NT Advanced Server

The Windows NT Workstation configuration is a single-user system which operates either stand-alone or as a client in a network. Utilities are included, such as performance/event monitoring, backup, remote access, network client support, disk maintenance, and user configuration/account profile utility. In addition, the product includes electronic mail and personal/workgroup scheduling applications. The Workstation is capable of supporting one or two microprocessors in the SMP (symmetric multiprocessing) mode of operation.

The Windows NT Advanced Server configuration is intended to act in a network as a multiuser applications and resource server. This version is a superset of the Workstation version, adding additional fault tolerance (disk mirroring/striping), enhanced user and server maintenance and account control utilities, and multiple-user RAS (remote access services). This version also includes the capability to interact with other servers in a group of servers and clients known as a *domain,* allowing a user to use a single network login to access all network resources. The Server is capable of supporting up to four microprocessors in the SMP mode.

6.5.1 End-user environment

Windows NT uses the Windows 3.1 GUI and can simultaneously run DOS, Windows 3.1, and native Windows NT applications using the Intel x86 CPU and Virtual 8086 environments. For DOS applications, Windows NT creates virtual DOS machines (VDMs) and provides each with a set of DOS resources, including the DOS API interfaces and functions.

Users familiar with the Windows user interface will recognize Windows NT's similar features, including the mouse and keyboard techniques for working with windows, menus, icons, and desktop tools.

Windows NT features advanced built-in network support, including security features. It has administrative tools group applications that enable users to manage user accounts, control network services, audit system events, and manage and back up files. It also includes the Windows NT file system (NTFS) that provides error-correction capabilities and security. Windows NT supports three types of file systems:

- File allocation table (FAT)
- High-performance file system (HPFS)
- Windows NT file system (NTFS)

FAT is the basic file system used in DOS and OS/2. HPFS is the augmented file system offered by OS/2. NTFS is Windows NT's native file system that is capable of C2 level security certification. It provides support for Unicode, recoverability, long file names, and POSIX file naming support.

A TrueType font containing Unicode extensions and providing internal support for Unicode is included with Windows NT. Windows NT has two points of entry for every function that requires a character string parameter. Header files perform program conversion functions so users do not have to convert their programs to one name or the other. To facilitate localization, the Win32 subsystem provides a national language support (NLS) API that gives applications access to culturally correct string comparisons; collation tables for sorting the characters of different languages; date, time, and currency formatting routines; and routines for determining the locale that is in effect and the other locales present on the system.

A unified command prompt is provided from which programs and batch files can be started and from which all Windows NT commands and most MS-DOS, OS/2, and POSIX commands can be issued.

6.5.2 Operating environment

Advanced operating system capabilities are available to applications by enabling multithreaded processed and enhanced synchronization, security, I/O, and object management. Windows NT is interoperable with other Microsoft systems, with the Apple Macintosh, and with UNIX-based operating systems on a Microsoft LAN manager or other network. When configured as a server, Windows NT can work as a multiuser operating system, enabling each workstation to support one interactive user and multiple remote users. Note that each user (or application) is required to log on before accessing the system.

Additional features include high-performance disk and network subsystems that can invoke sophisticated recovery mechanisms, such as a transaction log, and implement device drivers that directly manipulate disk hardware, resulting in better performance and more consistent throughput than what has been available on traditional PC-like operating systems. Windows NT's use of a flat memory model gives each application its own set of logical memory addresses, with up to 2 GB available for code and data.

Multitasking with Windows NT implies that an application thinks it's the only program running, so it's unaware of (and not likely to interfere with) other applications. Multitasking discourages applications attempting to write to a memory location holding another application's code or data. This dismissal of the cooperative system model for the preemptive system model means that NT's CPU retains control, determining how its time is allocated.

Windows NT's highly modular operating system implements operating system functions as a subsystem. Subsystems, in turn, are self-contained and easily updated, thus enabling portability, extensibility, compatibility, and reliability to the operating environment. See Fig. 6.12 for an illustration of the modular layout of Windows NT.

The infrastructure of Windows NT can be divided into two parts: the user-mode portion of the system (the Windows NT protected subsystems) and the kernel-mode portion (the Windows NT executive). Windows NT servers are called protected subsystems because each one resides in a separate process

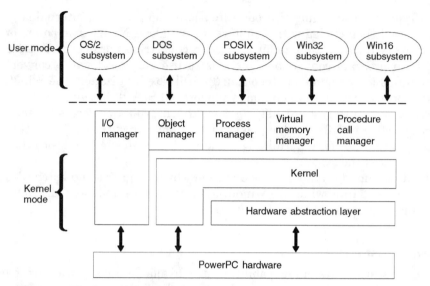

Figure 6.12 Windows NT modular architecture.

whose memory is protected from other processes by the Windows NT executive's virtual memory system. Because the subsystems do not automatically share memory, they communicate by passing messages. All messages pass through the Windows NT executive.

The *user-mode* domain of Windows NT supports the following subsystems, as depicted in Fig. 6.12:

OS/2 subsystem: This subsystem is automatically loaded at login time and always remains active. But like the POSIX subsystem, the OS/2 subsystem will get paged out of real memory if not accessed in a short while.

DOS subsystem: All MS-DOS applications run within the context of a process called virtual DOS machine (VDM). VDM is actually a Win32 application that emulates a virtual 80x86 computer running MS-DOS. Note that there is no limit on the number of VDMs that can be run. In the PowerPC environment, Windows NT emulates selected x86 instructions since real hardware support is not available. A hardware visualization is provided with the aid of a set of virtual device drivers (VDDs).

POSIX subsystem: POSIX.1, which is a standard that describes an operating system interface for C language programs written to be ported across diverse systems, is supported by the Windows NT subsystem in conjunction with the NTFS file system. This subsystem is loaded at login time (as in the case of the OS/2 subsystem).

Win32 subsystem: The Win32 subsystem is responsible for running the 32-bit applications, as well as managing the keyboard and mouse input and screen output (for all the subsystems). It collects all inputs and delivers them to the appropriate applications. The input model takes advantage of the preemptive multitasking capabilities that are available under Windows NT. A desynchronized input model is used to handle the I/O for 32-bit applications, as compared to a synchronized model for the 16-bit applications. This enables the Win32 subsystem to transfer a message to the input queue thread on the first available instant. By contrast, the input messages for 16-bit applications sit in a common queue, until the input queue is blocked.

Win16 subsystem: The Win16 subsystem is emulated using the MS-DOS–based VDM support. All Win16 applications run in one VDM. Note that only the Win16-on-Win32 subsystem (WOW) VDM is preemptively multitasked with respect to other processes running on the system. Each Win16 application is nonpreemptively multitasked with respect to another. In other words, only one application runs while the others are blocked, and if the WOW VDM is preempted when the system returns, it always unblocks the Win16 application that was running before the WOW VDM got preempted. The *thunking* process (i.e., translation to and from 16-bit) for application code and libraries is achieved with the use of WOW VDM stubs and APIs.

When an API call is made, the appropriate stub initiates the thunking process: parameters are pushed onto the stack and the call is converted into the equivalent 32-bit call and subsequently issued to the Win32 subsystem. Returned parameters are similarly converted back into 16 bits, thereafter being passed back to the original application.

The *kernel mode* includes the Windows NT Executive, the kernel, and the hardware abstraction layer, which resides on the PowerPC hardware. The *Windows NT Executive* includes:

I/O manager: The I/O manager is the part of the Windows NT Executive that manages all input and output for the operating system. A large part of the I/O manager's role is to manage communications between drivers—the I/O manager supports all file system drivers, hardware device drivers, and network device drivers and provides a heterogeneous environment for them while also providing a formal interface that all drivers can call. This uniform interface allows the I/O manager to communicate with all drivers in the same way, without any knowledge of how the devices they control actually work. The I/O manager also includes device driver help routines specifically designed for file system drivers, for hardware device drivers, and for network device drivers.

The Windows NT I/O model utilizes a layered architecture that allows separate drivers to implement each logically distinct layer of I/O processing. For example, drivers in the lowest layer manipulate the computer's physical devices (these are called device drivers). Other drivers are then layered on top of the device drivers. These higher-level drivers do not know any details about the physical devices. With the help of the I/O manager, they simply pass logical I/O requests down to the device drivers, which access the physical devices on their behalf. Installable file systems in Windows NT and network redirectors are examples of high-level drivers that work in this way.

Object manager: The Windows NT Executive object manager provides uniform rules for object retention, naming, and security. If a process wishes to manipulate a Windows NT object, it must first acquire a handle to the object. As far as the Executive is concerned, there is no difference between a file handle and a process handle, and thus the same routines that are used to create a file handle can be used to create a process handle. All object handle creation originates from the object manager; the object manager is thus able to satisfy some important Windows NT design requirements, including:

- A uniform, global name space for all objects. The object manager can track creation and the use of objects by any process.
- Uniform rules and mechanisms for protecting objects from unauthorized access.
- A uniform model for the safe sharing of objects.

 Like other Windows NT components, object manager is extensible, so that new object types can be defined as technology grows and changes. The object manager manages the global name space for Windows NT. This name space is used to access all named objects that are contained in the local machine. Some of the objects that can have names include the following:

Directory objects	Object type objects
Symbolic link objects	Semaphore and event objects
Process and thread objects	Section and segment objects
Port objects	Device objects
File system objects	File objects

The object name space is modeled after a hierarchical file system, where directory names in a path are separated by a backslash (\).

Process manager: The process manager manages the creation and deletion of processes. The process manager does not provide any hierarchical process structure or grouping or enforce any parent/child relationships. The Windows NT process structure includes only two types of objects: *process objects* and *thread objects.* A process object represents an address space, a set of objects (resources) visible to the process, and a set of threads that runs in the context of the process. A thread object represents the basic schedulable entity in the system. It contains its own set of machine registers, its own kernel stack, a thread environment block, and a user stack in the address space of its process. The Windows NT process structure works in conjunction with the security architecture and the virtual memory manager to provide interprocess protection. Each process is assigned a security-access token, called the primary token of the process. The token is used by the access-validation routines of Windows NT when threads in the process reference protected objects.

Virtual memory manager: The memory architecture of Windows NT is a demand-paged, virtual memory system based on a flat, linear address space accessed via 32-bit addresses. A process's virtual address space is a set of addresses available for the process's threads to use. Every process has a unique virtual address space that appears to be 4 GB in size, with 2 GB reserved for program storage and 2 GB reserved for system storage.

The virtual memory manager maps virtual addresses in the process's address space to physical pages in the computer's memory. In doing so, it hides the physical organization of memory from the process's threads. This ensures that the threads can access its process's memory as needed, but not the memory of other processes.

Procedure call manager: The procedure call manager provides the communication mechanism between client and server processes. Note that the client-server relationship exists between applications and environment subsystems. The Executive implements a message-passing facility called a local procedure call (LPC). The LPC facility works like an RPC but is optimized for two processes running on the same computer.

When an application makes an API call to the server, it is intercepted by a stub in the client process that packages up the parameters to the call and sends them to a server process that actually implements the API.

The Windows NT *kernel* layer resides below the Executive and is responsible for thread dispatching, multiprocessor synchronization, hardware exception handling, and the implementation of low-level machine-dependent functions. It is used by the executive layer of the system to synchronize its activities and to implement the higher levels of abstraction that are exported in user-level APIs. Generally speaking, the kernel does not implement any policy, since this is the province of the executive. However, policy decisions made by the kernel include the way in which thread priority is manipulated to maximize responsiveness to dispatching events (for example, the input of a character from the keyboard).

The *hardware abstraction layer* resides beneath the kernel and above the PowerPC hardware. The hardware abstraction layer is a layer of software provided by the hardware manufacturer that hides, or abstracts, hardware differences from higher layers of the operating system. Thus, through the filter provided by the hardware abstraction layer, different types of hardware look alike to the operating system, removing the need to specifically tailor the operating system to the hardware it communicates with. The goal of the hardware abstraction layer is to provide routines that allow a single device driver to support the same device on all platforms. The hardware abstraction layer allows a large number of variations in hardware platforms for a single-processor architecture without requiring a separate version of the operating system for each one.

The hardware abstraction layer routines are called from both the base operating system and from device drivers. For drivers, the hardware abstraction layer provides the ability to support a wide variety of I/O architectures, instead of being restricted to a single hardware model or performing extensive adaptation, as in the current PC industry. The hardware abstraction layer is also responsible for hiding the details of symmetric multiprocessing hardware from the rest of the system. For more information about the hardware abstraction layer, see Chap. 3.

6.6 WORKPLACE OS

Workplace OS is a general-user operating system which consists of the IBM Microkernel, Personality Neutral Services, and multiple Personalities. Personalities currently available on Workplace OS include OS/2 and MVM (DOS). Workplace OS with an OS/2 interface runs recompiled OS/2 applications natively.

Based on a core layer of services developed by IBM and Taligent, Workplace OS incorporates Taligent frameworks on top of the Carnegie Mellon University Mach microkernel (as depicted in Fig. 6.13). Workplace OS is portable across hardware architectures, including Intel, POWER, and PowerPC.

Workplace OS consists of a single scalable configuration which may be used as a client or developer workstation. It can also be used as a server through the addition of products such as the IBM LAN Server for Workplace OS. A Workplace OS client workstation requires at least 8 MB of main memory (note that 16 MB is recommended). A developer workstation requires 16 MB of main memory. The video system must be capable of showing 640×480×8. For better performance when emulating DOS applications which require planar graphics, all configurations should have a VGA-compatible video system. All Workplace OS configurations require a keyboard and a pointing device; a business audio device is recommended. Workplace OS supports one or more PCI buses; multiple SCSI interfaces; PCMCIA, including socket services; and IDE access to disks. Inclusion of an ISA bus is optional.

6.6.1 Operating environment

Due to the use of a microkernel as the foundation of the operating system, Workplace OS is portable to multiple hardware platforms. This microkernel-based architecture implements object orientation, portability, and support for multiple CPUs. OS offers memory protection, multitasking, and multithread-

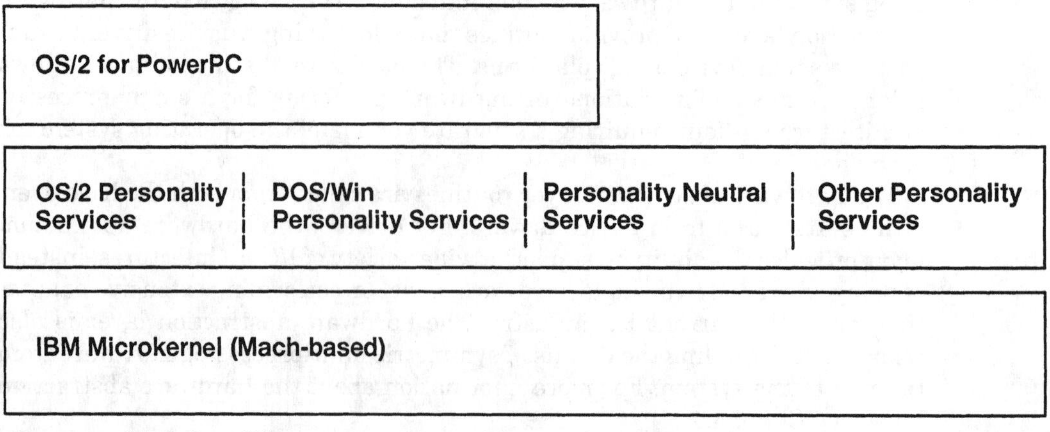

Figure 6.13 Workplace OS.

ing. OS also enables users to run other operating systems as personalities on top of the base system software layers, enabling PowerPC users to run Macintosh software without learning UNIX or figuring out Taligent.

The underlying hardware is managed by the microkernel. Device drivers, the file system, and the OS/2 personality are user-level processes, and applications are written to the interfaces exported by the OS/2 personality.

The term *microkernel* implies a highly modular and extensible architecture as compared to the traditional operating system kernel. Extensibility allows many of the traditional kernel-based operating services to reside outside the kernel at the user process level. In traditional operating systems like AIX or UNIX, standard services—such as process management, virtual memory management, and file and device management—are all built into the kernel.

6.6.2 End-user environment

The microkernel operates on system resource objects, such as virtual memory space, files, and processors. User-level tasks access these objects by sending messages over communication channels, called ports. Even the device drivers are implemented at the user process level, greatly increasing the ease of portability across heterogeneous hardware platforms.

6.7 SUMMARY

A variety of operating systems have been ported to the PowerPC—the PowerPC's ability to run a variety of operating systems is one of its greatest assets. The PowerPC's support of Taligent, Solaris, Windows NT, and Workplace OS gives users the ability to cut and paste between applications across operating systems. This chapter introduced the supported operating systems, emphasizing the importance of the PowerPC to users looking for a single integrated platform.

Early UNIX systems, such as UNIX Version 6, were much simpler than today's flavors of UNIX, requiring less configuring of devices and simpler execution environments for program execution. However, as the UNIX operating system evolved, its architectural layout increased in complexity. AIX is a fully PowerOpen compliant operating system based on the Common Open Software Environment's (COSE) version of UNIX. Based on System V Release 3, the AIX customization facility is tied in with the X11R5 implementation. From the X Windows desktop, it is possible to customize features of X Windows applications through a graphical interface. AIX also includes the AIX system management tool (*smit*), which consists of a series of menus linked to an object database that builds UNIX commands in an interactive way.

Taligent has applied the object-oriented paradigm and technology directly to the system architecture, creating a software platform designed for extension and innovation on three well-defined levels: applications, system software, and hardware. Code can be reused, industry extensions can be integrated without compromising either function or compatibility, and the encapsulated modular objects can be maintained in a structured and easy manner.

The ability to run Solaris on the PowerPC platform paves a path for the wide base of the existing SunOS user community to harness the power of the Power-PC processor. Its networking services and integration of a familiar GUI enable programmers to develop applications that can be distributed across multiple platforms while adhering to industry standards and complying with vendor demands for multiple-platform compatibility.

Windows NT supports high-performance disk and network subsystems while enabling users to continue to use DOS and/or Windows applications. NT's 32-bit environment lets applications address up to 4 GB of storage, making it a good choice for high-end applications. NT has removed the constraints of segmented memory management by implementing a flat memory model and giving each application its own set of logical memory addresses. NT is the operating system of choice for users wanting superior multiprocessor and security features at the cost of significant memory and disk size upgrades from existing PCs.

Workplace OS is a general-user operating system which consists of the IBM Microkernel, Personality Neutral Services, and multiple Personalities. Personalities currently available on Workplace OS include OS/2 and MVM (DOS). Workplace OS with an OS/2 interface runs recompiled OS/2 applications natively. Based on a core layer of services developed by IBM and Taligent, Workplace OS incorporates Taligent frameworks on top of the Carnegie Mellon University Mach microkernel. Workplace OS is portable across hardware architectures, including Intel, POWER, and PowerPC.

Development Tools

This chapter provides a brief overview of the most popular and standard development tools available for UNIX operating systems, specifically AIX. The advantages of using the XL C optimizing compiler (to exploit the fast PowerPC hardware) are discussed, followed by a brief discussion of the other compilers in the XL family. A look at how Assembler translates machine language into machine object code is also discussed. The review of debugging tools and facilities and the uses of source code debugging tools will foster an understanding of what troubleshooting options are available with AIX. We discuss **yacc, lex, make, imake, grep, sed,** and **awk,** highlighting the best uses of each. Finally, a quick overview of UNIX/AIX tuning theory and practices is provided.

7.1 COMPILERS

7.1.1 XL C compiler

The XL C, or C compiler, is an optimizing compiler. In addition to source code optimization, the compiler also performs certain preprocessor and common back-end optimization tasks. The architecture of the PowerPC demands that an optimizing compiler be used to make intelligent use of its underlying capabilities. Together, the POWER-based architecture and the XL optimizing compiler make possible an efficient computing environment, as depicted in Fig. 7.1.

The need for an optimizing compiler depends on the applications. For many general purpose applications, inherent efficiencies will provide a level of performance. However, for engineering and scientific applications that process

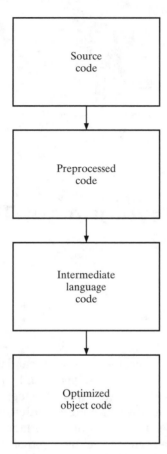

Figure 7.1 Optimizing compiler.

vast amounts of data and tend to perform repeated operations on each data element, a structured and methodical approach to compile-time optimization is required.

From a programmer's perspective, a program may be executing optimally. But, if tuned properly, even to a minuscule extent, its performance can be doubled or tripled. This is especially true of the PowerPC hardware performance due to the pipelined execution units in the central electronic complex of the PowerPC, and the central electronic complex dependency on the sequence of instructions. An instruction dependency between the currently executing instruction and its predecessor can cost precious cycles owing to data unavailability. A tight piece of code fragment spilling outside of the cache boundary can waste several cycles. The former can be controlled (to a certain extent) by implementing an optimized instruction-scheduling algorithm that resequences selected assembly language instructions to minimize idle machine cycles. The latter, however, is likely to require hand-optimization. The optimizing compiler on the PowerPC needs a great deal of built-in intelligence to identify potential hot spots during compile time and perform necessary tuning actions.

The instruction scheduling algorithm in the XL C compiler is its most significant component. The XL C compiler processes the output of the optimizer, constructing a dependency graph for each basic block of the code and finally arranges the instructions in the order in which they would execute the fastest. The algorithm used in the XL family of compilers is essentially the same.

The XL C compiler uses the **cc, xlc,** and **c89** commands to compile C source files. These commands are essentially the same except for the default language level. For **cc,** the default language level is *extended;* for **xlc** and **c89,** the default language level is *ansi.* These commands can also process assembler source files and object files. Unless the **-c** option is specified, these commands call the linkage editor to produce a single object file. The input file(s) can be a C language source file (file name with .c suffix), preprocessed C source (.i suffix), object file (.o suffix), or assembler source file (.s suffix).

7.1.2   C Set++ compiler

The C Set++ compiler is a native, optimizing compiler based on the common C and C++ front-end and the latest optimizing back-end technology. The C++ compiler, consisting of a browser, a HelpView debugger, a test coverage analyzer, and a set of class libraries, provides improved compilation speed, optimization, and debugging.

The C++ browser is a postcompilation static analysis tool which allows users to examine their programs by formulating queries of the program database. Using a menu-driven interface, the browser can be used to view and edit program source text, view lists of program elements, and display graphical relationships among program elements. The HelpView debugger enables users to debug difficult memory allocation errors and identify memory allocation problem areas. The **dbx** symbolic debugger is also supported. The test coverage tool provides information about how often different statements in the code are used when the program is executing.

The C Set++ includes the USL C++ Language System Release 3.0 Class Libraries and sample libraries including the NIH Library and the InterViews Library. National Language Support is also provided.

7.1.3   AIX XL FORTRAN and Pascal compilers

The XL family of compilers is designed to provide consistency and high performance across multiple programming languages by sharing the same code optimization technology.

The XL FORTRAN compiler conforms to the FORTRAN 90 standard, providing functionality such as array language, derived data types, pointed, modules, NAMELIST statement, defined operators, and dynamic storage allocation. Language extensions include facilities for interlanguage calls, extended precision floating point, optional checking of array bounds, typeless constants, and INTEGER*8 and LOGICAL*8. The XL FORTRAN three-pass compilation technology includes a front end which translates source into intermediate text (IL), optimizations applied to IL, allocation of hardware registers, and generation of an object file from the final form of IL.

The XL Pascal compiler is an enhanced version of the existing AIX XL Pascal compiler. The XL Pascal compiler provides 4-byte pointer support and National Language Support for single- and double-byte character sets.

7.2   ASSEMBLER

The assembler takes machine language instructions and translates them into machine object code. The assembler used on the PowerPC is a two-pass assembler, which refers to the fact that the assembler makes two passes over a source program. An assembler listing is produced in the first and second passes of the assembler.

On the first pass, the assembler (1) checks to see if the instructions are legal in the current assembly mode, (2) allocates space for instructions and storage area, (3) assigns the values of constants wherever appropriate, and (4) constructs a symbol table where an entry is made for symbols encountered in the label of statements. The source file is read a line at a time. For every new symbol encountered, an entry is added to the symbol table while assigning the value of the current location counter to the symbol.

Note: The only PowerPC instructions recognized by the assembler are those in the 32-bit subset PowerPC architecture.

Next, the assembler examines the instruction's mnemonic. If the mnemonic is for a machine instruction that is legal for the current assembly mode, the assembler determines the format of the instruction. The assembler then allocates the number of bytes necessary to hold the machine code for the instruction. The contents of the location counter are incremented by this number of bytes.

On the second pass, the assembler (1) examines the operands for symbolic references to storage locations and resolves these symbolic references using information in the symbol table, (2) ensures that no instructions contain an invalid instruction form, (3) translates source statements into machine code and constants, thus filling the allocated space with object code, and (4) produces a file containing error messages, if any have occurred.

Assembly language source code is assembled using the **as** command. The file that **as** reads and assembles ends with a .s suffix (by convention). Also, the file that **as** builds as its output is called a.out. If no source file is specified, **as** attempts to read and assemble standard input. A symbol cross-reference is also available. If the **-x** flag is used with the **as** command, a symbol cross-reference file is produced. This file contains information for all symbols defined and referenced in an assembler source program. However, if the **-x** flag is used, the assembly process terminates after the first pass and does not generate any object code.

The assembler command can also be used to produce an assembler listing. **as** gives a default name to the listing file, by replacing the suffix extension of the source file name with an .1st extension.

7.3 DEBUGGERS

Debuggers available with AIX include:

adb	Debugs executable binary files and examines non-ASCII data files
dbx	Allows source-level debugging for C, FORTRAN, Pascal, COBOL, and assembly language programs
xde	Provides windows for viewing source, context, and variables for application programs
kernel debugger	Determines errors in code running in the kernel

These debuggers as well as the *trace facility*, which helps isolate system problems by monitoring selected system events, are discussed as follows.

7.3.1 adb

adb is a general purpose debugging utility used to examine object files and core files, and to provide a controlled environment for running a program. Users can debug any executable C or assembly language program file by entering the following command:

```
adb FileName
```

where `FileName` is the name of the executable program file to be debugged. The **adb** program opens the file and prepares its text (instructions) and data for subsequent debugging.

When processing an executable program file that has been compiled, **adb** requires it to have a symbol table. Without the symbol table, **adb** will not be able to show the value of static, automatic, and external variables of the program. However, executable programs that have been stripped off the symbol table can still be examined for other information.

When no name is specified for the executable program, **adb** looks for the default file named `a.out`. If the `a.out` file does not exist, the **adb** program starts without a file and does not display an error message. **adb** may also be used

- to read core file images of programs that caused fatal system errors
- to examine data files containing non-ASCII data by giving the name of the data file in place of the program or core file
- with the -w flag to modify an executable file or a data file by writing directly to memory after running the program

adb can take input from standard input (keyboard) and write to standard output (terminal). One can also enter more than one command by separating each command with a semicolon as a delimiter. Use of expressions, operators, commands, variables, and addresses is supported. However, to use **adb** effectively and set breakpoints at appropriate places in the executable program, one has to be familiar with the assembly language instructions that the C compiler generates. One way to do this is to create an assembly language listing of a C program using the **-S** or **-qlist** flag of the **cc** command and then consulting the complete instruction set for the PowerPC described in Chap. 3.

adb features a set of subcommands for setting breakpoints and examining variables, including:

:r   Starts executing the program from the beginning

:b   Sets a breakpoint in a program

:k   Stops the program being debugged

7.3.2   fsdb

fsdb is a file system debug utility that can be used to examine and patch a damaged file system after a system crash. The **fsdb** command allows access to blocks and *inodes* and examines various parts of an *inode*. Components of the *inode* can be referenced symbolically. These features simplify procedures for correcting control-block entries and for descending the file system tree.

The file system to be examined can be specified by a block device name, a raw device name, or a mounted file system name. In the last case, the **fsdb** command determines the associated file system name by reading the `/etc/filesystems` file. Any numbers entered are considered decimal by default, unless it is prefixed with a 0 to indicate octal numbers or 0x to indicate hex numbers.

To examine a file system, specify it by a block device name, a raw device name, or a mounted file system name. In the last case, the **fsdb** command determines the associated file system name by reading the `/etc/filesystems` file. Mounted file systems cannot be modified.

The subcommands for **fsdb** allow you to access, view, or change the information in a file system. Any number you enter in the subcommand is considered decimal by default, unless you prefix it with either 0 to indicate an octal number or 0x to indicate a hexadecimal number. All addresses are printed in hexadecimal.

Because the **fsdb** command reads and writes one block at a time, it works with raw as well as with block I/O. It uses a buffer management routine to retain commonly used blocks of data in order to reduce the number of **read** subroutines. All assignment operations write the corresponding block immediately.

System information can be generated by specifying the following flags:

-     Disables the error-checking routines used to verify *inodes* and block addresses. The O subcommand switches these routines on and off. When these routines are running, the **fsdb** command reads the inode size and file system size entries from the superblock of the file system. The obtained information allows the **fsdb** command to access the various file system objects successfully and to perform various error checks.

The subcommands given to the **fsdb** command are requests to locate and display or modify information in the file system. Use the location subcommands to access the information in the file system, the display subcommands to view the information, and the modification subcommands to change the information. A location subcommand is made up of a number and is optionally followed by an address specification. The location subcommands are:

Number	Accesses data at the absolute disk address specified by the *Number* parameter
inode map-block-numberI	Accesses data at the *inode map* block # *inode-map-block number* parameter
Disk map-block-numberm	Accesses data at the *Disk map* block # *Disk-map-block number* parameter
I-Numberi	Accesses data at the *I-Number* parameter
Block-addressb	Accesses data at the *Block-address* parameter

These location subcommands can be combined with the **d** address specification to form a location subcommand that accesses information by directory entry. The form of the **d** address specification is:

d*Directory-slot-offset*	Accesses data at the *Directory-slot-offset* parameter.

To request information relative to the address specification, use a display subcommand made up of one of the display facilities in conjunction with one of the display formats. The display facilities are:

p	General facilities
f	File facility

If you enter a number after the **p** symbol, the **fsdb** command displays that number of entries. A check is made to detect block boundary overflows because logically sequential blocks are generally not physically sequential. If you enter a count of 0 or * (asterisk), the **fsdb** command displays all entries to the end of the current block.

Use the **f** symbol to display data blocks associated with the current inode. If you enter a number after the **f** symbol, the **fsdb** command displays that block of the file. Block numbering begins at 0. The desired display format follows the block number, or the **f** symbol.

The **fsdb** subcommands are requests to locate and display or modify information in the file system. The main categories of subcommands are:

Category	Function
Location	Access the information in the file system
Display	View the information in the file system
Modification	Change the information in the file system

7.3.3 dbx and xde

dbx is a full-featured symbolic debugger that supports debugging of a program at both a source level and assembler language level. Its source-level debugging features allows debugging of C, Pascal, COBOL, and FORTRAN programs; its assembler-language-level debug facility enables debugging of executable programs at the machine level. Standard operations the tool supports include:

- Examination of object and core files
- Controlled environment for running a program
- Setting of breakpoints at selected statements or running of the program one line at a time
- Analysis of symbolic variables

The **dbx** program can be started with several flags, including:

- Running the **dbx** command on a specified object file
- Using the **-r** flag to run the **dbx** command on a program that ended abnormally
- Using the **-a** flag to run the **dbx** command on a process that is already in progress

To use the **dbx** program, an executable file must be compiled with a debug flag to contain the symbol table information, and the symbol references must not be stripped from the executable file. **dbx** can be customized by including a set of **dbx** subcommands in a file named .dbxinit, enabling the included subcommands to execute automatically upon initiation of a debug session.

The **-c** option and .dbxinit provide mechanisms for executing *dbx* subcommands before reading from standard input. Use the source subcommand to read *dbx* subcommands from a file once the debugging session has begun.

Use the *dbx* subcommands for setting breakpoints, tracing program execution, displaying the source file, printing variables and expressions, handling signals, calling procedures, displaying and modifying memory addresses, displaying assembler instructions, and examining registers during machine-level debugging. Some of the commonly used subcommands include:

run	Begins running of the application program
step	Runs one source line
stepi	Runs one source instruction
stop	Stops execution of the application program
clear	Removes all stops at a given source line
cleari	Removes all breakpoints at an address
cont	Continues running of the program from the current breakpoint until another breakpoint is encountered or the program completes its execution
listi	Displays a specified set of instructions from the source file

next	Runs the application up to the next source line
nexti	Runs the application up to the next source instruction
trace	Displays tracing information
where	Displays all active procedures and functions
help	Displays an on-line list of **dbx** commands
quit	Quits **dbx**

An X Window interface for **dbx** called **xde** can also be used to debug application programs. **xde** provides an integrated debug environment with the X interface that allows viewing of the program's source code, stack traceback, and variables (shown in Fig. 7.2, 7.3, and 7.4, respectively). Other windows are available that enable users to issue **dbx** debug programs, view the output of these commands, and control the operating of the **xde** program.

The same prerequisites for **dbx** apply to **xde** (for example, an executable file must be compiled with a debug flag to contain the symbol table information, and the symbol references must not be stripped from the executable file). The

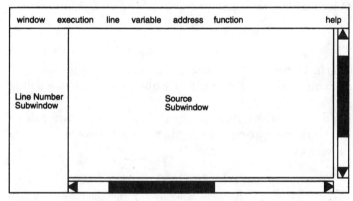

Figure 7.2 XDE file window. *(Copied with permission from IBM.)*

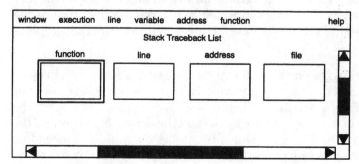

Figure 7.3 XDE context window. *(Copied with permission from IBM.)*

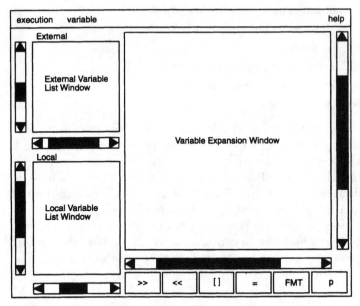

Figure 7.4 XDE variable window. *(Copied with permission from IBM.)*

xde tool and its X interface may be customized by modifying the `.dbxinit` and/or `.Xdefaults` files, which execute automatically upon initiation of a debug session.

The subcommands available in **dbx** appear as objects within pull-down menus in the **xde** environment. Thus, navigating within **xde** windows involves working with buttons and scroll bars.

7.3.4 Kernel debug program

The kernel debug program is used for debugging device drivers and kernel extensions. It provides an efficient mechanism for detecting errors in the code running in the kernel. The debug program can run in any configuration that includes an asynchronous terminal connected to a serial adapter. The debug program does not support any displays connected to any of the graphics adapters.

Note: The kernel debugger disables all external interrupts while it is in operation. The kernel debug program must be loaded by using the **bosboot** command before it can be started. Once loaded, users can start the debugger one of two ways. One way to start the debugger is through the use of breakpoints. These breakpoints can be set by either embedding static debugger program traps (SDTs) in the object code or by use of the **break** command. After the debug program is started, SDTs are treated the same as other processor instructions. Use the **step** command to step over SDTs; use the **go** or **loop** commands to resume execution at the instruction following the SDT. Using the break command sets a breakpoint from within the kernel debug program. If you use the **break** command, breakpoints will not display in the debug program code.

To set a breakpoint, do the following:

1. Locate the assembler instruction corresponding to the C standard.
2. Get the offset of the assembler instruction from the listing.
3. Locate the address of where the kernel extension is loaded.
4. Add the address of the assembler instruction to the kernel extension address.
5. Set the breakpoint with the **break** command.

Simultaneously pressing the Control, left Alternate key and the number 4 numeric pad keys also loads and starts the kernel debug program sending a nonmaskable interrupt to the processor. You can now use the kernel debugger interactively by entering kernel debugger commands at the system prompt.

Note: The kernel debugger is also executed as a result of a system crash. If a system crashes (and the debugger is available), the last line of the displayed text will normally describe the cause of the event and an 888 code will flash on the LED display of the operator panel. At that point, a dump may be taken if desired (using the quit dump command) and the system can subsequently be rebooted.

A full suite of interactive commands is available for use in kernel debugger. These commands can be used to set breakpoints, manipulate memory, and perform manipulation of variables and registers. An extensive reference of the commands may be found in the on-line help facility. Enter ? or Help to display the list of valid commands. Some commands are stand-alone, while others accept numeric and string arguments. Limited expression processing can also be performed using the addition, subtraction, multiplication, division, and reference operators. The program also allows use of variables to represent locations or values that are used repeatedly. Frequently used kernel debug commands include:

origin	Sets the origin of instruction address register
alter	Alters memory
xlate	Translates a virtual address to a real address
break	Sets a breakpoint
breaks	Lists the currently set breakpoints
user	Displays a formatted user area
proc	Displays the formatted process table

stack	Displays a formatted kernel stack trace
drivers	Displays the contents of the device driver table
tty	Displays the tty structure
find	Finds a string in memory
sregs	Displays segment registers
vmm	Displays the virtual memory data structure
help	Displays the on-line help commands
quit	Ends the debugging session

7.3.5 Trace facility

The trace facility helps isolate system problems by monitoring selected system events. Events that can be monitored include entry and exit to selected subroutines, kernel routines, kernel extension routines, and interrupt handlers. The trace facility captures a sequential flow of system events, providing a fine level of detail on system activity. Events are shown in time sequence and in the context of other events. The trace facility is useful in expanding the trace event information to understand who, when, how, and even why the event happened.

When the trace facility is active, information about system events is recorded in a system **trace** log file. This facility includes commands for activating and controlling traces and for generating trace reports. Applications and kernel extensions can use several subroutines to record additional events.

The data recorded for each traced event consist of a word containing the *trace hook identifier* and the *hook type* followed by a variable number of words of trace data optionally followed by a time stamp. The word containing the trace hook identifier and the hook type is called the *hook word*. The remaining two bytes of the hook word are called *hook data* and are available for recording event data.

The trace facility supports up to eight active trace sessions at a time. Each trace session uses a channel of the multiplexed trace special file /dev/systrace. Channel 0 is used by the trace facility to record system events. The tracing of system events is started and stopped by the **trace** and **trcstop** commands. Channels 1 through 7 are referred to as generic trace channels and may be used by subsystems for other types of tracing such as data link tracing.

When the trace is configured, the trace facility controls trigger the collection of data on or off and stop the trace facility (stop deconfigures the **trace** command and unpins buffers).

Frequently used trace commands include:

trace	Starts the tracing of system events
trcdead	Extracts trace information from a system dump
trcrpt	Formats reports of trace event data contained in the **trace** log file
trcstop	Stops the tracing of system events
trcupdate	Updates the trace formatting templates stored in the /etc/trcfmt file

7.4 SOURCE CODE ANALYSIS TOOLS

Source code analysis tools available under AIX aid in checking the source code for integrity and analyzing the flow of control. These tools are intended for use by software engineers and programmers to enhance productivity.

7.4.1 lint

The **lint** utility checks C source code for coding integrity. The benefit of using **lint** prior to compilation is significant, as it aids in identifying overlooked and trouble-prone code constructs. It also enforces orthodox type-checking rules that help in eliminating possible future bugs.

The **lint** tool also identifies the following:

- Source code and library incompatibility
- Potential problems with variables
- Potential problems with functions
- Problems with flow control
- Legal constructs that may be inefficient
- Unused variable and function declarations
- Nonportable code

To run **lint,** simply supply the source file as an argument to **lint.**

7.4.2 cflow

The **cflow** utility generates a flow graph of external references. It is capable of analyzing C assembler as well as object files, and producing a chart of their external references to the standard output.

The input file can be a C language source file (file name with .c suffix), a pre-processed C source (.i suffix), a **yacc** source file (.y suffix), a **lex** source file (.l suffix), an object file (.o suffix), or an assembler source file (.s suffix). Based on the kind of file it is, the contents of the file are sent to the C preprocessor **cpp,** the **yacc** compiler **yacc,** or the lexical analyzer **lex,** and subsequently run through the first pass of **lint.** Files suffixed with .s are assembled and information is extracted (as in .o files) from the symbol table.

The output of all this nontrivial processing is collected, converted into a graph of external references, and subsequently displayed with line numbers and indentation levels to show the flow of control and call sequences of functions and procedures.

7.4.3 cxref

cxref creates a C program cross-reference listing by analyzing C program files, creating a cross-reference table. **cxref** generates a list of all external references for each module of a C language source program, including where the reference is resolved (if it is resolved in the program). **cxref** uses the **cpp** command to include #define directives in its symbol table.

7.5   LEXICAL ANALYZER—lex

lex is a program-generating tool that produces code to handle lexical processing of character input streams. It accepts high-level, problem-oriented specifications for character string matching. The regular expressions are specified in the source specification to **lex.** The **lex** program generator is a table of regular expressions and corresponding program fragments. The table is translated to a program that reads an input stream, copies the input stream to an output stream, and partitions the inputs into strings that match the given expressions. As each string is recognized, the corresponding program fragment gets executed. This process of expression recognition is done by a deterministic finite state automation generated by **lex.** The program fragments written by the user are executed in the order in which the corresponding regular expressions occur in the input stream.

The **lex** command reads a file or standard input, generates a C language program, and writes it to a file named lex.yy.c. This file is a compilable C language program, which can be linked with or called from other routines.

7.6   PARSER GENERATOR—yacc

The name **yacc** is an acronym for "yet another compiler compiler." It is a general purpose tool used for imposing structure on the input to programs. A set of specifications (also referred to as the grammar rules) for the input process, prepared by the user, describes the input structure, code to be invoked when these rules get recognized, and a low-level routine (the lexical analyzer) to control the basic input. **yacc** then generates a function to parse the input process. This function calls the lexical analyzer to pick up the basic items (referred to as *tokens*) from the input stream. These tokens are organized according to the input structure rules. When one of these rules has been recognized, the corresponding user code (supplied for this rule as an action) gets invoked. In this way, **yacc** converts a context-free grammar specification into a set of tables for a simple automaton that executes a parsing algorithm.

The output generated by **yacc** (called y.tab.c) needs to be compiled with a C language compiler to produce a function *yyparse*. This function is loaded with the lexical analyzer function *yylex* and the user's main C routine.

7.7   PATTERN MATCHING LANGUAGE

sed and **awk** are tools used by programmers to edit text files. **sed,** a stream editor, is used to apply a series of edits to multiple files. **awk,** a programming language, allows manipulation of structured data and the generation of formatted reports. The following sections highlight the features of **sed** and **awk.**

7.7.1   awk

awk is a programming language that makes it possible to handle data manipulations efficiently. An **awk** program is a sequence of patterns and actions that tell what to look for in the input data and what to do when it is found. **awk**

searches a set of files for lines matched by any of the patterns; when a matching pattern is found, the corresponding action is performed. A pattern can select lines by combinations of regular expressions and comparison operations on strings, numbers, fields, variables, and array elements. Actions may perform arbitrary processing on selected lines. The action language looks like C, but there are no declarations. Strings and numbers are the built-in data types.

awk scans input files and splits each input line into fields automatically. Because of the automatic nature of its input, field splitting, storage management, and initialization, **awk** programs are usually much smaller than they would be in a more conventional language. The same brevity of expression and convenience of operations make **awk** valuable for prototyping larger programs. One starts with a few lines, then refines the program until it does the desired job, experimenting with designs by trying alternatives. Since programs are short, it is easy to get started, and easy to start over when experience suggests a different direction. It is straightforward to translate an **awk** program into another language once the design is right.

awk was originally designed and implemented by the authors of UNIX in 1977, in part as an experiment to see how the UNIX tools **grep** and **sed** could be generalized to deal with numbers as well as text. An enhanced version was made available in 1985. The main add-on feature in new **awk** (available in AIX and newer versions of UNIX) is the ability for users to define their own functions, support dynamic regular expressions with text substitution and pattern matching functions, and make use of additional built-in functions and variables.

7.7.2 sed

sed is a noninteractive stream editor that automates edits to be done on multiple files. As an editing filter, **sed** modifies a specified file according to an edit script and then writes the modified file to standard or redirected output. **sed** can also be used for writing conversion programs. For example, **sed** can translate formatting codes (such as Scribe/TeX) into troff. Invoke **sed** by entering:

```
command [-n, -e(script), -f(sourcefile)] file
```

The **-f** option is used to specify the name of the sourcefile, **-n** suppresses all information normally written to standard output, and **-e** uses the script string as the editing script. The script specifies to the program what instructions to perform. **sed** can also be invoked by putting your editing instructions in a file and then entering the name of the file.

How does **sed** work?

- All editing commands in an edit script are applied (in order) to each input line.
- Commands are globally applied to all lines.
- The original input file is unchanged by editing commands. The editing commands modify the copy of the original input line and then a copy is sent to standard output.

7.8   MACRO PROCESSOR—m4

m4 is a macro processor facility which is used as a preprocessor for C and other languages for expanding macro definitions. Built-in macros or user-defined macros can be processed using **m4. m4** processes each file in the order in which it is specified on the command line. A command reads standard input if a file is not specified or if a minus (–) is specified as a file name and writes the processed macros to standard output. To redirect the output to a file, enter:

```
m4 (FileName) >outputfile
```

m4 reads every alphanumeric token input and determines if the token is the name of a macro; if it is a macro, the name is replaced by its defining text and the resulting string is pushed back onto the input to be rescanned. Macros may also be called with arguments. The arguments are collected and substituted into the right places in the defining text before the defining text is rescanned.

The macro calls have the following syntax:

```
macroname(argument . . .)
```

A left parenthesis must immediately follow macroname. If the left parenthesis does not follow the name of a defined macro, the **m4** command reads it as a macro call with no arguments. Macro names consist of tokens: strings of ASCII alphabetic letters, digits, and the underscore character (_). Extended characters are not allowed in macro names. The first character cannot be a digit. While collecting arguments, the **m4** command ignores unquoted leading blanks, tabs, and newline characters. Use single quotation marks to quote strings. The value of a quoted string is the string with the quotation marks stripped off.

Users can also define macros using the define macro. For example:

```
define (option, misc)
```

m4 defines the string option as misc. Wherever option appears in the program, **m4** replaces it with misc. (The string name must comply with the conventions discussed previously.)

7.9   PROGRAM MODULES MANAGEMENT

7.9.1   make

The **make** program is primarily used for maintaining a set of programs by building up-to-date versions of programs. **make** simplifies the process of recompiling and relinking programs during software development by allowing programmers to record the specific relationships among files once only. The **make** command can then be used to automatically perform all the updates. Using this versatile utility, instructions can be combined to create large programs in a single file, macros can be defined to be used within the **make** command description file, and many basic types of files can be created.

To **make** the latest version of a program, enter:

```
make programname
```

make automates the compilation and linking required to update and create the `programname` file by carrying out tasks resulting from work done since the last issuance of the **make** command. **make** issues commands resulting from tracing dependencies of files being built.

The following example illustrates the relationship of **make** to its target.

```
       reads Makefile
make  ──►  program   (target of operation)
                │
                ▼
           builds on
        dependent files
```

make requires a description file (to build the target file), file names, specified sets of rules to construct many standard types of files, and time stamps of all system files. The description file tells the **make** command how to build the target file, which files are to be used, and what the file relationships are. The description file contains information on target and parent file name, macro definitions, commands and user-specified rules to build the target file. Each line in the description file involving target file is called a *dependency line*. If any parent file was changed more recently than the target file, **make** creates the files affected by the changes, including the target file. For example:

```
test:     dependency list1 ...
          command list1 ...
   .
   .
   .
test:     dependency list2 ...
          command list2 ...
```

defines two separate processes to create the target file, `test`. If any of the files in `dependency list1` changes, the **make** command runs `command list1`. If any of the files in `dependency list2` changes, the **make** command runs `command list2`. To avoid conflict, a parent file cannot appear in both `dependency list1` and `dependency list2`.

The **make** program does not perform any program operations; it simply writes all the steps to build the program, including outputs from lower-level calls to the **make** command. This makes it an extremely powerful and versatile tool for managing a large number of program modules.

7.9.2 imake

imake enables programmers to write portable software. Using **imake,** programmers can move software from one system to another without extensive code revision. **imake** aids in software portability by enabling programmers to avoid rewriting the *Makefile* (used by **make** to identify dependencies). Rather, programmers write an *Imakefile,* which is a machine-independent description of targets. An *Imakefile* localizes machine dependencies in configuration files. When you run **imake, imake** replicates the configuration files in the *Makefile.* For example:

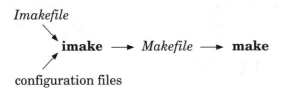

To use **imake,** programmers need **imake, cpp,** and **make,** a set of configuration files, and **xmkmf** (**xmkmf** uses **xmkmf** plus configuration files to generate a *Makefile* from an empty *Imakefile*). **imake** programming variants include a user environment, utilities for building programs, and an install method and location.

7.10   SOURCE CODE CONTROL SYSTEM

Source Code Control System (SCCS) is a complete system of commands that allows specified users to control and maintain an audit trail of changes made to an SCCS file. It allows simultaneous existence of multiple versions of a file and supports Multibyte Character Set (MBCS) characters. It provides a complete system for creating, converting, or changing controls on SCCS files. All SCCS files use the prefix .s.

An SCCS file is any text file controlled with SCCS commands. An SCCS file is made up of three parts: (1) a delta table, (2) access and tracking flags, and (3) the body of the text. Deltas are changes recorded for each version of a file. Tracking flags are essentially a list of flags with the @ designation; tracking flags define who may edit which files, which releases of files are available, and which files are available for joint editing. The body of an SCCS file contains information about all the versions of the file.

Frequently used SCCS commands include:

admin	Creates an SCCS file or changes an existing SCCS file
cdc	Changes the comments associated with delta
comb	Combines two or more consecutive deltas in an SCCS file
delta	Adds a set of changes (deltas) to the text of an SCCS file
get	Gets a specified version of an SCCS file for editing or compiling
rmdel	Removes the most recent delta on a branch from an SCCS file
sccs	Performs most SCCS services, using a set of pseudocommands (administrative program for the SCCS system)

7.11   AIX PERFORMANCE TOOLS

To maximize performance tuning, it is necessary to identify the critical resources on the system that can be tuned, improved, or upgraded, since it is the availability of these resources that determines the performance of a workload on a system. Tools, when used, usually report the availability and utilization of these resources.

It is a common practice to partition the resources into physical resources and logical resources. Physical resources are real components, while logical resources are programming abstractions. Physical and logical resources are identified as follows:

Physical resources	*Logical resources*
CPU	Process time slice
Memory	Page frames
	Stacks
	Buffers
	Queues
	Tables
I/O bus	_____
Adapters	_____
Disk	Logical volumes
	File systems
	Files
Network interface	Packets
	Channels

The tools of the trade in performance tuning do one or more of the following: timing, counting, and sampling. Based on how they work, they have been grouped under three categories: monitoring tools, analysis tools, and tuning tools.

7.11.1   Monitoring tools

Overviews of popular AIX monitoring and tuning tools follow. Details on flags and options are not included due to the variability of these commands. For "how to" information on these commands, refer to the AIX Commands Reference series.

7.11.1.1   iostat

The **iostat** command displays utilization data for CPU, disks, tty devices, and CDs. The command can be run singly to produce cumulative statistics since system boot, or it can be run repetitively to display statistics in real time for successive intervals over a defined duration of time. The report produced can have two types of format: the first type contains terminal-related and CPU statistics, and the second describes disk statistics. Sample output of both types of reports follows.

Type 1
```
tty:    tin      tout    cpu:    % user    % sys    % idle    % iowait
        0.4      30.2            1.4       1.7      96.3      0.6
        3.4      3.6             0.1       2.9      97.0      0.0
        2.3      73.4            1.2       2.0      96.4      0.4
        1.4      1.6             0.2       0.4      99.4      0.0
        0.5      616.6           2.0       7.4      90.1      0.5
        0.5      8.0             0.1       1.0      98.9      0.0
        0.9      0.9             0.2       1.2      95.3      3.3
```

Type 2
```
Disks:    % tm_act    Kbps    tps    Kb_read    Kb_wrtn
hdisk0    0.0         0.0     0.0    224        0
hdisk1    0.3         3.4     0.2    1713775    165156
hdisk2    0.3         3.2     0.2    1623159    126396
hdisk3    0.4         1.3     0.2    219649     479864
```

System information can be generated by specifying the following flags:

-d   The **-d** option is exclusive of the **-t** option and displays only the disk utilization report.

-t   The **-t** option is exclusive of the **-d** option and displays only the tty and CPU usage reports.

7.11.1.2 netstat

The **netstat** command presents statistics on network and communications activity including:

- Active sockets in use
- Contents of network data structures (which are specified in /etc/protocols), such as TCP, IP, UDP, and ICMP
- Packet traffic (inbound and outbound) distribution for each of the network adapter interfaces configured
- Statistics on participating network device drivers including the Ethernet adapter device driver, token-ring adapter device driver, and X.25 adapter device driver
- Utilization of assigned network memory management routines and size of the page pool being managed by network services

System information can be generated by specifying the following flags:

-A   Shows the address of any protocol control blocks associated with the sockets. This flag acts with the default display and is used for debugging purposes.

-a   Shows the state of all sockets. Without this flag, sockets used by server processes are not shown.

-f *AddressFamily*	Limits reports of statistics or address control blocks to those items specified by the *AddressFamily* variable. The following address families are recognized:

          inet   Indicates the AF_INET address family

          ns   Indicates the AF_NS address family

          unix   Indicates the AF_UNIX address family

-i	Shows the state of all configured interfaces. *Note:* The collision count for Ethernet interfaces is not supported.
-I *Interface*	Shows the state of the configured interface specified by the *Interface* variable.
-m	Shows statistics recorded by the memory management routines.
-n	Shows network addresses as numbers. When this flag is not specified, the **netstat** command interprets addresses where possible and displays them symbolically. This flag can be used with any of the display formats.
-p *Protocol*	Shows statistics about the value specified for the *Protocol* variable, which is either a well-known name for a protocol or an alias for it. Some protocol names and aliases are listed in the /etc/protocols file. A null response means that there are no numbers to report. The program report of the value specified for the *Protocol* variable is unknown if there is no statistics routine for it.
-r	Shows the routing tables. When used with the **-s** flag, the **-r** flag shows routing statistics.
-s	Shows statistics for each protocol.
-u	Dislays information about domain sockets.
-v	Shows statistics for the Ethernet adapter device driver, the token-ring adapter device driver, the X.25 adapter device driver, and the 802.3 adapter device driver.

7.11.1.3   nfsstat

The **nfsstat** utility is meant for displaying information about the server and client activity [the network file system (NFS) and the remote procedure calls used by it] The information reported relates to either NFS's server and/or client data, or the server and/or client data used by the remote procedure calls used in NFS.

System information can be generated by specifying the following flags:

-c	Allows the user to limit the report to client data only. The **nfsstat** command provides information about the number of RPC and NFS calls sent and rejected by the client. To limit the report exclusively to NFS or RPC data, combine this flag with the **-n** or **-r** option.
-s	Restricts the report to server data only. This option causes the **nfsstat** command to display information about the number of NFS and RPC calls received and rejected by the server. The user can also combine this option with the **-n** and **-r** options to further limit the report to NFS or RPC data.

-n   Displays and prints NFS information for both the client and server. To limit the report to NFS client or server information only combine this flag with the -c and -s options.

-r   Displays RPC information for the client and server. This option can be combined with the -c and -s options to limit the report to client or server data only.

-z   Initializes statistics. This flag is for use by the root user only and can be combined with any of the other flags listed here to zero particular sets of statistics after printing them.

7.11.1.4   no

This command displays (and changes) the values of network options including socket buffer sizes, low-water marks for the *mbuf* pools, and amount of memory used in *mbufs* in the AIX kernel.

System information can be generated by specifying the following flags:

-a   Prints a list of all configurable options and their current values.

-d *Option*   Sets the *Option* variable back to its default value.

-o *Option* [=*NewValue*]   Shows the value of the option specified by the *Option* variable if the *NewValue* variable is not specified. If a new value is specified, the *Option* variable is set to that value.

Note: When using the -o flag, do not enter space characters before or after the equal sign. If you do, the command will fail.

7.11.1.5   ps

The **ps** tool displays process status. Its multifarious options allow reporting of information on a variety of system resources, on a per process basis. Some of the key information reported for each process includes CPU usage, memory usage, nice value, number of I/O requests, resident set size, size of the code segment, amount of paging space used, and virtual size of the process.

System information can be generated by specifying the following flags:

-A   Writes to standard output information about all processes.

-a   Writes to standard output information about all processes, except the process group leaders and processes not associated with a terminal.

-d   Writes information to standard output about all processes, except the process group leaders.

-e   Writes information to standard output about all processes, except kernel processes.

-f   Generates a full listing.

-F-o *Format*   Displays information in the format specified by the *Format* variable. Multiple field specifiers can be specified for the *Format* variable. The *Format* variable is either a comma-separated list of field specifiers or a list of field specifiers enclosed within a set of " " (double quotation marks) and separated from one another by a comma or by one or more spaces, or both.

Each field specifier has a default header. The default header can be overridden by appending an = (equal sign) followed by the user-defined text for the header. The fields are written in the order specified on the command line in column format. The field widths are specified by the system to be at least as wide as the default or user-defined header text. If the header text is null, (such as, if -F -o user= is specified), the field width is at least as wide as the default header text. If all header fields are null, no header line is written.

7.11.1.6 sar

sar collects and exhibits system accounting reports and is very useful for obtaining an overall view of ongoing system activities and resource usage. It can be used as a display tool to monitor system performance as well as to view captured data from a previous date. Both the sampling interval as well as the granularity can be defined for **sar**. Internally, **sar** calls a program named **sadc** to access system data. Common information reported by **sar** includes CPU utilization, paging activity, disk access, system call frequency, kernel process statistics, request statistics on the run queue and the wait queue, process switching activity, message and semaphore operations, and terminal-related I/O activity.

System information can be generated by specifying the following flags:

-A	Reports all data.
-a	Reports use of file access system routines specifying how many times per second several of the system file access routines have been called.
-b	Reports buffer activity for transfers, accesses, and cache (kernel block buffer cache) hit ratios per second. Access to most files in AIX bypasses kernel block buffering, and therefore does not generate these statistics. However, if a program opens a block device or a raw character device for I/O, traditional access mechanisms are used, making the generated statistics meaningful.
-c	Reports system calls.
-e *hh[:mm[:ss]]*	Sets the ending time of the report. The default ending time is 18:00.
-f *File*	Extracts records from *File* (created by **-o** *File* flag). The default value of the *File* parameter is the current daily data file, the /var/adm/sa/sadd file.
-i *Seconds*	Selects data records at seconds as close as possible to the number specified by the *Seconds* parameter. Otherwise, the **sar** command reports all seconds found in the data file.
-k	Reports kernel process activity.
-m	Reports message and semaphore activities per second.
msg/s	Reports the number of IPC message primitives.

-o *File*	Saves the readings in the file in binary form. Each reading is in a separate record and each record contains a tag identifying the time of the reading.
-q	Reports queue statistics.
-r	Reports paging statistics.
-s *hh[:mm[:ss]]*	Sets the starting time of the data, causing the **sar** command to extract records time-tagged at, or following, the time specified. The default starting time is 08:00.
-u	Reports system unit activity.
-v	Reports status of the process, inode, and file tables.
-w	Reports system switching activity.
-y	Reports tty device activity per second.

7.11.1.7   schedtune

schedtune displays (and changes) the virtual memory manager's memory load control parameters and the paging-space-low retry level.

System information can be generated by specifying the following flags:

-D	Restores the default values (**h**=6, **p**=4, **w**=1, **m**=2, **e**=2, **f**=10, **t**=0).
-e *n*	Specifies that a recently resumed suspended process is eligible to be suspended again when it has been active for at least *n* seconds.
-f *n*	Specifies the number of (10-m) clock ticks to delay before retrying a **fork** call that has failed because of insufficient paging space. The system retires the **fork** call up to five times.
-h *n*	Specifies the systemwide criterion for determining when process suspension begins and ends. A value of zero effectively turns off memory load control.
-m *n*	Sets the minimum multiprogramming level.
-p *n*	Specifies the per-process criterion for determining which processes to suspend.
-t *n*	Increases the duration of the time slice—the maximum amount of time before another process is scheduled to run. The default time-slice duration is 10 m. The parameter *n* is in units of 10 ms each. If *n*=0, the time-slice duration is 10 ms. If *n*=2, the time-slice duration is 30 ms.
-w *n*	Specifies the number of seconds to wait, after thrashing ends, before reactivating any suspended processes.
-?	Displays a brief description of the command and its parameters.

7.11.1.8   vmstat

vmstat monitors memory statistics like page fault activity. In addition, it provides path lengths on disk transfers and system traps. Like **iostat,** this utility can be run singly or iteratively with a count to produce rate statistics. Common events reported include page ins and page outs by the virtual memory manager (VMM), paging space page ins and paging space page outs that depict the VMM initiated page ins/outs from/to paging space, address translation faults; device interrupts (related to hardware interrupts), and software interrupts.

System information can be generated by specifying the following flags:

Note: Both the **-f** and **-s** flags can be entered on the command line, but the system will only accept the first flag specified and override the second flag.

-f   Reports the number of forks since system start-up.

-i   Displays the number of interrupts taken by each device since system start-up.

-s   Writes to standard output the contents of the sum structure, which contains an absolute count of paging events since system initialization. The **-s** option is exclusive of the other **vmstat** command options. These events are described as follows.

7.11.1.9   vmtune

vmtune changes the parameters of the virtual memory manager page replacement algorithm. The virtual memory manager (VMM) maintains a list of free real-memory page frames. These page frames are available to hold virtual memory pages needed to satisfy a page fault. When the number of pages on the free list falls below that specified by the *MinFree* parameter, the VMM begins to steal pages to add to the free list. The VMM continues to steal pages until the free list has at least the number of pages specified by the *MaxFree* parameter.

If the number of file pages (permanent pages) in memory is less than the number specified by the *MinPerm* parameter, the VMM steals frames even-handedly from either computatonal or file pages. If the number of file pages is greater than the number specified by the *MaxPerm* parameter, the VMM steals frames only from file pages. Between the two, the VMM uses repaging rates to determine which frames are stolen.

If a process appears to be reading sequentially from a file, the values specified by the *MinPgAhead* parameter determine the number of pages to be read ahead when the condition is first detected. The value specified by the *MaxPgAhead* parameter sets the maximum number of pages that will be read ahead, regardless of the number of preceding sequential reads.

System information can be generated by specifying the following flags:

-f *MinFree*   Specifies the minimum number of frames on the free list. This number can range from 8 to 204800.

-F *MaxFree*   Specifies the number of frames on the free list at which page stealing is to stop. This number can range from 16 to 204800 but must be greater than the number specified by the *MinFree* parameter by at least the value of *MaxPgAhead*.

-p *MinPerm*   Specifies the point below which file pages are protected from the repage algorithm. This value is a percentage of the total real-memory page frames in the system. The specified value must be greater than or equal to 5.

-P *MaxPerm*   Specifies the point above which the page stealing algorithm steals only file pages. This value is expressed as a percentage of the total real-memory page frames in the system. The specified value must be greater than or equal to 5.

-r *MinPgAhead*	Specifies the number of pages with which sequential read-ahead starts. This value can range from 0 through 32. It should be a power of 2.
-R *MaxPgAhead*	Specifies the maximum number of pages to be read ahead. This value can range from 0 through 64. It should be a power of 2 and should be greater than or equal to *MinPgAhead*.

7.11.2   Analysis tools

For the following analysis tools to generate output, the accounting system must be running. It shoudl be noted that running the accounting system continuously slows system performance to a certain extent.

7.11.2.1   acctcoFm

acctcom reads from specific files (usually the /usr/adm/pacct) and provides accounting information on processes that have completed. Reporting statistics on the already completed processes is the main difference between this tool and **ps.** Typical information reported includes start time, stop time, CPU utilization, login name of the user who executed the process, the terminal on which the process was executed, and the status of how the process ended.

System information can be generated by specifying the following flags:

-a	Shows some average statistics about the processes selected. The statistics are displayed after the output records.
-b	Reads backwards, showing the most recent commands first. This flag has no effect when the **acctcom** command reads standard input.
-C *Seconds*	Shows only processes whose total CPU time (system time + user time) exceeds the value specified by the *Seconds* variable.
-e *Time*	Selects processes existing at or before the specified time. You can use the *NLTIME* environment variable to specify the order of hours, minutes, and seconds. The default order is *hh:mm:ss*.
-E *Time*	Selects processes ending at or before the specified time. You can use the *NLTIME* environment variable to specify the order of hours, minutes, and seconds. The default order is *hh:mm:ss*. If you specify the same time for both the **-E** and **-S** flags, the **acctcom** command displays the processes that existed at the specified time.
-f	Displays two columns related to the ac_flag field of the acct.h file: the first indicates use of the **fork** command to create a process; the second indicates the system exit value. Refer to the **acct** structure described in the **acct** file format in *AIX Version 3.2 Files Reference.*
-g *Group*	Selects processes belonging to the specified group. You can specify either the group ID or the group name.
-h	Instead of mean memory size, shows the fraction of total available CPU time consumed by the process (hog factor). This factor is computed as:

$$\frac{(\text{total CPU time})}{(\text{elapsed time})}$$

-H *Factor*	Shows only the processes that exceed the value of the *Factor* parameter. This factor, called the hog factor, is computed as:

$$\frac{(\text{total CPU time})}{(\text{elapsed time})}$$

-i	Displays columns showing the number of characters transferred in read or write operations (the I/O counts).
-k	Instead of memory size, shows total kcore minutes (memory measurement in kilobyte segments used per minute of run time).
-l *Line*	(lowercase L) Shows only processes belonging to workstation **/dev**/*Line*.
-I *Number*	(uppercase i) Shows only processes transferring more than the specified number of characters.
-m	Shows mean main memory size. This is the default. The **-h** flag or **-k** flag turn off the **-m** flag.
-n *Pattern*	Shows only commands matching the value of the *Pattern* variable, where *Pattern* is a regular expression. Regular expressions are described in the **ed** command. In addition to the usual characters, the **acctcom** command allows you to use a + (plus sign) as a special symbol for the preceding character.
-o *File*	Copies selected process records to the specified file, keeping the input data format. This flag suppresses writing to standard output. This flag cannot be used with the **-q** flag.
-O *Seconds*	Shows only processes with CPU system time exceeding the specified number of seconds.
-q	Displays statistics but not output records. The statistics are the same as those displayed using the **-a** flag. The **-q** flag cannot be used with the **-o** flag.
-r	Shows CPU factor. This factor is computed as:

$$\frac{(\text{user-time})}{(\text{system-time} + \text{user-time})}$$

-s *Time*	Shows only those processes that existed on or after the specified time. You can use the *NLTIME* environment variable to specify the order of hours, minutes, and seconds. The default order is *hh:mm:ss*.
-S *Time*	Shows only those processes starting at or after the specified time. You can use the *NLTIME* environment variable to specify the order of hours, minutes, and seconds. The default order is *hh:mm:ss*.
-t	Shows separate system and user CPU times.
-u *User*	Shows only processes belonging to the specified user. Enter one of the following for the *User* variable: a user ID, a login name to be converted to a user ID, a # (pound sign) to select processes run by the root user, or a ? (question mark) to select processes associated with unknown user IDs.
-v	Eliminates column headings from the output.

7.11.2.2 acctcms

acctcms provides accounting information on processes that have completed, in a manner similar to **acctcom.** The key difference is that this utility combines all the records for identically named processes and reports a combined total for that process name.

System information can be generated by specifying the following flags:

-a   Displays output in ASCII summary format rather than binary summary format. Each output line contains the command name, the number of times the command was run, total kcore time (memory measurement in kilobyte segments), total CPU time, total real time, mean memory size (in KB), mean CPU time per invocation of the command, and the CPU usage factor. The listed times are all in minutes. The **acctcms** command normally sorts its output by total kcore minutes. The unit kcore minutes is a measure of the amount of memory used (in kilobytes) multiplied by the amount of time it was in use. This flag cannot be used with the **-t** flag.

-c   Sorts by total CPU time rather than total kcore minutes. This flag cannot be used with the **-n** flag. When this flag is used with the **-n** flag, only the **-n** flag takes effect.

-j   Combines all commands called only once under the heading other.

-n   Sorts by the number of times the commands were called. This flag cannot be used with the **-c** flag. When this flag is used with the **-c** flag, only the **-n** flag takes effect.

-o   Displays a command summary of nonprime time commands. You can use this flag only when the **-a** flag is used.

-p   Displays a command summary of prime time commands. You can use this flag only when the **-a** flag is used.

-s   Assumes that any named files that follow this flag are already in binary format.

-t   Processes all records as total accounting records. The default binary format splits each field into prime and nonprime time sections. This flag cannot be used with the **-a** flag.

7.11.2.3 accton

accton works like a toggle switch in enabling and disabling the collection of process accounting statistics.

System information can be generated by specifying the following flags:

-l *File*   (lowercase L) Writes a line-usage summary file showing the line name, the number of minutes used, the percentage of total elapsed time, the number of sessions charged, the number of logins, and the number of logoffs. If you do not specify a file name, the system creates the information in the /var/adm/acct/nite/lineuse file.

-o *File*   Writes to the specified file an overall record for the accounting period, giving starting time, ending time, number of restarts, and number of date changes. If you do not specify a file name, the system creates the /var/adm/acct/nite/reboots file.

-p   Displays only input. Line name, login name, and time are shown in both numeric and date/time formats. Without the **-p** flag specified, the **acct-con1** command would display input, converting input to session records, and write reports.

-t   Uses the last time found in the input as the ending time for any current processes. This, rather than current time, is necessary in order to have reasonable and repeatable values for files that are not current.

7.11.2.4   filemon

The **filemon** command uses the trace facility to report I/O activity at four separate levels: logical file system, virtual memory segments, logical volumes, and physical volumes. Tracking at the logical file system level yields information on *read, write, open,* and *lseek* system calls. Analyzing the virtual memory system results in availability of physical I/O operations (for example, paging). Reporting of information at the logical volume level gives I/O statistics on a per-logical-volume basis. Monitoring at the physical volume level allows analyses of physical resource utilization enabling any combination of levels to be monitored. This tool normally runs in the background and monitors file system and I/O events in real time. An alternate way to use it is to use it like an offline monitor on previously collected trace files.

System information can be generated by specifying the following flags:

-i File   Reads the I/O trace data from the specified *File,* instead of from the real-time trace process. The **filemon** report summarizes the I/O activity for the system and period represented by the trace file.

Note: Trace data files are usually written in a circular manner. If the trace data has wrapped around, the chronological beginning and end of the trace may occur in the middle of the file. Use the raw mode of the **trcrpt** command to rewrite the data sequentially, before invoking the **filemon** command, as follows:

```
trcrpt -r file > new.file
```

For the report to be accurate, the trace file must contain all the hooks required by the **filemon** command.

-o *File*   Writes the I/O activity report to the specified *File,* instead of to the **stdout** file.

-d   Starts the **filemon** command, but defers tracing until the **trcon** command has been executed by the user. By default, tracing is started immediately.

-T *n*   Sets the kernel's trace buffer size to n bytes. The default size is 32,000 bytes. The buffer size can be increased to accommodate larger bursts of events, if any. (A typical event record size is 30 bytes.)

Note: The trace driver in the kernel uses double buffering, so, in fact, there will be two buffers allocated of size n bytes. Also, note that these buffers are pinned in memory, so they are not subject to paging. Large buffers may affect the performance of paging and other I/O.

-P   Pins monitor process in memory. The **-P** flag causes the **filemon** command's text and data pages to be pinned in memory for the duration of the monitoring period. This flag can be used to ensure that the real-time **filemon** process is not paged out when running in a memory-constrained environment.

-v   Prints extra information in the report. The most significant effect of the **-v** flag is that all logical files and all segments that were accessed are included in the I/O activity report, instead of only the 20 most active files and segments.

-O *Levels*   Monitors only the specified file system levels. Valid level identifiers are:

lf   Logical file level

vm   Virtual memory level

lv   Logical volume level

pv   Physical volume level

all   Short for **lf, vm, lv, pv**

The **vm, lv,** and **pv** levels are implied by default.

-u   Reports on files that were opened prior to the start of the **trace** daemon. The process ID (PID) and the file descriptor (FD) are substituted for the file name.

7.11.2.5 fileplace

fileplace shows the physical or logical placement of the blocks that constitute a file. This tool can also be made to report fragmented files within a volume, the indirect block numbers for the file, as well as the file's placement on physical volume blocks. Note that this tool is good for local files only; it does not report information on remote files that may be mounted over NFS file systems.

System information can be generated by specifying the following flags:

-i   Displays the indirect blocks for the file, if any. The indirect blocks are displayed in terms of either their logical or physical volume block addresses-numbers, depending on whether the **-l** or **-p** flag was specified.

-l   Displays file placement in terms of logical volume fragmentsblocks, for the logical volume containing the file. The **-l** and **-p** flags are mutually exclusive.

-p   Displays file placement in terms of physical volume blocks, for the physical volumes that contain the file. If the logical volume containing the file is mirrored, the physical placement is displayed for each mirror copy. The **-l** and **-p** flags are mutually exclusive.

-v   Displays more information about the file and its placement, including statistics on how widely the file is spread across the volume and the degree of fragmentation in the volume. The statistics are expressed in terms of either the logical or physical volume block numbers, depending on whether the **-l** or **-p** flag is specified.

7.11.2.6 gprof

gprof reports flow of control among subroutines of a program and the amount of CPU time consumed by each subroutine. It provides visibility to the sections of the code that are most active and points out spots that require optimization efforts. Two kinds of reports may be generated on a program's run-time behavior including (1) a flat profile showing the CPU time consumption along with frequency of occurrence on a per subroutine basis, and (2) a call-graph profile laying out the CPU time consumed by each subroutine plus its child subroutines.

The mechanics of how **gprof** works is straightforward. A special library function (called **mcount**) is embedded in the application code when the code is compiled for profiling. This causes a counter to increment each time a parent function calls a child function which enables tracking the frequency of subroutine calls. A second mechanism (also activated by **gprof**'s compile time option) facilitates sampling of the program's current program counter location each clock tick (every 10 ms) to quantify the time spent in each routine. Another command called **prof** is also available for profiling programs; however, data reported by it is a proper subset of the data available from **gprof.**

System information can be generated by specifying the following flags:

-b	Suppresses the printing of a description of each field in the profile.
-E *Name*	Suppresses the printing of the graph profile entry for routine *Name* and its descendants, similar to the **-e** flag, but excludes the time spent by routine *Name* and its descendants from the total and percentage time computations. (**-E** *MonitorCount* **-E** *MonitorCleanup* is the default.)
-e *Name*	Suppresses the printing of the graph profile entry for routine *Name* and all its descendants (unless they have other ancestors that are not suppressed). More than one **-e** flag can be given. Only one routine can be specified with each **-e** flag.
-F *Name*	Prints the graph profile entry of the routine *Name* and its descendants similar to the **-f** flag, but uses only the times of the printed routines in total time and percentage computations. More than one **-F** flag can be given. Only one routine can be specified with each **-F** flag. The **-F** flag overrides the **-E** flag.
-f *Name*	Prints the graph profile entry of the specified routine *Name* and its descendants. More than one **-f** flag can be given. Only one routine can be specified with each **-f** flag.
-L *PathName*	Uses an alternate pathname for locating shared objects.
-s	Produces the gmon.sum profile file, which represents the sum of the profile information in all the specified profile files. This summary profile file may be given to subsequent executions of the **gprof** command (using the **-s** flag) to accumulate profile data across several runs of an a.out file.
-z	Displays routines that have zero usage (as indicated by call counts and accumulated time).

7.11.2.7 lsattr

lsattr lists the attributes affecting performance, their current values, and whether or not they are tunable.

System information can be generated by specifying the following flags:

-a *Attribute*   Displays information for the specified attributes of a specific device or kind of device. You can use one **-a** flag for each attribute name or multiple attribute names. If you use one **-a** flag for multiple attribute names, the list of attribute names must be enclosed in quotes with spaces between the names. Using the **-R** flag, you must specify only one **-a** flag with only one attribute name. If you do not specify either the **-a** or **-R** flag, the **lsattr** command displays all information for all attributes of the specified device.

-c *Class*   Specifies a device class name. This flag can be used to restrict the output to that for devices of a specified class. This flag cannot be used with the **-E** or **-l** flags.

-D   Displays the attribute names, default values, descriptions, and user-settable flag values for a specific device when not used with the **-O** flag. The **-D** flag displays only the attribute name and default value in colon format when used with the **-O** flag. This flag can be used with any combination of the **-c, -s,** and **-t** flags that uniquely identifies a device from the *predefined devices* object class or with the **-l** flag. This flag cannot be used with the **-E, -F,** or **-R** flags.

-E   Displays the attribute names, current values, descriptions, and user-settable flag values for a specific device when not used with the **-O** flag. The **-E** flag displays only the attribute name and current value in colon format when used with the **-O** flag. This flag cannot be used with the **-c, -D, -F, -R, -s,** or **-t** flags.

-f *File*   Reads the needed flags from the *File* parameter.

-F *Format*   Displays the output in a user-specified format, where the *Format* parameter is a quoted list of column names separated by nonalphanumeric characters or white space. Using white space as the separator, the **lsattr** command displays the output in aligned columns. Only column names from the *predefined attributes* and *customized attributes* object classes can be specified. In addition to the column names, there are two special purpose names that can be used. The name *description* can be used to obtain a display of attribute descriptions and *user-settable* can be used to obtain an indication as to whether or not an attribute can be changed. This flag cannot be used with the **-E, -D, -O,** or **-R** flags.

-H   Displays headers above the column output. To use the **-H** flag with the **-O** flag is meaningless; the **-O** flag prevails. To use the **-H** flag with the **-R** flag is meaningless; the **-R** flag prevails.

-h   Displays the command usage message.

-l *Name*   Specifies the device logical name in the *customized devices* object class whose attribute names or values are to be displayed.

-O   Displays all attribute names separated by colons and, on the second line, displays all the corresponding attribute values separated by colons. The attribute values are current values when the **-E** flag is also specified and default values when the **-D** flag is specified. This flag cannot be used with the **-F** and **-R** flags.

| -R | Displays the legal values for an attribute name. The **-R** flag cannot be used with the **-D, -E, -F** and **-O** flags, but can be used with any combination of the **-c, -s,** and **-t** flags that uniquely identifies a device from the predefined devices object class or with the **-l** flag. The **-R** flag displays the list attribute values in a vertical column as follows: |

```
Value1
Value2
  .

  .
ValueN
```

The **-R** flag displays the range attribute values as `x...n(+i)` where `x` is the start of the range, `n` is the end of the range, and `i` is the increment.

| -s *Subclass* | Specifies a device subclass name. This flag can be used to restrict the output to that for devices of a specified subclass. This flag cannot be used with the **-E** or **-l** flags. |
| -t *Type* | Specifies a device type name. This flag can be used to restrict the output to that for devices of a specified class. This flag cannot be used with the **-E** or **-l** flags. |

7.11.2.8 nulladm

nulladm creates a process accounting file with the proper permissions.

7.11.2.9 netpmon

netpmon uses the trace facility to report network I/O and network-related CPU usage. Normally, this tool runs in the background and monitors network-related system events in real time. An alternate way to use it is as an off-line monitor on previously collected trace files. CPU-related information includes the amount of CPU consumed in network-related events and CPU idle due to network I/O. Device driver I/O related activities reflect statistics on I/O traffic through Ethernet and token-ring device drivers, and queue lengths for transmission I/O. Remote or NFS I/O statistics include remote procedure call requests on a per process, per file, per server basis. Communication interface data includes an inventory of socket-related system calls that have been issued, on a per protocol (such as TCP, UDP) basis.

System information can be generated by specifying the following flags:

-o *File*	Writes the reports to the specified *File,* instead of to standard output.
-d	Starts the **netpmon** command, but defers tracing until the **trcon** command has been executed by the user. By default, tracing is started immediately.
-O *ReportType* ...	Produces the specified report types. Valid report type values are:
	cpu CPU usage
	dd Network device driver I/O

so		Internet socket call I/O
nfs		NFS I/O
all		All reports are produced; this is the default value
-P		Pins monitor process in memory. This flag will cause the **netpmon** text and data pages to be pinned in memory for the duration of the monitoring period. This flag can be used to ensure that the real-time **netpmon** process does not run out of memory space when running in a memory-constrained environment.
-T *n*		Sets the kernel's trace buffer size to *n* bytes. The default size is 64000 bytes. The buffer size can be increased to accommodate larger bursts of events, if any. (A typical event record size is on the order of 30 bytes.)
	Note:	The trace driver in the kernel uses double buffering, so actually two buffers of size n bytes will be allocated. These buffers are pinned in memory, so they are not subject to paging.
-t		Prints CPU reports on a per-thread basis.
-v		Prints extra information in the report. All processes and all accessed remote files are included in the report instead of only the 20 most active processes and files.

7.11.2.10   rmap

rmap uses the trace facility to report system calls, process utilization, and I/O events.

System information can be generated by specifying the following flags:

-o *OutFile*		Redirects standard output to the specified file. The output generated by **rmap** will be formatted for either 80 columns and 66 lines or 138 columns and 88 lines depending on the reports selected.
-q		Suppresses the configuration file listing.
	Note:	One or more options may be present on the command line. However, each option should only appear once on the command. If an option appears more than once, only the last specification of the option is used.

7.11.2.11   rmss

rmss simulates various memory sizes. It temporarily reduces the effective RAM to assess the probable performance of a workload on smaller configurations. Although the tool tends to be optimistic for applications that access too many files, it comes across as a handy step-saver for scaling memory sizes to study the effect on a workload.

System information can be generated by specifying the following flags:

-c *MemSize*	Changes the simulated memory size to the *MemSize* value, which is an integer or decimal fraction in units of megabytes. The *MemSize* variable must be between 4 MB and the real memory size of the machine. There is no default for the **-c** flag.

-d *MemSize*	Specifies the increment between memory sizes to be simulated. The *MemSize* value is an integer or decimal fraction in units of megabytes. If the **-d** flag is omitted, the increment will be 8 MB.
-f *MemSize*	Specifies the final memory size. You should finish testing the simulated system by executing the command being tested at a simulated memory size given by the *MemSize* variable, which is an integer or decimal fraction in units of megabytes. The *MemSize* variable must be between 4 MB and the real memory size of the machine. If the **-f** flag is omitted, the final memory size will be 8 MB.
-n *NumIterations*	Specifies the number of times to run and measure the command, at each memory size. There is no default for the **-n** flag. If the **-n** flag is omitted, during **rmss** command initialization, the **rmss** command will determine how many iterations of the command being tested are necessary to accumulate a total run time of 10 s, and then run the command that many times at each memory size.
-o *OutputFile*	Specifies the file into which to write the **rmss** report. If the **-o** flag is omitted, then the **rmss** report is written to the file `rmss.out`. In addition, the **rmss** report is always written to standard output.
-p	Display the current simulated memory size.
-r	Reset the simulated memory size to the real memory size of the machine.
-s *MemSize*	Specifies the starting memory size. Start by executing the command at a simulated memory size specified by the *MemSize* variable, which is an integer or decimal fraction in units of megabytes. The *MemSize* variable must be between 4 MB and the real memory size of the machine. If the **-s** flag is omitted, the starting memory size will be the real memory size of the machine.
Command	Specifies the command to be run and measured at each memory size. The Command parameter may be an executable or shell script file, with or without command line arguments. There is no default command.

7.11.2.12   svmon

svmon reports memory status at system, process, and segment levels. It can create four types of reports: global, process, segment, and detailed segment, which are useful for analyzing memory statistics of varying granularities.

System information can be generated by specifying the following flags:

-D *sid1 . . . sidN*	Displays detailed memory-usage statistics for segments *sid1 . . . sidN*. If *N* sids are specified, then *N* detailed segment reports are displayed.
-G	Displays a global report.
-i *Interval [NumIntervals]*	Instructs the **svmon** command to print out statistics repetitively. Statistics are collected and printed every *Interval* seconds.

-P [n|s|a] *[pid1 ... pidN]*   Displays memory usage statistics for processes *pid1 ... pidN*. If no process IDs (PIDs) are specified, then memory usage statistics are displayed for all active processes.

-P [n|s|a] {u|p|g|r} *[Count]*   Sorts processes by memory usage and displays the memory usage statistics for the top *Count* processes. If a *Count* value is not specified, then memory usage statistics are displayed for all active processes.

-r   Displays statistics about the number of real memory frames with reference bits on. The refernce bit is used in the virtual memory manager (VMM) page-stealing algorithm. When the **-r** flag is specified, page space and address range statistics are replaced by statistics about the number of frames in use that have been recently referenced, and the number of pinned frames that have been recently referenced.

-S *sid1 ... sidN*   Displays memory-usage statistics for segments *sid1 ... sidN*. One segment report is printed.

-S {[n|s|a] [u|p|g|r]} *[Count]*   Sorts segments by memory usage and displays the memory usage statistics for the top *Count* segments. If *Count* is not specified, then a *Count* of 10 is implicit.

7.11.2.13   time/timex

These tools report elapsed time, user CPU time, and system CPU time used by the execution of a command.

System information can be generated by specifying the following flags:

-o   Reports the total number of blocks read or written and total characters transferred by a command and all its children.

-p   Lists process accounting records for a command and all its children. The number of blocks read or written and the number of characters transferred are reported. The **-p** flag takes the **f, h, k, m, r,** and **t** arguments defined in the **acctcom** command to modify other data items.

-s   Reports total system activity during the execution of the command. All the data items listed in the **sar** command are reported.

7.11.2.14   tprof

tprof reports utilization statistics for kernel services, library subroutines, application programs, and even individual lines of source code (of an application program) using the trace facility.

System information can be generated by specifying the following flags:

-d   This flag is not needed to microprofile shared libraries. It has been retained for compatibility purposes.

-e	Profiles the kernel extension.
-k	Profiles the kernel.
-p *Program*	Profiles the user program; also microprofiles the user program if that program is compiled with the **-g** flag.
-s	Profiles shared libraries.
-t *Process_ld*	Constrains reporting to the specified process and its children and parents.
-v	Specifies verbose mode, which creates additional files required when microprofiling shared libraries.
-x *Command*	Allows the execution of an arbitrary *Command*. Subprograms of the program specified by the **-p** flag are profiled.

7.11.3   Tuning tools

7.11.3.1   lvedit

lvedit alters the location and attributes of a logical volume.

7.11.3.2   nice

This utility executes a process with a specified priority level.

System information can be generated by specifying the following flags:

-Increment	Increments a command's priority up or down. You can specify a positive or negative number. Positive increment values lower priority. Negative increment values increase priority. Only users with root authority can specify a negative increment. If you specify an *Increment* variable that exceeds the range of 0 to 39, then the limit whose value was exceeded is used. This flag is equivalent to the **-n** *Increment* flag.
-n *Increment*	This flag is equivalent to the *-Increment* flag.

7.11.3.3   no

In addition to being an analysis tool, **no** is also used to change (and display) values of network parameters, including, among others, *mbufs, lowclust,* and *lowmbufs* in the running kernel of the PowerPC. Extreme care should be taken in using this command since there is no range checking in the values that one specifies for the kernel-tunable parameters.

System information can be generated by specifying the following flags:

-a	Prints a list of all configurable options and their current values.
-d *Option*	Sets the *Option* variable back to its default value.
-o *Option* [*=NewValue*]	Shows the value of the option specified by the *Option* variable if the *NewValue* variable is not specified. If a new value is specified, the *Option* variable is set to that value.

7.11.3.4   renice

This utility is similar to **nice**; it changes the priority of a process.

System information can be generated by specifying the following flags:

-g *GroupID*	Interprets numeric IDs as process group IDs.
-g	Interprets all IDs as unsigned decimal integer process group IDs.
-n *Increment*	Specifies how to alter the system scheduling priority. The *Increment* variable is a positive or negative decimal integer used to modify the scheduling priorities. Positive increment values cause a lower system scheduling priority. Negative increment values may require appropriate privileges and cause a higher system scheduling priority.
-p *ProcessID*	Interprets numeric IDs as process IDs (the default interpretation).
-p	Interprets all IDs as unsigned integer process IDs. The **-p** flag is the default if you specify no other flags.
-u *UserName*	Interprets user names.
-u	Interprets all IDs as user name or numerical user IDs.

7.11.3.5   reorgvg

This utility reorganizes elements of a volume group (the details on volume groups are covered in Chap. 11).

System information can be generated by specifying the following flags:

-i	Specifies physical volume names read from standard input. Only the partitions on these physical volumes are organized.

7.12   SUMMARY

The development tools reviewed in this chapter help create the optimal development environment for AIX programmers. This chapter discusses the XL family of compilers which provides source code and back-end optimization tasks, as well as the AIX two-pass Assembler which translates machine language instructions into machine object code.

Also discussed is the **dbx** or **xde** symbolic debugger which can be used to debug programs written in C, FORTRAN, Pascal, and Assembler languages; and the **adb** debugger which provides commands to examine, debug, and repair executable binary files and to examine non-ASCII data files, such as core dumps. The kernel debug program can help determine errors in code running in the operating system kernel, while the trace facility isolates system problems by monitoring and timestamping selected system events.

Source code analysis tools available under AIX aid in checking the source code for integrity and in analyzing the flow of control in the order of execution. **lex** is a program-generating tool that produces code to handle lexical processing of character input streams; **yacc** is a general purpose tool used for imposing structure on the input to programs; **awk** is a programming language that makes it possible to handle data manipulations efficiently.

We also review **m4,** which is a macro processor command used as a prepro-cessor for C and other languages for expanding macro definitions. As well as the *make* program, which is primarily used for maintaining a set of programs by building up-to-date versions of programs. The importance of *imake* to soft-ware portability and the role of SCCS as a file tracker is also discussed.

Finally, the suite of AIX performance-tuning tools, including monitoring tools, analysis tools, and tuning tools, are reviewed.

Standardization and Connectivity

Standardization and connectivity are discussed together because today's business environment relies on complex and diverse computer systems that, in order to be effective, must be open and integrated—an environment of *open systems*. System administrators need to ensure that a collection of personal computers, mainframes, and workstations can interact effectively and properly. Managers and system administrators must also have portable software—software that can be used in various environments on a variety of operating systems. A review of compatibility, portability, and interoperability standards is followed by a discussion of the interconnectivity functionalities of the PowerPC and AIX.

8.1 STANDARDIZATION

Standardization is necessary to realize the promise of open distributed systems and to take advantage of advanced networking technologies. Some of the standards groups discussed below have formed to promulgate their own standards while other standards groups and standards have evolved due to widespread industry use. Official standards organizations are discussed followed by a review of industry consensus standards.

8.1.1 Compatibility standards

8.1.1.1 International Organization for Standardization (ISO)

ISO is a Geneva-based agency created under the auspices of the United Nations. ISO is a nongovernment, independent agency which promotes standardization for materials and products traded internationally. Acceptance of ISO standards is the result of agreement by member bodies, leading to adoption worldwide by participating countries. Membership is composed of the national standards bodies of over 90 countries, including ANSI (American National Standards Institute) representing the United States, BSI (British Standards Institute) representing Great Britain, and DIN (Deutches Institut für Normung) representing Germany. These member groups represent the commercial and industrial interests of their respective countries. The work of ISO is divided across various technical committees (TCs), which are then divided into subcommittees (SCs) and work groups (WGs).

8.1.1.2   American National Standards Institute (ANSI)

ANSI, like all standards groups in the United States, is a voluntary organization and coordinates the activities of the various United States representatives to ISO. ANSI does not actually create standards itself, but oversees and accredits standards produced by Accredited Standards Committees (ASCs). ANSI also accredits trade organizations such as the the IEEE (Institute of Electrical and Electronics Engineers), the accredited body in the area of computer operating systems.

8.1.1.3   Institute of Electrical and Electronic Engineers (IEEE)

An ANSI-accredited professional society, the IEEE has over 325,000 members consisting of electrical and electronic engineers and computer professionals organized by subfield into approximately 35 "societies" (such as Aerospace and Electronic Systems, Antennas and Propagation, Consumer Electronics, Electromagnetic Compatibility, and Information Theory). The IEEE board approves IEEE standards developed by its member societies and forwards them to ANSI for approval as American National Standards. Until early 1993, the IEEE's Computer Society designated its TCOS (Technical Committee on Operating Systems) as the supervising body over the subcommittee that directed the POSIX (Portable Operating System Interface) effort. In early 1993, this responsibility was transferred to the newly formed PASC (Portable Applications Standards Committee).

8.1.2   Portability standards

8.1.2.1   Portable Operating System Interface for Computer Environments (POSIX)

The IEEE 1003.1 (POSIX.1) system application program interface (API), written assuming a C language interface, became a standard in 1988. (POSIX in the generic usually refers to POSIX 1003.1.) This initial POSIX standard spawned a family of open system standards related to the UNIX operating system. POSIX.1 was the basis for the Federal Information Processing Standard (FIPS) issued in 1989, as well as a point of reference for the development of the X/Open Portability Guide.

The full title of the current standard is "ISO/IEC 9945-1:1990 IEEE Standard 1003.1-1990 Information Technology—Portable Operating System Interface

(POSIX) Part 1: System Application Program Interface (API) (C Language)."
This standard, which most members of the POSIX community call dot1 (pro-
nounced "dot one"), is available from the IEEE Customer Service Department.*

POSIX is divided into roughly two dozen committees labeled from POSIX
1003.0 to 1003.19. Major POSIX committees, other than 1003.1, are 1003.2,
which deals with commands and utilities, as well as 1003.10, which deals with
systems administration. Many of the other working groups are defining Applications Environment Profiles (AEPs), which specify optional features that can
be added to a base standard (such as 1003.1). The POSIX Real-Time Working
Group (1003.4) enhanced POSIX.1 to include binary semaphores, process
memory locking, real-time signal extensions, timers, and interprocess communication.

A list of POSIX related committees follows:

1003.0	POSIX Guide
1003.1	System Interfaces
1003.2	Shell and Utilities
1003.3	Test Methods
1003.4	Real Time
1003.5	ADA Bindings
1003.6	POSIX Security
1003.10	System Administration
1003.8	Transparent File Access—Distribution Services
1003.9	FORTRAN Binding
1003.10	Supercomputing Application Environment Profile
1003.11	Transaction Processing Application Environment Profile
1003.12	Protocol Independent Interfaces
1003.13	Real-Time Application Environment Profile (Application Support)
1003.14	Multiprocessing Application Environment Profile (Application Support)
1003.15	Batch Services (Batch Environment Amendment)
1003.16	C Language Binding
1003.110	Directory Service Applications Programming Interface
1003.18	POSIX Platform Application Environment Profile
1003.19	POSIX ADA Language Interface BDG. for Real-Time Extensions
1201.1	Windowing Toolkit Applications Programming Interface Window Interface for User and Applications Portability
1201.2	User Interface Driveability Recommended Practice on Driveability
1224.0	X.400 and X.500 Object Management X.400 Mail Services Application Program Interface

---

* IEEE Customer Service, 445 Hoes Lane, Piscataway, New Jersey 08854.

1224.1	X.400 Gateway Applications Programming Interface
	OSI Applications Interface—X.400 Based Electronic Messaging
1238	Common OSI API and FTAM API
1238.1	Dependent Document

8.1.2.2 Federal Information Processing Standards (FIPS)

The FIPS define procurement requirements for the federal government. Those who work with the United States Federal Government should specifically refer to the FIPS, which are written by the NIST (National Institute for Standards and Technology) and are available from the National Technical Information Service. The current FIPS standard for POSIX.1 (ISO/IEC 9945-1 : 1990) is FIPS 151-2, issued in 1993, which specifies, with a few minor changes and clarifications, that the POSIX 1003.1 (issued in 1990) is to be used as the mandated federal standard. [Both FIPS 151-1 and 151-2 cite POSIX 1003.1. FIPS 151-1 maps to 1003.1 (1988) and FIPS 151-2 maps to POSIX 1003.1 (1990).] The differences between the 1988 and 1990 versions of POSIX 1003.1 consist primarily in corrections and clarification.

Those wishing to check their compliance with FIPS 151-1 should refer to the PCTS (POSIX Compliance Test Suite) that was developed by the NIST and can be administered by any one of seven accredited POSIX conformance test laboratories. NIST can supply the names of currently accredited test facilities, as well as information on the current requirements and test procedures.

8.1.2.3 X/Open

X/Open is an international consortium of hardware vendors, software vendors, and users who have developed and published the *X/Open Portability Guide* (XPG). XPG4, the fourth issue of the *X/Open Portability Guide,* was issued in 1992. Founded in 1984 by Bull, ICL, Siemends, Ollivetti, and Nixdorf, X/Open's mission is to broaden the market for open systems by developing and promoting Common Applications Environment (CAE) specifications. CAE specifications are a set of open, vendor-neutral specifications based on international and industry consensus standards.

X/Open brands products: products that comply with the XPG standards and have guaranteed to fix any errors (discovered by the rigorous independent compliance testing) may carry the X/Open seal. X/Open also ensures its alignment with emerging international standards by working closely with other formal standards organizations and by entering cooperative efforts with other groups to expedite high-priority standardization efforts. For example, in 1992 X/Open and OSF (discussed in 10.1.2.4) agreed to expedite OSF's Distributed Computing Environment Application Environment Specifications (DCE AES) for inclusion in X/Open's CAE.

8.1.2.4 Open Software Foundation (OSF)

OSF consists of approximately 350 members who input requirements and direction to OSF through special interest groups (SIGs). OSF is primarily concerned with determining the scope and requirements for new technology initiatives through the use of request for technology (RFT) solicitations to the computer industry. Organized in 1988 by seven major system vendors including DEC, HP, Apollo, IBM, Group Bull, Siemens, and Nixdorf, OSF uses RFT evaluation and testing to promote the development of portable software applications.

The OSF Application Environment Specifications (AES) are the specifications for the components making up OSF's operating system environment, which currently includes the OSF/1 operating system component, the Motif user interface component, and the distributed computing environment (DCE) interoperability component. OSF's AES describe portability interfaces for one functional area of the application environment including operating systems, network services, user environment services, graphics services, database management services, and programming languages. OSF's AES are used for compliance branding and certification.

Primary OSF offerings include the OSF/Motif, an X-based GUI (introduced in 1988), and DCE (introduced in 1992). OSF's operating system, OSF/1, is based on Carnegie-Mellon University's Mach microkernel architecture and implements the AES interface.

8.1.2.5 X Window System

The X Window System (or X) is a hardware, vendor-independent, and network-transparent operating environment developed at the Massachusetts Institute of Technology in 1984 as a cooperative effort funded by major computer manufacturers to build a network of graphical workstations. The enormous success of this program made the X Window System a UNIX based windowing standard which is now available on virtually every workstation in the industry. Several versions of X have been developed, of which X Version 11 (X11) is the most recent. The X Consortium was formed in 1988 to foster development and support of the X Window System.

X offers many benefits to users. It solves the problem of having a common interface across a heterogeneous range of computers and operating systems. It provides a mechanism upon which one can build different user interface styles. It also addresses the issue of sharing resources among multiple programs. X is operating-system-independent, encouraging the portability of its software to diverse platforms. Hence, X is one of the most popular and widely available user interface standards in the workstations arena.

X provides the ability to generate multifont text and graphics in monochrome or in color on a bitmap display. Graphics like points, lines, arcs, and polygons can be generated in a hierarchy of windows. Each window can be considered as a "virtual screen" and can, in turn, contain subwindows of an arbitrary depth. They may overlap each other and can be moved, resized, or restacked dynamically. Since windows are relatively inexpensive resources, applications utilizing several thousand subwindows are common and are often used to implement user interface components.

The X window system architecture is based on a simple client-server relationship. The display server is the program that controls and draws the output to the display monitors, tracks client input, and updates the windows accordingly. Clients are application programs that perform specific tasks. Since X is, by design, a distributed environment, its clients and server do not necessarily have to run on the same machine.

The terminology in the world of X may be somewhat misleading to programmers from the traditional host or mainframe environment. The word *server* in the context of X means the reverse of what servers mean in local area network environments. Consider a traditional database environment where the server lives on the remote host and the client application resides locally on the PCs that are attached to it. In X, the server lives on the local workstation, while the clients run on the remote host machines.

Although X is fundamentally defined by a network protocol, most application programmers think about it as a graphical user interface (GUI). For ease of use, a higher-level layer is used to abstract the protocol layer and insulate it from programmers building X-based interfaces. This higher-level layer is referred to as the Xlib or more correctly as the Xlib Interface Library (refer to Fig. 8.1). This library provides a familiar procedural interface that masks the detail of the protocol encoding and transport interactions. It also automatically handles the buffering of requests for efficient transport to the server, much as the C language standard I/O library buffers output to minimize system calls. The library also provides a suite of utility functions and primitive constructs that do not directly relate to the protocol but aid in building applications.

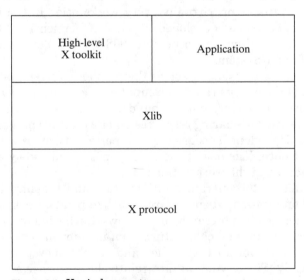

Figure 8.1 X window system.

8.1.3 Interoperability standards

8.1.3.1 Trusted Computing Base (TCB)

TCB is the aggregation of system mechanisms that enforce and ensure the AIX operating system's security policies. (A conceptual view of a TCB boundary is shown in Fig. 8.2.) Selected components from both the hardware as well as the software domains participate in the TCB's domain base to effectively police its compliance.

The TCB software includes:

- An operating system kernel that manages the system
- Configuration files that control system operation
- Programs executed with privilege or access permission to alter the kernel and/or configuration files

The hardware includes:

- A processor that operates in a dual execution mode: system mode and problem mode

The programs running in problem mode are functionally independent and can access only limited resources, whereas the programs running in system mode are relatively unconstrained. The kernel always runs in system mode and is henceforth considered a part of TCB. Processes running in problem mode interface to kernel modules through the system call mechanism, causing the processor to change to system mode. However, those processors are part of the TCB only if they run with kernel privilege.

The *system state* (information indicating the state of the system) consists of a static system state that may be changed only at system start time based on administrative privileges and a dynamic system state that may change at any

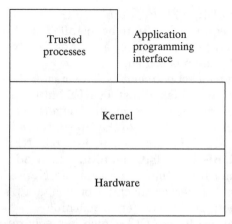

Figure 8.2 Conceptual base of trusted computer base.

time based on kernel privileges. The static system state is stored in configuration files such as /etc/master and /etc/system. The Dynamic system state is stored in kernel data structures and the state files of trusted programs such as kernel process table and the /etc/utmp file. The system security state is the part of the system state that handles security-relevant aspects of the system, the reading or modifying of which can be authorized by administrative or kernel privileges.

All programs that are installed with privilege or invoked by a privileged program are denoted as *trusted programs* (TPs). Additionally, a TP is any process that may alter or read the system security state.

There are three main components in the security policies identified in the AIX operating system, including:

Access control.   Addresses how information resources are created and distributed.

Accountability.   Addresses how users are identified on the system and for what actions they are accountable. Can detect actual and potential noncompliance.

Administrative.   Addresses issues pertaining to administrative users on the system, provides principle of least privilege, and ensures role separation.

8.1.3.2   Network File System (NFS)

Originally developed by Sun Microsystems, NFS has become a de facto networking standard. NFS's biggest asset is that it is independent of hardware, operating systems, and network architectures. This independence was achieved through the use of two sets of protocols:

- Remote procedure call (RPC) protocols
- Data standardizing External Data Representation (XDR) protocols

In addition to the RPC and XDR, NFS uses the TCP/IP protocol to implement data transmission. NFS requires TCP/IP to be installed, configured, and operational. The NFS facility can be started upon request or simply configured to start up when the operating system is booted.

NFS functions are controlled by a set of *daemons.* The master daemon associated with NFS is called **inetd. inetd** is not just for NFS but is also the master for all other daemons on the system. It essentially triggers the start-up of other daemons when or if needed. In addition to the **inetd,** there is a suite of daemons that are associated with NFS, as seen in Fig. 8.3. NFS daemons include: **portmapd, mounted, nfsd, pcnfsd,** and **biod.** The **biod** daemons is required to run on all of the machines that are serving as NFS clients. The **pcnfsd** daemon is needed on the server machine only if a PC's files are mounted. The rest of the daemons run on the server machine.

NFS also supports access control lists (ACL), which is a separate function handled by an RPC program to exchange information about ACLs between clients and servers.

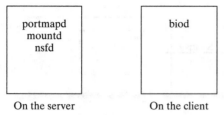

On the server   On the client

Figure 8.3 Participating daemons in NFS.

Mapped files are also supported under NFS on the PowerPC running AIX. This feature allows programs on clients to be accessed as if they were in real memory. Using the *shmat* system call, users can map areas of a file into their address space. As the program reads/writes into this region of memory, the file is read into the memory from the server or updated as needed. Multiple files on the same client can also share data effectively using a mapped file.

Secure NFS is also implemented under AIX in addition to the standard UNIX authentication. NFS uses the Data Encryption Standard (DES) and public key cryptography to authenticate users and machines in networks. A DES key is generated from two components: a public key published for general availability and a private key used to encrypt and decrypt data.

The NFS-compatible network lock manager supports file and record locking over the network. Local lock requests are handled by the kernel. When a lock is attempted on a remote file on an NFS-mounted directory, the kernel issues a local RPC request to **rpc.lockd,** the network lock daemon, to make a lock request to the network lock manager daemon on the NFS server. The network lock manager contains both the client and server functions. The client services requests from the kernel and sends them to the network server lock manager at the server end, while the server processes lock requests from the network and enforces lock operations in the kernel. Figure 8.4 delineates the coordination among the kernel and lock manager on individual machines at both ends, while showing the information exchange between the client and the server machines. The status monitor shown in the diagram performs *health-check* duties and keeps a record of relevant failures at the client and the server end, so that the lock information may be recovered if a crash occurs. When a lock request is issued, the kernel ascertains if it is a local request. If so, it processes the lock request itself. If not, it transmits the request to the network lock daemon. This locking system is essentially stateless.

Frequently used NFS commands follow:

Command	*Description*
exportfs	Exports and unexports directories to NFS clients.
mount	Makes a file system available for use.
nfsstat	Displays statistics pertaining to the ability of client/server to receive calls.
on	Executes commands on remote systems.

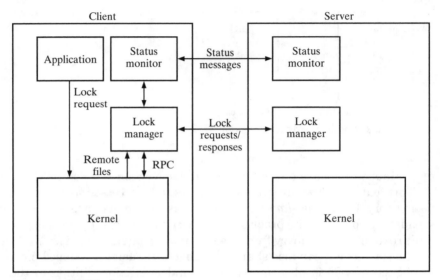

Figure 8.4 NFS lock manager.

rusers	Displays a list of users currently logged in on remote machines.
rup	Displays status of a remote host.
rpcinfo	Reports the status of RPC servers.
rpcgen	Generates C code to implement an RPC protocol.
rwall	Sends messages to all users on the network.
showmount	Displays a list of all clients that have remotely mounted a file system spray. Sends a specific number of packets to a host to report performance statistics.

8.1.3.3 Network Information Service (NIS)

NIS is a centralized database service that offers centralized control of networked machines. NIS was formerly known as "Yellow Pages" (YP). Rather than having to manage each host's files (for example /ets/hosts, /ets/passwd, and /etc/group), system administrators maintain one database for each file on one central server. Machines that are using NIS retrieve information as needed from these databases.

NIS consists of clients and servers, logically grouped together in domains using maps (databases) that provide information such as host names or passwords. An NIS server can be thought of as a host providing resources for other computers on the network. An NIS slave is a client that uses the maps to share information. These maps are essentially copies of the data to be shared, stored in a machine-independent standardized form called XDR format. The map files are created using the NIS command **makedbm.** After creation, each map has two files: a file named map.key.pag (containing key and value pairs) and a file named map.key.dir (containing index for large .pag files).

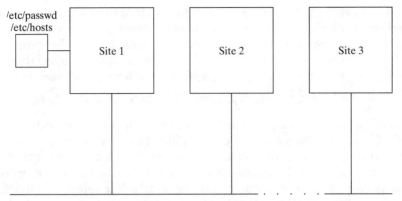

Figure 8.5 NIS: sharing user password and hostname information.

NIS reduces the effort of maintaining repetitive databases of information. It also helps users by making their password, directories, and files available on other systems. Network administration becomes easier and less time consuming. Typical information stored in an NIS database includes password files and host files (as seen in Fig. 8.5) whose contents are essentially the same for different nodes on a single network.

Frequently used NIS commands follow:

Commands	*Description*
domainname	Lists the name of the current NIS domain system for an NIS host.
makedbm	Creates the NIS database maps.
ypbind	Enables a client process to connect to a server.
ypcat	Lists the contents of NIS maps.
ypinit	Builds and installs NIS maps on an NIS server.
ypmatch	Displays the values of one or more keys within an NIS map.
yppasswd	Allows users to change NIS passwords from any NIS host.
yppoll	Identifies the version of a NIS map on the NIS server.
yppush	Forces propagation of updated NIS maps from the master server to slave servers.
ypserv	Looks up information in the local NIS databases.
ypset	Points the **ypbind** process to a specific server.
ypwhich	Identifies which machine is the NIS server of an NIS client.
ypxfr	Transfers an NIS map from an NIS server to a local host.

8.1.3.4 Andrew File System (AFS)

The AFS distributed file system joins the file systems of individual machines allowing users to access information stored anywhere on a network. AFS uses a client/server model: file server machines store data and transfer it to client machines, which perform computations for users. AFS uses a hierarchical file structure—a tree with */afs* as the root. The next level of directories consist of *cells*. Cells are subtrees of the AFS file space and consist of related directories and files. The cell controlling a specific user workstation is termed a local cell; other cells in the AFS file space are termed foreign cells. The directories and files under */afs* make up the AFS *file space*.

AFS client machines use a cache manager to access information stored in the AFS file space. When a user accesses a file, the cache manager requests the file from the file server machine and stores the file as a copy on the client workstation's local disk. This enables the client to use the local copy of the cached file rather than continuously sending network requests to the file server machines for data. When the file closes, the cache manager sends the changed file back to the appropriate file server, and the changed version replaces the file stored on the server.

Because AFS is a distributed file system, several security techniques are used to protect the many users, including passwords, mutual authentication, and access control lists (ACLs). Passwords and mutual authentication ensure that users accessing files are valid AFS users. ACLs allow individual users to restrict access to their own directories. Each ACL entry has two parts: a user or group name and the access control rights. Access control rights include:

r	read
l	lookup
i	insert
d	delete
w	write
k	lock
a	administer

For example

```
fs setacl . jenny rl
```

would give Jenny read permission only.

Frequently used AFS commands follow:

Command	Description
fs listacl	Lists a directory's ACL
fs setacl	Sets one directory's ACL
fs setacl-dir	Sets multiple directories' ACLs
fs copyacl	Copies a directory's ACL to one or more other directories
kpasswd	Changes AFS password
fs whereis	Lists the file server housing a file or directory

fs checkservers [-all] [<cell name>]	Checks the status of file servers
klog	Authenticates with authentication server to obtain tokens
tokens	Displays all tokens

8.1.3.5 Transmission Control Protocol/Internet Protocol (TCP/IP)

TCP/IP is a set of communication protocols that specify standards and conventions for routing and interconnecting computer networks. The de facto standard for local area networks, TCP/IP has proliferated to wide area network environments like the Internet. From a conceptual perspective, TCP and IP are two separate protocol layers. Figure 8.6 shows the protocol stack for TCP/IP. Applications use both the TCP and the IP layers to communicate with the network interface (which is the physical layer).

TCP/IP is a network technology independent of and capable of running on virtually all standard hardware platforms. It supports universal interconnection so that one computer may communicate with any other computer on the same network or another network. TCP/IP can handle a diverse variety of network-related tasks. Some of the routine uses of TCP/IP are for electronic mail, computer-to-computer file transfer, remote login, executing commands on a remote machine, printing files on remote systems, and managing a network. Frequently used TCP/IP commands follow:

Command	*Description*
finger	Displays user information on specified host
ftp	Utility is used to transfer files between hosts
host	Resolves a host name
ping	Determines status of a network or host

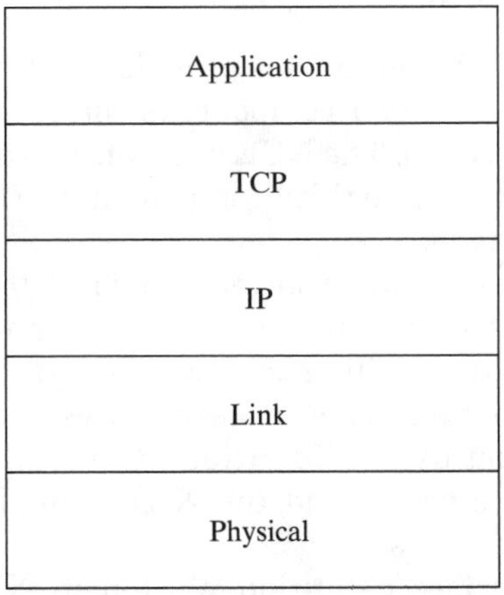

Application
TCP
IP
Link
Physical

Figure 8.6 TCP/IP protocol stack.

rcp	Copies one or more files between local and remote host, between two remote hosts, or between files at a single remote host
rexec	Allows a command to be executed on a remote machine
rlogin	Used to log in to a similar remote host
rsh	Used to execute commands on a foreign host
rwho	Displays user information on local area network hosts
telnet (tn)	Provides capability for a user to have a remote session on a similar or dissimilar remote host
tftp	Provides a minimal file transfer capability to transfer files to and from hosts; provides a stripped set of commands in ftp
whois	Identifies the owner of a user ID or nickname

Multiple sets of commands for remote file transfer, remote command execution, and remote login are found under most UNIX systems because each set of the utilities has descended from the System V and Berkeley domains. TCP/IP is mentioned here for reference only. To gain an understanding of the protocol suite, refer to product reference manuals.

8.1.3.6   Network Computing System (NCS)

NCS is a set of tools for distributing computer processing tasks across resources either in a network or several interconnected networks. NCS is an implementation of the network computing architecture, which distributes software applications across networks encompassing a variety of computers and programming environments. Programs based on Network Computing Architecture take advantage of computing resources throughout a network by allocating different parts of each program to be executed on host computers best suited for that task. NCS consists of three major components:

- Remote Procedure Call (RPC) run-time library
- Location broker
- Network Interface Definition Language (NIDL) compiler

The RPC run-time library and the location broker provide run-time support for network computing. Together, these two components make up what is called the *network computing kernel* (NCK). The NCK contains all the software required to run a distributed application. The third component, the NIDL compiler, is a tool for developing applications.

The RPC run-time library provides library routines for local programs to execute procedures on remote hosts. These routines transfer requests and responses between clients (the programs calling the procedures) and servers (the programs executing the procedures). When a user writes a distributed application, he or she usually need not use RPC routines directly. Instead, an interface definition in NIDL can be created, and the NIDL compiler can be used to generate the required RPC routines.

The NIDL compiler takes an interface definition written in NIDL as an input. An interface definition specifies the interface between the user and the provider of a service. Once the interface is established, the compiler defines the way in which a client application sees a remote service as well as the way in which a remote server sees requests for its service. From this definition, the NIDL compiler generates client and server stub source code and header files. The client stub program performs the conversion between requests (and responses) that are meaningful to the client and packets that are transmitted (and received) on the network. The server stub program provides similar support for the server. The stub programs produced by an NIDL compiler contain nearly all of the remoteness for a distributed application. They perform data conversions, assembly and disassembly of packets, and provide interaction with the RPC run-time library. It is much easier to write an interface definition in NIDL than it would be to write the stub code that the NIDL compiler generates from a definition.

The location broker provides information about the network or Internet resources to clients. It maintains a database that contains the identification and locations of objects on a network. Through a client agent, the location broker maintains information about the local brokers that manage information about resources on the local host, the global brokers that manage information about resources on all hosts, and the administrative tools.

Network communications between systems in an NCS environment are handled through the RPC run-time library. It is possible that one program can access different hosts that listen on two different ports or have two different addresses.

The remote procedure calls extend the procedure call mechanism from a single system to a distributed computing environment. The calls distribute the execution of a program among multiple computers in a way that is transparent to the application-level code. Figure 8.7 shows the flow of ordinary local procedure calls between the calling client and the called procedures.

Frequently used NCS commands follow:

Command	Description
lb_admin	Monitors and administers location broker registrations
libd	Manages the information in the local location broker database
nidl	Compiles program definitions written in NIDL
nrglbd	Manages the global location broker database

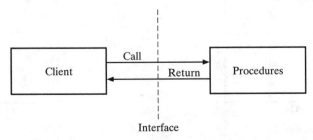

Figure 8.7 NCS single-process procedure call flow.

8.1.3.7   X.25 communications

X.25 is a communications protocol conforming to international standards that is particularly useful for communicating with diverse computer systems and for applications that access public databases. Both public networks and private networks can be based on X.25 protocol. Public networks are provided on a national basis by the National Post, Telegraph and Telecommunications authority. Private networks are operated by individual corporations.

X.25 is designed for a form of communication known as packet switching. Figure 8.8 presents a simplified view of how packet switching works. Data is sent in basic entities called frames. There are three main levels in X.25. The first level is the physical or electrical level. The second level is the frame level, also known as the data link or link level. The third level is called the packet level. Packets are sent to the network within the information frames of second level.

In a packet-switching network, the data to be sent is combined in a packet with addressing and control information. This results in an independent unit that can be sent through any suitable path in the network. Packets from many different users can share the same network routes and lines. X.25 uses the network user address to route both incoming and outgoing calls to the correct system.

In communication terminology, the computer or workstation that sends and receives data is known as data terminal equipment (DTE). The network equipment that is physically connected to the DTE is the data circuit-terminating equipment (DCE). When a user makes a call to another user over the X.25 network, one of the predefined number of logical channels is assigned to the call at each end. Each DTE includes a logical channel number in each packet sent. The number identifies the logical channel that connects the DTE with its DCE. The two logical channel numbers at two ends may be different, but each DTE needs to know only the number it assigned to the channel. When the two logical channels are assigned to a call, a virtual circuit is established from one DTE to the other by DCEs on the network. Each logical channel is either for outgoing calls only, incoming calls only, or two-way calls that are permanently connected. However, the virtual circuit is established only for two-way communication.

The virtual circuit may be either switched or permanent. A switched virtual circuit (SVC) is a virtual circuit that exists only for the duration of the call, act-

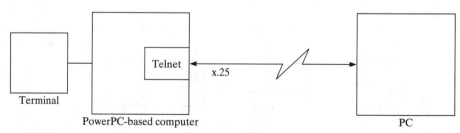

Figure 8.8 X.25 connection.

ing like a connection over a standard telephone network. A permanent virtual circuit (PVC) is like a leased line that can be established between two addresses, to save time in establishing calls. A PVC ties up a logical channel permanently.

Using X.25 on the PowerPC requires an X.25 adapter to connect to the X.25 network. Software requirements include the X.25 interface protocol code, real-time control microcode, applications programming interface, an X.25 device driver, and qualified logical link control (QLLC). X.25 commands which enable users to use the X.25 network without doing any application programming include:

Commands	Description
xcomms	Starts one of the other commands.
xtalk	Communicates with other systems and manages address lists for outgoing calls
xroute	Manages a routing list for incoming calls
xmanage	Displays status information for an X.25 port. Connects and disconnects an X.25 port. Gets statistics for an X.25 port.
xmonitor	Monitors the activity on an X.25 port.

8.1.3.8 Simple Network Management Protocol (SNMP)

The SNMP is used by network managers to troubleshoot, locate, and correct problems in a network. SNMP is also used by network hosts to exchange information used in management of networks.

In 1992, a security enhancement to SNMP was adopted, and an upgrade, known as SNMP version 2 (SNMP v2), was adopted in 1993. SNMP v2 runs on open systems interconnection-based networks as well as TCP/IP-based networks.

Network management for SNMP is based on a client-server model. The client agent is run on the local workstation that needs to be managed and used to contact one or more SNMP server agents that execute on remote machines, usually gateways. The server agent is a process that maintains certain databases for the host. Hosts involved in network management run a monitor process called *xgmon,* that generates requests for MIB (management information base) information and processes responses.

The MIB is a separate standard (from SNMP) that defines the set of variables and the semantics of each variable that SNMP servers maintain. The MIB database contains information pertinent to network management, which may be used to record the traffic statistics, error counts, and status of each connected network.

SNMP uses a formal specification language called Abstract Syntax Notation One (ASN.1) to define and specify the format of MIB variable names and messages. ASN.1 defines a hierarchical name space, so the name of each variable reflects its position in the hierarchy. The ASN.1 hierarchy carefully distributes authority to assign names to multiple organizations. The scheme allows many organizations to assign names concurrently while ensuring that the resulting names are unique and absolute.

Network management can be passive or active. Passive management involves the collection of statistical data so that network activity on each host can be profiled. Active network management, on the other hand, involves the use of a subset of the MIB variables that are designated read-write. The request sent to an SNMP server agent is accepted by the server, which performs the specified operations and returns a response to the requester. The SNMP server agent first parses the message sent by the client and translates it to internal form. SNMP then maps the MIB variable specification to the local data item that stores the needed information and then performs the fetch or store operations as requested. An information flow path illustrated in Fig. 8.9 shows how SNMP works in general.

For fetch operations, SNMP replaces the data area in the message with the new value that it has fetched. If more than one variable value was requested, SNMP fetches the value of each variable and replaces the value with the fetched value in the message. After all the specified operations are completed, the server translates the reply from its internal form to the external form and returns it to the client that requested the values.

8.1.3.9   Distributed Computing Environment (DCE)

DCE is a standardized approach to distributed computing that enables system administrators to create, use, support, and maintain distributed applications on a diverse network. DCE allows applications to exploit the potential resources in the network environment and thus improve the performance. Basic features of DCE include:

- Remote procedure call and presentation services
- Security services
- Management services

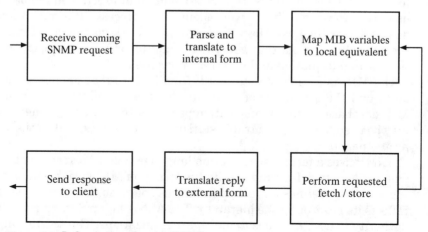

Figure 8.9 Information flow in SNMP.

RPC enables software developers to partition tasks in an application into separate procedure models that can be executed on different systems. It makes use of what are called threads to allow multiple sequential flows of execution within a single process. This feature provides better service availability by simultaneous handling multiple clients. The security services ensure against unauthorized access. Management services provide utilities to manage DCE.

DCE offers a whole suite of services, as seen in Fig. 8.10. The directory service assigns a unique name or attribute to a physical device, making it accessible from any location in the network. Within this paradigm, there are four components:

1. *DCE cell directory service* (CDS) stores names and attributes within a DCE cell, a group of systems administered as one entity.

2. *DCE global directory agent* (GDA) is a naming gateway connecting administrative domains through the X.500 worldwide directory service and domain name service (DNS).

3. *DCE global directory service* (GDS) is used to locate objects in a global environment.

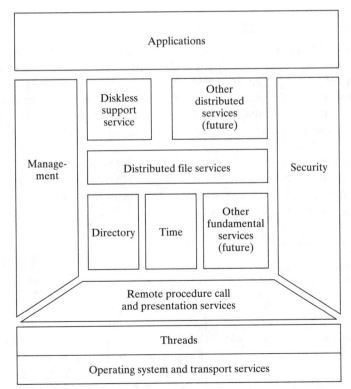

Figure 8.10 Distributed computing environment.

4. *X/Open directory service* (XDS) defines an application programming interface (API) that can be used to create, delete, modify, or search for directory service calls.

Several other services are also available, such as time services, which provide a consistent view of time. The distributed file system offers a consistent and unified view of all files in the distributed system. Diskless support service extends DCE to low-cost, diskless nodes.

A basic architectural difference between DCE and message I/O should be noted. DCE provides direct dialogue between the client and server application programs through RPCs, unlike message I/O where all interactions between the client and server applications are dependent on the communication service provider.

DCE for AIX is a layer between the AIX operating system and network and the distributed application (see Fig. 8.11). Built on a threads-based model, DCE provides support for remote procedure calls, the client functionality for cell directory service and security, time, and the basic distributed file system services.

DCE is used as a strategic base to build distributed applications, including on-line transaction processing (OLTP) for the AIX environment. Additionally, selected DCE interfaces and protocols are available on certain system application architecture (SAA) platforms.

8.1.3.10 Open Systems Interconnect (OSI)

In early 1977, ISO Technical Committee 97 on Information Processing formed a subcommittee on OSI to develop an architecture to serve as the reference for development of multivendor interconnectivity standards. However, the final ISO standard, ISO 7498, was not published until 1984. OSI is not concerned with the internal operations of individual systems; rather it is interested in promoting commonality and consistency among all standards related to systems interconnection.

The framework for standardization provided by OSI is based on the seven-layer OSI reference model (refer to Fig. 8.12). The OSI layers consists of the *physical* (transmission of an unstructured bit stream over a physical link); the *data link* (provides for the reliable transfer of data across the physical link);

Distributed applications
DCE
AIX and network services

Figure 8.11 DCE in relation to AIX.

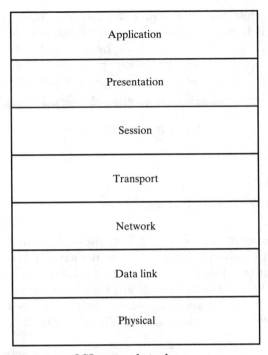

| Application |
| Presentation |
| Session |
| Transport |
| Network |
| Data link |
| Physical |

Figure 8.12 OSI protocol stack.

the *network* (provides a network connection path); *transport* (provides reliable, transparent transfer of data between end points); *session* (establishes, manages, and disconnects communicators); *presentation* (provides standardized application interface); and *application* (information processing applications including file-transfer protocol and network management).

OSI's primary contribution has been the identifying of functions that are necessary for effective network communication. And in conjunction with this contribution, the OSI conformance testing standards and the internationalized standardized profiles (ISPs) have enabled OSI to guarantee OSI-branded products as interoperable and compatible.

8.2 CONNECTIVITY

8.2.1 Connectivity with peer UNIX machines

Connectivity with peer nodes can be provided using the Basic Network Utilities programs (BNU) that are standard with the AIX regular distribution. BNU comprises a suite of utilities that are used to communicate with peer nodes. BNU is a version of UUCP and is often better known as UUCP in the traditional UNIX communities. The acronym UUCP stands for UNIX-to-UNIX Copy Program. It should be noted that, although the availability of the BNU or UUCP facility predates most networking suites, it is still one of the most widely used means of exchanging files across the Internet. Built in 1976 by Mike Lesk at AT&T Bell Labs, the research project became a de facto networking standard when it was shipped as part of the standard software distribution of UNIX Version 7 in 1977. An update was released in 1981. Although less sophisticated in terms of functionality, UUCP provides basic connectivity with peer machines over regular serial lines and does not require any additional network interface hardware.

UUCP performs the following primary functions:

- Electronic mail
- Transfer of files to and from remote systems
- Execution of commands on remote systems

UUCP is a store-and-forward network. That is, requests for mail forwarding, file transfers, or remote execution of commands are not executed immediately but are spooled for execution when communication is established between the two systems. Depending of how the configurations files have been set up, communication may be established immediately or may wait till a later time. Figure 8.13 presents a conceptual view of how UUCP works for forwarding electronic mail.

Although the suite of programs is referred to as UUCP, the actual UUCP program only participates in copying files. For mail handling, remote command execution, and other tasks, there are separate stand-alone program files (described later). Perhaps it would have been more appropriate to refer to the UUCP as UU because the name more clearly indicates that UUCP is a collection of many programs, all which have a name prefixed with the letters "uu." Referring to this suite of network utilities as BNU eliminates the misleading reference.

UUCP works in multiple steps. When mail is sent, a file transfer command is invoked, or a remote command execution request is issued, two things happen. First, a work file containing logistic information such as the name of the source file, name of the destination file, and command request type (for example, send file, receive file, or execute file) is created in a spooling directory on the PowerPC. The second phase involves starting a command called **uusched** to scan the contents of the work file, and subsequently invoking other programs like **uucico** if needed, to call another system, connect to it, and transfer the data in or out.

Requirements for BNU/UUCP installation are minimal. The simplest hardware requirement involves connecting a null-modem serial cable between the ports of two machines. A modem will be required at both ends if the connection is being made between two remote machines. There is no additional software requirement as such, but the software must be configured to define the machine name(s) to call or connect to, must place the phone call (if connecting to a remote machine over a modem), and optionally must specify when to call the remote machine to forward files and receive incoming files.

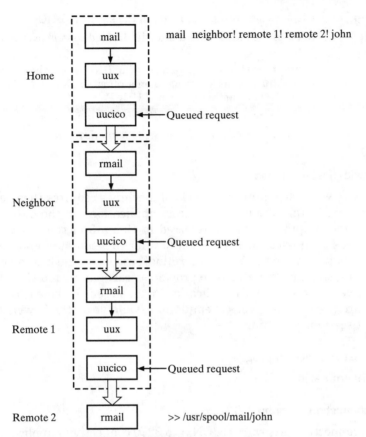

Figure 8.13 UUCP forwarding electronic mails.

Once UUCP/BNU is installed and configured, the following commands can be run by any AIX user to log in to remote systems, transfer files, run processes on remote systems, and report the status of jobs and transfers.

Command	*Description*
uucp	Copies file(s) to another AIX/UNIX system running BNU or another version of UUCP.
uuencode	Encodes a binary file.
uudecode	Decodes a binary file encoded by the **uuencode** command.
uuname	Provides information about peer systems accessible to the local system.
uupick	Completes the transfer of files sent by the **uuto** command.
uupoll	Forces a call to a remote system so queued jobs can be transferred.
uuq	Displays the BNU job queue.
uusend	Sends a file to a remote host that is running BNU or another version of UUCP.

uusnap	Displays a snapshot summary of the status of BNU.
uustat	Reports the status of and provides limited control over BNU operations.
uuto	Copies files to a peer system running BNU or another version of UUCP **uux.** Runs a command on a remote AIX or UNIX system running BNU or another version of UUCP.
ct	Dials a remote system and initiates a login process.
cu	Connects directly or indirectly to another system.

8.2.2 Connectivity with host machines

Connectivity with the mainframe world of machines requires the use of a software interface so that the user can access applications on the host. The hardware interface requirements are referred in Chap. 3 of this book. The term *emulator* has been used in this section to refer to a software application that allows the native system to mimic a terminal session on the host machine. The objective of using an emulator is to provide a transparent interface for a user on the PowerPC to work with applications resident on the host (Fig. 8.14).

There are two primary types of emulators available on the PowerPC to work with host sessions including:

- 3270 host connection program
- 3278/79 emulation

8.2.2.1 3270 host connection program (HCON)

The host connection program (HCON) is a 3270 connectivity application for the AIX environment. HCON emulates a subset of 327X functions and features, and allows end users at AIX terminals to connect to an IBM System/370 host and appear to the host as an attached IBM 3270 display terminal or printer. HCON facilitates file transfers between the workstation and the IBM System/370 host, allows printer emulation, and provides High-Level Language Application Programming Interface (HLLAPI) support for user-provided workstation applications to communicate with 3270 sessions. HCON connectivity can be:

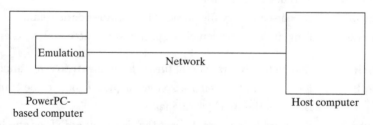

Figure 8.14 Connectivity with host.

- System network architecture (SNA) connection in a Type 2.1 low-entry networking (LEN) node attachment

- 5088/6098 graphics control unit attachment

- Distributed function terminal (DFT) SNA attachment to an IBM 3274/3174 or IBM 9370 workstation subsystem controller

- Transmission Control Protocol/Internet Protocol (TCP/IP) Telnet 3270 connection

HCON establishes multiple sessions with System/370 mainframes. Each session emulates either a 3278/79 display or a 3286/87 printer. A session emulating a display is a *display session*. A session emulating a printer is a *printer session*. HCON provides file transfer capabilities within display sessions. It also includes the HLLAPI to write programs that communicate with mainframe host programs.

Each HCON user can have up to 26 sessions, allowing one or more simultaneous invocations of sessions to communicate with one or more hosts using different session characteristics and communication protocols. The parameters defining the session characteristics are established by a *session profile*.

To communicate with a mainframe host, HCON uses one or more of the following:

- 3270 connection adapter in distributed function terminal (DFT) mode

- Host interface adapter (HIA)

- Group of adapters supported by System Network Architecture (SNA) Services/6000

- Group of adapters supported by Transmission Control Protocol/Internet Protocol (TCP/IP)

If the local system has more than one of these devices installed, users can implement different devices for different HCON sessions:

DFT sessions	Use the 3270 connection adapter. The 3270 connection adapter emulates a display (by establishing an SNA DFT or non-SNA DFT display session) or a printer (by establishing a non-SNA DFT printer session). The SNA Services/6000 is not required.
HIA sessions	Use the host interface adapter (HIA). The HIA emulates a display by establishing an HIA display session.
SNA stand-alone sessions	Use SNA Node Type 2.1 over SNA Services/6000. NO TAGHCON-supported adapters supported by SNA Services/6000 establish an SNA stand-alone printer session or SNA stand-alone display session.
TCP/IP sessions	Use TCP/IP with the appropriate adapters. HCON-supported adapters supported by TCP/IP emulate a 3270 display by establishing a TCP/IP display session.

The system can have any combination of supported adapters:

Each 3270 connection adapter supports up to five sessions.

HIA supports up to 16 sessions.

Each SNA Node T2.1 attachment supports up to 253 logical units (LUs) per connection.

For TCP/IP, the maximum number of sessions per connection depends upon the user's system resources.

8.2.2.2   3278/79 emulation (EM78)

The 3278/79 emulation (EM78) program allows your machine to imitate a 3278/79 device attached to a System 3270 computer. Emulators provide the functions of the device being emulated as if you were actually using that device. The emulator must be installed on your system.

The **em78** command invokes a 3278/79 emulation (EM78) session. At the beginning of an emulation session, the emulator acts as if you had just turned on a 3278/79 terminal. After you log in to the System 3270 host, you can run commands and programs from your workstation.

The **emrcv** and **emsend** commands upload and download files to and from a host, changing the format of the data in the files as you transfer them. Either an MVS/TSO host session or a VM/CMS host session can be specified during file transfer. For example, you can translate files from ASCII to EBCDIC or add or remove carriage-return characters.

You can customize the keyboard mapping, color, and field attributes for the EM78 emulator. To customize the emulator, you must edit a file following the EM78 customization file format and then install the changes with the **emkey** command.

8.2.3   Connectivity and access to PC-DOS

Using AIX Access for DOS Users (AADU), a product that provides transparent access to the AIX file system for PC-DOS users through the use of virtual drives, system administrators and programmers can use the PowerPC's disk space to store PC-DOS files. AADU allows PC-DOS users to share the AIX file system of the host machine without requiring knowledge of the AIX operating system. Access to printers on the PowerPC machine is also provided to PC-DOS users via network interface drivers. The minimum machine hardware requirements for AADU are 512 KB of physical memory and 1 MB of disk space on a PS/2, AT, or XT class machine that is equipped with an Ethernet, token-ring, or asynchronous serial connection. Performance is affected by the amount of memory and disk storage available on the PC-DOS. Software requirements call for DOS Version 3.3 or later and Microsoft Windows 3.1 or later. Figure 8.15 shows the connectivity layout of a PC-DOS and a PowerPC.

Standard AIX file permission modes are used by AADU to protect all the PC-DOS files stored on the AIX system disk. Users can selectively protect files and

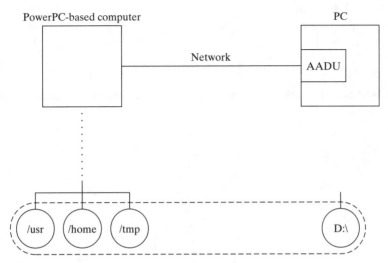

Figure 8.15 Connection with DOS-based PCs.

directories from other users. User management is responsible for evaluation, selection, and implementation of security features, administrative procedures, and communication facilities. Although files are accessible to users via the virtual drives, recognize that the AIX operating system will not be able to create file names which include PC-DOS graphic characters or use PC-DOS commands such as ASSIGN, FDISK, FORMAT, PRINT, SYS, BACKUP, RESTORE, JOIN, TREE, and SHARE on the virtual disk.

8.3   SUMMARY

Connectivity among systems must be maintained and fostered for smooth integration and operation of the wide variety of computers available to business and research communities. Standards must be complied with for the portability of application software systems and system networking. In an effort to emphasize the importance of open systems, this chapter has briefly reviewed the standards and standards groups shaping the details of open systems including ISO, ANSI, OSI, POSIX, DCE, TCP/IP, NFS, and AFS, among others. The ability of the PowerPC and the AIX operating system to interact with a variety of machines and other operating systems has also been discussed. The crucial elements of an open system—interoperability, portability, and integration—have been reviewed to demonstrate the ability of the PowerPC and its operating environment to interact with today's computing environment.

Design of AIX:
A PowerOpen Implementation

This chapter introduces a system perspective for the AIX based operating system. It introduces the kernel in light of its characteristic components, infrastructure, and communication mechanisms. Although some basic terms and concepts are reviewed, familiarity with "stock" UNIX is assumed.

9.1 COMPONENTS OF THE KERNEL

There have been references made about the fact that the AIX system supports the illusion that the processes have "life" and files have "places." These two entities, processes and files, are the central concepts in the AIX system model. A *file* (defined as a collection of bytes logically grouped together) and a *process* (defined as an instance of a program in its state of execution) together form an operational entity, in which the file is the piece of data and the process is the rule that acts upon the file. If the idea is extended further, it becomes evident that working with files involves devices and management of devices, while working with processes involves the management of processes. A logical block diagram of an AIX kernel displayed in Fig. 9.1 shows the two main subsystems for process and device management side-by-side. This well-known layout is similar to a traditional UNIX system. The vertical separation between the device management subsystem and the process management subsystem reflects their functional roles. The two horizontal separations emphasize the positioning of the functional components of AIX between the application level and the hardware level.

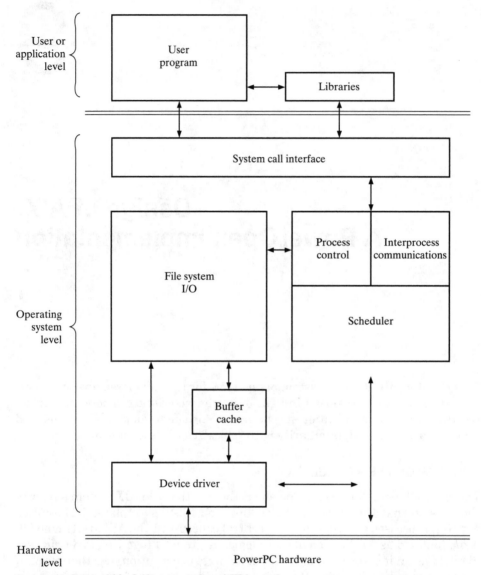

Figure 9.1 Logical block diagram of an AIX kernel.

The roles of each component are significant in their own ways as each affects the overall working of the operating system. User programs make use of libraries (using subroutine calls) to communicate with the kernel via *system calls*. Libraries are repositories for common routines that programs use to perform a task. They are linked with the programs at compile, load, or run time and become a part of the program. System calls are similar to ordinary functions in high-level languages like C. For the purpose of this discussion, they can be thought of as primitives that allow a program to enter the operating system. When a program enters the operating system, it accesses the file subsystem and/or the process subsystem. The *I/O subsystem* handles data flow and the file I/O aspect of program execution. It uses a buffered as well as a nonbuffered mode to interface with the I/O device drivers and coordinate file I/O. The *process subsystem,* on the other hand, handles the orchestration of processes. This orchestration is a top-level abstraction of all the tasks, including interprocess communication and process scheduling management.

9.2 Functions of the kernel

In generic operating system terminology, a *kernel* denotes a nucleus of software that plays the role of system orchestrator and provides facilities necessary for implementing system services. These services can be functions to access file systems, support for network protocols, or similar facilities.

From a structural perspective, the kernel is a single binary image that supervises all process management, scheduling, and I/O, using system calls to interface to the application world. The majority of the kernel source code is written in C, with a small amount in assembly language.

The kernel's responsibilities can be split up into the following functional domains: (1) task management and (2) I/O management.

9.3 KERNEL SERVICES

In order to understand how the numerous kernel services work, it is necessary to comprehend how the system calls operate.

9.3.1 System calls

Execution of a user process is divided into two levels: user and kernel. Whenever a user process requires an operating system service, it executes a system call. This system call performs a momentary *mode switch* from the *user mode* to the *kernel mode* in order to respond to the process's request (refer to Fig. 9.2). A mode switch is obligatory in order to make use of the privileged services that the kernel has access to, such as manipulation of the process status register. Although the kernel distinguishes one process from another by referencing its internal data structures, the underlying hardware has no clue about processes. The hardware merely views the system in terms of kernel mode and user mode. As illustrated in Fig. 9.3, a kernel is able to differentiate between processes P_1, P_2, P_3, and P_4 along the horizontal axis and the hardware distinguishes the mode of execution on the vertical axis. It should be understood that execution of a user process in two modes does not mean that there are two processes at any instant; it merely means that the kernel runs on behalf of the user process to handle allocation of resources, etc. For executing any simple program or command, mode switching happens more often than one would expect. Consider catenating a file called /tmp/foo and redi-

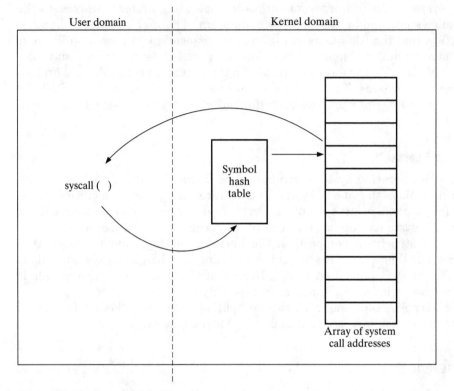

Figure 9.2 Mode switch in AIX.

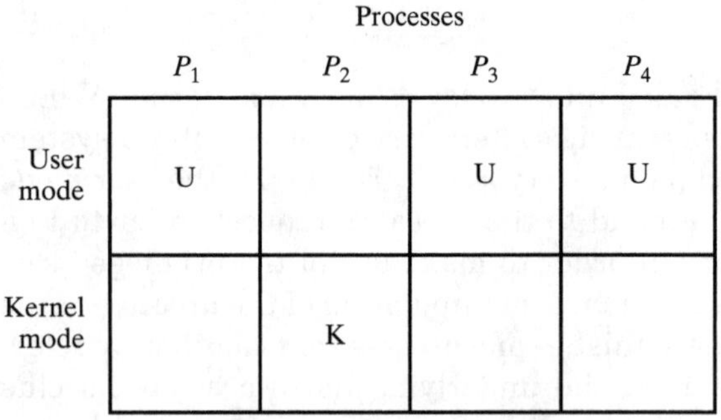

Processes

	P_1	P_2	P_3	P_4
User mode	U		U	U
Kernel mode		K		

Figure 9.3 Processes and modes of execution.

recting its contents to the terminal device /dev/tty01. The sequence of mode switches (system calls) that takes place is highlighted in boldfaced fonts within the algorithm that describes the example from the system perspective of AIX.

Command issued: cat /tmp/foo > /dev/tty01

Participating process	*Participant's action*
shell	**read** the command line
	parse the command line arguments
	fork a child process
	and **wait** for it to finish
child	**close** stdout and **open**/dev/tty01
	exit if open fails
	else **dup**/dev/tty01
child	**exec**/bin/cat
cat	**open**/tmp/foo
cat	**read**/tmp/foo
	write stdout (/dev/tty01)
cat	**exit** and **signal** the parent (the shell)
shell	**write** out a prompt for next command

This scenario of redirecting the contents of a file to a terminal device manifests several sets of underlying system calls. The process-related calls are *fork(), exec(), wait(), exit(),* and *signal().* File-related system calls used are *open(), dup(),* and *close().* The I/O-related system calls are *read()* and *write().* All of the system calls shown in this example are standard on traditional UNIX systems as well as AIX, and, hence, are not discussed in any further depth. When invoked from user programs, these system calls perform a mode switch, make use of the kernel services, and continue executing the user application.

Each mode switch from user mode to kernel mode can be categorized on the basis of the action that initiates it. There are two primary kinds of hardware and software actions that gain an entry into the kernel: (1) hardware interrupts and traps and (2) software interrupts and traps. System calls are referred to as being a special case of software interrupts. The CPU is allowed to be interrupted asynchronously. The occurrence of an interrupt normally causes the kernel to save its current context, service the interrupt, and then resume processing its current context.

Although system calls are invoked just like subroutines, there are some fundamental differences between them. It is necessary to reiterate that they run in the kernel mode when invoked. By doing so, they use certain kernel processes to perform miscellaneous asynchronous tasks. In addition to these basic traits, system calls on AIX are unique in the sense that they are pageable (with some restrictions). They are also preemptable by higher-priority processes to facilitate real-time processing support. Also, new system calls may be added dynamically. Recognize that adding a new system call essentially means extending the kernel by adding to its base set of kernel services.

9.3.2 Kernel facilities

AIX furnishes a set of routines that provide the run-time kernel environment to programs executing in kernel mode. This basic set of routines is referred to as *kernel facilities* or services. The programs that run in kernel mode are not conspicuously visible to the user, but they can be displayed using the **pstat** or **ps** commands, if required. Kernel services offered by AIX span a very wide range of functional areas. These services are primarily used by kernel extensions. The main categories of kernel services are shown in Fig. 9.4, and each is discussed in terms of its features, functions, and commonly used routines.

Process and exception management (P&EM) kernel services are provided by the base AIX kernel and are responsible for new kernel process creation, serialization of processes, and signal handling. In addition, certain traditional UNIX kernel services are also incorporated in here, in order to support ported code from other variants of UNIX and previous versions of AIX. Commonly used P&EM kernel services are:

creatp	Creates a new kernel process
initp	Initializes a kernel process after its creation
e_post	Notifies a process of the occurrence of event(s)
e_wait	Forces a process to wait for the occurrence of an event
wakeup	Activates processes sleeping on the specified channel
lockl	Imposes a lock to serialize access to a resource
unlockl	Releases a conventional process lock
setjmpx	Allows saving of the current execution state or context

Logical file system (LFS) services allow processes running in kernel mode to open and manipulate files in the same way that user-mode processes do. Since system calls can have data access limitations, a set of file system calls is provided with a kernel-only interface. Commonly used LFS kernel services are:

fp_open	Opens a regular file
fp_opendev	Opens a device special file
fp_close	Closes a file
fp_read	Performs a read operation on an open file
fp_write	Performs a write operation on an open file
fp_access	Checks for access permission to an open file
fp_fstat	Acquires the attributes of an open file
fp_ioctl	Issues a control command to an open file

Virtual file system (VFS) kernel services provide a standard interface and act as the basic building blocks for writing a virtual file system. They can be used to create and/or free *vnodes* across various file system types without having to worry about physical file system dependencies. VFS services that can be used across the various file system types to enable the logical file system to operate independently of the file system type are:

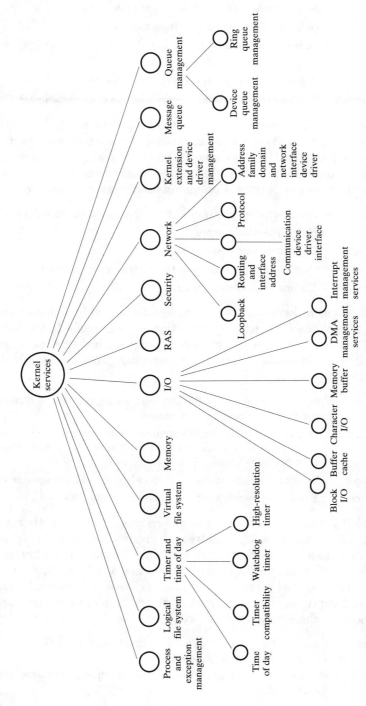

Figure 9.4 Taxonomy of kernel services.

gfsadd	Adds a file system type to the *gfs* table
gfsdel	Deletes a file system type from the *gfs* table
vn_get	Adds a vnode to the existing list of vnodes for the designated file system
vn_free	Frees a previously allocated vnode
vfsrele	Points to a virtual file system structure
lookupvp	Retrieves the vnode that corresponds to the named path

Memory kernel services offer the ability to dynamically allocate and free memory, pin and unpin processes, manipulate virtual memory objects, and move data between user and kernel memory. Data can also be moved between the kernel and an address space other than the current process address space, using a cross-memory service feature. Commonly used memory kernel services are:

xmalloc	Allocates memory (similar to *malloc* in the user mode)
xmfree	Frees allocated memory
init_heap	Initializes a new heap
pin	Pins the address range in the system address space
unpin	Unpins the address range

Message queue kernel services render the equivalent of normal message queuing functions for programs executing in user mode to the kernel extensions. The most frequent use for these message queue kernel services is as IPC channels to allied kernel processes or user-mode processes. Available message queue kernel services are:

kmsgctl	Queries the status of the message queue, sets selected status fields, or removes the queue, when needed
kmsgget	Opens or creates a message queue by traversing the message queue array to locate a possible match, and allocating a new queue structure if no match is found
kmsgsnd	Sends a message using a previously defined message queue
kmsgrcv	Receives a message from a message queue

Reliability-availability-serviceability services are collectively referred to as the RAS kernel services. They address the reliability, availability, and serviceability aspects of the software and hardware. Occurrences of errors and failures are recorded so that they may be examined at a later time. In the event of a fatal error, a kernel service called *panic* is invoked, which triggers a system dump and captures the data areas that are cataloged in the master dump table. Some of the RAS kernel services are:

panic	Crashes the system. (*Note:* It is invoked in the event of a catastrophic failure to perform a system dump.)
errsave	Writes an entry in the system error log when a hardware or software failure is detected.

Timing kernel services furnish an array of utilities that address various timing-related aspects of the global system. In order to structure their roles, the services are further grouped into four functional categories referred to as (1) *time-of-day* (TOD) kernel services, (2) *timer compatibility* kernel services, (3) *watchdog timer* kernel services, and (4) *high-resolution timer* (HRT) kernel services. Each type of service contributes to the time-and-timer-related issues of the kernel. The TOD service maintains the systemwide time-of-day timer values and can be used to access or set the time on the system. The timer compatibility service provides backward compatibility with earlier versions of AIX by handling application timeouts and the callout table entries. The watchdog timer service furnishes a low-overhead, moderate-resolution timer, which can be used to timestamp events without causing any serious overhead. The HRT services provide fine-grain timing functions that can be used to conduct critical measurements with as fine as 10 ms granularity. Following are the commonly used kernel services:

curtime	Reads the current time
ksettimer	Sets the systemwide TOD timer
tstart	Submits a timer request
tstop	Cancels a pending timer request
delay	Suspends the calling process for the specified number of timer ticks
talloc	Allocates a timer request block (structure is called *trb*)
tfree	Deallocates a timer request block

Security kernel services determine the privilege state of a process and, as a result, facilitate controlling the auditing system and access rights. There is only one security kernel service in the current implementation of AIX.

suser	Determines the privilege state of a process by checking to see if the process has any effective privilege

Network kernel services are a cluster of four types of network-related functions. The first is the *address family domain and network interface device driver* (AFD/NIDD) services, and this facilitates addition or removal of protocols and network interface drivers from network switching tables. The second set of functions is the *routing and interface address* kernel services, which support the network route addition and deletion functionalities for remote hosts and gateways. The third set of functions is referred to as the *loopback* kernel services; it allows debugging in a simulated environment for development of new network protocols without introducing network variables. The fourth function is the *protocol* kernel service, which enables a raw protocol handler to pass packets up through sockets so a protocol can be implemented in the user space. Finally, there is a set of functions called the *communications device handler interface* (CDHI) kernel service that provides a standardized interface between network interface drivers and AIX communications device drivers.
Commonly used Network kernel services are:

if_attach	Adds a network interface to the network interface list
if_detach	Removes a network interface from the network interface list

rtalloc	Allocates a route consisting of a destination address and a reference to a routing entry
rtfree	Frees the routing table entry by freeing the *mbuf* structure that is associated with the route
rtrequest	Carries out a request to alter the contents of the routing table
rtredirect	Forces a routing table entry to be redirected through a given gateway
net_attach	Opens a communications I/O device handler
net_detach	Closes a communications I/O device handler

I/O kernel services are better described as six separate categories: (1) *block* I/O services which enable asynchronous I/O transfers to take place in fixed-size blocks; (2) *buffer cache* services which manage user access to device drivers through block special files for file system compatibility services and mounts; (3) *character* I/O services that manage the read and write operations to character devices like keyboards, terminals, etc.; (4) *DMA management* services that coordinate the DMA operations between adapters and memory; (5) *interrupt management* services that enable and disable interrupt levels in the system; and, finally, (6) *memory buffer* services which provide facilities to acquire, release, and manipulate memory buffers.

Commonly used I/O kernel services are:

bread	Reads the specified block's data into a buffer.
bwrite	Writes the specified buffer's data.
getblk	Assigns a buffer to the specified block.
purblk	Purges the specified block from the buffer cache.
getc	Retrieves a character from a character list.
putc	Places a character at the end of a character list.
waitcfree	Checks the availability of a free character buffer.
m_get	Allocates a memory buffer from the memory buffer pool.
m_pullup	Shuffles an *mbuf* chain so that a given number of bytes is in contiguous memory in the data area of the head *mbuf* structure.
m_free	Frees an *mbuf* structure.
d_init	Initializes a DMA channel.
d_clear	Frees a DMA channel.
d_mask	Disables a DMA channel.
d_move	Provides a means of accessing the data while a DMA transfer is being performed on it. Since this service accesses the data through the same system hardware as that used to perform the DMA transfer, it can guarantee the data to be consistent.

device and ring queue kernel services are methods of queuing requests from one kernel process to another. They are based on a client-server model. These services primarily serve as compatibility structures for software ports from previous versions of the AIX operating system. Commonly used services are:

creatq	Creates a device queue
dstryq	Deletes the specified device queue
attchq	Creates a path to a device queue
detchq	Removes a path to a device queue
enque	Places a queue element into a specified device queue
deque	Removes an element from the device queue
waitq	Waits for a queue element to be placed on a device queue
queryi	Provides information about device queues
rqc	Creates a ring queue in the kernel heap
rqd	Deletes a ring queue from the kernel queue
rqputw	Puts a queue element on the specified ring queue
rqgetw	Returns the next element from the specified ring queue

Device driver management/kernel extension services include general purpose kernel loading and binding services and device driver binding services. Commonly used services are:

devswadd	Adds a device entry to the device switch table
devswdel	Removes a device driver entry from the device switch table
iostadd	Registers an I/O statistics structure used for updating I/O statistics reported by the *iostat* facility (covered in Chap. 8)
pio_assist	Provides a programmed I/O exception handling mechanism for routines performing programmed I/O
uexadd	Adds a systemwide exception handler for catching user-mode process exceptions
uexdel	Deletes a previously added systemwide exception handler

A kernel service, in general, can either be called in both the process and the interrupt environments or exclusively in the process environment. Table 9.1 provides the names of the available kernel services under AIX, along with the environment from which they can be called.

9.4 DISTINGUISHING FEATURES OF THE AIX KERNEL

The AIX kernel distinguishes itself from traditional UNIX systems by virtue of its unique characteristics. Although its infrastructure is based upon a System V Version 2 kernel, a myriad of characteristic features sets it apart from traditional UNIX systems.

The kernel structure in AIX has been extended to support *preemption* and *real-time processing* capabilities. The second distinguishing feature of the AIX operating system is that its kernel is *pageable*. The next noteworthy feature is its virtual memory management scheme, which provides support for an exceedingly large address space. Additionally, support for a *dynamic load* facility in AIX is adopted to allow parts of programs and kernel extensions to be

TABLE 9.1 Kernel Services

Command	Process environment	Interrupt environment	Command	Process environment	Interrupt environment
ackque	✓		devswadd	✓	
add_arp_iftype	✓	✓	devswdel	✓	
add_domain_af	✓	✓	devswqry	✓	✓
add_input_type	✓	✓	dmp_add	✓	
add_netisr	✓	✓	dmp_del	✓	
add_netopt	✓	✓	dmp_prinit	✓	
as_att	✓		dstryd	✓	
as_det	✓		DTOM *macro*	✓	✓
attchq	✓		epost	✓	✓
audit_svcbcopy	✓		e_sleep	✓	
audit_svcfinis	✓		e_sleepl	✓	
audit_svcstart	✓		e_wait	✓	
bawrite	✓		e_wakeup	✓	✓
bdwrite	✓	✓	enque	✓	
bflush	✓		errsave	✓	✓
binval	✓		find_arp_iftype	✓	✓
blkflush	✓		find_input_af	✓	✓
bread	✓		find_input_type	✓	✓
breada	✓		fp_access	✓	
brelse	✓	✓	fp_close	✓	
bwrite	✓		fp_fstat	✓	
canclq	✓		fp_getdevno	✓	
cfgnadd	✓		fp_getf	✓	
cfgndel	✓		fp_hold	✓	
clrbuf	✓	✓	fp_ioctl	✓	
clrjmpx	✓	✓	fp_lseek	✓	
copyin	✓		fp_open	✓	
copyinstr	✓		fp_opendev	✓	
copyout	✓		fp_poll	✓	
creatd	✓		fp_read	✓	
creatp	✓		fp_readv	✓	
creatq	✓		fp_rwuio	✓	
curtime	✓	✓	fp_select	✓	
d_align	✓	✓	fp_write	✓	
d_cflush	✓	✓	fp_writev	✓	
d_clear	✓	✓	fubyte	✓	
d_complete	✓	✓	fubyte	✓	
d_init	✓	✓	fuword	✓	
d_mask	✓	✓	getadsp	✓	
d_master	✓	✓	getblk	✓	
d_move	✓	✓	getc	✓	✓
d_roundup	✓	✓	getcb	✓	✓
d_slave	✓	✓	getcbp	✓	✓
d_unmask	✓	✓	getcf	✓	✓
del_arp_iftype	✓	✓	getcx	✓	✓
del_domain_af	✓	✓	geteblk	✓	
del_input_type	✓	✓	geterror	✓	✓
del_netisr	✓	✓	getexcept	✓	✓
del_netopt	✓	✓	getpid	✓	✓
delay	✓		getppidx	✓	
deque	✓		getuerror	✓	
detchq	✓		gfsadd	✓	
devdump	✓	✓	gfsdel	✓	
devstrat	✓	✓	i_clear	✓	

TABLE 9.1   Kernel Services (*Continued*)

Command	Process environment	Interrupt environment	Command	Process environment	Interrupt environment
i_disable	✓	✓	m_getclustm	✓	✓
i_enable	✓	✓	m_gethdr	✓	✓
i_init	✓		M_HASCL *macro*	✓	✓
i_mask	✓	✓	m_pullup	✓	✓
i_reset	✓	✓	m_reg	✓	
i_sched	✓	✓	MTOCL *macro*	✓	✓
i_unmask	✓	✓	MTOD *macro*	✓	✓
if_attach	✓	✓	M_XMEMD *macro*	✓	✓
if_detach	✓	✓	net_attach	✓	
if_down	✓	✓	net_detach	✓	
if_nostat	✓	✓	net_error	✓	✓
ifa_ifwithaddr	✓	✓	net_sleep	✓	
ifa_ifdstwithaddr	✓	✓	net_start	✓	
ifa_ifwithnet	✓	✓	net_start_done	✓	✓
ifunit	✓	✓	net_wakeup	✓	✓
init_heap	✓		net_xmit	✓	✓
initp	✓		net_xmit_trace	✓	✓
io_att	✓	✓	NLuprintf	✓	
io_det	✓	✓	panic	✓	✓
iodone	✓	✓	peekq	✓	✓
iostadd	✓		pfctlinput	✓	✓
iostdel	✓		pffindproto	✓	✓
iowait	✓		pidsig	✓	✓
kgethostname	✓	✓	pgsignal	✓	✓
kgettickd	✓	✓	pin	✓	
kmod_entrypt	✓		pincf	✓	
kmod_load	✓		pincode	✓	
kmod_unload	✓		pinu	✓	
kmsgctl	✓		pio_assist	✓	✓
kmsgget	✓		prochadd	✓	
kmsgsnd	✓		prochdel	✓	
ksettickd	✓		purblk	✓	
ksettimer	✓		putc	✓	✓
lockl	✓		putcb	✓	✓
loifp	✓	✓	putcbp	✓	✓
longjmpx	✓	✓	putcf	✓	✓
lookupvp	✓		putcfl	✓	✓
looutput	✓	✓	putcx	✓	✓
m_adj	✓	✓	qryds	✓	
m_cat	✓	✓	queryd	✓	
m_clattach	✓	✓	queryi	✓	✓
m_clget *macro*	✓	✓	queryp	✓	
m_clgetm	✓	✓	raw_input	✓	✓
m_clgetx	✓	✓	raw_usrreq	✓	✓
m_collapse	✓	✓	readq	✓	
m_copy *macro*	✓	✓	rqc	✓	
m_copydata	✓	✓	trqd	✓	
m_copym	✓	✓	rqgetw	✓	
m_dereg	✓		rqputw	✓	
m_free	✓	✓	rtalloc	✓	✓
m_freem	✓	✓	rtfree	✓	✓
m_get	✓	✓	rtinit	✓	✓
m_getclr	✓	✓	rtedirect	✓	✓
m_getclust *macro*	✓	✓	rtrequest	✓	✓

TABLE 9.1   Kernel Services (*Continued*)

Command	Process environment	Interrupt environment	Command	Process environment	Interrupt environment
schednetisr	✔	✔	vfsrele	✔	
selnotify	✔	✔	vm_att	✔	✔
setjmpx	✔	✔	vm_cflush	✔	
setpinit	✔	✔	vm_det	✔	✔
setuerror	✔		vm_handle	✔	
sig_chk	✔		vm_makep	✔	
sleep	✔		vm_mount	✔	
subyte	✔		vm_move	✔	
suser	✔		vm_protectp	✔	
suword	✔		vm_qmodify	✔	
talloc	✔		vm_release	✔	
tfree	✔	✔	vm_releasep	✔	
timeout	✔	✔	vm_unmount	✔	
timeoutcf	✔		vm_write	✔	
trcgenk	✔	✔	vm_writep	✔	
trcgenkt	✔	✔	vms_create	✔	
tstart	✔	✔	vms_delete	✔	
tstop	✔	✔	vms_iowait	✔	
uexadd	✔		vn_free	✔	
uexblock	✔	✔	vn_get	✔	
uexclear	✔	✔	w_clear	✔	✔
uexdel	✔		w_init	✔	✔
uiomove	✔		w_start	✔	✔
unlockl	✔		w_stop	✔	✔
unpin	✔	✔	waitcfree	✔	
unpincode	✔		waitq	✔	
unpinu	✔	✔	wakeup	✔	✔
uprintf	✔		xmalloc	✔	
untimeout	✔	✔	xmattach	✔	
uphysio	✔		xmdetach	✔	✔
ureadc	✔		xmemdma	✔	✔
uwritec	✔		xmemin	✔	✔
vec_clear	✔		xmemout	✔	
vec_init	✔		xmfree	✔	

dynamically loaded without intervention. Also, a true system management architecture is implemented to provide definition and management of the complex relationships of the objects in the system. In addition to the kernel structure modifications and support for *threads,* some of the key components, such as the file system, have been enhanced to provide greater reliability. The storage subsystem generalizes the storage space concept by implementing *logical volumes,* and optimizes the storage capacity by implementing *fragments.* The I/O subsystem of AIX supports functions like *mapped files, prepaging, data pacing,* and *asynchronous I/O.* Observe that, while a lot of the AIX kernel essentially adheres to the same concepts as traditional UNIX systems, much of it has been augmented to provide a superior environment above and beyond what UNIX had demonstrated before.

9.5 EXTENDING THE KERNEL

The kernel can be expanded by adding *kernel extensions.* This is a unique characteristic of AIX in which kernel extensions can be added to an operational environment without preempting any ongoing activity. Attributes such as new device drivers, system calls, kernel services, and private kernel routines can be added to the existing kernel to extend its functions. The direct benefit of being able to customize the kernel allows implementation of new timer services, customized interrupt handlers, pinned shared memory segments, and other useful facilities. Figure 9.5 demonstrates the different types of kernel extensions that can be implemented.

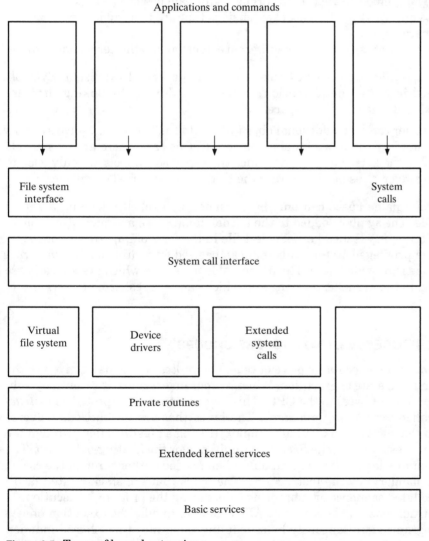

Figure 9.5 Types of kernel extensions.

Extending the kernel essentially means the same thing as altering the kernel. As useful as this feature is when correctly implemented, it can be equally as disadvantageous if exercised without caution. Any process executing in the user mode can extend (or alter) the kernel, provided it has *root* privilege. The operation is done by invoking a privileged subroutine called *sysconfig*. The other way of altering the kernel configuration is by changing the tunable parameters. Values of the tunable parameters, when modified, update the information in the ODM (object data manager) database.

The set of base kernel services available under AIX can be used by the kernel extensions. A kernel extension knows about these services by importing the symbols that are to be added to the kernel name space during the binding phase. The symbols are specified through a file called `kernex.exp`. This file also works as an export file for kernel extensions that are to be added to the kernel name space.

There are two ways to load a new kernel extension into the kernel name space:

1. The *sysconfig* routine can be used to load the kernel extension. Symbols defined in the kernel extension's exports file during the linking time are added to the kernel name space.

2. The loader can load additional object files into the kernel to resolve symbols referenced by the new kernel extension. In this case, there are no symbols added to the kernel name space since the exported symbols are only used to resolve references needed during the load of a new kernel extension.

The kernel name space can only be expanded by explicitly loading a kernel object file. The symbols added to the kernel name space are made available to any subsequently loaded kernel object file in the form of imported symbols.

A set of privileged system calls that can be used for writing one's own kernel extensions is provided here. The list in Table 9.2 shows which system calls are available to the kernel extensions and which ones are restricted to kernel processes.

9.6   PROGRAMS, PROCESSES, AND PROCESS GROUPS

A *program* is an executable piece of code, and *process* is the name given to the program in its state of execution. When a program executes, it essentially submits a pattern of bytes to the CPU. This byte stream is interpreted as *instructions* (called *text*), *data,* and *stack*. The bytes that are instructions traverse through the maze of the CPU subcomplex, tracing a pipelined flow through the branch processing unit, the fixed-point unit, and/or the floating-point unit. The bytes that are data are made available when needed (either through the cache, TLB, or memory) by the instructions. The bytes that are stack-related facilitate a collated sequence of subroutine calls during the program's execution.

Like traditional UNIX systems, AIX is able to handle the execution of several programs simultaneously by scheduling them in a time-shared manner. Just as several programs may be executed as multiple processes, multiple pro-

TABLE 9.2   System Calls

System calls	Kernel extensions	Kernel processes	System calls	Kernel extensions	Kernel processes
disclaim		✔	sethostid	✔	✔
getdomainname		✔	sethostname		✔
getgidx	✔	✔	setpgid	✔	✔
getgroups		✔	setpgrp	✔	✔
gethostid	✔	✔	setpri	✔	✔
gethostname		✔	setpriority	✔	✔
getpeername		✔	setreuid	✔	✔
getpgrp	✔	✔	setrlimit		✔
getppid	✔	✔	setsid	✔	✔
getpri	✔	✔	settimer		✔
getpriority	✔	✔	setuid	✔	✔
getrlimit		✔	setuidx	✔	✔
getrusage		✔	shmat		✔
getsockname		✔	shmctl		✔
getsockopt		✔	shmdt		✔
gettimer		✔	shmget		✔
getuidx	✔	✔	sigaction		✔
resabs		✔	sigprocmask		✔
resinc		✔	sigstack		✔
restimer		✔	sigsuspend		✔
semctl		✔	sysconfig		✔
semget	✔	✔	times		✔
semop		✔	ulimit	✔	✔
setdomainname		✔	umask	✔	✔
seteuid	✔	✔	uname		✔
setgid	✔	✔	unamex		✔
setgidx	✔	✔	usrinfo		✔
setgroups		✔	utimes		✔

cesses can also execute a copy of a single program. Since the sequence of instructions in an individual process is self-contained, one process does not cross over or violate another process's private space. When and if processes do need to communicate with each other, they do so via system calls.

An executable program is created by compiling a high-level language or assembly language source code. The process entity is created using system calls. The *fork* system call is the primary vehicle for creating user processes under UNIX and AIX systems. Every time a *fork* system call creates a new process, it invokes an internal routine called *newproc* to allocate and initialize a new *proc* structure. Subsequently, another internal routine, *procdup,* is invoked to create a new child process that is a duplicate of the caller (parent) process. Recognize that a parent may have more than one child. However, the converse is not true; a child cannot have more than one parent. The operating system tracks each process by a unique tag called the process identification number or *pid,* which is assigned to a newly created process as soon as it is created. As in the case of human reproduction, where a child inherits its parents' traits, the genealogy of inheritance in the case of process creation follows the same principle. A child process duplicates all of its parent's characteristics, except for the process identification number (*pid*).

An executable program is loaded into memory for execution using the *exec* system call. Once loaded, the program becomes a process and begins executing. During its execution, the process changes states constantly, depending on whether it is active or waiting with regard to the other processes on the system. It is often easier to think about processes being in a state of dynamic equilibrium. Every time a process changes its state, it follows a well-defined set of rules, as illustrated by the state transition digraph in Fig. 9.6. The nodes in the directed graph represent the permissible states that the process can assume. The edges in the graph represent the events in a process's state change. How does one determine what state transitions are permitted? A state transition between two states is legal as long as there is an edge from the first state to the second state.

A process is terminated using the *exit* system call. Usually the parent is notified upon the termination of a process. If a process needs to suspend execution until one of its child processes has terminated, it may do so using the *wait* system call. Sometimes a variation of *wait* is used, called *wait3,* which allows the parent process to acquire information about the cause of child process termination and resource utilization during its life span.

These mechanisms for process creation, suspension, and termination form the basics of how processes operate under AIX. Figure 9.7 illustrates the effect that *fork, exec, wait,* and *exit* have on the fate of a process. In fact, to execute any program on AIX, one has to make use of the *exec* system call (in one of its six variations). In a simple example of a user executing the *ls* command, the command language interpreter (i.e., the shell) first *fork*s off a child process, which subsequently *exec*s to overlay its image with that of the new program, *ls*. *ls* completes execution and exits thereafter; consequently, the parent process (the shell), whose execution was halted until now, comes out of the *wait* state.

Processes under AIX are organized into *process groups*. It is a term applied to a group of processes that are related. Typically, a set of processes under a process group have the same parent and, very often, they are associated with the same terminal. Process groups provide a means of communicating with a collection of related processes. The system never changes the process group of a process that has one. However, a new process group can be assigned to any process when there is a need to deliberately dissociate a process from its default process group. This is done with the help of a system call called *setpgrp*. Disassociating a process from its process group is a common practice in the writing of daemons or programs that need to remain detached from terminal(s).

9.7   AIX NOTIFIERS

AIX provides a number of ways to inform itself and the rest of the system about the occurrence of miscellaneous events. There are three primarily vehicles for notification: *signals,* interrupts, and *traps*.

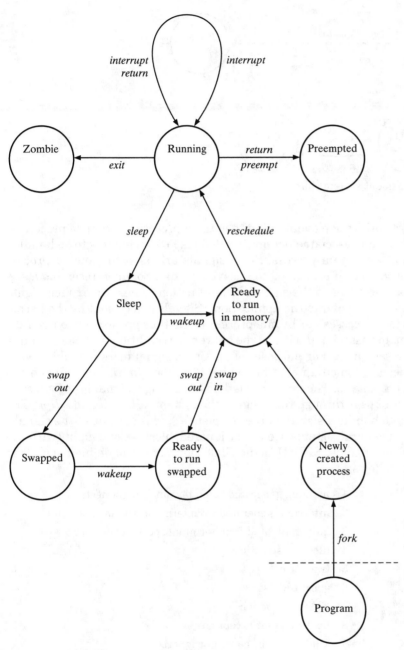

Figure 9.6 Digraph showing state transitions.

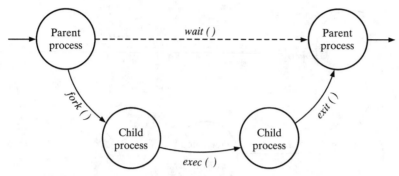

Figure 9.7 Process management system calls.

Signals are notification events used to notify a process or group of processes. Each signal has an associated action that defines how a signal is to be handled when it is delivered to a process. Since signals are asynchronous, a process never knows when or if it is going to receive a signal. So, upon receiving a signal, a process succumbs to the signal's default action (unless an explicit signal handler has been coded into the application). Signals can be sent by the kernel to a process (or processes), or by one process to another process (or to itself).

Every signal is associated with a type of event or condition and has a unique number representing it. For purposes of making a signal more readable, every signal has been assigned a name tag which is defined in a header file on the system called `signal.h`. The primary method of posting a signal for process(es) and process groups is through the usage of the system calls, *kill* and *killpg*. The method used to handle a signal on the recipient's side is specific to the signal's action. But, in general, signals are either ignored, blocked, or caught (with the exception of two signals, SIGKILL and SIGSTOP). A list of defined signals is presented as follows:*

SIGHUP	1	hangup, generated when terminal disconnects
SIGINT	2	interrupt, generated from terminal special character
SIGQUIT	3	quit, generated from terminal special character
SIGILL	4	illegal instruction
SIGTRAP	5	trace trap
SIGABRT	6	abort process
SIGEMT	7	EMT instruction
SIGFPE	8	floating-point exception
SIGKILL	9	kill (cannot be caught or ignored)
SIGBUS	10	bus error (specification exception)
SIGSEGV	11	segmentation violation

---

* The undefined values between 1 and 63 are reserved for future use.

SIGSYS	12	bad argument to system call
SIGPIPE	13	write on a *pipe* with no one to read it
SIGALRM	14	alarm clock timeout
SIGTERM	15	software termination signal
SIGURG	16	urgent contention on I/O channel
SIGSTOP	17	stop (cannot be caught or ignored)
SIGTSTP	18	interactive stop
SIGCONT	19	continue (cannot be caught or ignored)
SIGCHLD	20	sent to the parent process on child stop or exit
SIGTTIN	21	background read attempted from control terminal
SIGTTOU	22	background write attempted to control terminal
SIGIO	23	I/O possible, or completed
SIGXCPU	24	CPU time limit exceeded
SIGXFSZ	25	file size limit exceeded
SIGMSG	27	input data is in the HFT ring buffer
SIGWINCH	28	window size changed
SIGPWR	29	power-fail restart
SIGUSR1	30	user defined signal 1
SIGUSR2	31	user defined signal 2
SIGPROF	32	profiling time alarm
SIGDANGER	33	system crash imminent; free up some page space
SIGVTALRM	34	virtual time alarm
SIGMIGRATE	35	migrate process
SIGPRE	36	programming exception
SIGVIRT	37	AIX virtual time alarm
SIGALRM1	38	m:n condition variables
SIGWAITING	39	m:n scheduling
SIGKAP	60	keep alive poll from native keyboard (same as SIGGRANT)
SIGRETRACT	61	HFT monitor mode should be relinquished
SIGSOUND	62	HFT sound control has completed
SIGSAK	63	secure attention key

Interrupts are asynchronous events that are generated by the kernel or a device. The name is so given to them as they indeed "interrupt" the execution of the current process. When a process is preempted, the control is transferred to a special set of routines in the kernel called interrupt handlers. Interrupt handler routines service the interrupt and, after completion, transfer control back to the current process to continue execution.

Traps are synchronous events that are normally caused by the system hardware. As in the case of interrupts, a process may not decide how to react to the trap. Control is passed on to trap handlers in the kernel and the trap handler code takes control. In the case of a trap, a process may or may not resume execution, depending on the nature of the trap. There is a another type of notifier, *exceptions,* which are also synchronous events like the traps. They directly relate to the currently executing instruction. A common example is a divide-by-zero error. The only notable difference between exceptions and traps is in the resulting handler code modules.

9.8   INTERNAL REPRESENTATION OF FILES

AIX features a variety of files. The word *file* is so generic that one cannot be sure if a file is a piece of data on disk or the disk itself. Since the early days of UNIX, one of its hallmarks has been to treat files, disks, terminals, etc. the same way. The same is still true today. As much as this abstraction facilitates the portability of a UNIX system and application software, it can also confuse users. This section describes the different file types and explains how the kernel handles access to files.

9.8.1   File types

A *regular file* in AIX is not different from that in traditional UNIX systems. It is just a sequence of bytes with one or more names. A file can be created using either the *open* or *creat* system calls, and can be written to or read from using the basic *read* or *write* system calls. Directories that organize files hierarchically are no different than regular files, except they have a structure imposed on them by the system. They are commonly referred to as *directory files.*

AIX also supports two other file types: *pipes* and *device special files.* Pipes are like regular files and data is stored in them in the same manner as in the case of regular files. But they differ from regular files in that their data is ephemeral. The contents, being transient in nature, can only be read in a first-in first-out (FIFO) manner. Also, once the data is read from the pipe, the data disappears and cannot be read again. Pipes are useful in a variety of applications where a transient data stream makes more sense than a regular file, or in a situation where arbitrary processes need to be communicated with, even though one does not know the process(es) at the other end of the pipe (refer Fig. 9.8).

Hardware devices on AIX and other UNIX systems have file names and can be accessed by the same system calls that are used for regular files. The jargon used to refer to these devices is *device special files.* All device special files specify devices and, therefore, their file inodes do not reference any data. Instead, the inode indicates the device type and its logical unit number. Direct reference to these device special files is primarily made by the kernel. Users and applications never have to worry about these dependencies. Even the kernel does not care much about the device-specific dependencies—most dependencies are segregated in the device drivers. The kernel completely insulates the device dependencies from application programs.

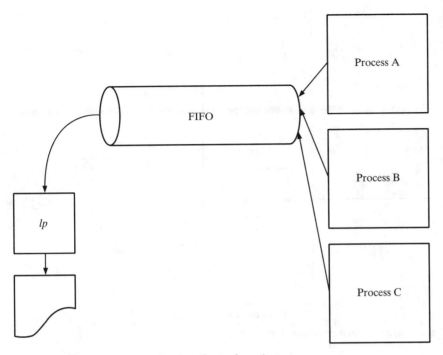

Figure 9.8 Process communicating through a pipe.

9.8.2   Inode and in-core inodes

The internal representation of a file on a UNIX system is specified in an *index block* (sometimes called an *index node*) which contains the description of the disk layout of the file data and allied information such as permissions and ownerships. The term *index node* has been abbreviated to *inode* over the years, and today most of the UNIX community knows it by this shortened name. This inode is the most precious structure as far as files are concerned. It holds information describing access permissions, ownership of the file, timestamps marking last modification and access times for the file, and an array of indices that point to the data blocks for the file. In essence, it contains all the pertinent information about the file, except for the file name. Initially, inodes exist in a static form on disk. Thereafter, they are read into an in-core inode table and remain resident in memory (see Fig. 9.9). Whenever a new file is created, an unused inode is assigned to it.

9.8.3   File links

In general, there is a one-to-one mapping (i.e., a single link) between a file and its referenced inode. But the file may have multiple names in the file system referencing it. This is the same as saying that multiple directories in the same file system may reference a file by multiple names. This is done by having the directory entry create a *hard link* of a file name to the inode that describes its

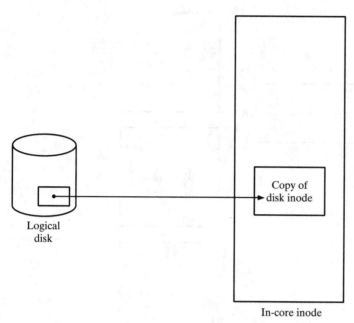

Figure 9.9 Two different representations of the same inode.

contents. In the case of a file having multiple names, all of the hard links map back into the same inode as shown in Fig. 9.10. Note that the reference count in the figure, as a result of this hard link, is 2.

The other kind of link is a *soft link* or a *symbolic link,* which uses a new inode for the file or directory being linked. It is treated like a regular file by the system, rather than as part of the file system structure. Therefore, this kind of link can point at files across file systems. A soft link is implemented as a file that contains a path name. The way it works is that the contents of the link are prepended to the rest of the path name, and this name is interpreted to yield the resulting path name.

The advantage of a soft link over a hard link is that a soft link can refer to a directory file or to a regular file on a different file system, whereas a hard link can only refer to regular files within the same file system. In contrast, the advantage of a hard link over a soft link is performance; resolving soft links are significantly slower because of housekeeping checks that have to be performed to ensure there are no loops in the file system resulting from the erroneous use of soft links.

9.8.4 Files to file system relationship

As far as accessing data is concerned, each inode contains eight pointers which point directly to data blocks. Each data block is 4 KB in size. For larger files, the inode contains a pointer which points to a block of indirect pointers; this block contains 1024 pointers which, in turn, point to data blocks. For even

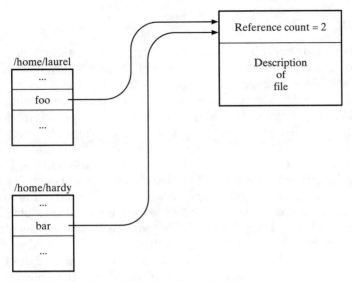

Invoking "ls-li" in hardy's directory shows:

```
399   -rwxr--r--   2   hardy   7512   Aug 15   07:35   bar
                      ↑
                  reference
                  count = 2
```

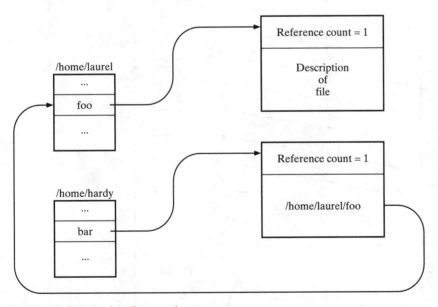

Invoking "ls-li" in hardy's directory shows:

```
568   -rwxr--r--   1   hardy   36   Jan 26   06:45   bar  →   /home/laurel/foo
                      ↑
                  reference
                  count = 1
```

Figure 9.10 Hard and soft file links.

larger files, the inode contains a pointer which points to a block of pointers (1024), each of which points to a further block of pointers (512), each of which points to a data block. Figure 9.11 represents the structural layout of how data block addresses are stored and accessed in the inode, depending on the size of the file. In principle, this single, double, and triple indirect access method can be extended to handle quadruple and quintuple indirect blocks, but the current structure has sufficed in practice and no immediate extension is deemed necessary, keeping in mind the current requirements of file sizes demanded by the computer industry. The size of data blocks is usually consistent within a file system, but may vary between two dissimilar file systems. For example, the size of each data block on the native AIX file system is 4 KB, whereas each data block of the CD-ROM file system is 512 bytes. Besides data blocks, a file system also contains what is called a *superblock* to describe the state of the file system. It contains information about the size of the file system, the number of inodes, the list of free inodes, and other housekeeping data.

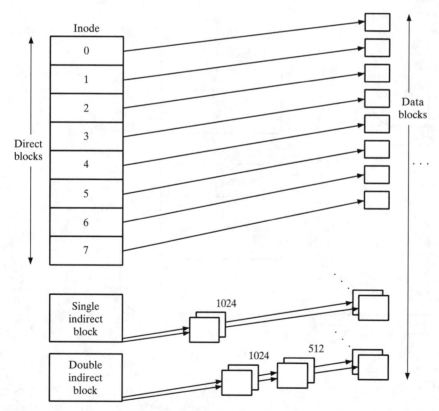

Figure 9.11 Three schemes for storing data block addresses, depending on the size of the file.

From the perspective of the kernel, there are three primary data structures associated with every opened file on the system:

- the file table
- the in-core inode table
- the user file descriptor table

The first two tables are global structures, while the third one is local to a user process. The user file descriptor table is organized using the file descriptors associated with opened files of that process as indices to each cell. By default, three file descriptors are assigned for every process in order to support the standard input (*stdin*), standard output (*stdout*), and standard error (*stderr*) streams. Whenever a file is opened by a process for reading or writing, a new entry is entered into this table. Each entry of this user file descriptor table indexes into the file table, which maintains the byte offset in the file where the subsequent read/write will start. This file table, in turn, points to the in-core inode table. Each entry of the in-core inode table is a generic inode and is rightfully referred to as a *gnode*. It is this gnode that locates the whereabouts of the data in the file. The three-step linkage of the tables for a traditional UNIX system is shown in Fig. 9.12. In the case of AIX, the file table to the in-core inode table mapping is further abstracted by indexing into a virtual file system structure called *vnode*, seen in Fig. 9.13. This abstraction of virtual inodes or vnodes allows the system to deal with remotely mounted non-AIX and non-UNIX file systems.

9.9   BUFFER CACHE

The design of the UNIX file systems implies a lot of disk I/O. If the UNIX kernel were really to perform every implied disk transfer, the CPU would be idling constantly, waiting for I/O. To address this issue, the kernel allocates a pool of buffers, called the *buffer cache*.* Its intent is twofold. The first is to minimize frequency of disk access by buffering read/write requests, and the second is to act as a cache of recently used disk blocks. A buffer cache is composed of two parts: (1) a *data buffer* that contains the disk I/O data and (2) a *buffer header* that points to the data array buffer. The buffer header also contains a (logical) device number field and a block number field that uniquely identifies the buffer, along with a status field summarizing the current status of the buffer, as seen in Fig. 9.14. Individual buffer headers are linked together in a buffer pool and remain connected through a doubly linked list.

The overall significance of the buffer cache has diminished in AIX, since AIX uses *mapped files* in its augmented file system. This concept of mapped files

---

* The buffer cache is a software data structure and should not be confused with the hardware caches.

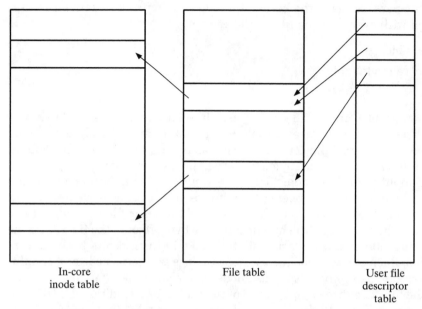

Figure 9.12 Three-step linkage and relationship of in-core inode table, file table, and user file descriptor table in UNIX.

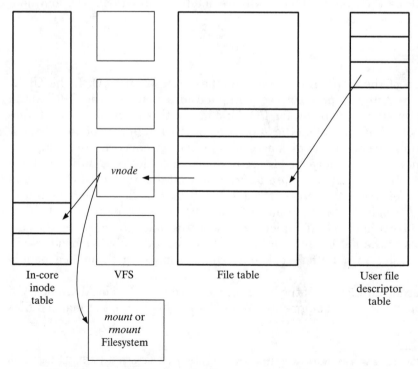

Figure 9.13 Four-step linkage and relationship of ICIT, FT, UFDT, and inode in AIX.

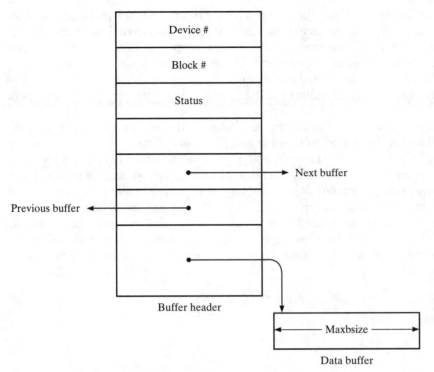

Figure 9.14 Structure of a buffer cache.

not only greatly minimizes disk access (when reading from or writing to a file), but also provides a better performance over the traditional buffer cache. The buffer cache continues to have responsibilities for the page device table lists and handling of the *superblock* during a file system mount operation. The buffer header part of the buffer cache is used to handle I/O requests to block devices.

9.10 SUMMARY

The seemingly mysterious properties of AIX can be understood in light of its infrastructure. Its architectural layout and the functional characteristics point to the fact that a lot of the AIX kernel is essentially the same as traditional UNIX systems, while much of its I/O subsystem components—like the virtual memory manager and the file system—have been enhanced to provide a superior environment above and beyond what UNIX vendors had attempted before.

Processes employ system calls to access the resources on the system. Since the kernel owns all the resources on the system, it becomes necessary for the user processes to go through a mode switch before being able to use the kernel's services. System calls on AIX are preemptable by higher-priority processes to facilitate real-time processing support. Also, the kernel can be dynamically extended beyond its base set of services. Extensions to the kernel are possible in any of the subsystems including device drivers, system calls, kernel services, and even private kernel routines. While some kernel services can be called in either by the process or the interrupt environment, others are restricted to the process environment. The set of base kernel services available under AIX are used by kernel extensions.

In addition to user processes on the system, there are privileged processes that run in the kernel address space, */unix*. These processes running in the kernel mode have access to additional system calls for carrying out privileged tasks. Even in the kernel address space, there is a distinction made between two types of system calls. There is a set of system calls that can be used by kernel extensions and another set that is available to kernel processes only. User mode processes in kernel mode can only use system calls that have their parameters passed by value, and the kernel routines executing under user mode processes can not directly use a system call having reference parameters. The latter restriction is imposed because when system calls with reference parameters access a caller's data, they are accessing storage across a protected domain.

Chapter 10

AIX Process Subsystem Internals

This chapter describes the process management subsystem for AIX. As such, the low-level process management tasks for AIX are not too different from traditional UNIX systems, but it is the availability of certain enhancements in the operating system that makes process control worth revisiting in AIX. The basic task management concepts are evolved and extended to provide an insight into process-level abstractions.

A section on thread-level abstraction is also included to explain the new paradigm introduced in the newer release of the AIX operating system to harness multiprocessor architectures. While the concept of threads (or *pthreads* as termed in the case of POSIX threads) introduces a layer of abstraction in terms of the dispatchable unit of work in the system, its implementation remains transparent when applied to a uniprocessor environment or previous implementations of AIX.

10.1 THE DIFFERENCE BETWEEN A PROGRAM AND A PROCESS

A source code is compiled to produce an executable file. This newly created file or program sits on a disk until ready to be used. The executable program on disk consists of three areas:

1. A text area which is the code

2. An initialized area consisting of the data

3. A noninitialized area known as the *bss** or heap

---

* This name comes from an assembly language pseudo-operator on the IBM 7090 machine, which was an acronym for "block started by symbol."

Different parts of the source code map to different areas of the executable file on disk. Refer to the example of C source code in Fig. 10.1 to understand the specific mappings. It is important to realize how static variables map differently than automatic variables, and how the stack is used differently than the heap.

10.2 PROCESS STRUCTURE

When an executable file is loaded into memory and undergoes transition to a process, the text area is mapped to one of the 16 segments of virtual memory accessible per process, known as the *text segment*. This segment is read-only and can be shared by other processes running the same code. The data and *bss*

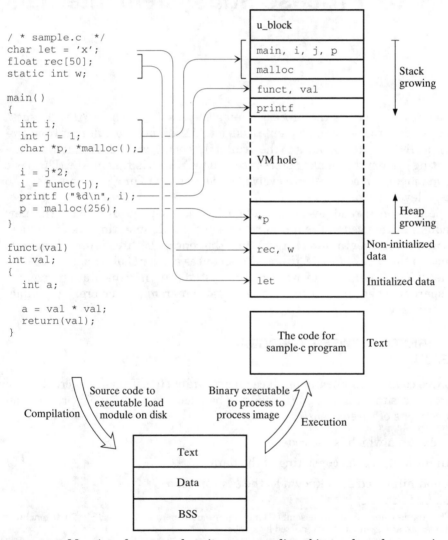

Figure 10.1 Mapping of source code to its corresponding object code and process image.

areas are mapped to another virtual memory segment referred to as the *data segment*. This segment is both readable and writable, and private to that process. This data segment can be further broken down into two areas: a *user area* (meant for use when a process is executing in user mode) and a *kernel area* (meant for use when the process has undergone a mode change and is executing in kernel mode). The kernel area, located at the end of the segment, contains machine-state information for that process, its file descriptor table, and environmental information such as the user-ID, current working directory, etc. The user area is at the start of the data segment; here space is allocated for initialized data used for variable declarations, noninitialized data used for function declarations, and dynamically allocated memory. Note that the stacks for the user area and the kernel area are separate.

The data segment is referred to as *working storage*. Unlike the text segment, it contains data which is created dynamically as the process runs. *Note* that this data has no persistent storage on the file system; therefore, if memory is overcommitted, its contents will be written out to the preallocated area on the paging space.

10.3 PROCESS-AFFILIATED KERNEL STRUCTURES

A process, when executing, has no knowledge of other processes on the system. It is the scheduler that manages how and when each process gets the CPU to execute its instructions.

Affiliated with each process is a set of data structures. The pertinent ones are *proc* and *user* (also referred to as *u_area* or user area). Each process is managed by the kernel through the global structure called *proc*. The *user* structure, which points to the *proc* structure, contains local data pertinent to that process.

Information contained in the *proc* structure includes:

- State of the process
- User identifier
- Process identifier
- Process identifier of the parent process
- Process priority
- *Nice* value of the process
- Process statistics
- Process link pointers pointing to child and sibling processes
- Number of threads in the process, etc.

The *user* structure, which points to the *proc* structure, includes information about

- signal management
- resource usage per process

- user-mode address space mapping
- controlling terminal (if any)
- user's file descriptor table
- pointer to the current directory of process
- cumulative number of ticks, etc.

Note that there is a *proc* structure for every process, including kernel processes, running in the system. Each structure is represented by a slot in the process table. There is also a *user* structure for every running process and it is stored in the process's private data segment. The difference in their contents is that the *proc* structure contains information that is needed in memory when a process is swapped out, while the *user* structure contains information that need not be in memory when the process is swapped out. Regardless, the processes that are in use remain pinned in order to avoid page faults in critical sections.

10.4   PROCESS STATES

A typical process moves through multiple states during its life cycle. Unlike the human life cycle, a process can revisit a state during its life. There are six possible states that are stored in the process table entry for every process, and these describe a process's state at any given time. The states are described below and their transition states are depicted in Fig. 10.2.

State	Description
SNONE	process slot available
SSLEEP	awaiting an event
SRUN	runnable
SIDL	being created
SZOMB	being terminated
SSTOP	stopped

The SNONE state is a part of the initialization of the *fork* system call that checks for an available process slot in the process table. The SIDL state indicates a process being created by allocation of space in memory to commence execution in the later part of the *fork* system call. The SRUN state can represent a new or a preempted process that is ready to run and is waiting for the CPU. If the process is not a new one, it can be a sleeping process returning to be scheduled again, or a waiting process resuming execution after having waited on a signal or event, or simply an exiting process from the run state reverting for its next time quantum (recall that exactly one process can run at any given time). The sleep state SSLEEP is encountered for processes that are waiting for an I/O to complete or a resource to become available. The stop state SSTOP represents processes which are waiting for a signal to transition them

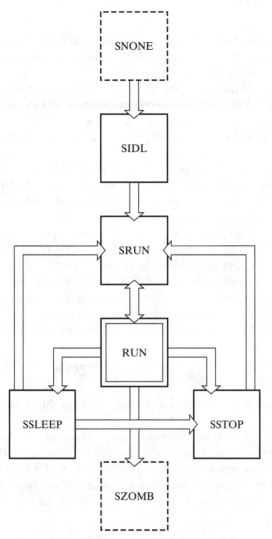

Figure 10.2 AIX process state transitions.

into the SRUN state. Note that a signal issued by the kernel can result in a sleeping process to transition into a stopped state, or a stopped process (that was previously in a sleep state) to transition to a sleep state. Last but not least, there is a terminating state called the zombie state, SZOMB, which indicates that a process is in a state of exiting, but is still occupying its process table slot. Although this SZOMB state ought to be short-lived, some processes hang around longer than desired, usually because of a parent process's failure to check on the death of its child. Zombie processes can be identified by displaying the process table entries and finding the processes that appear as `<defunct>` in the displayed output.

10.5   PRIORITY HANDLING

The *dispatcher* and the *scheduler* are the two main components of the kernel that drive a process. The dispatcher is a function which facilitates having the most-favored priority process run at any given time. The dispatcher is invoked at the occurrence of an interrupt or when the currently running process relinquishes control of the CPU in order to perform I/O or to time-slice with other processes. Note that the dispatcher does not recompute process priorities, but instead chooses the best-suited process to run, based on its existing priority.

The AIX scheduler consists of two parts. One of them is the real-time clock interrupt handler that executes every system timer tick (which is 10 ms). The second part recomputes the process priority every hundred clock ticks (which is 1 s). A nonfixed priority process is charged for every timer tick of CPU it uses by incrementing a field called *p_cpu* in the process table entry for that process. Then every hundredth timer tick (which is 1 s), the priority of all processes is recalculated. Subsequently, the dispatcher is called to ensure that a process which may now have a more-favored priority gets dispatched. Note that the recomputation task is performed by halving the CPU value (*p_cpu*) for all processes, be they in a runnable, sleep, or stopped state, and then converting the value into a new priority for each process. This explanation is better understood from the algorithm below.

$$priority = nice\ value + PUSER + \left(\frac{p\_cpu}{2} \right)$$

The value of PUSER is a constant, with a default value of 40. It is not a tunable parameter.

The scheduler is often referred to as the *swapper*. The duality of terms can lead to confusion. As stated before, the *swapper* is the process that handles context switching, i.e., it swaps processes in and out of the CPU and does so based on a priority scheme. A context switch does not, however, involve a swapping out of the process from main memory to disk. AIX implements two policies for managing memory:

- swapping
- demand paging

When the system is running normally—that is, it is not thrashing—the policy used is demand paging. This mechanism will, when memory is overcommitted, free up memory by "stealing" pages of memory belonging to a process. (Note that this may or may not involve I/O). When the system thrashes, the policy implemented is swapping. Here the most memory-intensive processes are suspended for a period of time until the system has recovered. When a process is suspended, all memory belonging to that process is freed up. So, the process is said to be swapped out of memory. In summary, the process named *swapper,* performs dispatching, scheduling, and swapping. It only performs swapping when the system is deemed to be thrashing.

What has been described until now pertains to normal processes only. For real-time processes, the priority has to remain unaffected—in other words, the value of *p_cpu* should not be subjected to recomputation. It becomes necessary that the real-time processes be run at a higher priority than the *swapper*. In general, the *swapper* process runs with an execution priority of 16. To avoid preemption by the *swapper,* the time-constrained real-time processes run at a fixed priority more favored than 16.

In the hierarchy ladder there are three categories of priorities: (1) *interrupt handler priority,* (2) *real-time priority,* and (3) *user process priority.* An interrupt handler enjoys the most-favored priority on the system in order for it to be able to preempt a running process to respond on time to an external event. The real-time processes have the next level of precedence in the priority hierarchy (Fig. 10.3). Any process that has been assigned a fixed value between 0 and 40 behaves as a real-time process. Such processes run until they voluntarily relinquish the CPU by entering a sleep state, or an interrupt causes it to get bumped by causing the dispatcher to run a process with a more-favored priority. Recollect that this trait of the dispatcher was mentioned earlier in this chapter, where a timer interrupt occurring every 10 ms was inevitable. Thus, it can be stated that the dispatcher's running of the most-favored process at least as frequently as 10 ms is tied to the inherent design of AIX. The user process priority is a volatile entity and is constantly redefined throughout its life span. At its birth, a process inherits its parent's priority and, over a period of time, its value changes based upon its CPU consumption. A process priority

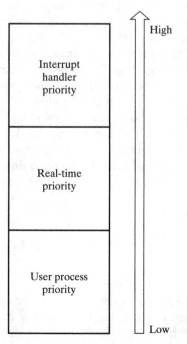

Low   **Figure 10.3** Priority hierarchy.

has a large degree of variance and can assume up to 86 possible values. There are several catalysts that govern a user process priority, the prime one being the CPU usage.

Permissible priority values for real-time processes = 0 to 40
Permissible priority values for user processes = 41 to 127

10.6   CONTEXT SWITCHING

Context switching is not specific to AIX or UNIX; instead, it is a generic phenomenon found in operating systems schedulers, in which, at the end of each time, quantum, an interrupt is generated from the timer. Processing the timer to switch the CPU to another process requires saving all the registers for the current process and loading the registers for the new process. This task is known as a *context switch*. Context switch time is pure overhead. The time required to perform a context switch depends on the cause of the context switch. The cost of a context switch owing to an external interrupt is different from that of one caused from expiration of a process's time-slice, which, in turn, is different from a context switch occurring due to voluntary sleep of a process. These varying costs of context switches directly affect the performance of the system.

AIX supports a set of unique features that enables it to achieve an exceedingly fast context switch time. Traditional UNIX systems do not allow a context switch while executing in the kernel mode. But AIX has a fully preemptable kernel which does permit such a context switch to happen. Not only is a context switch possible under AIX, but the mechanism is speeded up dramatically because of the presence of a unique data structure for the dispatcher.

There are 128 process-scheduling run queues under AIX that correspond directly to the 128 priorities supported by the dispatcher. Each run queue is a circularly linked list of runnable processes having the same priority. An array of pointers, called the *run queue pointer array* (RQ-PA), serves as the repository for head pointers to each of the circular doubly linked lists. The system maintains another array, called the *bit array*, with 1-bit flags to indicate which of the run queues are nonempty. This complex data structure is laid out in Fig. 10.4. As long as there is one process in the run queue of that priority level, the bit flag in the bit array remains enabled. So, when choosing which process should be run next, the dispatcher only has to look at the bit array to determine the most-favored priority run queue that is occupied. The algorithm is as follows:

```
compute the most favored priority level
index into the array of run queues
access the head pointer pointing to the run queue
select the process at the head of the run queue
dispatch the process
```

Following the expiration of the scheduler's time quantum, if the process is still runnable, it is placed at the end of the run queue, and the new head of the linked list is dispatched. In this way, the dispatcher is able to implement a

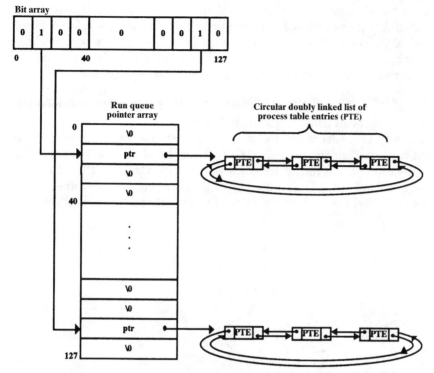

Figure 10.4 Data structure layout for the AIX process dispatcher. Indices 0 to 40 of the RQPA point to real-time processes and indices 41 to 127 point to user processes.

round robin scheme within processes of equal priority. The main gain of this implementation in AIX over traditional UNIX is an exceedingly fast context switch, since the dispatcher does not have to traverse through long queues, even if there were several runnable processes outstanding.

10.7 PROCESS SCHEDULING

The process scheduling mechanism in AIX is no different from that in traditional UNIX systems. The scheduler belongs to a general class of operating schedulers known as *round robin with multilevel feedback*. UNIX process management unifies the temporal diversification in the activities by merging all the computations as processes, thereby making a process the only schedulable entity. Processes are given a time quantum when the scheduler selects one for the CPU from its multilevel priority queue. The highest run-queue level at which incoming user processes can enter the process-scheduling subsystem is 40 (recall that all processes inherit a PUSER value of 40 plus a *nice* value varying between 0 or 39, which can be changed via the *nice* or *renice* system calls). New processes start life with a CPU value (p_cpu) of 0 as shown in Fig. 10.5. In all of the 128 circularly linked process scheduling run queues that correspond to the 128 permissible priorities supported by the dispatcher, the time quantum for time-slicing increases the lower the level. In other words, CPU-bound processes tend to stay at lower levels and I/O-bound processes hover around higher levels. A process is time-sliced every quantum, and the CPU time used in this interim is charged to that process.

When a context switch occurs to make another process runnable, the overhead encountered in the operation may or may not be charged to the right process. Although the enhanced context switch mechanism in AIX lessens the context switch overhead time, it does not eliminate it.

The process time measurement activity is tied to the clock handler and is carried out by sampling the usage of the CPU at the clock tick instants. The system keeps time with a hardware clock that interrupts the CPU at a fixed, hardware-dependent rate. The frequency of this interrupt is 100 times a second. This means that the best granularity of time that the AIX kernel can pro-

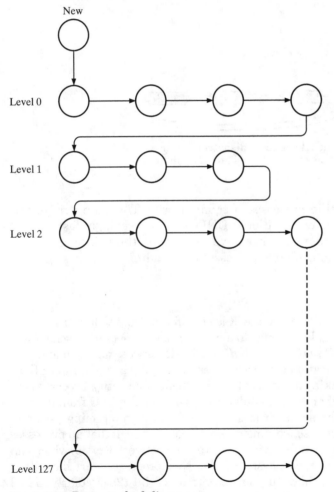

Figure 10.5 Process scheduling.

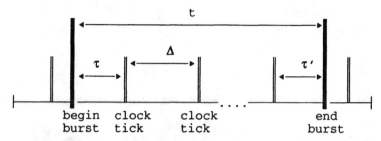

Figure 10.6 Process time measurement. Δ is the clock-tick interval (10 ms); *t* is the time quantum (CPU burst); τ and τ′ are the positive and negative errors created in measuring the interval.

vide is 10 ms. If a process is to wake up after one clock tick and then go away before the next tick, no CPU utilization would be attributed to its *p_cpu* field. Due to the coarse clock granularity and the snapshot-oriented mechanism of process timing in UNIX and AIX, errors occur easily, as depicted in the timeline in Fig. 10.6. The occurrence of an interrupt (such as the clock interrupt) affects the CPU utilization of the running process. But there is no feature to account for the time spent by the CPU in handling interrupts caused by other processes. The small magnitude of errors, when added up and compared against cumulative system statistics, results in a rather significant quantity—not small enough to be ignored, especially on loaded systems. Those familiar with the mainframe world may recall the problems of low resolution and large variability in time measurements.

Timing is done at three nested levels (diagrammed in Fig. 10.7)—i.e., the scheduler, the dispatcher, and the clock cycle level. While the scheduler recomputes the priority of all processes every second, and the dispatcher increments the utilization of the current process by one for every hundredth of a second, the system has several thousand opportunities in the interim to raise interrupt(s). In order to address finer time measurements, a hardware-based timer facility is available, which enables programs to measure time intervals with high resolution.

10.8 THE THREAD PARADIGM

Thread is a new paradigm planned for AIX version 4 and later releases. A thread is defined as an object that performs computations in the context of a process. The concept of thread* has descended from the Mach operating system which is based upon a set of programming abstractions to exploit multiprocessor environments.

Using the Mach design principles, traditional AIX processes have been divided into two separate components, emphasizing the notions of *tasks* and *threads*.

---

* *Threads* are often described as "lightweight processes." *Note:* This is not to be confused with Sun's lightweight processes (LWP).

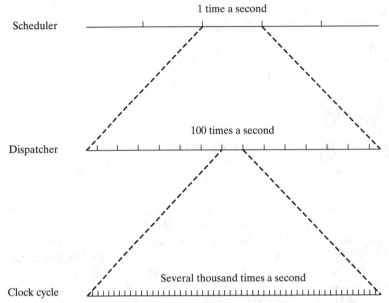

Figure 10.7 A conceptual layout for timing done at three nested levels—the scheduler, dispatcher, and the clock.

Both entities are intricately tied together. A task contains a passive collection of resources for a group of cooperating entities. Refer to Fig. 10.8 for an example. A thread is the active execution environment that is perceived as a basic schedulable entity. A task may have many threads, all running simultaneously.

Much of the power of the Mach programming model, which is supported by newer releases of AIX, comes from the fact that all threads in a task share the task's resources. For instance, the threads share the same virtual memory address space. However, each thread in a task has its own private execution state. Compared to a UNIX process, which encapsulates a processing state along with all of the resources required for execution, a thread has only one physical attribute (i.e., the processing state specified by the thread's program counter, stack pointer, and the hardware registers). From a performance standpoint, creation of a UNIX process is far more expensive than creation of a thread.

10.8.1   Thread-affiliated kernel structures

Just as there are global and local structures called *proc* and *user* affiliated with each process (discussed earlier in this chapter), there is a set of new data structures that relate to threads. Each thread is managed through a structure called *thread*. Associated with it is an allied structure called *uthread,* which is local in scope and contains data that is private to the thread. Figure 10.9 depicts the important relationship between processes and threads. Information contained in the *thread* structure includes:

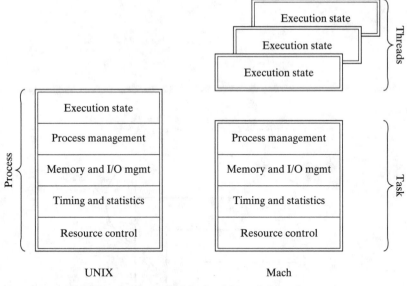

Figure 10.8 UNIX process versus Mach task and threads.

- State of the thread
- Pointer to the *proc* structure
- Pointer to the next thread
- Thread's priority
- Thread identifier
- Processor usage for the thread
- Processor ID to which the thread is bound

The *uthread* structure, which points to the *thread* structure, includes information about

- User mode-stack pointer
- User-mode machine state register value
- Pointer to the thread's kernel stack
- File system transaction identifier
- Timer structures

10.8.2 Thread states

Like processes, a thread may be represented with states. In the newer releases of AIX, threads happen to be the schedulable entity. This entity has an execution state that specifies whether or not the thread is executing or can be scheduled for execution. At any given time, a thread is in one of the following execution states:

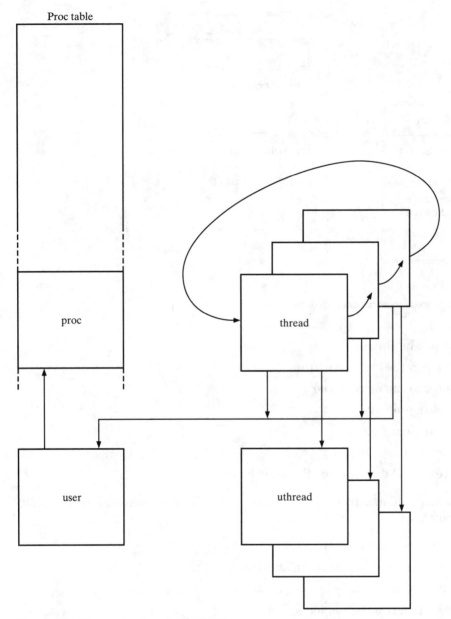

Figure 10.9 Process-to-thread relationship.

State	Description
TSNONE	thread does not exist
TSIDL	thread is being created
TSRUN and TWCPU	thread can be scheduled to execute
TSRUN and TNOWAIT	thread is executing

TSSWAP	thread is swapped and cannot be executed until it is swapped in by the scheduler or until a signal is posted to the thread or process
TSSLEEP	waiting for resource(s) to become available and cannot be executed until those are provided
TSSTOP	thread is suspended and cannot be scheduled to execute
TSZOMB	thread is being terminated

The TSNONE state indicates that a process slot is available in the process table, and the TSIDL state marks that a thread is in the process of being created. A thread that is runnable is represented by the TSRUN state. If a thread has been swapped out, it is indicated by the TSSWAP state. The TSSLEEP state is encountered for threads that are waiting on an I/O to complete or a resource to become available, while the TSSTOP state represents threads which have been stopped and are waiting on a signal to transition them into the TSRUN state. Last, there is a TSZOMB state, which indicates that a thread has exited. Figure 10.10 illustrates the possible state transitions of a thread.

10.8.3   *pid*s and *tid*s

Processes are the fundamental schedulable entities from the operating system's perspective in traditional UNIX and in AIX (up to Version 3). At birth, each process is assigned a unique process identifier number called its *pid*.

With the introduction of the thread paradigm and its consequent abstraction as being the schedulable entity, it becomes imperative that there be a thread identifier, *tid,* in addition to the *pid.* It is essential that one be able to distinguish between a *tid* and a *pid.* A *pid* on AIX is a 32-bit number derived from a combination of *proc* table slot* index and a generation count index that aids in avoiding rapid reallocation of *pid*s. By setting the least significant bit to 0, only even number *pid*s are generated (except for the *init* process). The opposite is true for *tid*; all *tid*s are odd number entities. *tid*s are derived from a combination of *thread* table slot† index and a generation count index that aids in avoiding rapid reallocation of *pid*s. In this way, one is able to tell the difference between a *pid* and a *tid.*

10.8.4   Context switching

With the implementations of threads, context switching happens at a thread level instead of at a process level. The context switching task consists of saving the user, kernel, and the hardware state of the currently executing thread, and restoring the corresponding state of a different thread. When a thread executes, its computational state is maintained in the hardware registers. When

---

* Slots in the *proc* table are recycled. They are made available to newborn processes on a first-come first-serve basis.

† Slots in the *thread* table are recycled. When a *tid* is to be allocated, its value is predicated on the first available *thread* table entry.

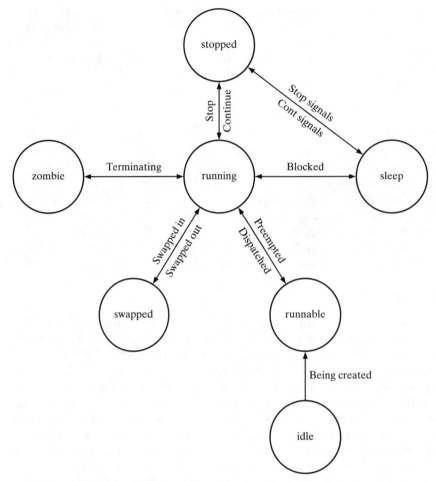

Figure 10.10 Possible state transitions of a thread.

the thread is not executing, its state information is held in a special area called its *mst* area (*mst* means *m*achine *st*ate). The *mst* is a data structure that specifies the value of the thread's stack pointer and the contents of its hardware registers. An abbreviated listing of the *mst* area is shown in Fig. 10.11.

Context switching may take place because of different situations. For example, the current thread may generate an interrupt due to a page fault and, in turn, block the thread's execution to allow another thread to execute. The current thread can issue a system call to access a resource that is not available. Furthermore, the current thread can be preempted by a hardware interrupt and, when the interrupt has been processed, a different thread is resumed.

10.8.5 Scheduling

With the support of threads, the scheduling becomes thread-based instead of process-based. The scheduler now traverses the thread table instead of the *proc* table.

```
            MSTSAVE AREA AT ADDRESS 0x00004100

curid:0x41424344  m/q:0x00000000  iar:0x00000000  cr:0x41424344
...

            MSTSAVE AREA AT ADDRESS 0x00264db0
...

Exception Struct
   0x00000000  0x00000000  0x00000000  0x00000000  0x00000000
...

            MSTSAVE AREA AT ADDRESS 0x2fee0000

curid:0x00001e24  m/q:0x000000bc  iar:0x41424344  cr:0x84242822
msr:0x400090b0    lr:0x01864370   xer:0x00000000  kjmpbuf:0x00000000
backtrack:0x00    tid:0x00000000  fpeu:0x01       excp_type:0x00000000
ctr:0x41424344
*prevmst:0x00000000  *stackfix:0x00000000  intpri:0x0b
o_iar:0x00000000  o_toc:0x00000000  o_arg1:0x00000000  excbranch:0x00000000
o_vaddr:0x41424344

Exception Struct
   0x41424344  0x400090b0  0x007fffff  0x41424344  0x00000106

Segment Regs
   0:0x00000000    1:0x007fffff    2:0x00003359    3:0x007fffff
   4:0x007fffff    5:0x007fffff    6:0x007fffff    7:0x007fffff
   8:0x007fffff    9:0x007fffff   10:0x007fffff   11:0x007fffff
  12:0x007fffff   13:0x4000140a   14:0x00000804   15:0x40001d4e

General Purpose Regs
   0:0x41424344    1:0x2fedff88    2:0x00000000    3:0x41424344
   4:0x00000001    5:0x01864468    6:0x0002f0b0    7:0xf00aaac8
...
  28:0xe3001e00   29:0xe6001220   30:0x0024d914   31:0x00039f0d

Floating Point Regs
    Fpscr: 0x00000000
  0:0x00000000 0x00000000   1:0x00000000 0x00000000   2:0x00000000 0x00000000
  3:0x00000000 0x00000000   4:0x00000000 0x00000000   5:0x00000000 0x00000000
...
 30:0x00000000 0x00000000  31:0x00000000 0x00000000
```

Figure 10.11 State information held in *mst* area (*mst* means *m*achine *st*ate).

10.9 PROCESS MONITORING

It makes understanding AIX even more meaningful if one is to monitor the dispatchable units of work at run-time.

Most information on processes can be obtained with the use of *crash*, which is a useful dump analyzer and operating system monitoring tool. Hard-to-find information includes process-subsystem-related details regarding sibling and child processes, state of signals, dispatcher- and scheduler-related information for the process, and memory subsystem details such as address space.

A *proc* structure is displayed in Fig. 10.12 from an AIX Version 3 system to show the kind of detailed information that is available about a process. The slot number (SLT) occupied by the process in the process table is displayed, along with its status (ST), process ID (PID), parent process ID (PPID), user ID (UID), effective user ID (EUID), and numerous affiliated fields pointing to vital information. The links are chain pointers. There is a *child pointer* that points to a child, a *sibling pointer* that links sibling processes together, and a *uidl pointer* that links processes for a given user ID. The dispatch fields are used by the dispatcher: the *prior* pointer links to a chain of processes with the same priority, the *next* pointer points to the succeeding process on the run list, and *pevent* and *wevent* are the pending and awaiting events, respectively. The *suspend* field shows the signal nesting level and the *process-waiting-for* field shows what the process is waiting for (in this example, events). The scheduler uses the scheduler fields in which the *pri* field marks the dispatch priority, *nice* gives the nice value, *lpri* gives the lock priority, and *wpri* gives the wait priority. In the miscellaneous field, the *adspace* represents the handle of the process private segment. The signal information field gives details about the pending, masked, caught, and ignored signals in double-word formats, where each bit represents a signal number. The statistics field displays information about the auditing flags and gives the size of the process image in terms of pages.

Recall that newer releases of the AIX operating system (i.e., beyond version 3) support threads. A *proc* structure listing in Fig. 10.13 shows the additional fields and points out the differences. Since the advent of threads has caused much of the vital information to be moved from the process table to the *threads* structure, a thread table entry listing is provided for gathering detailed information at a thread level. In addition to the process's slot number, status, process ID, etc., a new thread count (TCNT) field is present in the *proc* structure. An additional link, *ganchor,* points to the process group anchor. The dispatch and the scheduler fields' significance is reduced as processes are no longer the unit of dispatchable entity. A new set of thread fields is used to reference the process's threads: *threadcount* gives the number of threads for a process, *active* and *suspend* show the number of active and suspended threads, a *threadlist* pointer points to the list of threads for this process, and a *synch* pointer points to the threads waiting for this process to be suspended. In the miscellaneous

```
> proc - 1

SLT ST    PID   PPID   PGRP   UID   EUID   PRI    CPU    EVENT   NAME
  1 s      1      0      0     0      0     60      0             init
         FLAGS: swapped_in no_swap wake/sig locks

Links:  *child:0xe3003600  *siblings:0x00000000  *uid1:0xe3000100
    *wchan1(real):0x00000000  *lcklst:0x00000000
    selchn:0x00000000
Dispatch Fields:  *prior:0xe3000100  *next:0xe3000100
    pevent:0x00000020  wevent:0x00000004
    polevel:0x000000ad  *lockwait:0x00000000
    *eventlst:0x00000000  *wchan(hashed):0x00000000  suspend:0x0001
    process waiting for:  event(s)
Scheduler Fields:  pri: 60 nice: 20  lpri:127  wpri:127  flags:0x 0
  repage:0x00000000  scount:0x00000000  *snext:0x00000000  *sback:0x00000000
Misc:  adspace:0x00001004  *tty1:0x00000000
    *p_ipc:0x00000000  *p_dblist:0x00000000  *p_dbnext:0x00000000
Signal Information:  cursig:0x00  sigstate:0x00
    pending:hi 0x00000000,lo 0x00000000  sigmask:hi 0x00000000,lo 0x00000000
    sigcatch:hi 0x00000001,lo 0x18783eff  sigignore:hi 0x7fffffffe,lo 0xe786c000

Statistics:  size:0x0000008a(pages)  audit:0x00000000
```

Figure 10.12 *proc* structure of AIX version 3.

```
> proc - 24

SLT ST    PID   PPID   PGRP    UID   EUID   TCNT   NAME
 24 a     18e0   10cc   18e0      0      0      1
          FLAGS: swapped_in no_swap

Links:   *child:0x00000000   *siblings:0x00000000   *uidl:0xe3000000
    *ganchor:0xe3001800
Dispatch Fields:   pevent:0x00000000   wevent:0x00000000
    *p_synch:0xffffffff
Thread Fields:   *threadlist:0xe6000a00   threadcount:    1
    active:    1  suspended:    0  local:    0  localsleep:    0
    *synch:0xffffffff
Scheduler Fields:    nice: 20   repage:0x00000000   scount:0x00000000
Misc:  adspace:0x00000100   *ttyl:0x00000000
        *p_ipc:0x00000000   *p_dblist:0x00000000   *p_dbnext:0x00000000
    *lock:0x00000000   kstackseg:0x007fffff *pgrpl:0x08x
Signal Information:
    pending:hi 0x00000000,lo 0x00000000
    sigcatch:hi 0x00000000,lo 0x00086001  sigignore:hi 0x80000000,lo 0x18408006
Statistics:   size:0x00000026(pages)   audit:0x00000000
```

Figure 10.13 *proc* structure of AIX beyond version 3.

field, a set of new pointers, *lock* and *pgrpl,* point to the process lock and the process group list, while a *kstakseg* field points to the segment for additional kernel stacks. The signal information and the statistics fields remain unchanged.

Thread, which is a part of the process that gets scheduled to execute, can be thought about as a subprocess. The *thread* structure provides information that resembles the *proc* structure in AIX Version 3. Refer to Fig. 10.14 for an understanding of the *thread* structure. In addition to the thread's slot number, status, process ID, etc., several new fields are present that need mentioning. There is a thread ID (TID) field which has the same relation to its slot number as does the process ID. For example, the thread in slot 20 of the thread table will have a thread ID of 0x14*nn* (where 0x14 is 20 in a decimal system and *nn* is a sequence number). There is another new field indicating the type of scheduling policy (POLICY) in use by the operating system. Because the scheduler is a pluggable entity in terms of the kernel, any type of nonpreemptive scheduling algorithms such as FCFS (first-come first-serve) and SJF (shortest-job-first), or preemptive scheduling algorithms such as RR (round robin) or SRTF (shortest-remaining-time-first) can be noted by examining this POLICY field, if a custom scheduler is in use in a fault-tolerant or real-time environment. The next field of interest is PROCNAME which gives the name of the process for this relevant thread. The relevant link pointers consist of *procp,* pointing to the associated process block; *uthreadp,* pointing to the work area; and *userp* referring to the owing process's *u_block* structure. The *prevthread* and *nextthread* refer to the previous and subsequent threads. The dispatch fields, used by the dispatcher, are similar to the *proc* structure of AIX Version 3: the *prior* pointer links to a chain of threads with the same priority, and the *next* pointer points to the succeeding thread on the run or wait list. The SUSPEND field shows the signal nesting level and the THREAD-WAITING-FOR field shows what the thread is waiting for. The use of the scheduler fields

```
> thread - 16

SLT ST   TID    PID    CPUID  POLICY  PRI  CPU  EVENT  PROCNAME
 16 s    10e1   18e0     0    other   3c    0
         FLAGS: wakeonsig sel

Links:  *procp:0xe3001800  *uthreadp:0x2fee0000  *userp:0x2fee02e0
    *prevthread:0xe6000a00  *nextthread:0xe6000a00
    *wchan1(real):0x00000000  *wchan2(VMM):0x00000000
Dispatch Fields:  *prior:0xe6000a00  *next:0xe6000a00
    polevel:0x000001c4  ticks:0x0001  *synch:0xffffffff  result:0x08x
    *eventlst:0x00000000  *wchan(hashed):0x00000000  suspend:0x0001
    thread waiting for:  event(s)
Scheduler Fields:  cpuid:0x0000  scpuid:0x0000  pri: 60  policy:other
    lpri:127  wpri:127    time:0xff
Misc:  t_lockcount:0x00000000  t_lock:0x00000000
    t_dispct:0x00000044  t_fpuct:0x00000000
Signal Information:  cursig:0x00
    pending:hi 0x00000000,lo 0x00000000  sigmask:hi 0x00000000,lo 0x00000000
```

Figure 10.14 *thread* structure of AIX beyond version 3.

remains unchanged from that of the *proc* structure in AIX Version 3 where the *pri, lpri,* and *wpri* give the dispatch, lock, and wakeup priorities, respectively. Two new fields, *cpuid* and *scpuid,* specify the ID of the current and the previous processor to which the thread is/was bound to. The miscellaneous fields provide assorted information about the thread, including the number of dispatches, locks, and floating-point-unavailable interrupts. The signal information fields give details about the pending and masked signals in double-word formats, with each bit representing a signal number.

The *proc* and the thread structures described here are intended to serve the needs of beginner to advanced-level users. Using the *crash* tool, one can display any kernel data structure or memory locations in the system for debugging or learning purposes.

10.10 INTERRUPT AND EXCEPTION HANDLING

The hardware uses the same mechanism to report both *interrupts* and *exceptions*. When either event occurs, the machine saves its current state and takes an unconditional branch to a special location, where the handler code is located. Depending on the cause for the preemption, the handler code determines whether the event is an exception or an interrupt, and, consequently, performs different processings accordingly.

Interrupts are triggered asynchronously and seldom have anything to do with the currently executing instruction. Exceptions are synchronous events and are directly related to the currently executing instruction. Timer ticks are interrupts and the divide-by-zero operation is an example of an exception. *Page faults* are also treated like interrupts, with the difference being that the interrupted program is made nondispatchable until the page fault is resolved.

Interrupts are asynchronous events that are generated by the operating system or a device. The occurrence of an interrupt indeed interrupts the execution of the current process.* The process* is preempted and the control is transferred to what are called *interrupt handlers.* The appropriate interrupt handler routine services the interrupt and, after its completion, it transfers control back to the current process* to continue execution. Since an interrupt itself can be interrupted by a higher-priority interrupt, AIX saves an abbreviated context for the interrupt and links a representation of each one together using a region called *current machine state area* or *csa.* The system tracks these regions by the user's *user* structure and a pointer to the *csa* area. Although there are numerous types of interrupts with different interrupt priorities on the system, there are essentially two types of interrupt levels (see Fig. 10.15) associated with them. The first is called a *system interrupt;* these are generated by base hardware components, such as the real-time clock. The second kind of interrupt is referred to as a *device interrupt,* and these are caused as a result of the system's interaction with assorted devices. Interrupt priorities associated with the individual interrupts are essentially hierarchies by which pending interrupts are serviced. A device's interrupt is selected based on its maximum interrupt latency requirements and the corresponding device driver's interrupt execution time. As far as interrupt processing within the system is concerned, this operation is provided by the branch processing unit hardware and its three registers, namely, the MSR (machine status register), the SRR0 (save and restore register), and the SRR1.

The exception handling mechanism enables the executing instruction to specify the type of action to take. Exceptions are handled differently depending on whether they occur while executing in user mode or kernel mode. The default consequence of an exception in user mode causes a signal to be sent to the process* indicating the type of exception. If an exception handler is defined, cleanup action is taken to free up the process's storage and affiliated resources. Exception handling in the kernel mode extends the capability of the traditional UNIX mechanism by allowing these exception handlers to be stacked on a per-process or per-interrupt handler basis.

---

* Thread in the case of AIX beyond version 3.

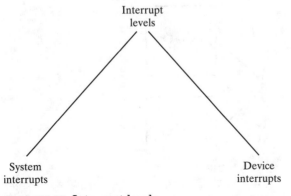

Figure 10.15 Interrupt levels.

10.11   INTERPROCESS COMMUNICATION

The choice of interprocess communication (IPC) is generally governed by the quantity of data to be communicated between processes, and the frequency of exchange between processes. No matter which IPC mechanism is used, each has a minimum overhead cost associated with it and an upper limit on the bandwidth that it can handle gracefully. In the context of IPCs, *overhead* refers to the time required to transfer the smallest message, and *bandwidth* refers to the maximum permissible rate at which transfer can occur.

There are several IPC mechanisms available under AIX. The list includes:

Pipes

Message queues

Shared memory

Semaphores

Sockets

Streams

10.11.1   Pipes

Pipes are the most basic of the IPC mechanisms. They are like regular files, and data is stored in them in the same manner. Where they differ from regular files is that their data is ephemeral. Their contents are transient in nature and can only be read in a first-in first-out manner. Once the data is read from pipes, the data disappears and cannot be read again.

Pipes are used in applications where a simple transient data stream makes more sense than a regular file, or in situations where arbitrary processes need to communicate, even though the processes at the other end of the pipe are unknown (refer to Fig. 10.16). When multiple processes write to a pipe, the write operations remain atomic and data from one write operation never gets interleaved with data from other processes. However, it should be noted that

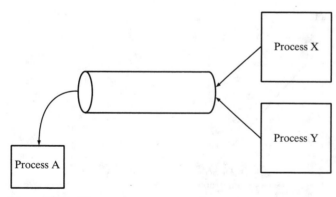

Figure 10.16   Pipes.

the pipes do not preserve message boundaries. So, if one process is to write two 32-byte messages into the pipe, the reader process at the other end of the pipe has no way of interpreting whether the contents represent two 32-byte messages or four 16-byte messages. Here the application needs to do its own housekeeping for maintaining message boundaries.

There are two kinds of pipes, *unnamed pipes* and *named pipes*. When using unnamed pipes there is no way for processes without a common ancestor to communicate. So a process has to create a pipe and then fork off a child process, in order to be able to have both processes (i.e., the parent and the child) share the same set of file descriptors to read and write from the pipe. Named pipes (also called FIFOs) overcome this shortcoming. Since they are identified by a file name, the file descriptor information can be passed to another process which may be unrelated.

- unnamed pipes
- named pipes

Unnamed pipes are opened using the *pipe* system call and named pipes are created using the *mknod* system call.

10.11.2 Message queues

Message queues provide a more flexible means of communications than pipes or sockets. Unlike pipes or sockets, message queues do not require a process to be waiting on a message.

All messages have an associated message queue identifier, using which, processes can read or write messages to arbitrary queues. This identifier is like a file descriptor in the case of an *open* system call, and is used to reference the queue header. In comparison to pipes, there is no requirement that a process be waiting for a message on a particular queue before another process can write a message to that queue. This means that a process is able to write a message to a queue and exit, and have the message read by another process at some later time. Unlike pipes, messages provide a specific header format so that applications do not have to worry about interpreting message boundaries. Every message on a queue has three attributes: a message *type, length* of the data portion of the message, and the *data* itself. With a variable-length data field available, it is easier to structure and manage the data using message queues.

A message queue is a linked list of messages which has been grouped and named as a set. Figure 10.17 exhibits messages on a queue, showing queue headers, a linked list of message headers, and pointers from the message headers to a data area.

The most frequent operations performed with this IPC facility are (1) creating or accessing a message queue, (2) removing or controlling the parameters associated with a message descriptor, and (3) transmitting (sending or receiving) a message. There are four system calls to handle these operations. The *msgget* system call opens or creates a message queue by traversing the mes-

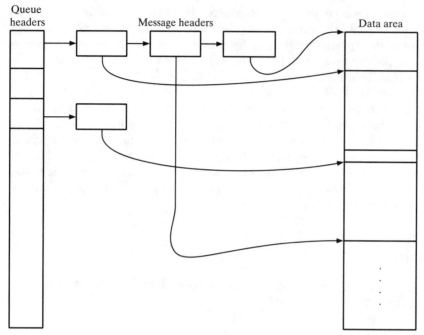

Figure 10.17 Messages on a queue showing queue headers, a linked list of message headers, and pointers from the message area to a data area.

sage queue array to locate a possible match, and allocating a new queue structure if no match is found. The *msgctl* system call is used to query the status of the message queue, set selected status fields, or to remove the queue, when needed. The remaining two system calls, *msgsnd* and *msgrcv*, are similar; one sends and the other receives a message.

10.11.3 Shared memory

Shared memory provides IPC capability to processes. It is unique in that it is the only IPC method that does not require the data to be communicated between processes to be copied. For large chunks of data this is ideal, as it eliminates severe performance problems that can arise from large data movements inside the system. Although AIX protects one process from accessing the memory space of another process, a common memory space can be made available among multiple processes using a set of special system calls. Even though a shared memory capability allows data sharing under AIX, it remains the responsibility of the processes sharing the memory to devise a synchronization scheme to serialize access to it. On its own, this IPC facility does not provide locks or access control among the processes. Although reading from shared memory may be safe, writing to it can result in severe contention problems leading to deadlocks if proper care is not taken. A conceptual diagram of how shared memory works is given in Fig. 10.18.

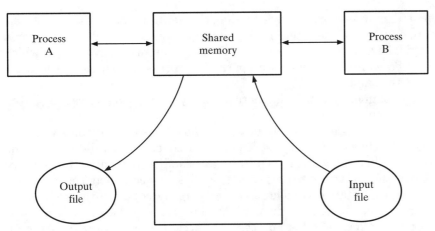

Figure 10.18 Data movement between two cooperating processes using shared memory.

The system calls for manipulating shared memory are similar to the system calls for messages queues. The *shmget* system call creates a new region of shared memory or returns an existing one; the *shmat* system call logically attaches a region to the virtual address space of a process; the *shmdt* system call detaches a region from the virtual address space of a process; and the *shmctl* manipulates various parameters associated with the shared memory. Note that the low-level instructions to read/write to shared memory are no different from how processes read from and write to standard memory.

Access to a shared memory region is gained by invoking the *shmget* system call that searches the shared memory table for a matching key and subsequently returns a numeric id. A per-process segment table entry provides access to the descriptor associated with the id. The id references entries in the kernel's segment information table, which, in turn, describes a segment of memory. Under the current implementation of AIX, a process may attach to a maximum of ten shared memory segments at any given time. Chapter 11 elaborates on the memory segments and explains how a memory of a process is divided into sixteen segments of which eight (segments 3 to 10) are always available for shared memory and two more (segments 11 and 12) can be made available, if needed.

10.11.4 Semaphores

Semaphores are a synchronization primitive. Although semaphores are not exactly IPC mechanisms, they can be regarded as IPC catalysts, since they provide a means to synchronize access to shared resources (most commonly, shared memory segments). Semaphores can be used by a variable number of unrelated processes. The semaphore facilities found in AIX have their earliest root going back to Dijkstra's Dekker algorithm, published in 1968, which described an implementation of two atomic operations which incremented and decremented an integer counter, depending on the value. Being atomic in their operation, only one of them could succeed at any given time. The semaphores in AIX and UNIX are a generalization of Dijkstra's atomic operations, in which they are used as flags to prevent cooperating processes from using the same resource at the same time.

The most common use of semaphores is in synchronizing access to shared memory segments. A semaphore's value can be 1 when memory is available and its value can toggle to 0 when the memory becomes unavailable. A process accessing this shared memory is required to check the availability of the resource (i.e., when the value is 1) prior to accessing it. Assuming the resource is available, the first thing the process does is to decrement the value (to ensure that it can retain exclusive access to the resource). After the process has finished modifying the shared memory, the last thing it does is to increment the value (to allow another process to access the resource). When a semaphore's value toggles between 0 and 1, as seen in the preceding example, the type of semaphore is referred to as a *binary semaphore*. On the other hand, when a semaphore takes up general values (0 or positive) to deal with situations with more than two participants, it is called a *counting semaphore*.

The semaphore-related system calls are similar to the system calls for message queues and shared memory. Allocation of and access to semaphores is based on possession of a *key*, so that processes without a common ancestry can coordinate use of the same sets of semaphores. The *semget* system call creates and gains access to a semaphore set associated with the key; the system returns an integer that serves as the semaphore identifier (called *semid*) for the semaphore set created. Each *semid* points to a set of semaphores and a data structure that contain information about the semaphores. There is a *semop* system call which performs an atomic set of operations on the semaphores associated with the *semid*. It reads the list of semaphore operations (supplied to *semop* as a parameter), verifies that the semaphore numbers are legal, and ensures that there is permission to perform the operations. In case of a violation, the *semop* request fails. The third semaphore-related system call is *semctl,* and it controls miscellaneous operations on the set, such as initialization or removal of a set. The basic data structures for semaphores are illustrated in Fig. 10.19.

Of the IPC mechanisms discussed so far, the message queues, shared memory, and semaphores are exceedingly similar in their implementation. Each of them features an equivalent set of system calls, as shown in Fig. 10.20.

10.11.5   Sockets

Sockets are communication channels that enable unrelated processes to exchange data locally or over networks. They are invoked using the *socket* system call. Although they can be used for IPC on the local machine, their primary use has been for remote communications across hosts.

Sockets move associated data in accordance with a referenced protocol. They make use of underlying drivers to transport information from a process on one system to a participating process on the other, as seen in Fig. 10.21.

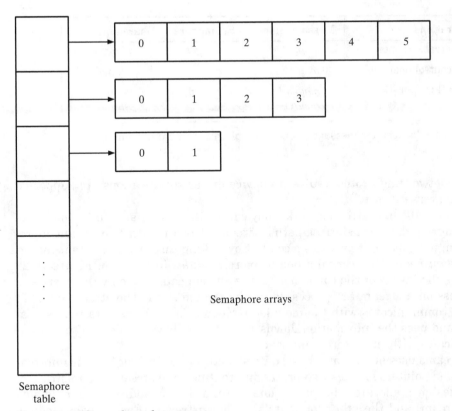

Figure 10.19 Semaphore data structures.

The kernel structure for a socket consists of a layered implementation. It has three layers: a *socket layer* which provides the interface with the system calls, a *protocol layer* containing the protocol modules for communication, and a *device layer* holding the drivers that control the network devices. Using sockets, processes can communicate in a client-server mode: a server process listens to a socket from one end of a bidirectional communications path, and client processes communicate with the server via another socket on the other end of a communications path (which may be on a different machine). The internal connections and routing of data from client to the server is maintained by the kernel itself.

10.11.6 Streams

Streams is an adaptable suite of tools and facilities for development of AIX and traditional UNIX system communication services. It supports implementation of services ranging from networking protocol suites to device drivers. Streams allow one to define standard interfaces for I/O within the kernel and between the kernel and the rest of the AIX system. The key benefit is that the association mechanism is simple and open-ended. A plethora of applications ranging

Operations	Message queue	Semaphore	Shared memory
system calls to create or open	*msgget*	*semget*	*shmget*
system call for control operations	*msgctl*	*semctl*	*shmctl*
system calls for IPC operations	*msgsnd* *msgrcv*	*semop*	*shmat* *shmdt*

Figure 10.20 System calls used for message queue, semaphore, and shared memory.

from networking protocol suites to device driver specifications are supported by this versatile set.

To describe how streams work, they can be thought of as a full-duplex processing and data transferring path between a driver in kernel space and a process in user space. It provides a conduit by linking three components together: a *stream head,* a *driver,* and one or more *modules* in between. Figure 10.22 shows the layout of the components. The system calls made by the user-level process on a stream are processed by the stream head. The stream head, in turn, communicates with the module(s). Modules modify the data representation and pass the information downstream to the driver, which, in turn, communicates with the external interface.

Streams uses queues as a basic data structure that includes status information and pointers for message-processing routines and stream administration. Queues are allocated in pairs, one with a lower address for read-side (upstream) and the other for write-side (downstream). Each driver, module, and the stream head are assigned a pair of queues, as a module is added to the stream. Data is passed between the driver, stream head, and modules in sets

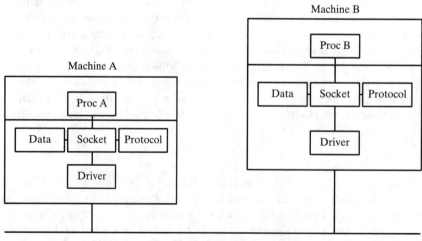

Physical network

Figure 10.21 Socket.

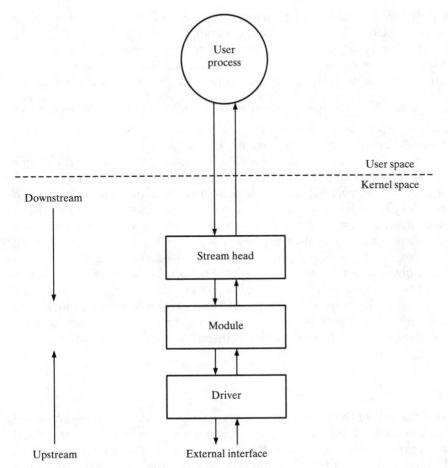

Figure 10.22 Structure of a simple stream.

of data structures, called *messages*. A streams message consists of one or more message blocks, each forming a triplet consisting of a header, a data block, and a data buffer. Within a stream, messages are distinguished by a *type* indicator. Some message types sent upstream may induce specific action by the stream head, such as sending a signal to the user process, while others carry information only within the stream.

The basic operation of a streams driver is similar to that of a traditional I/O driver. It consists of multiple associated nodes accessed by using an *open* system call. Typically, each file system node corresponds to a separate minor device for that driver. If one minor device is opened multiple times, subsequent *open* calls return a file descriptor referencing the stream. Processes sharing the same minor device share the same stream to the device driver. A user process sends data to the device using a *write* system call, and receives data from the device using a *read* system call once the device is open. These calls are compatible with the traditional character of the I/O mechanism. A *close* system call closes the driver and dismantles the associated streams once the last open reference to the stream is completed. The rate of message transfer between modules, drivers, stream head, and the processes is controlled by a mechanism called *flow control*. It is a local and voluntary process to each stream that limits the number of characters that can be queued for processing. This, in turn, limits buffer and related processing at any queue. If the stream exercises flow control on the user, the *write* call blocks until flow control is relinquished, and does not return until count bytes are sent to the device. Then *exit* is called to finish the user process, close open files, and dismantle the stream, if appropriate.

The benefit of streams is that it provides a flexible, reusable, and portable set of tools for development. It standardizes service interfaces that are governed by a set of protocols. It creates data communication service modules and provides the capability to manipulate modules from user level. This allows interchange of modules with common service interfaces and changes the service interface to a streams user process. Thus, user-level programs, network architectures, and higher-level protocols can be independent of underlying protocols and physical communication media. Further, higher-level services can be created by selecting and connecting lower-level services and protocols. The same protocol module can be used with different drivers on different machines by implementing compatible service interfaces. From a user's perspective, modules can be dynamically selected and interconnected without the hassle of kernel programming, assembly, or linking.

10.12   SUMMARY

An understanding of the concept of a program or process is only complete when one is able to understand not only the structure of a process but also the allied data structures in the user's and the kernel's world. The process life cycle under AIX is no different than traditional UNIX systems, but it is the presence of advanced context switching mechanisms, priority queue handling, and a preemptable kernel that makes the AIX process different in terms of process subsystem internals.

The basics of UNIX process management concepts have been kept concise here, as that material can be found in any of the numerous textbooks on the UNIX operating system. Concepts that highlight the unique capabilities of the operating system in areas such as support for real-time computing, threads (also called *pthreads*), and support for multiprocessor platforms have been emphasized in this discussion.

11

AIX File, Memory, and I/O Subsystem Internals

This chapter provides a tour of the I/O subsystem of AIX. Internal data structures related to file, I/O, and memory are explained in light of their functions, features, and benefits. The discussion begins with a design overview of the file system and is followed by a detailed description of the logical file system, physical file system, mapped files, and journaled file system. The virtual memory subsystem is discussed next, with regard to its page replacement, memory load control, and code pinning policies. Finally, a description of the I/O management and its key features is presented from a systems point of view.

11.1 AIX FILE SYSTEM

The AIX file system can be described through a logical view of the file layout, as well as through a physical view of the file organization. The logical perspective is referred to as the *logical file system,* and the physical view of the file layout is called AIX's *physical file system.* The logical file system includes the traditional inverted tree structure as seen on all UNIX systems. Directories, links, etc. are all considered a part of the logical file system. Three different file system types are supported by AIX:

- Journaled file system
- Network file system
- CD-ROM file system

The journaled file system specifies the native AIX file system. The network file system specifies the file system type that permits files residing on remote machines to be accessed as though they resided on a local machine. The CD-ROM file system allows the contents of a CD-ROM to be accessed through the normal file system interface (such as *open, read,* and *close*).

11.1.1 Physical file system

The physical file system maintains the system's perspective of the devices. To interface the logical file system with the physical file system, an intermediate layer of abstraction is introduced, which is the *virtual file system.* Because of this abstraction, AIX is able to support foreign file and file system types. Figure 11.1 illustrates the interfacing role of the virtual file system. The virtual file system permits user processes to access files using a universal system call interface, regardless of the location or the type of the file. Figure 11.2 demonstrates how the presence of a virtual file system changes the "standard UNIX" access to a file.

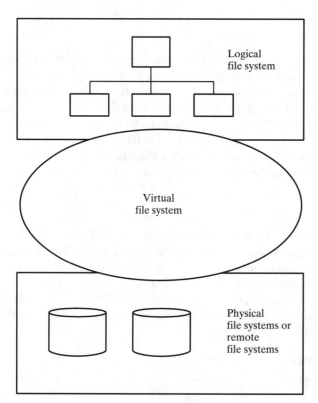

Figure 11.1 Virtual file system.

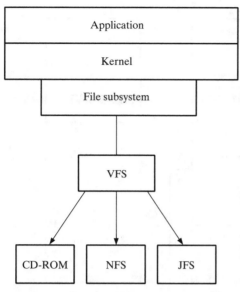

Figure 11.2 Virtual file system permitting generalization for file access.

Access to a file begins with one of the user file descriptors pointing to the file table, and the file table, in turn, pointing to the vnodes. The vnode references an affiliated gnode in the in-core inode table and also points to a structure called *vfs* that describes the mount (for example /*home* or /*usr*) that supports the file in question. This *vfs* structure has a reference pointing to a data structure called *gfs,* which describes the type of the file system, and another reference pointing back to the directory vnode upon which it is mounted. The *gfs* structure states whether the file system in question is a journaled file system, a network file system, or a CD-ROM file system. Depending on which file system type is being pointed to, the *gfs* structure indexes into two structures: a structure called *vfsops* that determines the set of operations apropos to this file system (such as mount, unmount, sync, etc.), and a structure named *vnodeops* that describes a set of functions (such as *link, mkdir, mknod*) that can be performed on vnodes from this file system. Figure 11.3 represents the tour through the tables and structures that completes the picture.

11.1.2 Memory mapped files

When one opens a normal file under AIX to read from, write to, or append to, the file is automatically mapped to memory to provide what are called *mapped files*. That is, normal file access under AIX bypasses the buffer cache subsystem that traditional UNIX systems use. By having files mapped to the system memory, the cost for a read-from or write-to a file is diminished to merely the cost for a memory write. This greatly enhances I/O performance. Although,

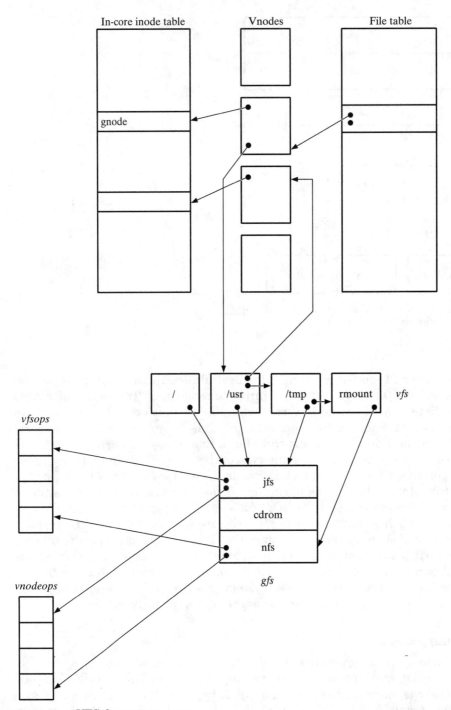

Figure 11.3 VFS data structures.

upon being opened, files get mapped implicitly by default, explicit mapping can also be requested using a set of special purpose system calls.

There are two system calls, *mmap* and *shmat,* that provide the capability for multiple processes to map the same region of an object such that they share addressability to that object. As far as choosing one over the other, the *shmat* call is used when there are a few files to be mapped simultaneously to their entirety and memory regions need to be shared among unrelated processes. The *mmap* call, on the other hand, is used when many files are to be mapped simultaneously, portability of the application is vital across other UNIX plat-forms, and there is a need to map a portion of the file.

If mapped explicitly, the file is accessed by address rather than by *read* and/or *write* system calls. There could be a performance tradeoff here; while explicitly mapped files save on the overhead cost of the *read/write* system calls, they lose the benefit of the system write-behind feature.

11.2 JOURNALED FILE SYSTEM

Traditional UNIX systems could not guarantee recovery from a crash without loss of files. The method of recovery depended excessively on utilities and the savvy of the system administrator. AIX does away with the UNIX-like way of storing and recovering information by implementing a persistent storage man-agement scheme. The mechanisms implemented by AIX in this area are radi-cally different from those in traditional UNIX systems. AIX implements a level of abstraction on top of the physical media called *logical volume.* This logical volume not only enhances the reliability of the files in the file systems but also eradicates the limitations of static file system size.

11.2.1 Logical volume manager

The logical volume manager (referred to as LVM from here on) is a paradigm that addresses the concept of virtual disks (called logical volumes) to address the evolving need of the storage subsystem. The LVM provides a layer of abstraction between the logical partition perceived by the users and the actual physical partition viewed by the operating system (refer to Fig. 11.4). LVM con-sists of two major subsystems:

- LVM subroutines
- Logical volume device driver (LVDD)

The LVM subroutines can be accessed through the logical volume data struc-tures and the logical volume device driver configuration routines, as seen in Fig. 11.5. The logical volume device driver interface is at a higher level than that of a physical device and allows an abstraction of device-specific dependen-cies (refer to Fig. 11.6 for viewing the interface layout).

The principal benefit of implementing the LVM paradigm is that it allows the extension of files, file systems, and raw partitions to multiple physical

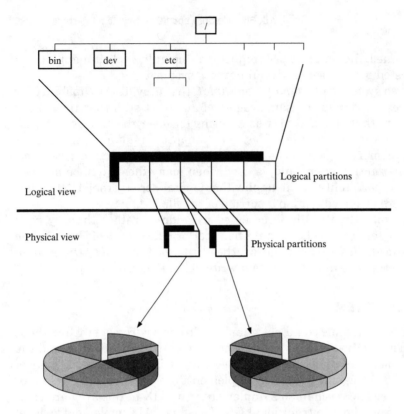

Figure 11.4 Abstraction of logical and physical partitions using the LVM.

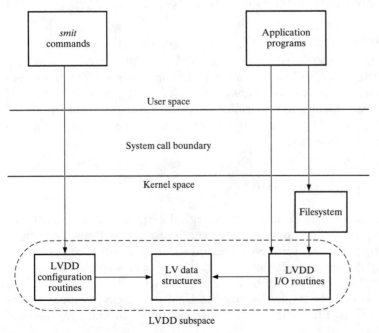

Figure 11.5 LVM execution model.

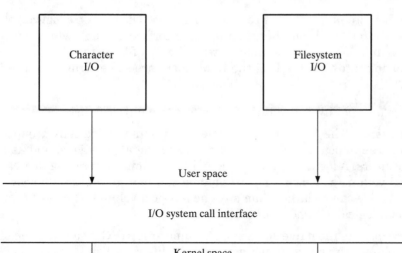

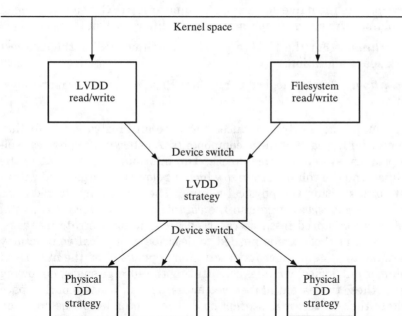

Figure 11.6 Logical volume device driver interface.

media, without modification to the existing system or application software. Since the logical volume is an abstraction, it can be made larger than the underlying physical volumes. Logical volumes can also be mirrored on multiple physical volumes to improve performance for data access and provide a greater reliability for sensitive data sets. The LVM supports transparent software bad-sector remapping, which means that it has the ability to detect and relocate bad sectors autonomously. The size of a logical volume can be increased dynamically on a running system without impacting logged-on users. The only thing a user notices is that, before increasing the logical volume size, the file system is fuller than it is after the resizing operation. The access to logical volumes is transparent with no alteration to the interface through which users and system administrators communicate with the AIX file system.

Before delving into the details of the LVM, there are some terms that need explaining.

- *Physical volume.*   Physical volume (PV) refers to a physical disk.
- *Logical volume.*   The term logical volume (LV) refers to a logically grouped area. This area appears as if it were a device to the applications, and as a disk to the users. A logical volume, in actuality, is simply a mapping to areas of physical volume(s). Since a logical volume can map to multiple physical volumes, its size can be larger than any one physical volume. The most common use of a logical volume is for a file system.
- *Volume group.*   As the name suggests, a volume group (VG) is a collection of physical volumes. A volume group may contain different disk types.
- *Physical partition.*   For the LVM, a physical partition (PP) is the smallest unit of disk space allocation.
- *Logical partition.*   A single logical partition (LP) points to one or more physical partitions

Figure 11.7 maps the newly introduced terms to an illustration to further explain the positioning each of these components. As shown, the physical volume is the primary system storage device. The information pertinent to the physical volume and the volume group to which it belongs are organized within selected data areas within the physical volume. The areas are referred to as the *physical volume reserved area* and the *volume group reserved area.* LVM uses the information stored in these reserved areas to orchestrate its tasks. Note that the size of these areas needed to describe a physical volume may vary from system to system, since its description depends upon the number of physical volumes and logical volumes constituting the storage space. Following the contents of these two essential reserved areas, a small fraction of the space is used to store the *bad sector relocation pool.* The remainder of the space on the physical volume stores the user data. Figure 11.8 shows the organization of the data area, bad-sector relocation pool, volume group reserved area, and physical volume reserved area on a physical volume.

The LVM acts as a device driver. It receives requests like *open, read, write, ioctl,* and *close,* and performs the necessary tasks to complete the operations. For example, a *read* call to a logical volume is converted to the appropriate operation on physical volumes, and is subsequently passed to the physical device driver. The LVM synchronizes the I/O and, in turn, responds to the initial logical request for that *read* operation.

In general, applications use the logical volume device nodes as a "normal device" and access it using standard *read, write,* and *ioctl* system calls. The flow of block as well as character (raw) I/O are handled by the LVDD's *strategy* routine. The driver *strategy* entry point then translates the logical address to a

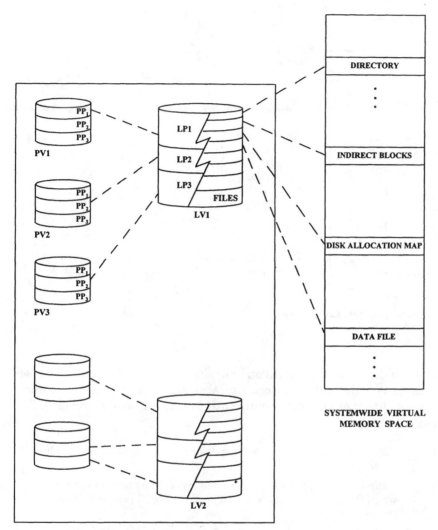

Figure 11.7 Mapping of physical and logical volumes.

physical address (handling bad-sector relocation and mirroring) and calls the appropriate physical disk device drivers. Once the I/O has completed, the physical device driver calls a routine named *biodone,* which, in turn, invokes the LV I/O completion handling routine. Once this has been completed, *biodone* is called upon again to notify the requester that the I/O is now completed.

Like any regular device driver, the LVM driver is split into two parts, the top half and the bottom half. The top half contains the *open, close, read, write,* and *ioctl* entry points. The bottom half contains the *strategy* entry point—block read and write code.

The code in the top half of the LVM device driver runs in the context of a user process address space. When commands like *ioctl* are used to manipulate a vol-

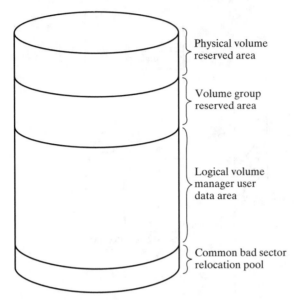

Physical volume
reserved area

Volume group
reserved area

Logical volume
manager user
data area

Common bad sector
relocation pool

Figure 11.8 Physical volume organization.

ume group and its associated logical and physical volumes, the *ioctl* call passes
through an entry point called *lv_ioctl* (an abstraction for the logical volume
layer) A complete set of I/O entry point routines like this one is provided. The
entry points are:

lv_open	Called by the file system when a device is opened or a logical volume is mounted
lv_close	Called by the file system when a logical volume is unmounted or when the last *close* has occurred on the open file corresponding to the device
lv_read	Called by the *read* system call to translate character I/O to block I/O requests
lv_write	Called by the *write* system call to translate character I/O to block I/O requests
lv_ioctl	Serves as an entry point for the *ioctl* call and also implements most of the driver programming interface

The bottom half of the LVM device driver features several layers, including
the device *strategy* entry point. This *strategy* routine is a code that is called to
process all logical block requests. This part of the LVM, the bottom half, vali-
dates I/O requests, translates logical addresses to physical addresses, handles
mirroring and bad-sector relocation, and actually starts the I/O. Unlike the top
half of the LVM device driver, this part runs in the interrupt context and is not
permitted to block.

The different layers of the bottom half of the LVM device driver are:

- *Strategy.*   Performs logical request validation, initialization, termination, and serialization of logical requests (when block ranges overlap).

- *Mirror consistency manager.*   Ensures integrity of the mirrored data (i.e., if mirroring is enabled on the system).

- *Scheduler.*   Schedules physical requests for logical operations.

- *Status area manager.*   Tracks availability of physical volumes and the state of physical extents.

11.2.2   Disk mirroring

Mirroring refers to the replication of data stored in a logical block. The LVM controls mirroring through the use of *ioctl* system call, as seen in Fig. 11.9. AIX can be *singly mirrored,* i.e., configured to maintain two copies of a data. If there

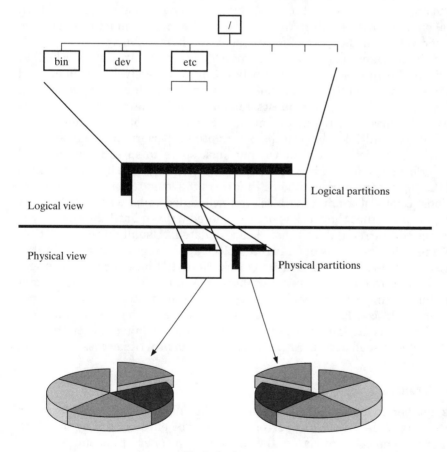

Physical volumes

Figure 11.9 Disk mirroring (singly mirrored).

are three copies, then data is said to be *doubly mirrored*. As implied from its definition, mirroring, if enabled, requires double the disk space (at a minimum) for the mirrored data. This feature remains disabled by default. If required, mirroring may be enabled using the *smit* tool. Data may be mirrored for high availability or for higher performance.

Mirroring for high availability is done to deal with situations when or if data becomes unavailable owing to media defects, a catastrophic drive failure, controller malfunction, etc. By mirroring data, the LVM is able to transparently recover from the loss of one copy of the data. When access to one copy of data is denied, the LVM redirects I/O intended for the missing data to the secondary or tertiary copy. Although this is a very useful feature for handling critical data, careful planning is a prerequisite when setting up the volume group for mirroring. Consider an example, where a configuration of two physical volumes is being used with a file system that has been singly mirrored for a total of two separate copies of the file system. If the two copies of the file system are housed on separate disks, then one disk's failure would still mean retaining access to an alternate copy of the data. But had only one disk maintained both physical volumes, a disk failure would have resulted in a complete loss of data, thereby defeating the purpose of mirroring for high availability.

Mirroring for higher performance is carried out if there are data blocks that are subjected to intensive I/O, primarily owing to excessively frequent read operations. Having multiple copies of a data block which can be accessed in parallel by concurrent read requests renders quicker data access than one without disk mirroring. If implemented, the mirrored copies should be distributed across multiple physical disks for optimal performance. On systems equipped with sufficient hard drives and disk space to spread the mirrored blocks, performance for read access is achieved by the system by scheduling to access the copy of the mirrored block that costs the least to retrieve. For write operations, copies of a mirrored block get scheduled to be written whenever feasible, meaning that the block is not considered written until the last copy of its associated mirrored block has been updated. Usually the total time required to write the copies of a mirrored block approximates the time it takes to write the slowest copy of a mirrored block. Note that lack of careful configuration planning to ensure proper distribution of mirror copies across disjoint physical disks can result in performance degradation instead of performance enhancement. In conclusion, mirroring is not always the best way to achieve high performance. Its gain is significant when data is mirrored for the purposes of frequent read access, rather than for frequent write access.

11.2.3 Bad block relocation

This is another configurable feature that can be enabled or disabled based on the need. There are two kinds of errors that may be encountered by the LVM: (1) soft errors and (2) hard errors. Based on the type of error encountered, the LVM takes the appropriate actions.

When the LVM detects a soft (correctable) read error, it attempts to rewrite the data, with write verification to the physical drive, potentially correcting the error. Either of two things can happen. If there is no support for write verification on the disk drive and the LVM rewrite fails, the soft error gets treated as a hard error. On the other hand, if the disk drive supports write verification, the read succeeds; this is followed by the LVM performing a write operation to the relocated area and relocating the sector.

When the LVM detects a hard (uncorrectable) error, it relocates the sector. The operation is performed using a pool of data sectors that is maintained for this purpose. All subsequent I/O is then directed to the new sector. If the data is mirrored, then LVM redirects the failed read to another copy of the data and subsequently relocates and rewrites the relocated bad sector. When no mirroring of the data is available, the LVM returns an error. Later, when the sector is updated, it gets relocated and is again capable of storing data.

11.3   MEMORY SUBSYSTEM

The memory subsystem internals of AIX is one of the areas that differs fundamentally from traditional UNIX operating systems. The memory management scheme of the operating system was rearchitected to make the best use of the processor's architectural features. In regard to the storage space, there are three fundamental objects that form the infrastructure of the memory subsystem: (1) real memory, (2) virtual memory, and (3) disk space. The real memory frames and the virtual memory pages are divided up into basic units, each of which is 4 KB in size. The disk space is also partitioned into basic units called blocks, each of which is 4 KB.

real memory → frames (each 4 KB in size)

virtual memory → pages (each 4 KB in size)

page space → blocks (each 4 KB in size)

From the system's perspective, virtual memory encompasses both real memory and disk (the file system and the paging space). A virtual memory address may point to a page on disk or to a page in real memory, depending on whether the reference is being made to an active or an inactive portion of the program. A road map of the general page mapping concept is illustrated in Fig. 11.10, where a virtual page number from the virtual address space indexes into a table called the external page table (XPT) to resolve whether to go to the paging area or to go to the real memory. If the address is meant for the paging space, then it directly points to the location on the paging space. But if the address were to point to the real memory, it must derive its real page number prior to accessing the real memory. This real page number is generated from a structure called the page frame table (PFT).

11.3.1   Memory addressability

As far as addressability goes, the AIX kernel, in conjunction with the processor, provides a per-process address space of 4 GB (2^{32}) and a total system address space of 4 PB (2^{52}). Note that the upper limit on real memory supported by the

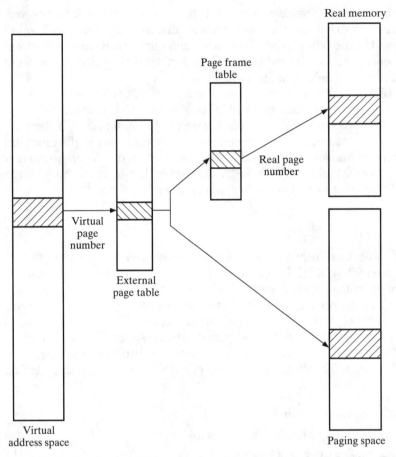

Figure 11.10 Road map of the general page mapping mechanism.

32-bit implementation of the POWER and PowerPC architectures is 4 GB, whereas the upper limit on real memory supported by the 64-bit implementation of the PowerPC architecture is 16 EB. Think about the total systemwide virtual address space consisting of 2^{52} bytes that is divided into approximately 2^{24} segments for a 32-bit implementation. In the future, when AIX offers a 64-bit implementation, the total systemwide virtual address space will consist of 2^{80} bytes that is divided into 2^{52} segments. To understand the hardware architectural dependencies on memory addressability, refer to Sec. 3.3.3.4 and Fig. 3.8.

11.3.2 Segmented memory

Associated with each process is an array that holds the addresses of 16 segments, which happen to be the range of virtual memory addressable by that process. For a running process, its array containing the addresses of the 16 segments addressable by the process itself are held in the 16 segment registers.

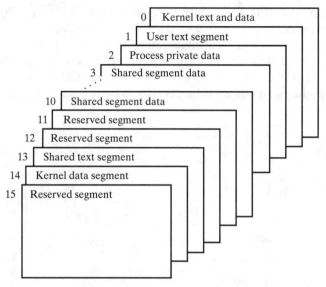

Figure 11.11 Segmented memory.

Access to segments is regulated by the mode (i.e., kernel mode versus user mode) in which the process is serving at that instant. For kernel processes, this is not a problem, as they always run in kernel mode. But processes executing in user mode have access to a limited number of segments; they have read/write access to segment 2 and any shared data segments that the process may have attached, and read access to segments 1 and 13. The remaining segments cannot be accessed by user-mode processes directly.* This description of the process address space is better understood with the help of a diagram; the layout of the segments is illustrated in Fig. 11.11.

From the kernel's perspective, text and data in segments 0 and 11 through 15 serve all processes, while the other segments are process-specific. Segment 0 houses the text and data for the base kernel along with kernel extensions (if any). Segments 1 and 2 are private for each process and remain protected from being accessed by other processes. Segments 3 through 10 are shared data segments and can be used to hold explicitly mapped files, or as shared memory for processes that have requested access via a shared memory system call (refer to Sec. 11.1.2). Segments 11 and 12 are used to manage the kernel structures used by the virtual memory manager (VMM). Segment 13 is the shared text segment and holds text loaded from shared objects, such as *libc.a*. Segment 14 serves as the kernel data segment, which holds kernel structures, data, and, most important of all, the *proc* table. Last, segment 15 is reserved for I/O

---

* In order to access an area other than what is referenced by segments 1, 2, 13, and shared data segments (if attached), a user process has to either be in kernel mode or access an address in the virtual memory address space indirectly by opening a pseudodevice called *kmem,* located in the /*dev* directory.

addresses. Figure 11.12 is a graphical depiction of where each of the sixteen segments points to.

Segments which point to additional data structures require some more explanation. Segment 0, which contains the kernel text and data, includes the heap and its allied control structures. Segment 1 contains the user process text—i.e., the code. Segment 2 is the process private segment and it includes the initialized data, uninitialized data (*bss*), user heap, user stack, system call

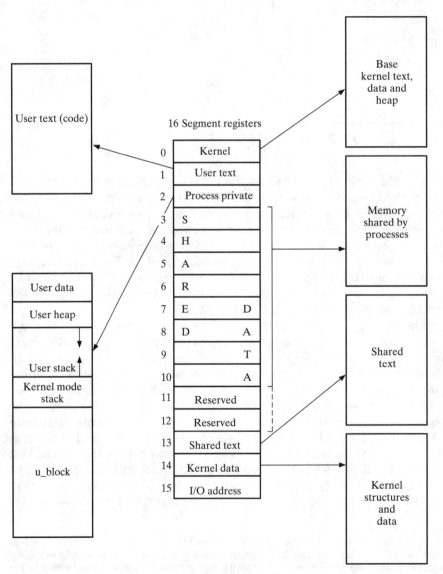

Figure 11.12 Segmented memory of the AIX kernel.

error code variable *errno,** kernel mode stack (used by auto variables in kernel extensions), user block, and kernel mode heap. Segment 11 is allocated for use by the VMM to refer to kernel structures such as the page frame table, hash anchor table, page device table, and segment control block. The page frame table (PFT) is a structure that is allocated at boot time with one entry for each frame of physical memory. This PFT is referenced whenever the cache and the TLB[†] has failed to provide a real address. The PFT is actually two parallel non-pageable tables with a hash anchor table to hold the hashed list of pages and to refer back to a segment information table. This segment information table contains entries (each of which is called a *segment control block*) to describe each segment in the system. The different kinds of segments recognized by the VMM are discussed later in this section.

Continuing with the description of subsequent segments, segment 12 is allocated for use by the VMM to reference the page table area containing the external page table and area page map. The external page table (XPT) is a collection of structures that is used to construct an external page table for every working segment by having each of its entries describe the location of that page, primarily pointing out whether the page in question is in real memory or on the paging space. References made by the remaining segments are straightforward and has been discussed in the previous paragraph.

11.3.3 Virtual memory management

As described earlier, virtual memory segments are partitioned into fixed-size units called *pages.* Each page's size is 4 KB. A page can be in real memory or on disk until needed. Similarly, real memory is divided into fixed-sized units called *page frames.* The role of the virtual memory manager (VMM) is to manage the allocation of real memory page frames and to resolve process references to virtual memory pages that are not currently in real memory. Figure 11.13 shows how a 4-bit index into the segment registers is used and a page offset into the virtual segment table is derived from an effective address, to access an element.

There are several subcomponents within the VMM. They are:

- Segment manager
- Virtual page manager
- Page frame manager
- Page fault handler
- Persistent storage manager

---

* It is a global variable that holds an error code to indicate why a system call failed.

[†] TLB is an acronym for translation lookaside buffer, a hardware structure which is responsible for translating virtual page numbers to real page numbers.

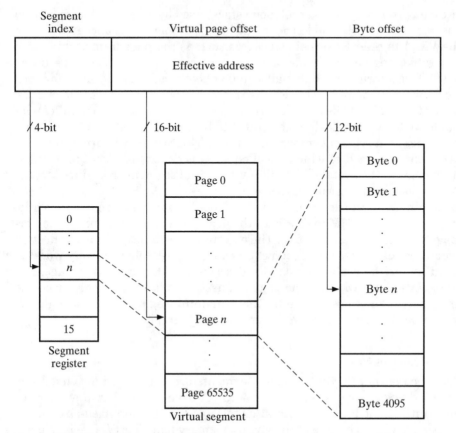

Figure 11.13 Accessing an element in virtual memory using the 16 segment registers, virtual segment, and byte offset.

The segment manager provides functions to create, modify, copy, and destroy virtual memory segments. The virtual page manager manages the mapping of virtual memory pages to disk slots on external storage. The page frame manager orchestrates the allocation and deallocation of physical memory page frames to virtual pages, and the lists of free page frames, mapped page frames, and page frames in use, for I/O operations. The page fault handler is responsible for handling the page faults which occur when a referenced virtual address is not mapped within the PFT. The persistent storage manager providesatabase memory, transaction processing, locking, and logging services for the physical file system.

The VMM distinguishes between types of segments based upon the function performed by them and the way they are backed to external storage when paging occurs. There are three kinds of segments that are recognized by the VMM:

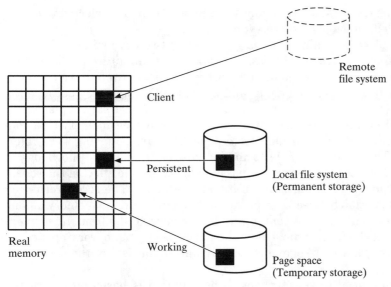

Figure 11.14 Different segment types supported by AIX.

- *Working storage segments.* These include dynamically allocated structures and variables, and copy-on-write mapped pages* that do not have a permanent backing storage.

- *Persistent storage segments.* AIX accesses all files as mapped files. This means that program and/or file access begins with a few initial pages getting copied into virtual storage segments. Subsequent pages are "page-faulted in" on demand.

- *Client segments.* This type of segment includes pages that are brought in via NFS or any other type of remote file system.

Figure 11.14 shows the different segment types supported by AIX.

11.3.4 Page replacement

The VMM maintains a list of free page frames that it uses to accommodate pages that must be brought into memory. Unless a virtual memory page is pinned, it may become paged out when extra memory frames are needed. In a memory-constrained environment, the VMM occasionally replenishes the free list (number of empty page frames in memory) by removing some of the current data from real memory, effectively "stealing" the real memory frames. The vir-

---

* Mapped files may be read-only, read-write, or copy-on-write. The phrase "copy-on-write" refers to the fact that any changes made to the data are stored in the paging area and not written back to the original file. Only an *fsync* system call will cause the pages to be written back to disk.

tual memory pages, whose page frames are to be stolen, are selected using an algorithm called the *page replacement algorithm*.

The page replacement algorithm is governed by two key artifacts. The first one is the use of repaging statistics. A *repage fault* differs from a new *page fault* in the sense that the page in question, which is known to have been referenced recently, is referenced again and is not found in memory because the page has been replaced since it was last accessed. A perfect page replacement scheme would eliminate repage faults entirely (excluding memory-size constraints) by always stealing frames from pages that are not going to be referenced again. This is not feasible to implement, as it requires knowledge of future page references. However, it is possible to reduce the effect of the repaging phenomenon by using statistics of its past behavior. The second criterion used is the distinction between computational memory and file memory among the memory-resident pages. A *computational memory* differs from *file memory* in the sense that the former consists of the pages belonging to working storage segments or program text segments and the latter consists of the remaining pages.

The technique used to select pages to be replaced is based on one of the generic page replacement algorithms known as the *clock hand algorithm*. It makes use of a referenced bit for each page to determine what pages have been used, or referenced recently. When the page replacement routine is invoked, it cycles through the page frame table, examining each page's referenced bit. If a page is found unreferenced and is replaceable, it is placed on the free list. If a selected page is found modified since it was last written to the disk (file system space or the page space), the page is written out prior to being placed on the free list. If a page was referenced, it is not selected for page out; instead, its reference bit is reset. Additional intelligence, added to the page replacement policy under AIX, ensures that the computational pages get fair treatment. What this means is that, if a huge data file was to be read into memory sequentially, it ought not to page out text pages which are likely to be reused soon. The VMM attempts to keep the size of the free list around a fixed range. If page faults or system demands cause the free list size to fall below the low threshold, the page replacement algorithm frees up enough pages to make the free list larger than the high threshold, thus maintaining a consistent size for the free list.

11.3.5 Memory load control

When a process references virtual memory pages that are on disk, the referenced page must be paged in. This creates I/O traffic and delay. If the main memory is fully occupied and there aren't any free pages left, *thrashing* may happen. Thrashing is the result of incessant I/O to the paging disk, wherein processes encounter page faults almost as soon as they are dispatched. To eradicate this phenomenon, a load control algorithm is implemented that detects when the system is beginning to thrash, and consequently suspends active processes (by putting them to sleep and freeing up all the memory they are using) until the system has recovered from thrashing.

This load control feature is settable as well as tunable. This means that one can disable the memory load control feature of the operating system if no suspension of active processes owing to detection of thrashing is desired, or if compatibility with earlier versions of AIX, which lacked this load control feature, is needed. As far as tuning goes, the memory load control feature can be fine-tuned to best meet the requirements of an individual system and its workload.

The memory load control mechanism works by attempting to determine if there is a scarcity of memory frames for the set of active processes on the system. This inference is made by the scheduler once every second. Based on an analysis of the previous second's snapshot, the scheduler determines if processes are to be suspended or activated. If it is to suspend processes, the nominated processes are marked up and are consequently suspended at the earliest opportunity that the system gets to have the processes in user mode.

11.3.6   Code pinning

When code and data associated with a device driver is pinned in real memory—that is, it is exempt from being paged out to disk—response time for that device improves dramatically, as there is no time lost to page faults. If not used properly, pinning can result in serious performance problems on the system throughput.

11.4   I/O SUBSYSTEM

I/O management under AIX has two characteristic traits, namely an asynchronous I/O facility and a page-hiding property. Other functionalities are no different than on traditional UNIX systems.

11.4.1   Asynchronous I/O

The term *synchronous I/O* alludes to the notion that I/O occurs while one waits for it to complete. In contrast, asynchronous I/O does not cause applications to wait. This, in general, improves performance, since the I/O operations and the applications can both progress at the same time. Transaction-processing applications like databases are able to take generous advantage of this feature for performing overlapped compute tasks and I/O.

This facility is an implementation of the POSIX Asynchronous Input and Output Interface 1003.4 document. The functions provided by the asynchronous I/O facilities are (1) nonblocking I/O, (2) cancellation of I/O requests, and (3) notification of I/O event completions. The nonblocking I/O facility allows the applications to proceed with their execution without being blocked; it does so, by queuing the requests and allowing the application to continue execution. Cancellation of I/O requests works only if the request is still in the queue and its I/O operations have not yet started. Notification of I/O event completions are handled by either having the application poll for the status of that I/O operation periodically, or by sending an asynchronous notification status to the application.

Multiple asynchronous I/O requests may be issued on the same device by one or more applications. But remember that, since the operations are performed asynchronously, the order in which the I/O calls are handled may not be the order in which they were issued.

11.4.2 I/O pacing

Interactive processes on the system occasionally suffer from long response times when used in environments with heavy I/O on a moderately loaded system. Although this is quite normal in multiuser time-sliced environments, the interactive applications in particular are noticed by the user community. The reason for this symptom should be evident: it has to do with pending I/O requests being the bottleneck. *I/O pacing* is a feature of the memory manager that can put an upper limit on the number of I/O requests that can be outstanding against a file at any given time. When this limit is exceeded, the process with pending I/O requests is suspended (by putting it to sleep) long enough so that the outstanding requests can be processed and a lower threshold level is reached. In traditional UNIX systems, including previous releases of AIX, users occasionally encountered a multiple-second delay when another application was performing a large number of writes to disk. As most writes are asynchronous, long queues can build up, which cause several seconds worth of delay. The disk I/O pacing feature eliminates this problem. However, there may be instances with real-time computing requirements where this feature can hurt processes performing intensive I/O. Keeping in mind the diverse requirements for response time, this feature has been made a selectable option rather than hard-coded.

By default, pacing remains disabled. One may enable pacing in AIX using *smit* and specifying the number of pages for upper and lower limits to suitable values, if large I/O-intensive jobs on the system inhibit interactive response time.

11.5 DEVICE SUBSYSTEM

The device I/O subsystem allows a process to communicate with devices such as disks, tapes, terminals, printers, and networks. Its low-level modules, which actually control these devices, are referred to as *device drivers*. In its simplest form, a device driver moves data between hardware devices and user applications, where the user applications supply and consume information. In general, there is a one-to-one correspondence between device drivers and device types: systems may contain one disk driver to control all disk drives, one terminal driver to control all terminals, etc. But note that installations that have devices from more than one manufacturer—for example, two brands of 4-mm tape drives—may treat the devices as two different device types and have two separate drivers, because such devices may require different command sequences to operate properly. The system also supports software devices that have no associated physical device. For instance, the kernel treats the physical memory as a device to allow a process access to physical memory outside its address space, even though memory is not a physical device.

11.5.1 Device drivers overview

Device drivers run in a privileged state as kernel extensions. This implicitly indicates that device drivers have access to a number of functions or services that are not available to normal application programs.

11.5.2 Major and minor numbers

Devices are identified in the kernel through major and minor numbers. Usually a major number identifies a particular device driver. A minor number identifies various device instances known to the device driver. Note that a device driver may be assigned multiple major numbers. Also, minor numbers can be used to identify different modes of operation for a device as well as different device instances.

11.5.3 Character and block device drivers

There are two types of devices: *block* devices and *character* devices. Devices such as disk that appear like random-access storage are denoted as block devices, whereas devices like terminals and network interfaces are referred to as character (or raw) devices. Note that those which act as block devices may have a separate character device interface, too.

11.5.4 Device switch table

The kernel-to-driver interface is described by a structure called the *device switch table*. Each device type has entries in that table that direct the kernel to the appropriate driver interfaces for the system calls.

11.5.5 Device head and device handler

A device driver consists of a *device head* and a *device handler*. A device head is the portion of a driver that provides interfaces to application programs through the standard *open, close, read, write,* and related system calls. The device head accepts I/O requests from application programs and communicates them to a device handler. The interface between application programs and a device head is rigidly defined by the kernel. Its prime functions are converting requests from the form of a file I/O function call to a form that is recognizable by the device handler, performing I/O blocking and data buffering, handling error recovery, and managing the I/O request queues.

Device handler is the portion of a device driver that communicates with the actual device and/or adapter. It takes requests from a device head and implements the requests on actual hardware. It should be noted that the interface between a device head and a device handler is not defined, though the operating system provides a large number of primitives to assist in constructing an interface. The details are always device-driver-specific, and are mostly left up to the preference of the device driver author.

Device driver routines providing support for physical devices typically run in two different types of environments. The top half of the driver always runs in the environment of the calling process. This is normally pageable. The bottom part of the device driver runs in the process or interrupt environment. This performs the actual I/O and needs to be pinned so that page faults are not taken in the interrupt execution environment.

11.6 OBJECT DATA MANAGER

ODM (object data manager) is an object-oriented database. It is sort of like an unsung hero, as it maintains all the metadata on a running system in the background at all times, but no one directly sees its contribution.

The ODM fully supports the concepts of object classes and objects. An *object class* is a group of objects with the same definition. An *object,* a member of a defined object class, is an entity that needs storage and management of data. In fact, an object class is conceptually similar to an array of structures, with each object being a structure that is an element of the array. A given object class is also associated with a set of descriptor(s). These descriptors take up values when the object is added to an object class.

Although ODM's configuration information in its entirety is complex, it can be viewed as a set of predefined and customized information. The predefined information pertains to all the possible devices (and their default configurations) that AIX supports, while the customized information includes the actually installed devices along with their current configurations. In other words, the predefined object class defines what can be there, while the customized object class describes what is actually there. Unlike traditional UNIX, AIX categorizes devices hierarchically, allowing for structured device management. Not only are similar devices clustered under the same functional class, but their dependencies with allied devices are also mapped out. The benefit of this is in the degree of control that devices have with one another. This scheme guarantees that a higher-level device such as a SCSI adapter always retains a cohesive bond with all its lower-level members such as disk drives and tape drives, and does not get reconfigured or unconfigured by accident. In order to store these device-to-device mappings, the location of devices is also stored by ODM. As a result, the location code becomes handy for identifying the paths and dependencies of each device. A typical location code looks as follows:

DD-SS-CC-PP

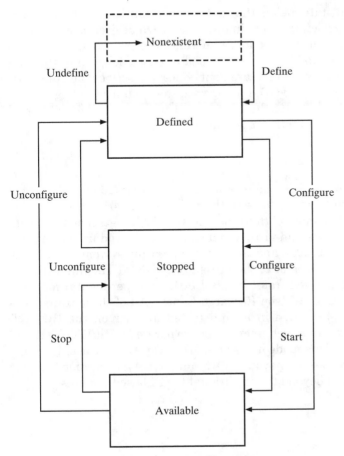

Figure 11.15 Device-state transition diagram.

In it, PP gives the port number,* CC points out the connector location, SS represents the slot in which the adapter is installed, and DD indicates the drawer number.

While using *smit* (system management interface tool) to install and/or configure devices, one may find that devices are either "available" or "defined" in the ODM database of the system. There is a subtle difference between the two states which is often confusing. Overall, a device may be either usable or unusable on the system, based on its state. This state is a function of the object classes of the ODM. As seen in the device state transition diagram in Fig. 11.15, a state can be defined, configured, reconfigured (changed), undefined, or unconfigured. When undefined, a device implicates that the entry is in the predefined object class of the ODM, but it is not resident in the customized object

---

* This convention has a slight exception for SCSI devices. The two digits of the PP field identify the SCSI id number and logical unit number (LUN).

class. An unconfigured state means that a device's definition has been moved from the available to the defined state in the customized devices object class. A device becomes defined upon detection, and this happens when the ODM's device-specific define method is invoked to load a device driver into the running kernel. This is a very powerful statement, since it describes the automatic device definition property of the ODM along with the dynamic binding feature of the AIX kernel. This ability of the base kernel to dynamically load kernel extensions sets AIX apart from the other variants of UNIX.

11.7 SUMMARY

The three key concepts used in the evolution of the augmented I/O storage facility of AIX are derivatives of some of the well-known early computer systems. The large virtual memory of this machine and the integration of file subsystem with logical volumes and virtual memory were evolved from computer systems like the IBM System/38 and the earlier operating system, MULTICS, which is regarded as the ancestor of the present-day UNIX. The innovation of database memory was derived from the IBM 801, an experimental machine developed at the Thomas J. Watson Research Center. All of these traits were combined and first implemented in an integrated manner on the IBM RT. Later, the concepts were improved upon and incorporated in the POWER and PowerPC architectures. This made it possible to deliver AIX as the only implementation of the UNIX operating system with unique I/O and storage features that stand out above and beyond the traditional UNIX based systems.

What You Need to Build a PowerPC

This chapter provides a description of the devices, interfaces, and data formats required to design and build a PowerPC based industry standard computer system. The hardware standard, when coupled with the hardware abstraction software of operating systems, enables one to build PowerPC systems which run compliant operating systems and shrink-wrapped applications for those operating environments.

Today's diverse base of computer systems limits the system designer's ability to add new features without jeopardizing compatibility and interoperability. To sustain and continue to grow, one has to be able to construct computer architectures that are modular in nature and provided scalable scope of growth, expansion, and upgrade.

Any computer system has a set of key subsystems like the memory, connectivity, storage, expansion, and human interface, which are independent of the processor type and can be characterized on their own accord. There is always a variety of options available as to how to implement these subsystems. For example, the requirements for the system expansion bus subsystem can be met using a VME, EISA, ISA, NUBUS, or MCA bus. However, what kind of bus is to be used is left up to the vendor or integrator.

The guidelines provided here are intended to make the reader's choices easier regarding the selections of each of the subsystems. Note that this information can also be found in the *PowerPC Reference Platform Specification Guide*. This chapter includes excerpts that provide an overview of what it would take to build a PowerPC based computer system.

Dataflow through the computer emphasizes a hierarchical pyramid of resources (depicted in Fig. 12.1). The highest level resource is the processor. It is followed by the cache subsystem, and, subsequently, the memory subsystem. Beyond that, there is the connectivity subsystem, followed by the storage and expansion subsystems. As stated before, there can be a choice for implementing each of the levels in the hierarchical pyramid. To understand the positioning of the various types of buses that link the different subsystems in the computer with one another, refer to Fig. 12.2.

12.1 MEMORY SUBSYSTEMS

The memory subsystems are broken down into the subcomponents discussed in the following subsections.

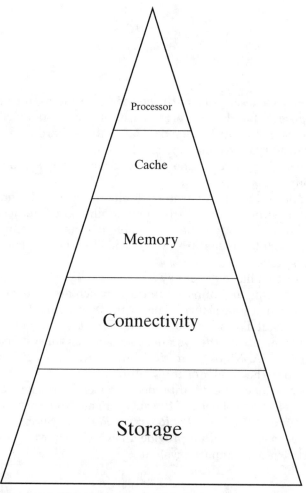

Figure 12.1 Hierarchical pyramid of resources.

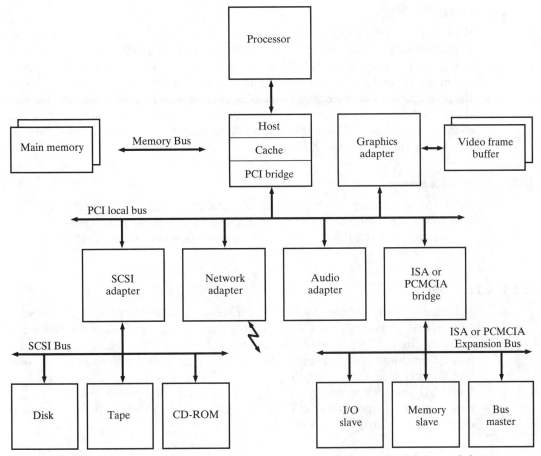

Figure 12.2 Positioning of various buses in a typical system. Hierarchical layout of the processor bus, memory bus, PCI bus, SCSI bus, and the system expansion buses (e.g., ISA or PCMCIA).

12.1.1 System memory

PowerPC Reference Platform (PReP) system configurations require a minimum of 8 MB of system memory with at least 8 MB of expansion capability. It is recommended that a minimum of at least 16 MB of memory be supplied on a system which is to support any of the operating systems. In addition, at least 24 MB of system memory expansion capability is advised beyond the minimum of 8 MB that is implemented. Expansions to system memory are added directly to the same bus on which the base system memory exists. System memory and expansions to system memory may be located elsewhere as long as coherency is maintained. The systems processor must be able to read and write system memory. The state of this memory must be valid as long as power is applied to the memory subsystem. The system memory must also support cache line burst operations from the target processor.

12.1.2 System ROM

System ROM contains the firmware required by the system. Typically, system ROM is implemented using ROM, EPROM, or flash ROM. It is strongly recommended that system ROM be writable by the system processor. This memory must be readable by the system processors, but it may not be accessible to the system I/O processors. The size of this memory is dictated by the size required to implement the systems firmware. Normally, system ROM is not cached. If system ROM is cached, then system ROM must support burst transfers to the target processor.

12.1.3 Nonvolatile memory

Nonvolatile memory is required to maintain the system in the absence of system power. This memory must be readable and writable by the system processor. A minimum of 4 KB of nonvolatile memory is required for the PReP system configuration.

12.1.4 I/O memory

I/O memory can exist on the system expansion bus and is part of the I/O subsystems. It is typically not cached. If an implementor chooses to cache I/O memory, then software must manage the coherence. I/O memory may also be located on the primary processor bus. If it is located on the primary processor bus, the I/O memory will participate in the hardware managed coherency protocol. I/O memory is configured separately from the system memory in the memory map. Candidates for I/O memory include graphics buffers, communications buffers, and I/O processor memory.

12.1.5 Memory mapped system I/O

Part of the memory subsystem is the addressing and communications with diverse I/O devices. Within the PowerPC architecture, I/O is performed by loads and stores to or from areas of the memory space, which are mapped to the I/O addresses. To communicate with I/O on a secondary bus, PReP systems are required to generate I/O addresses. Addresses in the memory space must be converted by the bus bridges to the addresses of the I/O on the bus. These I/O addresses must be compatible with existing adaptors and be configurable at boot time.

12.1.6 Secondary cache

A secondary (also referred to as L2) cache may be included as an optional part of the system.

12.2 STORAGE SUBSYSTEMS

The following components are included in the storage subsystems.

12.2.1 Interface

The storage subsystem should use a fast SCSI-2 interface to support hardfiles and CD-ROMs. This interface will also support scanners, tapes, optical storage, and RAID based storage systems.

12.2.2 Hardfile

PReP system configurations should have either a hardfile or hardfile capability (which is storage provided remotely via a network). In either case, the minimum size for this storage is 80 MB. Systems requiring hardfile capability can achieve this by direct connection through SCSI or IDE, networking, or an expansion adapter. It is strongly recommended that PReP systems capable of containing a hardfile have one with a capacity greater than 200 MBs. This size will be sufficient to support any of the operating systems in their basic configurations.

12.2.3 Diskette

Diskette drives must support 3.5-in, 1.44-MB MFM format diskettes achieved through direct connection to a floppy drive. Optional features of the floppy drive include autoeject, which allows the software to control ejection of the media and media presence detection.

12.2.4 CD-ROM

The CD-ROM device should support, at a minimum, the ISO 9660 standard which is achieved through direct connection, such as SCSI or IDE. It may also be achieved through networking or expansion adaptor connection.

12.3 HUMAN INTERFACE SUBSYSTEMS

The human interface subsystem consists of an alphanumeric input device, pointing device, audio capability, and graphics options as discussed in the following subsections.

12.3.1 Alphanumeric input device

PReP system configurations require an alphanumeric input device, typically a keyboard. Even though no particular keyboard interface is specified, it is essential that the input device be capable of generating at least 101 scan codes that can be interpreted by the machine-specific layer of the device driver. Typically, most system environments require a direct attached keyboard; those that do not include servers or multiuser systems with terminals attached.

12.3.2 Pointer device

Some of the system configurations such as workstations, which have directly attached keyboards, typically require a pointing device, like a mouse, tablet, or touch screen. The pointing device is required to provide two-dimensional positioning as well as the capability of generating at least mouse up and down events. Some operating systems may require additional scan codes. The pointing device should be able to report the positioning information with at least the pixel resolution of the largest display supported by that system.

12.3.3 Audio

PReP compliant configurations require audio capability. Audio must be capable of analog audio in and out. The audio capability should provide 16-bit stereo samples at sample rates of 44.1KHz and 22.05 KHz.

12.3.4 Graphics

Configurations in an operating environment that requires directly attached graphics subsystems must support at least a 640×480, direct-mapped, 8-bit-per-pixel display device. The software interface to the graphics subsystem is accomplished through an implementation-bus-interface-specific device driver. Most systems require directly attached graphics systems. An example of a system that does not require a directly attached graphics device is a server (data server or a computer screen).

For the colors and resolution capabilities, the graphics subsystem should support color depth of 16 or 24 bits and higher resolutions of at least 1024×768 pixels. Note that these graphics resolution specification requirements apply to the graphics adapter and frame buffer, and not to the graphics mode or display requirements. It is also recommended that the graphics subsystem support Big-Endian operations to allow the *Endianness* of the graphics frame buffer and registers to be set independently of the Endian mode of the processor.

12.4 REAL-TIME CLOCK

PReP compliant configurations require a real-time clock (RTC). The RTC must operate in the absence of external power via a battery power source. It is required that the RTC provide the necessary information to determine year, month, day, hour, minutes, and seconds. The recommended day accuracy of the RTC should be at least +/– .001 percent, which is about one second per day.

12.5 CONNECTIVITY SUBSYSTEMS

The following components are included in the connectivity subsystems.

12.5.1 Serial

All configurations require at least one serial port. Compliant systems should implement this serial port using EIA-232C signal compatibility. This serial port must support asynchronous protocol with Baud rates up to at least 19.2 K. Console functionality via an ASCII terminal may be provided by this serial port.

12.5.2 Parallel

A minimum of one parallel port is required on the compliant systems. The parallel port should use the Centronics 8-bit bidirectional protocol. However, it is recommended that the Extended Capability Port (ECP) protocol be used if possible instead of the Centronics protocol.

12.5.3 Network

LocalTalk (EIA-422) is a direct network connection recommended for low-end connections. LocalTalk is compatible with the SCC 8530 controller and is defined by interface standards and protocols. A LAN connectivity option is recommended for high-performance environments, preferably Ethernet or Token Ring. Additional options for network connections include ATM, ISDN, FDDI, and Isochronous Ethernet.

12.6 EXPANSION BUS OPTIONS

No particular expansion bus is mandatory. It is recommended that systems implementing an expansion bus should probably use PCI, PCMCIA, and/or an ISA bus. These buses are supported by the current operating system ports to PReP systems. Other buses which could be used with modifications to the abstraction software of each hosted operating system include VME, EISA, NUBUS, VL, and MCA.

12.7 INTERFACE STANDARDS

This sections lists and describes standards applicable to the PowerPC Reference Platform subsystems. Implementation recommendations for these standards are also provided.

12.7.1 SCSI

Small computer system interface (SCSI) is an ANSI standard specification for a peripheral bus. PowerPC based systems that implement SCSI must comply with the ANSI standard X3.131-1990 (Revision 10c) for SCSI-2 (Fast SCSI). This standard specifies the electrical interface as well as the internal system connector. It is recommended that SCSI implementations use nondifferential signaling with active termination. Use of this standard provides a convenient method for accessing CD-ROM, tape, hardfile, scanner, optical, and floptical drives.

12.7.2 IDE

IDE is an optional interface for hardfiles. IDE implementations should comply with the X3.221 AT Attachment: Proposed American National Standards. A local-bus, enhanced-IDE standard has been developed for PowerPC systems using IDE.

12.7.3 Ethernet

If Ethernet is implemented, it must adhere to the Ethernet and IEEE 802.3 standards. This specification covers both the electrical interface and the connectors. Refer to Fig. 12.2 to understand the positioning of the Ethernet network adapter.

12.7.4 Token ring

If Token Ring is implemented, it must adhere to IEEE 802.5 standards. This specification covers both the electrical interface and the connector. Refer to Fig. 12.2 to understand the positioning of the token-ring adapter.

12.7.5 Serial

The EIA-232C standard for computer serial port connectors should be used. It is recommended that compliant systems implement EIA-232C using a 9-pin D-shell male connector and pin assignments as defined in Fig. 12.3.

12.7.6 LocalTalk

LocalTalk is the standard Macintosh serial port. It is recommended that compliant systems implement EIA-422 using the 9-pin connector and the pin-out, as shown in Fig. 12.4.

12.7.7 Parallel port

This port is specified by IEEE P1284, Standard Signaling Method for a Bidirectional Parallel Peripheral Interface for Personal Computers. P1284 is the formalized and enhanced version of the popular Centronics interface.

12.7.8 PCI bus

The PCI (peripheral component interconnect) bus is a system board-resident bus that can be populated with adapters requiring fast accesses to each other and/or system memory. Refer to Fig. 12.2 to understand the positioning of a PCI

Figure 12.3 9-pin D-shell serial connector.

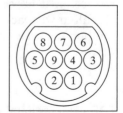

Figure 12.4 9-pin LocalTalk connector.

with respect to other buses in a system. One of the characteristic features of this bus is that all its read/write transfers are burst transfers and the variable-size length of the bursts are negotiated between the initiator and target devices.

The PCI bus, if implemented, must adhere to its standards developed by Intel Corporation, and now managed by a consortium known as the PCI Special Interest Group.

12.7.9   PCMCIA bus

The PCMCIA standard defines the physical requirements, electrical specifications, and software architecture for the 68-pin cards and their sockets. Release 1.0 cards and sockets of the PCMCIA supported only memory operations and had no I/O capabilities. Release 2.0 and later releases of the specification allow the full range of I/O capabilities. The PReP compliant systems should support the sockets that are Release 2.0 and beyond compatible.

The PCMCIA software architecture has two key elements: Socket Services and Card Services. Socket Services is a hardware-dependent interface that masks the socket's actual hardware implementation from higher-level software components that utilize it. Card Services is a software layer that sits above the Socket Services, coordinating access among the cards, the sockets, and system resources, such as interrupts and memory map. Card Services accesses cards via Socket Services. The card drivers interact with the car via Card Services. Card Services is generally operating-system-dependent.

For maximum compatibility and interoperability, PowerPC system platform vendors should provide Socket Services and the operating system vendors should provide the Card Services extension. For PowerPC Reference Platform compliant systems, both Socket Services and Card Services should be provided in the system abstraction layer.

12.7.10   ISA bus

The ISA (Industry Standard Architecture) bus is the most widely used system bus in the PC industry. Originally, the ISA bus was referred to as the PC-AT bus, and there were no official definition or standards for it. Later on, its specifications were defined by the IEEE standards group. The ISA bus, if implemented, allows a transfer rate of up to 8.3 MB/s. Transfers over the ISA bus are synchronized around 8 MHz, and they usually take a minimum of two cycles of the bus clock to perform a data transfer. As the data path of an ISA bus is 16 bits wide, up to 2 bytes may be transferred during each transaction.

The IEEE definition of ISA is used to implement ISA buses for the PReP systems.

12.7.11   Input device interface

This is the interface for the alphanumeric and pointing devices; for example, the ADB standard as used in Apple computers or the PC/AT, PS/2 interface as used in an Intel 8042AH chip.

12.8   SYSTEM CONFIGURATIONS

Configurations of PowerPC Reference Platform systems include:

Portable System	A PowerPC compliant machine that is capable of battery operation.
Medialess System	A PowerPC compliant medialess system that relies on network connections for storage. Boot is from the network; software, data, and paging space are attained from the network.
Desktop System	A PowerPC compliant desktop system that is an entry level system for commercial or technical applications.
Technical Workstation System	A PowerPC compliant technical workstation configuration that specifies a technical user's desktop or deskside machine.
Server System	A PowerPC compliant server configuration specifies a machine that serves multiple users and does not required a locally attached keyboard and display.

12.9   SUMMARY

The information included in this chapter provides an introduction to the aspects to be considered when building a PowerPC system. The memory subsystem, storage subsystem, and computer-human interface subsystem that form the infrastructure of any nascent system are addressed. The discussion of the connectivity subsystem and expansion buses form the next level of building a system, where one decides on the choices of expandability (networking and interfacing with exiting bases). The information on storage subsystem addresses the industry-standard interfaces. Together, the discussion on different subsystems provides a thorough and comprehensive overview of what it would take for you to build your own PowerPC.

PowerPC Models

The PowerPC microprocessor has been used to build a wide array of computer systems by a diverse number of companies. Apple and IBM are among the first companies to have built complete computer systems using the PowerPC 601 processor as the core of the computer system. Existing models of complete computer systems, such as the RISC System/6000 200 series and the Macintosh series are described here.

A.1 CHIP VERSUS SYSTEM

Recognize that PowerPC is an architecture and the 601 processor is one of its many implementations that can be manufactured to run at varying clock speeds to deliver optimal performance with multifarious I/O subsystems (buses). Therefore, it makes sense to keep the discussion of PowerPC-based computer systems separate from discussions of the PowerPC chip's concepts, facilities, and architecture, which has been the main premise of this book.

A.2 IBM IMPLEMENTATIONS

The 7011 RISC System/6000 POWERstation/POWERserver 200 series is a set of low-priced, entry-level desktop workstations or servers with multiuser, commercial applicability. They are binary-compatible with the other RISC System/6000 POWERstation/POWERserver family of systems and the AIX/6000 operating system, with support for paging over LANs and remote boot. In the 200 series, some models are based on the POWER RSC processor (the predecessor to the PowerPC), while others are based on the PowerPC 601 processor.

The 220 and 230 feature the POWER RSC processor with 16-MB to 64-MB memory, optional internal fixed disk up to 2 GB, two Micro Channel slots, one Gt1 graphics card slot, one integrated SCSI controller, one Ethernet controller, one diskette drive bay, and standard device ports/connectors. The 230 series offers an additional 128-KB level-2 cache. (Note that the level-2 cache is also referred to as a secondary cache.)

The 250 series offers a range of models featuring the PowerPC 601 processor, along with some additional features, including 16-MB to 256-MB memory and provision for a GXT graphics card and integrated SCSI-2 controller (over SCSI-1 controller). Each model can be enhanced to include more features in place of the standard ones. With an optional diskette drive and fixed disk, these systems can operate stand-alone or can be attached to a LAN for diskless or dataless configurations. In terms of connecting the computer to different Ethernet media, one can use any of the thick (10Base5), thin (10Base2), or twisted pair (10BaseT) interfaces.

Highlights of the POWERstation/POWERserver 200 series include:

- The introduction of the PowerPC 601 microprocessor and the first implementation of the PowerPC architecture in the System/6000 product line

- High-performance graphics adapters which connect directly to the PowerPC 601 local processor bus and provide accelerated 2-D performance

- Binary compatibility with the current family of RISC System/6000 systems and the latest version of AIX

- Industry-standard memory and SCSI-2 and Ethernet controllers for additional growth capability

- The ability to function as LAN-dependent, LAN-attached, or stand-alone workstations

A.2.1   RISC System/6000 POWERstation N40

The RISC System/6000 N40 is the industry's first PowerPC-based notebook workstation. It combines the power of the PowerPC 601 microprocessor and the AIX operating system in a lightweight color notebook computer. Running at 50 MHz, the N40 achieves an exceedingly high level of performance, making it more powerful than not only any notebook computer but also many desktop workstations.

The 6.9-lb N40 features a 9.4-in TFT (thin-film transistor) active matrix color screen that offers wide-angle viewing in 256 colors. The N40's video memory supports up to a 1280×1024 image, which can be viewed via a pan-and-zoom feature on the TFT display or via an externally connected monitor. Also featured is a pointing device, which is located in the center of the keyboard and eliminates the need for a separate mouse. The N40 operates from an external battery pack that has a battery life of up to four hours.

Highlights of the N40 include:

- 50-MHz PowerPC 601 processor

- Main memory support from 16 MB to 64 MB

- SCSI-2 diskette drive support

- Removable disk drive with a 340-MB capacity

- Ethernet network support

- Support for PCMCIA adapters providing token-ring network support

- An external display port supporting 1280 × 1024 resolution and up to 256 colors

- Ports for an external mouse, keyboard, and Appletalk printers, and a built-in speaker and microphone

The N40 also features Tadpole's Nomadic Computing Environment, providing users with a rapid save-and-resume, power management, portability tools, and other UNIX mobile computing innovations.

A.2.2   RISC System/6000 POWERstation/POWERserver 25S

The RISC System/6000 POWERserver 25S is an entry server model with 16 MB of memory, 1 GB of internal fixed disk, and an 8-port EIA-232 adapter with fan-out cable. This entry-level configuration can function without a fixed disk in a LAN environment or, with a fixed disk and diskette drive added, in a stand-alone environment. Customers can upgrade memory and add features to enhance the system, making the system ideal for attaching multiple async terminals such as in retail, data entry, small office, banking, and insurance environments.

Highlights of the 25S include:

- 66-MHz PowerPC 601 processor

- 16-MB memory

- One integrated SCSI-2 controller

- One integrated Ethernet controller

- Standard device ports/connectors:

  Keyboard/speaker port

  Mouse port

  Tablet port

  Two serial ports

  Parallel port

  SCSI-2 port

  Ethernet port

- Two Micro Channel card slots (form factor 3) for expansion

- One PowerPC 601 local processor bus slot for an optional graphics adapter
- 1-GB SCSI-2 disk drive
- 2-GB SCSI-2 disk drive select option
- 8-port async adapter with the multiport interface cable
- Async select options for 16- and 128-port configurations

A.2.3   RISC System/6000 POWERstation/POWERserver 25W

The RISC System/6000 POWERstation 25W is a midrange graphics workstation in the 250 series that offers the same base function as the 250, as well as the POWER GXT100 graphics adapter, 16 MB of memory, 540 MB of internal fixed disk, keyboard, and mouse.

Highlights of the 25W include:

- 66-MHz PowerPC 601 processor
- POWERGXT100 graphics adapter
- Keyboard and mouse
- Graphics select options—POWER GXT150 graphics adapter, POWERGt4e or GTO accelerator
- 540-MB SCSI-2 disk drive
- Disk drive select options—1 GB, 2 GB
- Eight slots for SIMM memory cards
- 16-MB memory
- One integrated SCSI-2 controller
- One integrated Ethernet controller
- Standard device ports/connectors:

  Keyboard/speaker port
  Mouse port
  Tablet port
  Two serial ports
  Parallel port
  SCSI-2 port
  Ethernet port
- Two Micro Channel card slots (form factor 3) for expansion
- One PowerPC 601 local processor bus slot for an optional graphics adapter

A.2.4   RISC System/6000 POWERstation/POWERserver 250

The RISC System/6000 POWERstation/POWERserver 250 has a 66-MHz PowerPC 601 processor which offers the highest performance of the 200 series family. It has extensive expansion capability from 16 MB up to 256 MB of memory, optional internal fixed disk up to 2 GB, up to a maximum of seven SCSI devices on the SCSI bus, an optional 2.88-MB diskette drive, an optional graphics adapter, and two 32-bit Micro Channel card slots.

Highlights of the 250 include:

- 66-MHz PowerPC 601 processor
- 16-MB memory
- Eight slots for SIMM memory cards
- One integrated SCSI-2 controller
- One integrated Ethernet controller
- Standard device ports/connectors:

  Keyboard/speaker port

  Mouse port

  Tablet port

  Two serial ports

  Parallel port

  SCSI-2 port

  Ethernet port

- Two Micro Channel card slots (form factor 3) for expansion
- One PowerPC 601 local processor bus slot for an optional graphics adapter

A.2.5   RISC System/6000 POWERstation/POWERserver 25T

The IBM RISC System/6000 POWERstation 25T is a high-performance graphics workstation that offers the same base function as the POWERstation/ POWERserver 250, as well as the POWER GXT150 graphics adapter with appropriate cable, 16 MB of memory, 540 MB of internal fixed disk, keyboard, mouse, and 17-in display.

Highlights of the 25T include:

- 66-MHz PowerPC 601 processor
- 16-MB memory
- Eight slots for SIMM memory cards
- One integrated SCSI-2 controller
- One integrated Ethernet controller
- Standard device ports/connectors:

  Keyboard/speaker port

  Mouse port

  Tablet port

  Two serial ports

  Parallel printer port

SCSI-2 port

Ethernet port

- Two Micro Channel card slots (form factor 3) for expansion
- One PowerPC 601 local processor bus slot for an optional graphics adapter
- POWER GXT150 graphics adapter and cable that attaches to the display
- POWERdisplay 17 (17-in display)
- Graphics select options—POWER Gt4e or GTO accelerator
- 540-MB SCSI-2 disk drive
- Display select option POWERdisplay 19
- Disk drive select options—1 GB, 2 GB

A.3   APPLE IMPLEMENTATIONS

PowerPC based systems offered by Apple consist of the following:

A.3.1   Power Macintosh 6100/60

The Apple Power Macintosh 6100/60 is an entry-level workstation that offers the performance of a 601 processor in Apple's System 7 environment.
Highlights of the 6100/60 include:

- 60-MHz PowerPC 601 processor
- 8 MB of memory, expandable to 72 MB
- 2 SIMM slots
- 17-in Nu-Bus expansion slot
- On-board Ethernet controller
- Integrated SCSI controller
- Disk drive select options—160 to 250 MB
- Standard video support

A.3.2   Power Macintosh 7100/66

The Apple Power Macintosh 7100/66 is a midrange workstation that offers the performance of a 601 processor under Apple's System 7 environment.
Highlights of the 7100/66 include:

- 66-MHz PowerPC 601 processor
- 8 MB of memory, expandable to 136 MB
- 4 SIMM slots
- 3 full-size Nu-Bus expansion slots
- On-board Ethernet controller

- Integrated SCSI controller
- Disk drive select options—250 to 500 MB
- Standard video support with 1 MB of VRAM

A.3.3   Power Macintosh 8100/80

The Apple Power Macintosh 8100/80 is a high-end workstation that offers the performance of a 601 processor under Apple's System 7 environment.
   Highlights of the 8100/80 include:

- 80-MHz PowerPC 601 processor
- 256-KB secondary cache
- 8 MB of memory, expandable to 256 MB
- 8 SIMM slots
- 3 full-size Nu-Bus expansion slots
- On-board Ethernet controller
- Integrated SCSI controller
- Disk drive select options—250 MB to 1 GB
- Standard video support with 2 MB of VRAM

Acronyms Used in This Book

The following acronyms have been referred to in this book:

Acronym	Definition
AA	Absolute Address
AADU	AIX Access for DOS Users
AIX	Advanced Interactive Executive
ABI	Application Binary Interface
ACL	Access Control List
AES	Application Environment Specifications
AES/OS	Application Environment Specifications
AFS	Andrew File System
AIC	AIXwindows Interface Composer
AIX	Advanced Interactive Executive
ALU	Arithmetic Logic Unit
ANSI	American National Standards Institute
API	Application Programming Interface
ASCII	American National Standard Code for Information Interchange
ASIC	Application Specific Integrated Circuit
ATM	Asynchronous Transfer Mode
BAT	Block Address Translation
BE	Big-Endian

Acronym	Definition
BICMOS	Bipolar Complementary Metal-oxide Semiconductor
BCD	Binary Coded Decimal
BIST	Built-in Self-test
BNU	Basic Network Utilities
BPU	Branch Processing Unit
BSC	Bisync Binary Synchronous Communications
BSI	British Standards Institute
CAE	Common Applications Environment
CAR	Cache Address Register
CCITT	Comite Consultatif Internationale de Telegraphique et Telephonique
CDE	Common Desktop Environment
CDS	DCE Cell Directory Service
CICS	Customer Information Control System
CISC	Complex Instruction Set Computer
CMOS	Complementary Metal-oxide Semiconductor
COP	Common On-chip Processor
COSE	Common Open Software Environment
CPI	Cycles Per Instruction
CPU	Central Process Unit
CR	Condition Register
CRC	Cyclic Redundancy Check
CSMA	Carrier Sense Multiple Access
CSMA/CD	Carrier Sense Multiple Access with Collision Detection
CTR	Count Register
CUA	Common User Access
DCE	Distributed Computing Environment Data Circuit-terminating Equipment
DCE AES	Distributed Computing Environment Application Environment Specifications
DDE	Dynamic Data Exchange
DEC	Digital Equipment Corporation
DES	Data Encryption Standard
DFT	Distributed Function Terminal
DIN	Deutches Institut für Normung
DMA	Direct Memory Access
DRAM	Dynamic Random Access Memory
DSSC	Distributed Services Steering Committee

DTE	Data Terminal Equipment
EB	Exabyte
EBCDIC	Extended Binary Coded Decimal Interchange Code
ECC	Error Checking and Correcting
EIA	External Interface Adapter
	Electronic Interface Adapter
	Electronics Industries Association
EM78	3278/79 Emulation
EPROM	Erasable Programmable Read Only Memory
EEPROM	Electrically Erasable Programmable Read-Only Memory
EISA	Extension to Industry Standard Architecture
EPOST	Extended Power-on Self-test
FAL	Firmware Abstraction Layer
FDDI	Fiber Distributed Data Interface
FIFO	First-In First-Out
FIPS	Federal Information Processing Standard
FPR	Floating-point Register
FPU	Floating-point Unit
FXU	Fixed-point Unit
GDA	DCE Global Directory Agent
GDS	DCE Global Directory Service
GL	Graphics Library
GPR	General Purpose Register
GUI	Graphical User Interface
HAL	Hardware Abstraction Layer
HANFS	High Availability for Network File System
HAS	Hardware Abstraction Software
HCON	Host Connection Program
HIA	Host Interface Adapter
HLLAPI	High-Level Language Application Programming Interface
HP	Hewlett-Packard
I/O	Input/Output
IBM	International Business Machines
ICCCM	Inter-Client Communication Conventions Manual.
IDE	Integrated Device Electronics
IEC	International Electrotechnical Commission
IEEE	Institute of Electrical and Electronics Engineers
IEEE-CS	IEEE Computer Society
IPI	Initial Program Load

Acronym	Definition
ISA	Industry Standard Architecture
	Instrument Society of America
	Initial Storage Area
	Invalid Storage Address
ISDN	Integrated-Services Digital Network
ISE	Instruction Set Emulator
ISO	International Organization for Standards
ISP	Internationalized Standardized Profiles
ISV	Independent Software Vendor
KB	Kilobyte
L1	First-level Cache
L2	Second-level Cache
LAN	Local Area Network
LE	Little-Endian
LED	Light-emitting Diode
LEN	Low Entry Networking
LRU	Least Recently Used
LU	Logical Units
LVM	Logical Volume Manager
MB	Megabyte
MBCS	Multibyte Character Set
MCA	Micro Channel Architecture
	Machine Check Analysis
	Machine Configuration Analysis
	Machine Check Adapter
MESI	Modified-exclusive-shared-invalid Protocol
MFM	Modified Frequency Modulation (Recording)
MHz	Megahertz
MIB	Management Information Base
MIPS	Millions of Instructions per Second
MMIO	Memory Mapped Input/Output
MMU	Memory Management Unit
MP	Multiprocessing
	Massively Parallel
MS-DOS	Microsoft Disk Operating System
NCK	Network Computing Kernel
NCS	Network Computing System
NFS	Network File System
NIC	Numerically Intensive Computing
	Network Information Center

NIDL	Network Interface Definition Language
NIS	Network Information Service
NIST	National Institute for Standards and Technology
NLS	National Language Support
NVRAM	Non-Volatile Random Access Memory
ODM	Object Data Manager
OEM	Original Equipment Manufacturer
OLE	Object-linking and Embedding Operations
OLTP	On-line Transaction Processing
ONC	Open Network Computing
OS	Operating System
OSF	Open Software Foundation
OSI	Open Systems Interconnect
PAD	Packet Assembler/Disassembler
PAL	Portability Assist Layer
PASC	Portable Applications Standards Committee
PB	Petabyte
PCD	POSIX Conformance Document
PCI	Program Controlled Interrupt
	Peripheral Component Interconnect
PCMCIA	Personal Computer Memory Card Interface Association
PMC	Project Management Committee
POE	PowerOpen Environment
POSIX	Portable Operating System Interface
POST	Power-on Self-test
POWER	Performance Optimized With Enhanced RISC
PSC	Profiles Steering Committee
PVC	Permanent Virtual Circuit
QIC	Quarter Inch Cartridge
QLLC	Qualified Logical Link Control
RAID	Redundant Array of Independent Disks
REX	Remote Execution Service
RFT	Request for Technology
RISC	Reduced Instruction Set Computer
ROM	Read Only Memory
RPC	Remote Procedure Call
RSC	Remote Service Console
	Remote Support Center
RT	RISC Technology/Model of the PC (PC/RT)

Acronym	Definition
RTC	Real Time Clock
	Real Time Controller
SAA	System Application Architecture
SANE	Standard Apple Numerics Environment
SCCS	Source Code Control System
SCCT	Steering Committee on Conformance Testing
SCSI	Small Computer System Interface
SCWUI	Steering Committee on Windowing User Interfaces
SDN	Software Defined Network
	System Defined Network
	Software Designed Network (AT&T)
SDO	Standards Development Organization
SDT	Static Debugger Program Traps
SEC	Sponsor Executive Committee
SGFS	Special Group on Functional Standards
SICC	Systems Interface Coordination Committee
SIG	Special Interest Group
SMP	System Modification Program
	Symmetric Multiprocessor
SNA	System Network Architecture
SNMP	Simple Network Management Protocol
SPRG	Special Purpose Register Group
SRAM	Static Random Access Memory
SVC	Switched Virtual Circuit
	Supervisory Call
TAG	Technical Advisory Group
TCB	Trusted Computing Base
TCF	Transparent Computing Facility
TCOS	Technical Committee on Operating Systems
TCP/IP	Transmission Control Protocol/Internet Protocol
TEA	Transaction Error Acknowledgment
TFA	Transparent File Access
TLB	Translation Lookaside Buffer
TP	Trusted Programs
TPWG	Transaction Processing Working Group
UART	Universal Asynchronous Receiver/Transmitter
UDP	User Datagram Protocol
ULSI	Ultra Large-scale Integration
UMCU	Universal Micro Control Unit
UUCP	UNIX-to-UNIX Copy Program

VESA	Video Electronics Standards Association
VL	Volume License
VLSI	Very Large Scale Integration
VMD	Vector Memory Display
VME	VERSA Module Eurocard
VMM	Virtual Memory Manager
VPD	Vital Product Data
VUE	Visual User Environment
WAN	Wide Area Network
WOW	Windows-16 on Windows-32
X	X Window System
XDR	External Data Representation
XDS	X/Open Directory Service
XNFS	Network File System for X Windows System
XPG	X/Open Portability Guide
X11R5	X Windows Release 5

PowerPC and POWER Instruction Sets

PowerPC Instruction Set

Instruction	Mnemonic
Add	add[o][–]
Add carrying	addc[o][–]
Add extended	adde[o][–]
Add immediate	addi
Add immediate carrying	addic
Add immediate carrying and record	addic.
Add immediate shifted	addis
Add to minus one extended	addme[o][–]
Add to zero extended	addze[o][–]
AND	and[–]
AND with complement	andc[–]
AND immediate	andi.
AND immediate shifted	andis.
Branch	b[l][a]
Branch conditional	bc[l][a]
Branch conditional to count register	bcctr[l]
Branch conditional to link register	bclr[l]
Compare	cmp
Compare immediate	cmpi
Compare logical	cmpl
Compare logical immediate	cmpli
Count leading zeros doubleword	cntlzd[–]
Count leading zeros word	cntlzw[–]
Condition register AND	crand
Condition register AND with complement	crandc
Condition register equivalent	creqv
Condition register NAND	crnand

PowerPC Instruction Set (*Continued*)

Instruction	Mnemonic
Condition register NOR	crnor
Condition register OR	cror
Condition register OR with complement	crorc
Condition register XOR	crxor
Data cache block flush	dcbf
Data cache block invalidate	dcbi
Data cache block store	dcbst
Data cache block touch	dcbt
Data cache block touch for store	dcbtst
Data cache block set to zero	dcbz
Divide doubleword	divd[o][–]
Divide doubleword unsigned	divdu[o][–]
Divide word	divw[o][–]
Divide word unsigned	divwu[o][–]
External control in word indexed	eciwx
External control out word indexed	ecowx
Enforce in-order execution of I/O	eieio
Equivalent	eqv[–]
Extend sign byte	extsb[–]
Extend sign halfword	extsh[–]
Extend sign word	extsw[–]
Floating absolute value	fabs[–]
Floating add	fadd[–]
Floating add single	fadds[–]
Floating convert from integer doubleword	fcfid[–]
Floating compare ordered	fcmpo
Floating compare unordered	fcmpu
Floating convert to integer doubleword	fctid[–]
Floating convert to integer doubleword with round toward Zero	fctidz[–]
Floating convert to integer word	fctiw[–]
Floating convert to integer word with round toward zero	fctiwz[–]
Floating divide	fdiv[–]
Floating divide single	fdivs[–]
Floating multiply-add	fmadd[–]
Floating multiply-add single	fmadds[–]
Floating move register	fmr[–]
Floating multiply-subtract	fmsub[–]
Floating multiply-subtract single	fmsubs[–]
Floating multiply	fmul[–]
Floating multiply single	fmuls[–]
Floating negative absolute value	fnabs[–]
Floating negate	fneg[–]
Floating negative multiply-add	fnmadd[–]
Floating negative multiply-add single	fnmadds[–]
Floating negative multiply-subtract	fnmsub[–]
Floating negative multiply-subtract single	fnmsubs[–]
Floating reciprocal estimate single	fres[–]
Floating round to single-precision	frsp[–]
Floating reciprocal square root estimate	frsqrte[–]
Floating select	fsel[–]
Floating square root	fsqrt[–]
Floating square root single	fsqrts[–]
Floating subtract	fsub[–]

PowerPC Instruction Set (*Continued*)

Instruction	Mnemonic
Floating subtract single	fsubs[−]
Instruction cache block invalidate	icbi
Instruction synchronize	isync
Load byte and zero	lbz
Load byte and zero with update	lbzu
Load byte and zero with update indexed	lbzux
Load byte and zero indexed	lbzx
Load doubleword	ld
Load doubleword and reserve indexed	ldarx
Load doubleword with update	ldu
Load doubleword with update indexed	ldux
Load doubleword indexed	ldx
Load floating-point double	lfd
Load floating-point double with update	lfdu
Load floating-point double with update indexed	lfdux
Load floating-point double indexed	lfdx
Load floating-point single	lfs
Load floating-point single with update	lfsu
Load floating-point single with update indexed	lfsux
Load floating-point single indexed	lfsx
Load halfword algebraic	lha
Load halfword algebraic with update	lhau
Load halfword algebraic with update indexed	lhaux
Load halfword algebraic indexed	lhax
Load halfword byte-reverse indexed	lhbrx
Load halfword and zero	lhz
Load halfword and zero with update	lhzu
Load halfword and zero with update indexed	lhzux
Load halfword and zero indexed	lhzx
Load multiple word	lmw
Load string word immediate	lswi
Load string word indexed	lswx
Load word algebraic	lwa
Load word and reserve indexed	lwarx
Load word algebraic with update indexed	lwaux
Load word algebraic indexed	lwax
Load word byte-reverse indexed	lwbrx
Load word and zero	lwz
Load word and zero with update	lwzu
Load word and zero with update indexed	lwzux
Load word and zero indexed	lwzx
Move condition register field	mcrf
Move to condition register from FPSCR	mcrfs
Move to condition register from XER	mcrxr
Move from condition register	mfcr
Move from FPSCR	mffs[−]
Move from machine state register	mfmsr
Move from special purpose register	mfspr
Move from segment register	mfsr
Move from segment register indirect	mfsrin
Move from time base	mftb
Move to condition register fields	mtcrf
Move to FPSCR bit 0	mtfsb0[−]
Move to FPSCR bit 1	mtfsb1[−]
Move to FPSCR fields	mtfsf[−]

PowerPC Instruction Set (*Continued*)

Instruction	Mnemonic
Move to FPSCR field immediate	mtfsfi[–]
Move to machine state register	mtmsr
Move to special purpose register	mtspr
Move to segment register	mtsr
Move to segment register indirect	mtsrin
Multiply high doubleword	mulhd[–]
Multiply high doubleword unsigned	mulhdu[–]
Multiply high word	mulhw[–]
Multiply high word unsigned	mulhwu[–]
Multiply low doubleword	mulld[o][–]
Multiply low immediate	mulli
Multiply low word	mullw[o][–]
NAND	nand[–]
Negate	neg[o][–]
NOR	nor[–]
OR	or[–]
OR with complement	orc[–]
OR immediate	ori
OR immediate shifted	oris
Return from interrupt	rfi
Rotate left doubleword then clear left	rldcl[–]
Rotate left doubleword then clear right	rldcr[–]
Rotate left doubleword immediate then clear	rldic[–]
Rotate left doubleword immediate then clear left	rldicl[–]
Rotate left doubleword immediate then clear right	rldicr[–]
Rotate left doubleword immediate then mask insert	rldimi[–]
Rotate left word immediate then mask insert	rlwimi[–]
Rotate left word immediate then AND with mask	rlwinm[–]
Rotate left word then AND with mask	rlwnm[–]
System call	sc
SLB invalidate all	slbia
SLB invalidate entry	slbie
Shift left doubleword	sld[–]
Shift left word	slw[–]
Shift right algebraic doubleword	srad[–]
Shift right algebraic doubleword immediate	sradi[–]
Shift right algebraic word	sraw[–]
Shift right algebraic word immediate	srawi[–]
Shift right doubleword	srd[–]
Shift right word	srw[–]
Store byte	stb
Store byte with update	stbu
Store byte with update indexed	stbux
Store byte indexed	stbx
Store doubleword	std
Store doubleword conditional indexed	stdcx.
Store doubleword with update	stdu
Store doubleword indexed with update	stdux
Store doubleword indexed	stdx
Store floating-point double	stfd
Store floating-point double with update	stfdu
Store floating-point double with update indexed	stfdux
Store floating-point double indexed	stfdx
Store floating-point as integer word indexed	stfiwx
Store floating-point single	stfs

PowerPC Instruction Set (*Continued*)

Instruction	Mnemonic
Store floating-point single with update	stfsu
Store floating-point single with update indexed	stfsux
Store floating-point single indexed	stfsx
Store halfword	sth
Store halfword byte-reverse indexed	sthbrx
Store halfword with update	sthu
Store halfword with update indexed	sthux
Store halfword indexed	sthx
Store multiple word	stmw
Store string word immediate	stswi
Store string word indexed	stswx
Store word	stw
Store word byte-reverse indexed	stwbrx
Store word conditional indexed	stwcx.
Store word with update	stwu
Store word with update indexed	stwux
Store word indexed	stwx
Subtract from	subf[o][−]
Subtract from carrying	subfc[o][−]
Subtract from extended	subfe[o][−]
Subtract from immediate carrying	subfic
Subtract from minus one extended	subfme[o][−]
Subtract from zero extended	subfze[o][−]
Synchronize	sync
Trap doubleword	td
Trap doubleword immediate	tdi
TLB invalidate all	tlbia
TLB invalidate entry	tlbie
TLB synchronize	tlbsync
Trap word	tw
Trap word immediate	twi
XOR	xor[−]
XOR immediate	xori
XOR immediate shifted	xoris

POWER Instruction Set

Command	Mnemonic
Add	a
Absolute	abs
Add extended	ae
Add immediate	ai
Add immediate and record	ai.
Add to minus one extended	ame
AND	and
AND with complement	andc
AND immediate lower	andil.
AND immediate upper	andiu.
Add to zero extended	aze
Branch	b
Branch conditional	bc
Branch conditional to count register	bcc
Branch conditional register	bcr
Compute address lower	cal
Compute address upper	cau
Compute address	cax
Cache line compute size	clcs
Cache line flush	clf
Cache line invalidate	cli
Compare	cmp
Compare immediate	cmpi
Compare logical	cmpl
Compare logical immediate	cmpli
Count leading zeroes	cntlz
Condition register AND	crand
Condition register AND with complement	crandc
Condition register equivalent	creqv
Condition register NAND	cmand
Condition register NOR	cmor
Condition register OR	cror
Condition register OR with complement	crorc
Condition register XOR	crxor
Data cache line store	dclst
Data cache line set to zero	dclz
Data cache synchronize	dcs
Divide	div
Divide short	divs
Difference or zero	doz
Difference or zero immediate	dozi
Equivalent	eqv
Extend sign	exts
Floating add	fa
Floating absolute value	fabs
Floating compare ordered	fcmpo
Floating compare unordered	fcmpu
Floating divide	fd
Floating multiply	fm
Floating multiply add	fma
Floating move register	fmr
Floating multiply subtract	fms
Negative absolute value	fnabs
Floating negate	fneg

POWER Instruction Set (*Continued*)

Command	Mnemonic
Floating negative multiply add	fnma
Floating negative multiply subtract	fnms
Floating round to single precision	frsp
Floating subtract	fs
Instruction cache synchronize	ics
Load	l
Load byte reverse indexed	lbrx
Load byte and zero	lbz
Load byte and zero with update	lbzu
Load byte and zero with update indexed	lbzux
Load byte and zero indexed	lbzx
Load floating-point double	lfd
Load floating-point double with update	lfdu
Load floating-point double with update indexed	lfdux
Load floating-point double indexed	lfdx
Load floating-point single	lfs
Load floating-point single with update	lfsu
Load floating-point single with update indexed	lfsux
Load floating-point single indexed	lfsx
Load half algebraic	lha
Load half algebraic with update	lhau
Load half algebraic with update indexed	lhaux
Load half algebraic indexed	lhax
Load half byte reverse indexed	lhbrx0
Load half and zero	lhz
Load half and zero with update	lhzu
Load half and zero with update indexed	lhzux
Load half and zero indexed	lhzx
Load multiple	lm
Load string and compare bytes indexed	lscbx
Load string immediate	lsi
Load string indexed	lsx
Load with update	lu
Load with update indexed	lux
Load indexed	lx
Mask generate	maskq
Mask insert from register	maskir
Move condition register field	mcrf
Move to condition register from FPSCR	mcrfs
Move to condition register from XER	mcrxr
Move from condition register from XER	mfcr
Move from FPSCR	mffs
Move from machine state register	mfmsr
Move from special purpose register	mfspr
Move from segment register	mfsr
Move from segment register indirect	mfsri
Move to condition register fields	mtcrf
Move to FPSCR bit 0	mtfsb0
Move to FPSCR bit 1	mtfsb1
Move to FPSCR fields	mtfsf
Move to FPSCR field immediate	mtfsfi
Move to machine state register	mtmsr
Move to special purpose register	mtspr
Move to segment register	mtsr

POWER Instruction Set (*Continued*)

Command	Mnemonic
Move to segment register indirect	mtsri
Multiply	mul
Multiply immediate	muli
Multiply short	muls
Negative absolute	nabs
NAND	nand
Negate	neg
NOR	nor
OR	or
OR with complement	orc
OR immediate lower	oril
OR immediate upper	oriu
Real address compute	rac
Return from interrupt	rfi
Return from SVC	rfsvc
Rotate left immediate then mask insert	rlimi
Rotate left immediate then AND with mask	rlinmlux
Rotate left then mask insert	rlmi
Rotate left then AND with mask	rinmq
Rotate right and insert bit	rrib
Subtract from	sf
Subtract from extended	sfe
Subtract from immediate	sfi
Subtract from minus one extended	sfme
Subtract from zero extended	sfze
Shift left	sl
Shift left extended	sle
Shift left extended with MQ	sleq
Shift left immediate with MQ	sliq
Shift left long immediate with MQ	slliq
Shift left long with MQ	sllq
Shift left with MQ	slq
Shift right	sr
Shift right algebraic	sra
Shift right algebraic immediate	srai
Shift right algebraic immediate with MQ	sraiq
Shift right algebraic with MQ	sraq
Shift right extended	sre
Shift right extended algebraic	srea
Shift right extended with MQ	sreq
Shift right immediate with MQ	sriq
Shift right long immediate with MQ	srliq
Shift right long with MQ	srlq
Shift right with MQ	srq
Store	st
Store byte	stb
Store byte reverse indexed	stbrx
Store byte with update	stbu
Store byte with update indexed	stbux
Store byte indexed	stbx
Store floating-point double	stfd
Store floating-point double with update	stfdu
Store floating-point double with update indexed	stfdux
Store floating-point double indexed	stfdx
Store floating-point single	stfs

POWER Instruction Set (*Continued*)

Command	Mnemonic
Store floating-point single with update	stfsu
Store floating-point single with update indexed	stfsux
Store floating-point single indexed	stfsx
Store half	sth
Store half byte reverse indexed	sthbrx
Store half with update	sthu
Store half with update indexed	sthux
Store half indexed	sthx
Store multiple	stm
Store string immediate	stsi
Store string indexed	stsx
Store with update	stu
Store with update indexed	stux
Store indexed	stx
Supervisor call	svc
Trap	t
Trap immediate	ti
TLB invalidate entry	tlbi
XOR	xor
XOR immediate lower	xoril
XOR immediate upper	xoriu

Bibliography

Adkins, A., and M. Dean, *PowerPC Reference Platform: Specifications Guide* (beta version), IBM Corporation, Mar. 1994.

Agarwal, A., J. Hennessy, and M. Horowitz, "Cache Performance of Operating Systems and Multi-programming Workloads," *ACM Transactions on Computer Systems,* **6**(4):393–431 (Nov. 1988).

AIX Version 3.1 RISC System/6000 As A Real Time System, IBM Corporation, 1991.

AIX Version 3.2 Commands Reference, IBM Corporation, 1994.

AIX Version 3.2 for RISC System/6000: Assembly Language Reference, IBM Corporation, 1992.

AIX Version 3.2 for RISC System/6000: Technical Reference: Kernel and Subsystems, Volume 4, IBM Corporation, 1992.

AIX Version 3.2 Performance Monitoring and Tuning Guide, IBM Corporation, 1993.

AIX Version 3.2 Problem Solving Guide and Reference, IBM Corporation, 1994.

AIX Version 3.2 System Management Guide: Communications and Networks, IBM Corporation, 1993.

Allen, M., and M. Becker, "Multiprocessing Aspects of the PowerPC 601 Microprocessor," *Proceedings of COMPCON 1993,* Feb. 1993

Alpert, D., "Memory Hierarchies for Directly Executed Language Microprocessors," Ph.D. thesis, Stanford University, 1984.

Anderson, D., and T. Shanley, *Pentium Processor System Architecture,* MindShare, Inc., Richardson, TX, 1993.

Appel, A. W., and K. Li, "Virtual Memory Primitives for User Programs," *Proceedings of ACM Fourth Symposium on Architectural Support for Programming Languages and Operating Systems* (ASPLOS IV), Apr. 1991, pp. 96–107.

Auslander, M. A., "Managing Programs and Libraries in AIX Version 3 for RISC System/6000 Processors," *IBM Journal of Research and Technology* **34** (Jan. 1990).

Bach, M. J., *The Design of the UNIX Operating System,* Prentice-Hall, Englewood Cliffs, N.J., 1986.

Boykin, J., D. Kirschen, A. Langerman, and S. LoVerso, *Programming Under Mach,* Addison-Wesley, Reading, 1993.

Cannon, C., and D. Chakravarty, "PowerPC—Architecture and Design," *Worldwide Software Development Conference,* San Jose, 1994.

Chakravarty, D., "The AIX Process Structure," *AIXpert,* Nov. 1993.

Chakravarty, D., "Automation in Clinical Biochemistry and Laboratory: Computer Applications in Medicine," in K. L. Mukherjee (ed.), *Medical Laboratory Technology: Procedure Manual for Routine Diagnostic Tests,* Tata-McGraw-Hill, vol. 3, chap. 32, pp. 960–984, 1988.

Chakravarty, D., "Benchmarking Under AIX," *Focus J, 1* (4) (1989).

Chakravarty, D., *POWER RISC System/6000 Concepts, Facilities, and Architecture,* McGraw-Hill, New York, 1993.

Chakravarty, D., and A. Chakravarty, "Architectural Dependencies Related to Performance Measurements Under UNIX," *Computer Measurements Group Transactions,* Summer 1992. Republished in *International CMG Conference Proceedings,* Dec. 1992.

Cocke, J., and V. Markstein, "The Evolution of RISC Technology at IBM," *IBM Journal of Research and Technology* **34** (Jan. 1990).

Common Desktop Environment: Getting Started Using ToolTalk Messaging, Sun Microsystems, Inc., 1994.

Diefendorff, K., and M. Allen, "Organization of the Motorola 88110 Superscalar RISC Microprocessor," *IEEE Micro,* **12**(2):40–63 (Apr. 1992).

Guide to OSF/1: A Technical Synopsis, O'Reilly & Associates, Inc., Sebastopol, Calif., 1991.

Handy, J., *The Cache Memory Handbook,* Academic Press, San Diego, 1993.

Hennessy, J. L., and D. A. Patterson, *Computer Architecture: A Quantitative Approach,* Morgan Kaufmann Publishers, Palo Alto, 1990.

P. D. Hester, "RISC System 6000 Hardware Background and Philosophies," *IBM RISC System/6000 Technology,* IBM Corporation, Austin, Texas, 1990.

Hester, P. D., J. T. Hollaway, and F. T. May, "Hardware Description," *RT Personal Computer Technology,* IBM Corporation, 1986.

Hill, M. D., "Aspects of Cache Memory and Instruction Buffer Performance," Ph.D. thesis, University of California, Berkeley, 1989.

Hill, M. D., and A. J. Smith, "Evaluating Associativity in CPU Caches," *IEEE Transactions on Computers* 38(12):1612–1630 (Dec. 1989).

Host Connection Program/6000 Guide and Reference, IBM Corporation, 1993.

Hwang, K., *Advanced Computer Architecture: Parallelism Scalability, Programmability,* McGraw-Hill, New York, 1993.

Hwang, K., and F. Briggs, *Computer Architecture and Parallel Processing,* McGraw-Hill, New York, 1984.

Jain, R., *The Art of Computer Systems Performance Analysis,* John Wiley & Sons, New York, 1991.

Kahle, J. A., and D. Ogden, "PowerPC 603 Microprocessor," *IBM RISC System/6000 Technology: Volume II,* Prentice-Hall, Englewood Cliffs, N.J., 1994.

Keller, T. W., "AIX 3.2 Memory Load Control," *AIXpert,* pp. 17–25, Feb. 1992

Lewis, E., "Performance Tuning: Theory and Practice," *AIXtra,* Mar. 1993, pp. 48–56.

McKusick, M. K., and M. Karels, "Performance Improvements and Functional Enhancements in 4.3BSD," Computer System Research Group, Dept. of CS and EE, University of California at Berkeley, Calif.

Microsoft Windows NT Resource Guide, Microsoft Press, Redmond, Wash., 1993.

Montoye, R. K., E. Hokenek, and S. L. Runyon, "Design of the IBM RISC System/6000 Floating Point Execution Unit," *IBM Journal of Research and Technology* 34 (Jan. 1990).

Moore, C. R., "PowerPC 601 Microprocessor," *IBM RISC System/6000 Technology: Volume II,* Prentice-Hall, Englewood Cliffs, N.J., 1994.

Moore, C. R., D. M. Balser, J. S. Muhich, and R. E. East, "IBM Single Chip RISC Microprocessor (RSC)," *Proceedings of the 1992 International Conference on Computer Design,* 1992

Patterson, D. A., and J. L. Hennessy, *Computer Organization and Design: The Hardware/Software Interface,* Morgan Kaufmann Publishers, Palo Alto, 1994.

Patterson, D. A., and C. N. Sequin, "A VLSI RISC," *Computer* 15(9):8–21 (Sep. 1982).

PowerPC Architecture, IBM Corporation, 1993.

PowerPC 601 RISC Microprocessor User's Manual, Motorola Press, 1993.

Przybylski, S. A., *Cache and Memory Hierarchy Design: A Performance-Directed Approach,* Morgan Kaufmann Publishers, 1990.

Przybylski, S. A., "Performance-Directed Memory Hierarchy Design," Ph.D. thesis, Stanford University, 1988.

Puzak, T. R., "Cache Memory Design," Ph.D. diss., University of Massachusetts, 1985.

Rashid, R. F., et al., "Mach—A Foundation for Open Systems," *Proceedings of Second IEEE Computer Society Workshop on Workstation Operating Systems* (WWOS-II), Sep. 1989, pp. 109–113.

Ritchie, D. M., and K. Thompson, "UNIX Timesharing," *CACM* 57 (6) part 2:1931–1946 (Jul. 1978).

SCSI—Architecture and Implementation, IBM Corporation, 1990.

SCSI—Understanding the Small Computer System Interface, NCR Corporation, Prentice-Hall, Englewood Cliffs, N.J., 1990.

Silha, E., and G. Paap, "PowerPC: A High-Performance Architecture," *Proceedings of COMPCON 1993,* Feb. 1993.

Special Issue on Software Performance Engineering of CMG Transactions, No. 60, Spring 1988.

Stone, H. S., *High-Performance Computer Architecture,* Addison-Wesley Series in Electrical and Computer Engineering, 1987.

Tims, S., and M. Chow, "Apple's Macintosh Application Services: A Component of the PowerOpen Environment," *AIXtra,* Mar. 1994, pp. 51–58.

UNIX Programmer's Reference Manual (PRM), 4.3 Berkeley Software Distribution, Computer Systems Research Group, Computer Science Division, University of California, Berkeley, 1986.

Wabi 1.1 for AIX: User's Guide, IBM Corporation, 1994.

Writing Applications for the Solaris Environment: A Guide for Windows Programmers, Volume II, Sun Microsystems, Inc., Addison Wesley, 1992.

Index

ABOUT THE AUTHOR

DIPTO CHAKRAVARTY has been a developer and an instructor of AIX and POWER architectures for the IBM Advanced Workstation Division and worldwide. His prior experience includes expert consulting with Bellcore, DEC, HP, Intel, Motorola, OSF, Sun, and several other organizations. A recognized expert in performance tuning of Unix on RISC architectures, he is the author of *POWER RISC System/6000: Concepts, Facilities, and Architecture,* also available from McGraw-Hill. His research interests include performance monitoring of massively parallel systems, microarchitectures, and VLSI.

CASEY CANNON is in AIX and RISC System/6000 information design and development. She is the project lead for Wabi, RAS architecture, multimedia, and 3D graphics as well as the lead IBM writer for the Common Desktop Environment. She has authored multiple publications on topics ranging from multimedia and object-oriented applications to problem solving and system recovery. Ms. Cannon is also a faculty member at Austin Community College.

ABOUT THE SERIES

The J. Ranade Workstations Series is McGraw-Hill's primary vehicle for providing professionals with timely concepts, solutions, and applications. Jay Ranade is also Series Editor in Chief of more than 100 books in the J. Ranade IBM and DEC Series and Series Advisor to the McGraw-Hill Series on Computer Communications.

Jay Ranade, Series Editor in Chief and best-selling computer author, is a Senior Systems Architect and Assistant V.P. at Merrill Lynch.